FLAGS OF FAME

SOUTH ASIA INSTITUTE, NEW DELHI BRANCH
HEIDELBERG UNIVERSITY
SOUTH ASIAN STUDIES NO. XXVII

Flags of Fame

STUDIES IN SOUTH ASIAN FOLK CULTURE

Edited by

HEIDRUN BRÜCKNER
LOTHAR LUTZE
ADITYA MALIK

MANOHAR
2023

First published 1993
Reprinted 2019, 2020, 2021, 2023

ISBN 978-81-7304-049-8

Published by
Ajay Kumar Jain *for*
Manohar Publishers & Distributors
4753/23 Ansari Road, Daryaganj
New Delhi 110 002

Printed at
Replika Press Pvt. Ltd.

For Günther-Dietz Sontheimer (1934-1992)

SONG IN PRAISE OF THE LORD'S FLAG

Give me the flag of fame, o king Malu, the Sun
Give me the flag of favour
This is all I beg from you
Don't let me be humbled
Lest people laugh at you
I don't want to be saved nor freed from death
May your well-known sword shine forever!

Give me family, kith and kin, may my tribe grow
May none of us have to wander for food
Lest your name be blackened
O Lord, your sword rules the three worlds
Give me the flag of fame, o king Malu, the Sun!

Keep Śivājī Vāghyā forever in your shade
Loved and blessed
In the company of his fellow singer Rāmacandra!
People will flock to your feet
May your well-known sword shine forever!

(From a song of a divine 'dog-man' of Lord Khaṇḍobā; translated from the Marāṭhī by Günther-Dietz Sontheimer with Dilip Chitre)

CONTENTS

II TEXTUAL NETWORKS

FOREWORD

The present volume is based on the papers of two 'inter-regional' seminars and a two day conference conducted by Lothar Lutze and Heidrun Brückner at the South Asia Institute, Heidelberg University, in summer 1988 and 1989. The theme of the seminar was: "South Asian Folklore: Regional Varieties, Modes of Transmission and Performance." The majority of contributions focussed on descriptions and analyses of rituals and oral texts in a ritual context, all within the framework of the folk level of Hinduism. The term "folk culture" in the subtitle of the volume is meant to encompass folk religion, folk literature and folk performances.

The backgrounds of the contributors are Indology, literature, linguistics, folklore, history and anthropology. Generally speaking, the book is expressive of an approach to South Asian studies which tries to cut across narrow compartmentalizations of disciplines in order to do justice to the continuity of Indian culture. This approach has been cultivated at the South Asia Institute from its inception in the early sixties; since the seventies the inter-regional seminars conducted by the Department of Indology have been a forum for discussions and publications along these lines.

The editors would like to express their gratitude to Klaus Werner Müller for his editorial assistance; to Shirley Langwiesner for taking special efforts in preparing the index; and to Sandra Joost and Srilata Müller for carefully and promptly reading through the proofs. We would also like to thank Anne Feldhaus for her suggestions and support.

Günther-Dietz Sontheimer died in Heidelberg on June 1, 1992, while this volume was under preparation. We dedicate the book to him.

The editors *Heidelberg, February 1993*

Note on transliteration and transcription

The use of diacritics in transliteration and transcription follows generally acknowledged Indological conventions as found in the dictionaries of the respective languages. The application of diacritics with regard to place names, proper names, the names and epithets of deities, as well the use in the transcription of non-written languages and dialects of phonetic symbols based on linguistic conventions, has been left to the choice of individual authors.

List of Plates

INTRODUCTION

I. Contents and Scope of the Present Volume
(*Heidrun Brückner, Aditya Malik*)

The fifteen articles of the present volume cover a wide geographic area from Kerala to coastal Karnataka, Maharashtra, Rajasthan, Garhwal, the Gangetic plain, Bengal, Orissa, and Nepal. They have been organized into two groups: I *Divine Performances* focusing mainly on ritual performance, and II *Textual Networks* centering on (mostly oral) texts. Needless to say, textual evidence is also included in part I, and, conversely, ritual data in part II. The present volume is — among other things — part of a larger project to work out a morphology of the folk level of Hinduism in relation to its other layers. To this end the common features have to be identified and, simultaneously, regional and subregional variation has to be studied in relation to context. The material presented in this book shows that the folk religious level of Hinduism has many elements in common in different regions of South Asia. A systematic analysis of these elements and the identification of factors that determine variation would be a next step. By providing some new data and fresh approaches the editors hope that the present book will be an incentive towards that end. As a working model for a differentiated and yet "open" approach to Hinduism, we have chosen a notion developed by Günther Sontheimer which he most recently elucidated in his contribution to *Hinduism Reconsidered*.[1] The notion is that of the "five components" of Hinduism. The components are (1) The

---

[1] *Hinduism Reconsidered* is based on papers delivered during the IXth European Conference on Modern South Asian Studies at Heidelberg (Wilhelmsfeld) in 1986. The contributors to the panel "Hinduism Reconsidered" not only attempted a critical review of existing notions and theories on Hinduism, but also tried out new models and perceptions — such as von Stietencron's provocative view of Hinduism as a group of several "religions," Eichinger Ferro-Luzzi's much debated "polythetic-prototype" approach, and Burghart's concept of "translations" of Hinduism.

work and teachings of the Brahmans, (2) asceticism and renunciation, (3) tribal religion, (4) folk religion, and (5) bhakti. Sontheimer stresses that these components are not to be viewed as "watertight compartments, but rather as presenting a continuum and as interacting among themselves in a fluctuating process..." Taking the Khaṇḍobā cult of Maharashtra as an example of "folk religion," Sontheimer shows how other components are integrated into the cult and thus make it "a mirror of Hinduism." There is special need to work out such categories of description and analysis because folk religion does not explain itself.[2] Therefore Sontheimer's pragmatic approach is particularly useful. Thus typical features of folk religion identified by him overlap with traits that connect the materials of most contributions (Zoller, Sontheimer, Malik, Singh, Freeman, Nambiar, Tarabout): references to a royal and martial paradigm expressed by the perception of god as a king and hero; possession as a way of direct communication with the divine, and the stress on the immediate presence of the god. While local deities often combine both negative and positive characteristics, these tend to be split up into a benevolent god and his demonic counterpart as the social and territorial domain of the deity expands. This state of affairs is the central theme of *Criminal Gods and Demon Devotees. Essays on the Guardians of Popular Hinduism* (A. Hiltebeitel (ed.) Albany 1989).[3]

---

[2] In this context see, for example, A. Piatigorsky: Some phenomenological observations on the study of Indian religion. In Audrey Cantlie and Richard Burghart (eds.) *Indian Religion* (London 1985). The book contains religious, anthropological and Indological studies of Hindu and Buddhist cults and concepts.

[3] The editor of this book views "criminal gods" as a possibly "worldwide phenomenon" whose Hindu varieties are distinguished mainly by "the specifically Indian codes they violate... and the ways they violate them." Their counterparts, however, the "demon devotees," might perhaps be "uniquely Indian... for their mythologies are shaped by a theology of *bhakti*, or devotion, in which the gods repeatedly convert their demon adversaries — sometimes by defeating them, but more often by killing them... — into their devotees." Michaels' paper in the present volume presents an interesting variation, Śiva being perceived both as God and as *piśāca*.

The West Coast material not only shares the royal and martial aspects and the feature of possession with the data from other regions, but Tulunad, North and Central Kerala are further related by similar ecological and economic conditions, as well as by the matrilinearity of the castes involved in the cults. With the gods being placed in the specific setting of "small kingdoms" we encounter a variety of highly localized cults — the realm of the gods often consisting of no more than a few villages — which are at the same time "royal."

The first article, by Günther D. Sontheimer, combines the study of scriptural, historical, and oral literary sources with a detailed documentation and analysis of the Somvati Amāvāsyā festival in the cult of the folk deity Khaṇḍobā in Maharashtra. Sontheimer takes up a special facet of the cult, namely the god's hunting expedition. On the lines of a number of earlier studies of his, he not only describes the event in the immediate context of the procession and the festival rituals of which it forms an integral part, but also analyses it as a typical feature of folk religion, characterized by antagonistic rituals, a perception of god as king and the notion that the annual renewal of fertility is the task of the kingly god who recreates life out of death. The rituals of folk religion distinguished by pomp, festivity, drama and play form a contrast to the Vedic *śrauta* ritual. At the same time, elements of the hunting expedition have parallels with Vedic rituals such as the Aśvamedha: Khaṇḍobā's horse is sent ahead of the procession, recalling the sacrificial horse which is made to roam through the realm of the sacrificer/king. Besides explicating this and other Vedic connections, Sontheimer describes the forest in which the hunting expedition is undertaken as the locus both of fights against "demons" and of royal erotic adventures.

The cults and rituals of central and northern Kerala studied in the three following papers have a number of features in common with the cult of Khaṇḍobā in Maharashtra and the cults of related folk deities of the Deccan as well as with the neighbouring Tuluva cults.

In his paper on "ritual rivalry" in Kerala, Gilles Tarabout emphasizes the sacrificial nature of religious festivals conducted by two competing social factions. The social identity of castes, such as the Nayar and Namputiri, who participate in these festivals, are marked by a "locality component." Thus, in order to preserve certain social, ritual, and political privileges, more importance is given to the institution of "Houses" rather than to kinship based on blood relationships. The festivals involving two related groups or "Houses" in a symbolic enactment of battle are reminiscent of the agonistic component of Vedic ritual as described by Heesterman. On a higher level, however, the factions form a dynamic whole within the unit of the cult. It is the fame, prestige, and power of the "Houses" and of the cult that is at stake when the festivals are performed. Tarabout concludes by mentioning parallel festivals in the Tulu region and in Buddhist Sri Lanka. Here too the "locality component" is important in the social definition of the groups involved.

Both J. Richardson Freeman's and Balan Nambiar's papers deal with the Teyyam complex of Kerala. Whereas Nambiar offers a detailed descriptive account of the ritual itself, Freeman raises some important questions about social science perspectives on the phenomenon of possession. His analysis, which stresses the inclusion of the actors' viewpoint, links up with Schoembucher's plea for a cosmological and performative model of possession (see below). In this context Freeman writes: "...there are few attempts at a cultural comprehension...of how possession is conceptually constituted, behaviourally induced, and morally evaluated by its actual practitioners." He points out that the Teyyam complex is based on a belief in powers and beings capable of "possessing" people, possession itself being brought on either intentionally or spontaneously. Freeman gives a brief description of the ritual sequence itself, thereby stating what is perhaps the central idea underlying the notion of possession as performative act: the actor is "acted upon far more than he acts...the Teyyam, as a collective representation, performs itself through him." By delineating the ritual process within the context of the conventions that generate it, he is able to demonstrate the "high degree of culturally structured determinacy" involved. The "possessing entities" range from *yakṣis* ("bloodthirsty vampires") to *paradēvata* ("paramount goddesses"). Both psychopathology and the interpretation of possession as "desperate strategies of the socially oppressed," would be completely out of place.

Balan Nambiar, as a painter and sculptor brought up in the environment of the cult, has been inspired in his own work by its aesthetic qualities. His rich description of the ritual impersonation of a goddess *(paradēvata)* substantiates both Freeman's and Schoembucher's claim: elaborate costumes and settings, various actors, a specific time and place, and the presence of the community all constitute the Teyyam of Tāi Paradēvata, the goddess whose ritual Nambiar describes. After a brief overview of the Teyyam complex in general, Nambiar turns to a narration in chronological order of the rituals in this particular Teyyam. Tāi Paradēvata, who is a multiform of Bhadrakāḷi, the goddess created by Śiva to destroy the demon Dāruka, is performed by members of the Vaṇṇān community in Kerala. There are three phases to the performance: (a) *tiṭaṅṅal* or beginning, in which legends of the Teyyam are sung and the performers ask for blessings; (b) *eḷamkōlam*, which is a "junior" form of the main performance and is usually performed in the evening before the main performance; (c) *Tāi Paradēvata* or the main performance done on the day following *eḷamkōlam*.

Axel Michaels and Claus Peter Zoller take us to the heights of the Himalayas. Michaels, in his paper on the "Hidden" Mahādeva and protective stones in Nepal, raises some important issues about the nature of religion in Nepal and in India, questioning the validitiy of Western concepts and models in understanding and describing Hinduism. If the festival of Lukumahādyaḥ cannot be represented in terms of a tension between the high and the low, or the simple and the complex, or the local and the supralocal, or Sanskritization and parochialization, then how does one talk about it? Showing how various lines of meaning converge in the cult — *liṅgam* and unhewn stone, Śiva and Śakti, Siva and the *piśāca*, tantrism and Brahmanism, vegetarian and non-vegetarian deities, the city and its outskirts etc. — Michaels concludes that the generating principle behind religious configurations in Hinduism is one of "unlimited and reciprocal substitutions," thereby recalling Eichinger Ferro-Luzzi's approach (see above).

Beginning with a description of Himalayan ball games, Zoller proceeds to show how these games reflect and form part of the social order of Himalayan tribes, in particular the Baṅgāṇis. Warfare, headhunting and wife-capture represent the martial layer of social exchange, which seems to be more dominant in myths and in people's minds than the peaceful one. Zoller views Baṅgāṇi society as based on an exchange of life and death, destruction and creation of life being co-terminous. His observations on the hero in Baṅgāṇ and in particular his analysis of "battle intoxication" substantially contribute to the understanding of the processes that permit a warrior to disregard his own life as well as that of his enemy. Agonistic rituals and the martial paradigm are elements this Himalayan religion shares with folk cults in other parts of India.

The first part of the book is rounded up by Elisabeth Schoembucher, who provides the theoretical perspective for dealing with possession. She stresses the need for developing alternative models in place of reductionist theories about possession that harbour little understanding of the participants' own perception of the phenomenon. Beginning with a brief overview of possession under the headings of "the term," "the person," and "the possessing entities" as they are used in anthropological literature, Schoembucher goes on to develop a cosmological and performative approach to the phenomenon. In contrast to psychological and sociological theories that tend to reduce forms of possession to "illness" or "ritual," Schoembucher's approach views possession on the whole as an ecstatic religious experience. Functional models have the limitation of being based on the premises of Western rationality and related notions of the individual and personhood. An Indian view of personhood would result in a different explanation of possession. Schoembucher points out that persons who become possessed and the entities that possess them can have a common origin: the entities are usually spirits of *people* who have died. Furthermore, even within the domain of these entities, there is a hierarchy in which the scale runs from malevolent spirits of the "disgruntled dead" (cp. Knipe in Hiltebeitel 1989) to higher beings who need to be persuaded to participate in earthly events. Schoembucher builds on this to develop her notion of possession as a performative process/act or "divine performance," in which possession can be seen as a central constituent of an entire performative event. In this sense spirit mediumship and spirit possession are part of performative acts which are "highly structured," involving both a degree of predictability and a knowledge about the agents.

Part II opens with three papers focusing on the Tulu culture of South Kanara. The papers are authored by a folklorist (Rai), an anthropologist (Claus), and an Indologist (Brückner) respectively. Viveka Rai takes up the problem of relating regional forms of folklore to "universal" genres. He illustrates his point with material from Tulu oral literature, in particular from the Tulu genre of *pāḍdana* which is also dealt with in Peter Claus' and Heidrun Brückner's contributions. By placing the *pāḍdanas* in a wider context, Rai provides the background for the other two articles; these, as micro-studies, treat two sub-genres of the larger class of *pāḍdanas*. Rai relates his observations to ongoing discussions in the field of folklore studies.

Brückner's examination of a *pāḍdana* from a bardic male tradition shows how far a text which at first sight appears unique — its hero being worshipped only at a single locality — forms part of a larger textual tradition and contains hardly any detail not found in other texts. She points out that this very fact also establishes the validity of the text. In the context of the cult, however, its authority is constituted by its functioning at the ritual level. Complementing her first point, Brückner also shows that, although the elements that constitute the text are familiar in other contexts, in the text itself they combine to form a unique entity. The change of a single element can then change the meaning and impact of the entire text. Lastly, she tries to identify motives of the Tulu story as variations of elements found in the cults of village goddesses of the Deccan.

Whereas Brückner analyses a number of relatively short texts with mostly men as heroes, the texts being recited by male specialists in a ritual context, Claus examines *pāḍdana* texts of epic dimension which focus on heroines and are recited by women. Both authors are concerned with the processes, range and significance of variation in oral texts, as well as with questions of authenticity and localization. Claus' study complements his earlier work on the epic narrative of Kordabbu; this work was published in the volume *Oral Epics in India*, which he edited along with Blackburn, Flueckiger, and Wadley (Blackburn *et al.* 1989). His examination of the Siri *pāḍdanas* leads him to the conclusion that the texts and the rituals of the possession cult "are both in very dynamic states and each has a contextual existance partially independent of the other in which their continual development takes place." The epic dimension of Claus's material links it to the papers of Malik and Singh.

Bahadur Singh and Aditya Malik discuss different aspects of the epic tradition of the Rājasthānī folk deity Devnārāyaṇ. Whereas Singh focuses on one episode in the "first" part of the oral epic called the Bagaṛāvat, Malik examines a story that falls in the "second" part of the epic that essentially deals with the circumstances of the deity's birth, childhood and marriage(s). Malik analyses the structure and values represented in Devnārāyaṇ's *byāvlo*, a relatively short narrative. Here again, as in the case of other pastoral and folk deities, it is the heroic and martial paradigm that is emphasized. Brahmanical notions about ritual purity and impurity receive scant attention. Like the traditional king, the deity is accessible to all sections of society, regardless of their status in terms of the *varṇa* hierarchy. Analogous to the system of reciprocal obligations that binds king and populace together, relationships between the deity and devotees are determined by degrees of reciprocal devotion. Besides containing several elements common to other "martial" epic traditions in India, the narrative structure of the story also reflects the growth of the deity in terms of a tension between feminine and masculine power, ending in the god's decision to pursue the male heroic quest. His multiple marriages echo a widespread pattern found in folk cults of Maharashtra, Tamil Nadu and other parts of India.

Singh analyses the narrative purpose and sense of ethics expressed in the episode of the 'golden Śiva image.' The narrative has a double characteristic: it embodies both a prefiguration of future events in the epic and an 'intergenerational' aspect that refers to events of the past that have led to the present episode. The ethics stand in contrast to clichés about Indian "otherworldliness," exhorting the epic's listeners to heroic abandon and to a celebration of life in the face of its impermanence. Once again, this articulates what is perhaps a singular feature of folk religion, namely, its "earthboundness."

Richard Burghart's article deals with a caste of itinerant Brahman genealogists associated with different Vaiṣṇavite ascetic orders. He combines an historical account with observations gained through ethnographic fieldwork. After describing the history, social organization and professional activity of the caste in question, he analyses the purpose and function of their work, which he considers to be twofold, fixing identities and transforming identities: "On the one hand, genealogists keep records in order to fix identities, thereby enabling others to control membership and entitlements within Vaiṣṇavism; on the other hand, they use their knowledge to magnify persons, make saintly reputations and in this way transform identities."

The hagiographic aspect of the genealogical accounts forms a link to Hugh van Skyhawk's contribution, which is also the result of a textual study combined with observations gained in field research. He juxtaposes two contemporary Marathi narratives, written down by a Muslim Śekh and a Marathi Brahman respectively, thereby documenting a variety of Hindu-Muslim syncretism. Both stories deal with saints and their marvellous deeds. They not only have several narrative elements in common, but also follow widespread patterns of Indian hagiographical literature.

The volume ends with Alokaranjan Dasgupta's article. It takes us to the east of India, namely to Orissa and Bengal, and deals with the lyric genre of Adivasi protest poetry. Dasgupta, who is not only a scholar but also a poet and writer, presents specimens of Santal poetry, especially riddles, which he places in their socio-political context. In particular he discusses a prose narrative belonging to the compositions of a tribal group of the Mayurbhanj district of Orissa. The narrative, which is interspersed with popular rhyming, deals with the subtle way in which a tribal bard questions the authority of a king.

We have chosen the "Song of a divine dog-man" of Lord Khaṇḍobā of Maharashtra as a motto for our book because it conveys in poetic terms what we have tried to circumscribe as "folk religion." The song expresses no concern with other wordly matters — the devotee does not ask his Lord for "liberation." He asks for the welfare of his family and tribe in this world, and he wants "fame," which — in being granted to him — also adds to the fame of his Lord, symbolized by his "shining sword" and the "flags" or banners carried in his honour. The relationship between Lord and devotee is characterized by an affectionate intimacy and a strong sense of reciprocity. The imagery evoked by the song is familiar in most of the cults discussed in the following pages: not only in the Khaṇḍobā cult studied by Sontheimer, but also in Tarabout's material with its central concern for fame, prestige and power; in the Teyyam cult studied by Freeman and Nambiar; in the cults of the princely *daivas* of Tulunad; in the ritual Himalayan games analysed by Zoller; and in the world of the oral Rājasthānī epic of Devnārāyaṇ examined by Malik and Singh.

II. Some contextual and theoretical considerations (*Lothar Lutze*)

In the inter-regional seminars at the South Asia Institute three concepts came up time and again: "tradition," "myth," and "folk." The following is an attempt to elucidate the meaning of these terms with reference to South Asian culture.

Tradition[4]

The concept of tradition and its dialectics appear to be most adequately circumscribed by two Sanskritic terms, *paramparā* and *sātatya*. The former, which refers to the handing-on of cultural content such as myths, is dynamic and allows of change; it may be visualized as a river capable of changing its bed. *Sātatya*, its static counterpart, may be likened to a *sarovar*, a reservoir permanently at people's disposal.

---

[4] The remarks on *Tradition* and *Myth* are based on material from an essay by L. Lutze, "Kṛṣṇa's death: Variations on a Mahābhārata episode in contemporary Indian poetry," (South Asian Digest of Regional Writing, Vol. 12, 1987) especially the introduction on myth and modernity in Western and Indian literature.

In the light of this dualism, we may distinguish between two ways of looking at the application of tradition, such as in religion or art. One of them would see it as *the actualization of sātatya.* In this view, a *rāga* - to use an example from Indian classical music - is a melodic idea, a potential actualized in each individual musical performance. Similarly, a myth may be seen as a narrative idea waiting for actualization in a story-telling performance, a comic strip, a novel, or a T.V. serial.

The other approach would be to see the application of tradition as *the fixation of paramparā* - either, in an oral culture, through memorization (1); or through visualization, pictorial or in writing (2); or, last but not least of late, through technical recording (3).[5] (1), (2) and (3) should be seen as three basically equivalent conditions in which myths and other cultural content may be encountered, their respective prestige depending on the preference given to one of them by a certain cultural community at a certain point in time. The acceptance of the basic equivalences of these three conditions is one of the cornerstones of an unbiased, non-hierarchical approach to South Asian culture.[6]

Myth

In the present context, 'myth' is used in the sense of a set of mental images arranged in narrative sequences and shared by a community of people; 'mythology' may refer (1) to the totality of such myths within that community or (2) to the scholarly - i.e., as a rule, logical - treatment of myth(s).

---

[5] Cf. James Monaco's distinction between performance art, representational art and recording art (Monaco, J., How to read a film: The art, technology, language, history and theory of film and media. New York, 1977: 7).

[6] Cf. the concept of 'text' in Lotman, Ju. M., Pjatigorskij, A. M., Tekst i funkcija (Text and function). In Eimermacher, K. (ed.) *Teksty sovetskogo literaturovedéeskogo strukturalizma* (Text of Soviet literary structuralism), München, 1971: 483-497.

In traditional thinking, myth is the substance of religious imagination and practice (ritual) and hence part of everyday life, where it converts into narrative the interplay *(līlā, kheḷ)* between the divine and the human, with gods approaching and turning into, human beings and vice versa, with the resulting augmentation and glorification of things human in general and the affairs of a certain community in particular. As to the role of time in myth, it is traditionally described as a suspension of the time flow; in myth, the past is ever present, and present and future events are determined by that past; in fact, present and past are merged into each other.

What is perhaps most remarkable about Hindu mythology, at least to the Western observer, is its functioning throughout South Asian culture. 'Functioning' here would mean being shared by *all* the members of a cultural community, regardless of social standing, and being a part of their everyday reality.

There are several obstacles to the functioning of myth in modern Western culture. One of them is what Uvo Hölscher, in a different context,[7] has called the process of *literarization*. Though not identical with the transition from orality to writing, it is certainly connected to it. Greek tragedy had been ritual practice as part of the annual Dionysia before it reached its height in the 5th century B.C. when its "real existence" was "an oral one"; the texts written and circulated in the following century "acquire a literary existence independant of its possible productions in the theatre"; — people want to re-read what has been successful on the stage. Lyrical poetry in the 7th-century-B.C. Greece, according to Hölscher, retains the "character of the unliterary and occasion-bound" of the preceding folk forms. "It is a kind of poetry which lives, which actually exists only as the fulfilment of the life that fundamentally was 'social' life' and orality was its medium. At the end of this process, Hölscher

---

[7] Hölscher, U. *Die Odysee: Epos zwischen Märchen und Roman*. München, 1989: 35-41.

welcomes "the specific qualities and potentialities of literature," such as "the acquirement of the poetic as pure art, the transformation of myth into a separate domain of poetry and imagination."

Hölscher, of course, must be aware that the process of literization - or artification, as it concerns art in general - is bound to involve loss and sacrifice. After all, it is a process of separation from everyday reality and community life; "the domain of poetry and imagination," welcome as it may be as a sanctuary, has also become the *Spielraum* of a sublime non-seriousness, of the ultimately non-commital - which does not exclude that art, in its turn, may be accepted by many as token and instrument of human survival.

To students of South Asian culture, the correspondences are obvious, but so are the differences. Such students would hesitate to oppose "the purely functional of ritual and folk poetry" to "the poetic as pure art": what strikes them as characteristic of their regions is prevalence of mixed forms as well as functions. And above all, what Hölscher describes as a historical process, if not as progress, is *simultaneously* present and alive on the South Asian cultural scene, for the mutual benefit of élite culture no less than of folk (or popular) culture.

Literization has brought about ways of manipulating myth which are possible only when it has lost its universal validity and become art in oppostion to reality in the sense of non-art. Once myth is literature, the boundaries within which it originally would be actualized can and will be transgressed, it can be toyed with, be made the subject matter of irony and satire and, eventually, of 'de-mythication. At this stage, the original augmentation and glorification of things divine and human will be replaced by their reduction to the banal, the pedestrian, the all-too-human.

As cosmopolitans and intellectuals, as passive and active participants in *Weltliteratur*, major South Asian writers of today are no less aware of the potentialities and pitfalls of literization than their colleagues in the West - they have long since made them their own. At the same time, as we have seen, they were born into a culture in which myth is still the substance of religion and co-exists with a mythology which has never ceased to function; and the best among them move freely and sovereignly on a continuum with local tradition at one end and world literature at the other. As a result, in South Asia élite literature has never been quite as élitist, and popular literature never quite as trivial as in the West. It is myth that bridges the difference of caste and class, of community and region.

This is where the South Asian writer of today has an advantage over his Western counterpart. The fiction writer, just like the village story-teller, can indulge in 'pure' story-telling if he has a mind to, for he needs no digressions. Thus, whenever he feels like moralizing, he can, instead of ethical prescriptions (Vor*schriften*), introduce mythical prototypes (Vor*bilder*) without interrupting the flow of his narrative. Similarly, poetry, be it rural or urban, has at its disposal an inexhaustible store of poetic imagery which will be understood and appreciated by all.

In applied mythology, it will be useful to distinguish between (1) the overtly and (2) the covertly mythological treatment of a subject. The second variety is not necessarily a conscious artifice; it may as well be the subconscious re-constitution (by the maker) and re-cognition (by the recipient) of certain visual configurations. The scene in Raj Khosla's "Merā gā̃v merā deś" (My village, my country) where Dharmendra, an earthly latter-day Kṛṣṇa, hides in a tree and watches the village girls bathing in the river is one example out of many which could be taken from commercial Hindi films, which are certainly, along with T.V., the most popular field of myth application in contemporary South Asia.[8]

---

[8] Cf. Lutze, L. From Bharata to Bombay: Change in continuity in Hindi film aesthetics. In L. Lutze (ed.) *Drama in contemporary South Asia: Varieties and settings.*

Folk

Who then, in this comprehensive system of culture, are the folk? Alan Dundes, who asks this question in his well-known article,[9] offers a "flexible definition of folk": "the term 'folk' can refer to *any group of people whatsoever* who share at least one common factor. It does not matter what the linking factor is - it could be a common occupation, language or religion - but what is important is that a group formed for whatever reason will have some traditions which it calls its own. In theory a group must consist of at least two persons, but generally most groups consist of many individuals. A member of the group may not know all other members, but he will probably know the common core of traditions belonging to the group, traditions which help the group to have a sense of group identity."

This definition is indeed quite flexible; some may find it too vague. What Dundes is trying to do is of course widen the folk concept so that it includes new varieties of folk, in particular those that have come into being along with urbanization and industrialization, and in doing so to de-ruralize folklore studies, an academic discipline which some fear might otherwise die out one day for dearth of subject matter. "From this perspective, it would be absurd to argue... that industrialization stamps out folk groups and folklore. There may be a diminution in the number of peasants, but peasants constitute only one type of folk. Industrialization has in fact created new folklore, e.g., the folklore of computers."[10]

These quotations should be seen against the background of the stand Dundes has taken throughout his writings against what he

---

South Asian Digest of Regional Writing, Vol. 10, 1981: 57-69, esp. 64f.

[9] Dundes, A. Who are the folk? In *Essays in folkloristics,* Meerut 1978: 1-21.

[10] Dundes, A. *ibid.*, p. 8.

calls "The devolutionary premise in folklore theory."[11] When he condemns "the past-oriented Weltanschauung of most folklorists" and their "endless quest for the land of 'ur'," every unbiased student of folk-culture, especially those with a German background, will wholeheartedly agree. Still, in the South Asian context, it may be useful to distiguish between (1) folk-culture, which is predominantly rural and oral, and (2) popular or mass culture, which is predominantly urban and technical; both (1) and (2) make use of fixation through writing and/or print.[12]

In this distinction, (1) and (2) are seen as basically equivalent. (1) does not necessarily precede (2); in contemporary South Asian culture - and, one hopes, for some time to come - they will coexist and stimulate each other. What they have in common is their tendency towards collective identity (as opposed to individual originality).

The emphasis on the basic equivalence and simultaneity of folk and popular cultures in present-day South Asia is meant to avoid nostalgic idealization of the former; on the other hand, it may also help to avoid the opposite: the derogation of folk-culture as primitive, especially in its association with illiteracy.[13] Every serious student of South Asian folk-culture has long since learnt to tell apart illiteracy and lack of education, and will agree with the late S.H. Vatsyayan that "it happens that an illiterate in the sense of unlettered audience is educated in the sense that, having still remained in an oral tradition, it does have a sense of judgement and of literary

---

[11] Dundes, A. The devolutionary premise in folklore theory. In Richard M. Dorson (ed.) *Analytic essays in folklore. Studies in Folkore 2.* The Hague 1975: 17-27.

[12] Cf. also A.K. Ramanujan and Stuart Blackburn *Another Harmony* (Berkeley 1986). In their introduction the editors review the history of the study of Indian folklore and develop a new methodological and analytical approach of their own which stresses the inter-relatedness of folk and classical traditions without assigning a "higher" value to any of the two.

[13] Cf. Dundes (1978: 18): "Partly because folkore was wrongly tied to illiteracy, it was wrongly assumed that as literacy increased, folklore would decrease."

values; while those literate - who can read and write and sign their name - may have no sense of these and may therefore in fact be less educated."[14]

What, in our view, distinguishes folk-culture from mass-culture is, quite simply, the fact that the two of them take place under totally different communicative and performative circumstances. On the basis of J. Monaco's distinction between performance arts and recording arts, we would differentiate between oral tradition as a performance art representing folk-culture, which is produced in the presence of a more or less homogenous audience and affected by its immediate response, and cinema and T.V. as recording arts representing mass-culture, in which immediate - "live" - interventions are technically impossible and recipients condemned, at least temporarily, to passivity.

In this context it is a mere statement of fact that in the long run the communicative and performative circumstances which are characteristic of folk-culture are threatened in their existence by the general technicalization of culture, which has been going on for quite some time now and will gain in intensity in the future. Mass-culture, undoubtedly a fascinating object of study in the South Asian context, will take care of itself; on the other hand, there is no reason not to admit that the editors of, as well the contributors to, the present volume have been partial to varieties of cultural activity which may sooner or later be lost.

---

[14] Vatsyayan, S.H. The role of the writer in contemporary Indian society. In *South Asian Digest of Regional Writing*, Vol. 1, 1972: 4-17, here: p. 12.

I *Divine Performances*

KING KHAṆḌOBĀ'S HUNT
AND HIS ENCOUNTER WITH BĀṆĀĪ, THE SHEPHERDESS*

Günther D. Sontheimer

I. *The Somvatī Amāvāsyā festival in the Khaṇḍobā cult: Two strands*

One of the most important festivals in the Khaṇḍobā cult of Maharashtra is observed on Somvatī Amāvāsyā, that is, on a new moon day which falls on a Monday. The major centre of the cult is Jejurī in the Pune district and it is here that the festival is observed most conspicuously and elaborately. The festival is also observed in other places where Khaṇḍobā and similar Śaivite folk deities are worshipped, but it is only of local importance.[1] There are many dimensions of this festival (see Stanley 1977), but we shall emphasise here the hunting excursion of the Lord, and the folk-religious and royal character of this day. Though outwardly there is little to show that the royal god actually goes for a hunt, this is a frequent explanation given by participants in the festival.

---

* Acknowledgments:
This paper draws on material collected during two stays in India which were respectively financed by the German Research Association (DFG; 1985/86) and the Volkswagen-Stiftung e.V. (1990/91). I am grateful to both institutions.

[1] For instance in the cases of Mhaskobā (Vir, Purandar taluka, Pune distr.), Siddhanāth (Javali, Phaltan taluka, Satara district), Dhuḷobā (Vidhni, near Phaltan), Khaṇḍobā (Budh, Khatav taluka, Satara district). Whereas in these places the god is taken to the river, in Dhok Sāngli, Shirur taluka, Ahmadnagar district, we have the widespread custom that water is *brought* to Khaṇḍobā from the (Bhimā) river in order to bathe the god.

Before we proceed, it is necessary to point out that the festival incorporates two main religious orientations, which at times coalesce and at other times stand apart, maintaining more or less a dynamically fluctuating relationship. From the point of view of the brahmanical texts, though not one which is necessarily shared by all Brahmans who are also devotees of Khaṇḍobā, the essence of the festival would be that it is a purifying ritual at an inauspicious point of time, namely the conjunction of the sun and the moon on a Monday. Terms like *snāna, śuddhi, pāpa* are used in expressing this attitude. The other orientation belongs to the realm of folk religion. The god's exit into the "forest" is dramatically performed and the devotees participate in the royal "hunt", which culminates in a common bath of the god and his devotees in the Karhā river.

The motives of the devotees who participate in the festival are variously expressed, but can be summarised by the desire to secure "life and prosperity" (Heesterman 1985:31), or to seek the values of "bodily existence and well-being" or "auspiciousness," or "higher quality of life" (Marriott 1976:194). Both orientations, the brahmanical and the folk, and the rites connected with them are, of course, pervaded by the peculiar sacredness of Somvatī Amāvāsyā, a day on which the "fluidity of power" (Stanley 1977:30) is "unambivalently auspicious" (Stanley 1977:42) in the Khaṇḍobā cult. In the following article we shall also try to explore some of the dimensions of these attitudes and their mutual interaction, as they are expressed in oral folk myths, scriptural brahmanical texts, and in the dramatic performances and rituals of the festival. We shall spread our net rather wide, to draw together scattered and variegated materials which may eventually provide the background to the festival, especially the hunting excursion of the god. In passing, we should like to point out the pervasiveness and spatial spread of the incidents of the Khaṇḍobā cult and whatsoever its relationship and/or indebtedness to similar cults, especially in Tamilnadu, Karnataka, and Andhra Pradesh. Future research will probably have to concentrate on parallels between similar folk cults in different regions: too often the local or regional data are taken to be unique, without comparative scrutiny to show whether this is true or not.

II. *Somvatī Amāvāsyā in the Jayādri Māhātmya, Mārtaṇḍavijaya and other scriptural sources*

The *Jayādri Māhātmya* is an unpublished Sankrit text which describes literally "the Greatness of Jejurī." It links the Jejurī (Jayādri) cult firmly to the *Mahābhārata* and to purāṇic precedents while heavily aetiologising local events and incidents pertaining to Jejurī and to another important place of the cult, namely Naḷdurg, in the Usmanabad district. The oldest Ms. is dated *śake* 1678 (1756 A.D.).[2] It was around this time, namely between 1635-1790 A.D., that an increased building activity is recorded in inscriptions in the temple complex of Jejurī (Potdar 1914:265-272; Khare 1958:91-93). Other scriptural sources are the *Mārtaṇḍavijaya* (1823 A.D.),[3] and the *Śrīkṣetra-Jejurī-Māhātmya* (1925),[4] both in Marathi.

The *JM* basically relates a conversation between the five Pāṇḍavas and Śiva. The Pāṇḍavas have arrived at Jejurī and Dharmarāja asks a host of questions which are mostly answered by Śiva or Vaiśampāyana. The questions resemble a checklist of the mythical and ritual constituents of the cult of Jejurī. It appears that Jejurī as a *kṣetra* was given its scriptural sanction in the 17th and 18th century, though the *JM* presupposes an earlier cult, and the earliest

---

[2] A xerocopy was obtained of the Ms. in the possession of R.C. Dhere, to whom I am most grateful. The *Jayādri Māhātmya* purports to belong to the *Pātālakhaṇḍa* of the *Padmapurāṇa*.

[3] The *MV* by Gaṅgādhara is a reworking of the *MM* and *JM* and has important additional information.

[4] This work gathers all the important mythological and ritual matters from the *MM, JM,* and the *MV*. See Khāḍe 1925.

inscribed reference to the deity at Jejurī probably dates to the 13th century (Potdār 1933:265; Sontheimer 1987:13). Dharmarāja enquires about the cause of the important festivals *(utsava)* of Campaṣaṣṭhī and the full moon *(pūrṇimā)* festivals in the month of Pauṣa (Dec.-Jan.), Māgha (Jan.-Feb.), and Caitra (Mar.-Apr.), but the equally important Somvatī Amāvāsyā is not included in his questionnaire. The *JM* makes him ask about the origin *(utpatti)* of the river Karhā and why a particular spot on the bank is called "Ghoḍe-uḍḍān". While answering these questions, Śiva also narrates the aetiology of Somvatī Amāvāsyā. The question about the origin of the Karhā seems somewhat inconsistent and illogical when we come to know that the Pāṇḍavas have been the cause of the origin of the river. We summarise the passage (Khāḍe 1925:16):

At the time when the Pāṇḍavas were to perform their sacrifice *(yajña)*, there was no water for the sacred bath of Brahmans, and water is necessary for a *yajña*. Bhīma manages to topple over the *kamaṇḍalū* of Brahmadeva who was in engaged in meditation.[5] From the enraged Brahmadeva's pot flowed the river. Brahmadeva eventually came from the (Mountain) Brahmādri to Pāṇḍeśvar (a village near the Karhā river) where the *yajña* was to be performed. He was reconciled with Bhīma because it was for the sake of *yajña* that Bhīma had committed a mistake *(aparādha)*. This happened in the month of Phālgun (Feb.-Mar.) on Somvatī Amāvāsyā. When Mārtaṇḍa Bhairava saw the river "flow like the Gaṅgā" he went to have a purifying bath *(snāna)*. Brahmadeva and Nārada also came for a bath. The spot where they bathed is also known as Ghoḍe-uḍḍān.[6] It was at this spot that "the *tīrtha* which destroys

---

[5] This is according to *MV* 27.85. The *JM* says that he poured the water over Brahmadeva's head (Khāḍe 1925:28).

[6] Lit.:"the place where the god's horse 'pranced' or 'rose', or 'landed after having flown through the air." For the first time Khaṇḍobā arrives on horseback at the mountain plateau (Kaḍe Paṭhār) which is situated higher up, about three miles beyond the main temple, called Gaḍkot or Khillā (both meaning 'fort'). This spot, marked by "hoof-prints" in the rock, is also called Ghoḍe Uḍḍān. The second

sins" *(pāpa-nāśana-tīrtha)* originated. Ever since, when there is Amāvāsyā on a Monday, Mārtaṇḍa Bhairava *(alias* Khaṇḍobā) comes for a purifying bath *(snāna)* from the Jayādri Mountain.

The *MV* (28, 76-95) tells us very much the same myth in Marathi and adds:

Brahmadeva was reconciled to the idea that the water was needed to perform the *yajña* with the connivance of Mhāḷsākānt ("the husband of Mhāḷsā"). Mhāḷsākānt, alias Khaṇḍobā, came on horseback and had a bath in the river. The gods followed him and became purified by the water of his feet *(śrīcaraṇodakeṃ)*. They threw turmeric dust (Ma. *bhaṇḍār)* on the Lord. The site where Nārada bathed is called Ghoḍe-uḍān *[sic]*. It is the "sin-destroying *tīrtha.*" Ever since that day, known as Somvatī Amāvāsyā *parva,* Mhāḷsākānt comes from the Jayādri Mountain. The river was called Mandākinī or "Brahmā's vessel" by gods and Ṛṣis, which changed into "Karhā" in Prākṛt *(Karhā nāṃva Prākṛta jāṇa bolīṃ)*. Somvatī Amāvāsyā is an auspicious day and extremely pure *(paramapāvana)*, increases *puṇya (puṇyavardhana)* and is suitable for *snāna* and *dāna.*

Thus we have a myth which proposes to serve as an epic and purāṇic "pretext" for the Somvatī Amāvāsyā festival. The Vedic *yajña* is replaced by the *yātrā* or *utsava* during which Mārtaṇḍa Bhairava has a ritual bath, *snāna,* in the Karhā river. The day is also said to be fit for making over gifts *(dāna)*. Besides Somvatī Amāvāsyā, the four annual festivals in the months of Pauṣ, Māgh, Caitra, and at Caṃpaṣaṣṭhī in the month of Mārgaśīrṣa (Nov.-Dec.) are mentioned. In the *JM* or *MV* we do not find a particular emphasis on Mārtaṇḍa Bhairava in his capacity as a king, let

---

Ghoḍe Uḍḍān on the river bank is probably the spot where he lands with his horse starting off from the Gaḍkoṭ. Khaṇḍobā is often said to fly with his horse which is called "wind" (Ma. *vāru)*.

alone as a hunter, nor is the hunt mentioned. The only passages in which a hunter is mentioned are found in the *MV* and the *MM*. Here Malla, the Daitya, goes for a hunt which turns into a raid on the *āśrama* of the Seven Ṛṣis.[7] Those Brahmans and others who believe in the efficacy of the scriptures would be satisfied with reading or listening to them, even if they are in Marathi, because they promise to yield the desired *phala*. This may include enjoyment of life as well as the goods of life *(bhukti)*, the acquisition of "supernatural" worldly power *(siddhi)*, and may extend to final salvation *(mukti)*.

We could have let the matter rest at this point and conclude that the scriptural aetiology is firmly entrenched and the festival has its brahmanical sanction. But, in fact, the participants in the festival never refer to this aetiology, nor do they refer to the *JM* or *MV* in the way one would refer to the Veda (or *śruti)* as an authority, even if its contents are not known. Even the Brahmans do not refer to it and participate in the festival during the moments where their ritual expertise is needed, e.g. to fix the exact astrological time for the conjunction of the sun and the moon, though they abstain from the tumultous, playful performance of the festival.

III. *Khaṇḍobā as a folk deity, king and hunter*

In folk perception Khaṇḍobā reflects the traditional king, though this image may have become elusive in modern times. He is responsible for the welfare of the people and is endowed with divine powers to bestow fertility on his realm, and to redistribute "the goods of life" which he obtains through the efforts of his followers. There is

---

[7] *MV* 1.88: under "the pretext of hunting" the *Daitya* Malla left with his army. Observing the rite of hunting *(mṛgayāvīdhī saṃpādūn)* he came to the *āśram* of the Ṛṣis.

some reason to hold that one of the origins of the Khaṇḍobā cult is found in the charismatic heroic chieftain or *rājā* or local potentate, who was believed to be divine by his followers because of his prowess and resourcefulness. An early inscription of the last quarter of the 7th cent. A.D. from Ājaṇṭā mentions a certain ruler Khaṇḍeśvara ("the lord of the sword"), and calls him Mallayeśa-kārttānta, "the destroyer of Mallayeśa" (Chabra 1955:124; Malandru 1982). It is characteristic of the folk attitude to deify successful living heroes or heroes, who died a violent death. Heroes who performed a heroic feat and survived could become local rulers as a next step in their career and were considered divine by their folk. The beginnings of the dynasties of the Hoyṣalas and the Yādavas of Devgiri are attributed to legendary heroic feats of the founders of these dynasties — the killing of tigers (Derrett 1957:7) and the defence of village cattle (Verma 1970:14). In the early medieval period heroes died for their master or king who was considered divine, if not *quasi* a deity. In other words, loyalty to the king or chieftain was expressed by unflinching bhakti leading to self-immolation at times (Sontheimer 1991b:23). This bhakti was eventually directed towards gods like Mallanna, Mailāra or Khaṇḍobā, or a goddess worshipped in temples. These deities were also *quasi* royal masters. Self-immolation became a sacrifice, an extreme form of bhakti, which was now directed to the god as king on earth. Memorials depicting heads of heroes and oral myths in the Khaṇḍobā-Mailāra cult still testify to these acts of bravery and the defiance of death. Perhaps this is meant by the *MV*, when it says: "For the hero god is king."[8]

---

[8] *MV* 16.30:
pāhā rājyanītī | vīrāsa īśvara bhūpati |
svāmikāryāta sanmāna pāhatī |
te dhanya hotī trijagīṃ |
The phrase could possibly be also inverted and translated: "For the hero the king is god." Following Stein (1983:88) one could say: Kingship and "sovereignty" were transferred to the deity Khaṇḍobā and shared by powerful devotees like King Śāhū Mahārāj of Satara, Brahman Sardārs, and rulers like the Hoḷkars and the Gāykvāḍs and many Marāṭhā *śiledārs*. The relationship between Khaṇḍobā as the divine king

The objection of the *MM* and *MV* to the demon kings, Malla and Maṇi, was not so much directed to their bravery and heroism — their tremendous prowess, though unethical as it were, is stressed — but to the fact that they would let themselves be worshipped as gods (*MM* 7.13-36). The *MM* and the *MV* emphasize the point that it is a purāṇic deity, namely Śiva, who descends to become an *avatāra* and even "condescends" to become a king on earth. The historical elevation of a hero and local ruler to a god, who would eventually attain the status of Indra, Śiva or Viṣṇu, was ignored. Folk deities who were claimed to be Śiva by their followers and had, for example, a historical root — like in the death of a hero in a battle — could be ridiculed, especially by sectarians. Followers of Mailāra, for instance, when challenged by the Liṅgāyat saint Dāsimayya claimed that the deity was none other but Śiva himself. But in this they were rebuked by the saint, who argued that Mailāra was a warrior killed by hunters (Sontheimer 1987:14). The attitude in the *MM* and *MV* seems to have been to assimilate the local or regional folk cult of the king by splitting it into halves which were then hierarchized: the local king was demonized and the demon was defeated by an *avatāra* of Viṣṇu or Śiva. The purāṇic deity now became god as king on earth and he assumed the court and regalia of his mundane, demonized predecessor, who would become his demon devotee, flunkey, or a subordinate deity. The local folk cult, whether it was related to a living royal master or to a hero deified after his death, as some opponents of folk deities would claim was the case with Mailāra (Sontheimer 1987:13) or even Viṭhobā (for instance, Sontheimer 1989c:70), acquired a new vertical, even transcendent purāṇic or "sectarian" dimension. The god was now worshipped as Śiva or Viṣṇu or a form of them. He could not only grant *bhukti*, but also *mukti*, which otherwise had been possible only by violent

---

and his powerful devotees is reflected, in the cult, in the relationship between Khaṇḍobā and Heggaḍe Pradhān (Ka. = "Headman" and Skt. = "Minister"). The main cult at Jejurī was often duplicated by bhaktas, including headmen, in their villages.

self-immolation. As in the scriptural texts relating to the Khaṇḍobā cult *bhukti* and *mukti* were not values which were delinked from each other, but constituted a continuum. *Bhukti* implies mundane values like prosperity etc. which we have referred to above. Though the two values are not delinked from each other, there is an emphasis on reading and listening to scriptures, and individual worship through *pūjā,* in the brahmanical attitude. However, the folk traditions and the oral texts about Khaṇḍobā, for example, emphasize the dramatic rather than the scriptural and ritual enactment of bhakti.

In folk perception Khaṇḍobā, Khaṇḍerāyā or Khaṇḍerāv, as these popular appellations indicate, is not just viewed as an *avatār,* but he is Śiva himself as king on earth - "here and now" - in order to look after the welfare of his followers or devotees. It is pre-eminently a cult of folk bhakti and therefore we have to shift into the realm of folk culture with its dramatic performances and oral literature. Again, however, we do not want to postulate a dichotomy between the scriptural texts and oral folk literature, or between ritual emphasized in the brahmanical sphere and dramatic folk performances. There is a constant interaction between these two realms. It may be advisable not to generalize about the cult on the basis of either points of view, but to try to inquire contextually when, how, and where, one or the other realm stands forth. For instance, one of the tasks of the scriptural text of the local *Māhātmya* is to explain the existence of the typical dramatically performed folk rites and oral myths, to devalue them by hierarchization within the framework of the brahmanical system, or even to ignore them. Hook-swinging, possession, walking on fire, breaking of chains etc. are thus hierarchized, by classifying them as *rākṣasī, piśācī* or *rājasī* rather than *sāttvikī* bhakti.[9] In folk bhakti, however, such rites are considered to be *sāttvikī. Sattva* is often taken to mean *sattā* which, essentially, means "power." This power is often gained by acts of

[9] See the discussion in Sontheimer 1991a.

violent, vehement, and insistent bhakti. It provokes the *sattva* of the god, his powerful presence which lends strength and renewal to the devotee as well as to the god. For instance, the Vāghyās, who are the "dog-men" or "tiger-men" of Khaṇḍobā, and also the Dhangar shepherds, break their iron chains on Somvatī Amāvāsyā. The breaking is a sure sign that they are infused with Khaṇḍobā's *sattva* and that he will remove all obstacles. Hookswinging (Ma. *bagāḍ)* which exists now only in a mild form at some places, shows the serious will of the devotee to honour his pledges (Ma. *navas)* and to elicit Khaṇḍobā's *sattva.* In an old song of the Vāghyās we hear *(pad* 8):[10]

> The Lord of the earth is the ruling force in the Deccan
> The thunder of King Malhār resounds all over the world.
> Great noblemen come.
> The devotees wear *bhaṇḍār* (turmeric dust) on their fore-head and
> show their fierce will by circling
> in the air suspended by a hook.
> His *sattva* is great
> They raise cries of "Yeḷkoṭ" ("Seven Crores"),
> And sins and faults are removed.

In the *MM,* on the other hand, Śiva is seated on the distant Kailāsa looking from far away on his *kṣetra* on earth. The primordial events which led to its establishment are also far removed in time. His other self, so to say, rules as Mārtaṇḍa Bhairava on Earth. In folk perception, on the other hand, Jejurī is the very Kailās on earth and it is Śaṅkar who rules there as King Khaṇḍobā. Thus we hear in another Vāghyā song *(pad* 24):

> He is the Lord of the Three Worlds
> He resides in happiness

---

[10] Here the songs are numbered according to the collection *Khaṇḍobācīṃ paḍeṃ* (see References) by Śrī Sadguru Bhāūmahārājā. My translations were revised with the help of the eminent Marathi and English poet Dilip Chitre.

Have faith in him
Malhārī (Khaṇḍobā)
will fulfill your wishes.
Jejurī is Kailās.

An oral legend tells how a devotee, who belonged to the Māṅg caste, prompted Śiva to stay on earth by self-sacrifice after he had defeated the demons Maṇi and Malla (Sontheimer 1989b:313). Characteristic of folk religion this violent act of suicidal self-sacrifice leads to the deification of the devotee. He did not even have to travel to the Kailāsa and get his celestial legitimation to return as a deified hero to earth, as is sometimes required in folk religion (Blackburn 1985). Today he is known as Yeśvant Rāv and he is said to be the Havaldār[11] of the temple fort in Jejurī. He has his shrine near the main entrance of the fort (Gaḍkoṭ). Such devotees are said to practise *ugra bhakti.* The term *ugra* lends itself to negative interpretations and may mean "terrible," "wrathful," "hideous," in the view of Brahmanical scripture and ritual, or from a modern reformist perspective. But *ugra* for the bhakta, who may even call his god or goddess *ugra,* has no negative connotations and means "fearful," "powerful," "mighty," "strong," high," "noble."[12] This epithet was even shared by a king who was not yet hedged by brahmanical norms. Thus Mārtaṇḍa Bhairava is *ugra* when he battles the demons Maṇi and Malla, and he also appears in his *ugra* form when he goes on a hunt.

In the past at ieast Khaṇḍobā was involved in all spheres of the human life of his devotees, for example, in legal, social, psychological, medical, artistic, entertaining or soteriological matters. Khaṇḍobā is the family deity of groups ranging from the (formerly untouchable) Māṅgs to the Brahmans, and the spectrum included

---

[11] An officer attached to a fort. His duty was to arrange for the guards etc.

[12] Cp. the parallel concept of *maṟam* in early Tamil literature which can mean "heroism, bravery (usually with the added connotation of fierceness or even cruelty)." (Shulman 1980:288f.; 1985:350).

nobles, warriors, robbers, merchants, nomads, forest dwellers, farmers, pastoralists, Muslims and so on. As a family god he has assumed all the characteristics of most of his followers and their caste professions.

The immanence of the divine in the world of humans, according to folk religion, is also reflected in the cosmology and the experience of time which prevailed in folk belief. The classical theory of four *yugas* of long duration is replaced by the simple notion of the Satyayuga ("the *yuga* of truth") and the Kaliyuga ("the *yuga* of vice") in the folk religious experience. Moreover, there is still co-inherence of the Satyayuga in the Kaliyuga. The Satyayuga prevails on certain occasions, for instance, on Somvatī Amāvāsyā. The qualities of both ages mingle the further we turn away from the influence of the brahmanical ritual and texts. A Dhangar shepherd and devotee of Khaṇḍobā can still say about Somvatī Amāvāsyā:

> "On that day we go to Jejurī. If there were no Satyayuga we would not go to Jejurī."

Because the cosmos of folk religion is preponderantly horizontal, and god is immanent in this world, oral literature tends to reflect life on earth and its environment. The songs of the bards of Khaṇḍobā or the myths *(ovīs)* sung by the Dhangar shepherds reflect an enchanted and yet, often realistic, intimate view of their traditional life. Oral literature may use images and ideas from scriptural texts in Sanskrit and Marathi, or from the Bhakti literature of the Maharashtrian saints, but such borrowings are marginal, often transformed and interpreted in the context of folk culture. In the songs of the Vāghyās, who are the bards of Khaṇḍobās and sing his miraculous deeds, the Lord is a king who goes for a hunt on Somvatī Amāvāsyā day.

IV. *The historical background of the hunting excursion*

Thus in the matrix of the festival we find the idea that Khaṇḍobā goes for a hunt. Nowadays this idea may become disfunctional and evanescent. There is no game to be hunted by hunters and foodgatherers, or by sedentary communities who enrich their settled life and supplement their food by hunting in the wilderness. There are no kings and princes who practise the royal pastime of hunting. Yet the old notion that hunting involves excitement or even eroticism, besides food, and generation of life out of death, is still reflected in the oral literature and casual statements made on Somvatī Amāvāsyā, when it is said that the Lord "goes for a hunt" or "plays hunting." Folk religion is sensitive to the environmental, social, historical, and local context more than the written brahmanical text which tries to disentangle the cult from the phenomenological world. One may ask why Khaṇḍobā's hunt is traditionally emphasized. And we may answer that he is, like Rudra, the "Lord of the hunters" and like Mallanna in Warangal (Sontheimer 1985:148), "the Lord of those who hunt with spears," and that this was instrumental in celebrating a common epithet or mythologeme in the festival. Or we may say: after all Khaṇḍobā is a king, and kings must go hunting according to their dharma and have erotic adventures in the forest. It seems, however, that such traditions are not simply observed for these reasons, but go back to an environmental core and to ancient, if not prehistorical roots which have survived. In fact, the whole cult is a mirror of survivals. For example, if Khaṇḍobā is (or rather was) the "Lord of Robbers," i.e. of the Rāmośīs, the environmental and historical core is the fact that robber chieftains and heroes like Umājī Naik would raid merchant caravans passing Jejurī, which was situated at a crossroad. The legend of Vālmīki, "the robber," could be localized near Jejurī for the same reason (Sontheimer 1991:120f).

Hunting wild boars was quite common amongst the villagers around Jejurī. A 52 year old member of the Māḷī ("gardener") caste tells how his father used to go hunting near his village Sākurḍe, close to Jejurī. He would use a spear or an axe to hunt wild boars. Not only was the "mutton" a supplementary diet, but oil extracted while cooking the meat had medicinal properties against rheumatism etc. Within living memory the Karhā valley and in particular, the eastern part of it up to Baramati was covered with trees and bushes typical of the pastoral area in Maharashtra. They are all mentioned in the songs of the Vāghyās, in the description of the forest(s) which Khaṇḍobā traverses while on the hunt: the Bābhūḷ *(Acacia Arabica)*, the Nīm *(Azadirachta Indica)*, the Bor or Jujube *(Zyzyphus Jujuba)*, the Khair *(Acacia catechu)*, the Hivar *(Mimosa* or *Acacia Tomentosa)*, the Murmuti (?; a bush), the Nivaḍuṅg (Prickly Pear; *Cactus Indicus)*, the Tarvaḍ (a bush rather than a tree; *Cassia Auriculata)* and so on.[13] In prehistoric times hunting and fishing communities must have frequented the area. Microliths can be found along the banks on the eastern part of the river, mostly on its northern bank. D.D. Kosambi in his study on the microlithic tracks in the Poona District mentions: "The finest technique belongs to the Karhā track, and may be seen at its highest development in Deuḷgav-Gāḍā." (Kosambi 1962:128). Subsequently, a rather casual search at the spot (Ghoḍe-uḍḍān) where Khaṇḍobā terminates his hunt with a bath in the river, again yielded microliths of the finest quality. Formerly, according to oral sources, the hunt would lead across the river upto the northern margin of the valley and the ancient Yādava temple of Bhuleśvar. This is an area where many Dhangars still have their seasonal monsoon camps. Today the god still crosses the Karhā river after his bath and visits the village of Dhālavḍi. Here he is "shown" *nived* (= Skt. *naivedya)* consisting mainly of millet bread and his entourage is given a meal by the villagers at the shrine of the god Bābīr. This shrine is flanked by ancestor stones showing a warrior and his wife seated on a horse, in imitation of the popular representations of Khaṇḍobā and his wife Mhāḷsā, or Bāṇāī, his second wife from the Dhangar shepherd com-

[13] For instance in a performance of a *jāgraṇ* ("vigil") by Shankar Dhondiba Jadhav, a famous Vāghyā (Marāṭhā) from Dhāmni (Khed taluka, Pune distr.).

munity. Bābīr was originally a deity of the Gavḷīs, a widespread community of keepers of buffaloes and large cattle in the semi-arid southern parts of Maharashtra. Because of deteriorating pastures they were replaced by the sheep-breeding Dhangars. Bābīr himself was a cowherd boy. He was slain by Rāmośīs who protected standing crops in the fields belonging to the farmers. After his death he was deified. A major shrine with a festival *(jatrā)* for this god is found at Nhāī Rūī between Indāpūr and Bārāmati (Sontheimer 1989:87). The survival of the "tribal" element may be seen in the Mahādev Koḷīs. They were the traditional hunters and, when forced by circumstances, the traditional robbers of Maharashtra, before they were absorbed by the rural populace as a caste of boatmen and water carriers, or survived as "tribes" in the forested parts of the Western Ghats.

The tradition of the "God as King" going for a hunt is also attested by two stone panels which are found in the village of Sākurḍe, to which we have already referred, and in the village of Mūrti Moḍhve situated about 5 kms to the east of Jejuri. The panels show a hunter with a bow who wears large earrings and a halo typical of Bhairava. He is followed by a woman who wears a crown *(kirīṭa,* in Mūrti Moḍhve) or a similar halo like Bhairava (in Sākurḍe). She may be his *śakti.* In front of the hunter, who holds a raised bow, wild boars and antelopes are in flight, pursued by dogs. Several emaciated followers are indicated. The god is now locally called *Vandev* (the god of the forest) or Bhairava. The sculptures are characteristic of the Yādava period (c. 14th or 13th cent.). In Mūrti Moḍhve hero-stones of the same period also exist in considerable number. Some of them depict the defence of cattle and the death of the hero. Wild cows or *vangāys* were still plentiful around Mūrti Moḍhve a few decades ago. At the instance of the villagers they had to be chased away by members of the itinerant hunter caste, the Rās Phāse Pārḍhīs, because they damaged the standing crops. Now only an occasional pack of wolves and rabbits can be met in this area. Amongst the famous royal devotees of the Khaṇḍobā of Jejurī were King Śāhū (1709-1749), who was an "avid hunter" (Sontheimer 1989c:217), and Malhārrāv Hoḷkar (Sontheimer 1989a:308).

Thus the excursion on Somvatī Amāvāsyā may be a reflection of this situational core of hunting which is deeply embedded in the natural environment and the local hunting traditions.

V. *Khaṇḍoba's hunt in the oral traditions of the Vāghyās and Dhangars*

In an old Vāghyā song called the *Somvatī pad (pad* 22) we have the description of the hunting procession of the Lord.[14] The song is at least as old as 1823.

> ... I see the splendid procession going to the Karhā river
> The sparkling vanguard at the Wednesday Bazaar
> The Lord goes to meet the Hoḷkar
> They run, push, jostle, choke the whole road
> What crowds! What throngs!
> It's a glorious multitude
> *Breaking away the king flashes and vanishes*
> *eluding all his horsemen*
> Nīlgāy, spotted deer, sāṃbar take flight in fear
> The hunting dogs are unleashed
> Antelopes, leopards, sāṃbars, deer stampede away
> Enjoying his hunting game the Lord
> arrives at the Karhā river.
> (Emphasis added).

The longest song of the Vāghyās *(pad* 48) describes the exit of Khaṇḍobā alias Malukhān into the forest, his hunt, and his stay at Bāṇāī's shepherd camp. It is again a song at least as old as 1823.

[14] I generally prefer to use the term "Lord" for Ma. *dev* rather than the "god" or "God." Khaṇḍobā has many names, for example Mārt(t)aṇḍa Bhairava, Khaṇḍerāv/Khaṇḍerāyā, Mallarī, Malhār(ī), Mālu, Mallukhān, which are all used in certain contexts by certain people.

Here is the beginning:

The Mahārāj of Fort Jejurī, Savāī Malukhān,
Leads a hunting expedition to the forest,
He rides a horse, the Minister by his side
Among his retinue of titled nobles *(mānkarīs)*,
[and] strong heroes *(vīr baḷivān)* is
Yeśvant Rāv with his flame-red banner in front.
Battle music sounds, the hunting pack growls,
The god hunts and plays among the shadows of the forest.
Surrounded by mountains and cliffs the thirsty Malhār
Searches rivers and lakes. And he finds Cannāpur.
The shepherds' town with nine lakh sheep.
...

There are many versions of the story of Bāṇāī, the shepherdess whom Khaṇḍobā meets and marries after he has traversed the forest. The parallels to the story of Śakuntalā, according to the *Mahābhārata*, are evident. We shall give a representative excerpt from a long version of the myth told by a Dhangar informant, the late Limba Torve:

What happened now while the god was sulking? He said: "Pārdhān (Minister), call the people of the town. After calling them we shall go hunting. Let's go hunting." Then what did the Pārdhān do? He loaded the cannons and guns. He called the people of the town: "Come, the god is going to go hunting." There was an army of 12,000 men. The god was on his way. He left the fort of Jejurī. And the army came down...
The god started hunting. The first time he shouted. His shouting made the forest tremble. The second time he shouted. Trees and bushes were shaken. The third time he shouted. Cliffs and rocks loosened. The fourth time he shouted [in a retold version: he rounded up the herds of game: Sāṃbar, spotted deer, and wild boar] and began to hunt. The sixth time he shouted. He made heaps of the hunted animals. He piled the meat on a wooden scaffold. The god started hunting. The army of the 12,000 became thirsty. The 12,000 became very thirsty. Nowhere there

> was water. And thus the army of 12,000 went back to the fort of Jejurī...[15]

Khaṇḍobā has to cross five or more different "frightful" forests. Finally even his Minister (Heggaḍe-Pradhān) is sent back before they arrive at Bāṇāī's shepherds camp or settlement (Ma. *vāḍā).* According to the *Mahābhārata,* King Duḥṣanta [sic] has to cross several forests during his hunt, makes a virtual slaughter of the animals of the forest and finally reaches the *āśrama* of the Ṛṣi Kaṇva (1.63-67, Crit. Edn.). During his march he is accompanied by his army, the people of the town, the ministers *(āmātya)* and his "chaplin" *(purohita).* Like Khaṇḍobā he leaves them behind one by one, and when he reaches Kaṇva's hermitage within the *āśrama* (similarly to Bāṇāī's *vāḍā* in the encampment or settlement of the Dhangars) he meets Śakuntalā who was abandoned by Menakā (of Indra's heaven) in the forest. Bāṇāī or Raṃbhāī (one of Indra's daughters, see below) was similarly "abandoned" in the forest according to Dhangar stories (Sontheimer 1989a).

But, independent of the similarity of incidents in the Śakuntalā story and the myth of Bāṇāī, we find a basic structure wherever we look at in our materials and obtain what could perhaps be called the meta-contextual text of the king's hunt and the encounter with the girl from the wilderness. The components of the text would be: Crossing the threshold — hunting (which merges into the cattle raids, capture of women, and conquests) — snatching life out of the jaws of death — eroticism — *vanvās* — winning life and the goods of life (e.g. the prey, which is hunted for food, *vīrya,* fertility etc.) — the extension or restoration of *sva* or the renewal of life — triumphant return.

---

[15] For text and translation of the full story see Sontheimer (1989a:7-62).

VI. *Hunting and eroticism in the forest*

Wilderness, its dangers and ambivalence, hunting, the passion and excitement of hunting, death and fertility, eroticism and the adventures of the hero, king, or god are all invariably linked in actual hunting practises, ritual hunts, and literature. These pervasive themes occur *mutatis mutandis* in hunting practises of "tribals" and in their oral literature, in temple rituals and temple legends, in the two epics, and in purāṇic and poetic Sanskrit literature,[16] in classical Tamil literature, and in South Indian medieval literature. A few examples may illustrate this point.

In the eastern Ghats in Andhra Pradesh shifting cultivators like the Koṇḍu Reḍḍis associate hunting with eroticism. In their hunting practises, herbal juices, expressly called "love potions" (Tel. *valapu mandu)* are used while tracing the footprints of the wild boar (Tel. *aḍavi pandi)*. The hunter sprinkles the herbal juice on its footprints and waits for the prey to return. The beast is attracted by the love potion and returns to the hunter who kills it with bow and arrow. The Koṇḍu Reḍḍis make it explicit that the wild boar develops love (Tel. *valapu)* for the hunter and comes towards him thereby facing death.[17]

The ritual hunt of the goddess Bharāḍī in the village Angevadi (Malvan taluka) in the Sindhudurg district of Maharashtra is an example of an event which in other places now only lives in memory. Annually, the young male population of the village has to go for a wild boar hunt. The actual village festival *(jatrā)* cannot begin

---

[16] For a highly informative paper on the evidence in Sanskrit literature, see Friedrich Wilhelm (1991:7-16). Daśaratha's addiction to hunting and his passion for a lovely woman were comparable appetites for Kālidāsa in his *Raghuvaṃśa* (IX.69). Wilhelm 1991:10. For the theme of hunting and eroticism see also Hofstetter 1980:130ff. Another reference may serve for many: In the *Vetālapañcaviṃśatikā* (XIX,51ff.) King Rūpasena forgoes hunting and receives the daughter of the Ṛṣi in return. He marries her according to the Gāndharva rites.

[17] Information received from Prof. M.L.K. Murty (Hyderabad).

unless a boar is shot. Some of the hunters are equipped with guns and are, as it were, led and inspired by the goddess. That is, if no beast can be tracked down, one of the hunters will be possessed by the goddess and she will direct the way through her medium. The whole hunt — which may take several days — is felt as fraught with horripilation, especially if a whole troop of wild boars turns up "like an avalanche of stones." The stay in the jungle (Ma. *rān),* the communal meals, and drinking the water of the forest is an experience which transcends the normal flow of village life. The hunter who first sights a boar receives special honours. The women of the village, meanwhile, prepare garlands of flowers. When the wild boar or "he who presides over the village border" (Ma. *sīmecā adhikārī)* is carried into the village — tied upside down to a pole — he is garlanded by the villagers. The young women of the village perform the ceremony of lights' *(ārati)* by waving lights around the beast. The "hero" who has sighted the boar first will get the best piece of the meat, whereas the other parts will be distributed amongst all the households. The "hero" is asked to give a common dinner for the small village community (Sāvant 1985:77-80). The goddess Bharāḍī is identified with the "Jagadaṃbā Māyabhavānī", the Maharashtrian Durgāmahiṣāsuramardinī, who has her centre in Tuljapur in the Osmanabad district. An erotic relationship between the Devī and the buffalo demon is suggested in Sanskrit texts (Shulman 1980:178), in the desire of Mahiṣa to marry the goddess. A similar relationship is continued on the level of South Indian village religion where the goddess' desire for her lover, the buffalo victim, provides a pervasive theme in ritual and legend (Brubaker 1978; Shulman 1980). Bharāḍī is a village goddess who annually goes for a hunt and possesses the hunters before and during the hunt. Her dead prey is received and worshipped by the festive women of the village who seem to represent the goddess. Though there is no marriage between the two, the case reminds us of the intruding god = Mhasobā/Mhaskobā of Vir (Purandar taluka, Pune district) who is first killed by the goddess at the border of the village and then married to the village goddess (Kosambi 1962:122; Shulman 1980:178; Sontheimer 1989:57). The goddess, and the village represented by her, need the stimulus of the outsider coming from the wilderness. In the context of agriculture the fertility of the fields increases. The success or failure of crops depends on hunting, as amongst the Murias of Bastar (Elwin 1947:204) who also enact a communal hunt which precedes the ceremonial eating of the first mangoes of the year (Elwin 1947:214). The nature of the wild-boar is thus frequently seen as ambivalent: he destroys crops, but he also ploughs (for example, Gonda 1954:128ff.; Oppitz 1983).

The hunting in the wilderness usually ends with an erotic adventure for the hunter, hero, king, or god who meets the beautiful girl in the forest and falls in love with her. The most famous example in South India is, of course, Murukaṉ's courtship of Vaḷḷi. The earliest reference to Murukaṉ and Vaḷḷi in personified form is found in an early poem of the Caṅkam period (*naṟṟiṇai* 82.4; Zvelebil 1977:233). Ever since the theme is perpetuated in Tamil culture and has its climax in the Kantapurāṇam of Kaciyappa Civācāriyar (see, e.g. Zvelebil 1977:228-246; Shulman 1980: ch.8) — composed around 1550 A.D. (Zvelebil 1974:186). According to the Kantapurāṇam, two daughters of Viṣṇu performed *tapas* near Caravaṇappokai to be wed to Murukaṉ. By the grace of Murukaṉ, one of them was born as the daughter of Indra and raised by his white elephant; hence she was named Teyvayāṉai [...] The second daughter of Viṣṇu is born to a deer which was impregnated by the lustful glance of the sage Civamuṉi. The deer abandoned her in a pit where she was found by Nampi, the lord of the Kuṟuvai hunters, who longed for a daughter. The hunter chief adopted her and named her Vaḷḷi, since she was born in a pit from which old men scrape the roots of the Vaḷḷi [...] Eventually, after many obstacles and mutual lovesickness Murukaṉ married Vaḷḷi (Shulman 1980:275).

Arjuna during his sojourn in the forest is known for four encounters with women: Ulūpī, a Nāga princess, Citrāngadā, with five Apsarases, and with Kṛṣṇa's sister Subhadrā whom he fell in love with (Ruben 1962:7). Bhīma marries the demoness Hiḍimbā who fell in love with him. His reputation has spread far amongst the tribes.

Amongst the Koyi tribe in Andhra Pradesh there is a tradition that Bhīma while hunting in the jungle met a tribal woman and married her. The Koyis trace their ancestry to this liaison (Thurston 1909: Vol IV, 56, 71). In the myth of Ceñcūlakṣmī and Narasiṃha, the heroine is the daughter of a Ceñcū "chief" or "king." She was a huntress and when she saw a lion in the forest of the Eastern Ghats, she shot him with bow and arrow. From the dead lion the handsome Narasiṃha arose and they fell in love with each other (Sontheimer 1985:146). The story of Narasiṃha and Ceñcūlakṣmī is associated, for instance, with Ahobilam, an important centre of the Narasiṃha cult in Andhra Pradesh. Here in the heavily forested upper part of Ahobilam, Narasiṃha is said to be *ugra*, whereas in the temple complex of the *kṣetra* in the valley he is said to be *saumya*. A vivid panel in one of the shrines shows a huge Ceñcūlakṣmī with leaf skirt, who leans on her bow. A miniature Narasiṃha kneels before her and removes a thorn from her foot.

The myth of the god or king and his two wives is one of the most widespread in India and its most famous example is Murukaṉ, Teyvayāṉai and Vaḷḷi, who belongs to the tribal Kuṟuvars. In Tirupati Veṅkaṭeśvar fell in love with Padmāvatī while on hunt in the forest according to the temple *Māhātmya (Śri Venkateshwara Leela Mahatmyamu*, ch. xvi). In every cult of a folk deity similar to the one of Khaṇḍobā, for example in the Mallanna cult (Andhra Pradesh), Mailāra cult (Karṇataka) etc., the oral myth of the second "wife" is very elaborate. The second wife comes from or is brought up amongst forest tribals, fisherfolk, hunters, pastoralists, or even itinerant merchants: Khaṇḍobā's second wife in Malegaon (Nanded district) comes from the once itinerant merchant groups of the Bañjāras. The more we move away from the folk traditions into a structured, stratified or hierarchized context, the first wife would be assigned a vertical, celestial, scriptural-purāṇic background. She would be a manifestation of Pārvatī and at the same belong to a dominant caste. Thus Mhāḷsā, the first wife of Khaṇḍobā is said to belong to the once influential caste of the Liṅgāyat merchants (Liṅgāyat Vāṇīs), and she is brought up by the rich merchant prince

Timmāśeṭ of Nevāsā. The second "wife" would become a manifestation of another celestial female, for example, of the heavenly courtezan Rambhā of Indra's court, or of Gaṅgā, who is assigned a place in the forest or in the underworld (as Patālagaṅgā). Thus Gaṅgā is often said to be "reborn" on earth as Bāṇāī.

Inevitably the hunt of the god leads to the encounter with Bāṇāī and their subsequent "marriage," which causes a sustained tension and open quarrel between the wives.[18] Apparently, the second wife is given a lower status in the *kṣetra* of the god. For instance, Bāṇāī is assigned a place in a temple which has been built over what is actually a little "cave." It is situated outside the temple fort, halfway up the stairs leading to the hillfort. But this does not reflect the importance of Bāṇāī in the Khaṇḍobā cult. It seems that — as has also been demonstrated in the context of other royal cults and ritual kingship — the values of eroticism and fertility which Bāṇāī stands for are given a higher rank than ritual purity.[19] These values account also for the reproach which is sometimes levelled at the "rustic" (Kosambi 1962:86) Khaṇḍobā cult in which — as a Maharashtrian brahman noted at the end of the last century — non-brahmanical priests "were *pūjārīs* and ritual purity was very little respected" (Sontheimer 1989b:333). Modern authorities like the historian G.H. Khare could, moreover, categorically hold that it is only a cult of *sakāma bhakti* (Khare 1958:88). Thus, in certain contexts the status of the two women seems to be equal and at times the status of the resolute, "rustic" Bāṇāī seems to be even higher. It is Bāṇāī, besides Khaṇḍobā, to whom wishes for cattle and fertility of crops are directed rather than to Mhāḷsā. Nonvegetarian offerings are sent to her. The purity of the *kṣetra* is represented by Mhāḷsā, and Bāṇāī introduces the pollution of the wilderness. Thus a Vāghyā song *(pad* 14) describes the anger of Mhāḷsā:

---

[18] For the popularity of the *ēcal* genre in Tamilnadu which deals with the quarrels of the co-wives of the god, see Shulman 1980:294f.

[19] See Marglin 1985, and the essays in Carman 1985.

We are Lingāyat Vāṇīs
We are Lingāyat Vāṇīs
We follow the Śiva-Dharma, O Woman,
We follow the Śiva-Dharma,
We constantly contemplate Śiva,
        We keep our food and water covered.

There are mirrors inlaid in our courtyard walls,
        where we count our diamonds and precious stones
After bathing with Gaṅgā water
After bathing with Gaṅgā water, we worship the Tuḷsi plant,
        smearing ashes on the forehead.
Your entry
        has polluted our house,
        has polluted our house,
        has polluted our house,
Oh my, oh my, what spell you have cast on the Lord.
O Woman, how did you make Mallārī crazy,
        Mhāḷsā said: O Bāṇu, O Woman,
        you have made Mallārī crazy

Yet in other contexts, as we have said, the two women are equal, and stand in a complementary relationship, and even cooperate in ritual contexts, for example during Divāḷī. In fact all the king's wives and courtezans (the Muraḷīs) cooperate in perfect harmony. We quote the first stanza of a Vāghyā song *(pad* 40):

Parrots chatter among the trees
Crows caw, sparrows twitter at the doorstep
Herons at the reservoir, Kokilas in the mango grove
High on the tree Blue Jays and Little Spotted Owls
The peacock's cries!
The celestial maidens go to fetch water with their pots.
Jejurī, the city of birds, where the water of the River
        Karhā is like nectar.
Bāṇu and Mhāḷsā anoint the Lord with fragrant pastes
Seated on a square wooden platform the Lord bathes
        with hot water from the two-handled vessel.
He wears a silken, yellow dhoti, a musk mark
        on his forehead
Phulāī, the gardener woman, garlands him

Raṃbhāī, the tailor woman, embroiders his shawl.
In a chamber a Muraḷī lovingly sings his praise
His ornaments are golden, golden is his silken upper garment.
He is offered a seat of sandalwood, with coloured
powders they draw decorative
patterns in front of him.
Wake up, quick! It's Divālī, says Mhāḷsā to Lord Mālu
Wake up, let me put collyrium into your eyes
Divāli has come.

At times the "vegetarian" Mhāḷsā even catches fish while Bāṇāī watches this reversal of roles. At other times Bāṇāī and Mhāḷsā even eat from the same plate, a scene which can otherwise only be seen amongst "uncouth" Dhangar children.

Thus the hunt leads to the encounter with Bāṇāī which can be viewed from various related points of view. The fixed settlement, the village or the *kṣetra* needs the complementarity of the forest. The king has to dominate the forests as part of his kingdom or extend his kingdom into it. The sacrifice of the animals (which may merge into a battle against enemies or demons) may amount to the assimilation of powers of the wild animals to the personal powers of the king, but hunting is also a sacrifice to enhance the fertility of the fields and often, incidentally, fields are temporarily turned into a forest for the purposes of the hunt (see below and cp. Höfer 1968:74). After the hunt follows the erotic adventure or even direct love relationship by which the king or god binds to himself the powers and riches of the forest, or in the case of Bāṇāī, of her habitat, the pastoral area. Bāṇāī is often the rich, beautiful "Mirdhīn" (Head) of twelve Dhangar *vāḍas* or settlements who owns 900,000 sheep. From another point of view the erotic relationship turns into emotional bhakti. Bāṇāī is the epitome of that emotional love which drives the Lord "crazy." Along with her come her followers, the Dhangars, who become the most faithful bhaktas of the Lord and would not miss attending a single Somvatī Amāvāsyā. We might also conclude that Khaṇḍobā now dominates the forest and the pastoral world and has becoming the Lord of the pastoralists, whereas he has converted the pastoralists into "hunters," if only in the ritual drama of the Somvatī Amāvāsyā festival.

Mhāḷsā — in the songs of the Vāghyās — insists in vain on her prior, "legal," and superior rights and status, her domestic qualities, her excellent food, and her intrinsic love for her protector. From her point of view Mhāḷsā cannot resign to the fact that Khaṇḍobā goes for a hunt. At times she seems to accompany him, because on the level of the *Māhātmya* and certain ritual contexts she can also be called the *ardhāṅginī* of Śiva. Or she actively helps him as his *śakti* according to the more śāktic versions of the myth of his battle against the demon kings Maṇi and Malla.[20] But in the story of the hunt and encounter of Bāṇāī she remains at home trying to put obstacles in his way by magical means, which could kill him, or so it seems. She is sorry to have caused the exit of the Lord into the wilderness and she experiences a kind of *viraha*, a separation from the distant hunter traversing the five forests and the pastoral area. In the song which narrates the sojourn of the Lord in the wilderness Mhāḷsā expresses her anxiety to her female confidante. It is a constant refrain at the end of each stanza (*pad* 48):

> Says the graceful Mhāḷsā: "Listen, oh Raṃbhāī,
> The Lord has gone for a hunt,
> why isn't he back yet?"

Yet it is not just Mhāḷsā who drives him out into the wilderness. Actually it is the standstill of the world, the stagnation of life. Life has become insipid in the *kṣetra* and this leads to Khaṇḍobā's exit. Thus, in the version of the Bāṇāī legend told by Limba Torve (see above) we hear (in short):

> Khaṇḍobā and his wife Mhāḷsā: What did they do? They were sitting side by side — somewhere. At that time they used to sit like this somewhere every day ...
> The Minister was worried by their idleness and brought the game of chess in order to create a quarrel between the two.

---

[20] The myth is reflected visually in the ubiquitous depiction of Mallārī: Khaṇḍobā and Mhāḷsā seated on a horse defeating the demons Maṇi and Malla. It is Mhāḷsā who is shown shedding the blood of the demons.

> Khaṇḍobā lost and had to surrender all his clothes, his ornaments, and even his dogs to Mhāḷsā. He retained only his pouch containing magical turmeric dust *(bhaṇḍār)* and his spear *(jheṇḍā)*. Sulking he ordered his minister to call the 12,000 inhabitants of the town and went with them for a hunt in the wilderness (ctd. above, p. 35).

In another version he loses not only his crown "worked with golden threads," but also his kingdom including Pāli (Pāli-Pember), Naḷdurg, and Jejurī.[21]

VII. *The encounter with Bāṇāī*

1. The origins of Bāṇāī

About Mhāḷsā's purāṇic background there is unanimity in the scriptural and oral texts in Maharashtra: Pārvatī is "born" as Mhāḷsā on earth. The sources also basically agree that Mhāḷsā was brought up by her foster father Timmaśeṭ at Nevāsā (Aurangabad district) and married at Pāli (Satara district) where her marriage to Khaṇḍobā is celebrated annually on the 15th of the light half of the month of Pauṣ (Dec.-Jan.). This is also told in the *JM* (Khāḍe 1925:44). Historically, Mhāḷsā seems to have been an independent goddess who had her own cult before it was absorbed by the Khaṇḍobā cult by identifying her with Pārvatī and naming Khaṇḍobā Mhāḷsākānt, "the husband of Mhāḷsā." In the *Līḷācaritra* (13th cent.) which records the life of Cakradhara, the "founder" of the Mahānubhāva sect, Mhāḷsā is an independent goddess at Nevāsā *(Uttarārdha* 331; Ḍhere 1961:74) and even today separate temples for her continue to exist (Ḍhere 1961:67).

The sources on Bāṇāī's background tell a much more chequered story. Whereas one would think that the dominant view in *all* the

---

[21] Nāmdev Vāghe Śingṇāpūrkar, caste: Gopāl.

oral versions we have come across so far, makes Bāṇāī the *second* wife of Khaṇḍobā, the *JM* and the *MV* strike a discordant note. Here Bāṇāī is the *third* wife of Mārtaṇḍa Bhairava. She was Jayā, a friend or *dāsī* of Pārvatī. We shall give a summary of the version in the *MV* (27.35ff):

> Pārvatī promised Jayā, her favourite friend *(sakhī)* who is as if a "creeper of beauty" *(lāvaṇyalatikā)* and has "eyes like a doe" *(mṛgākṣī)* that she would also become Paśupatī's husband *(bhartā)* on earth. Śiva warns that another wife will cause her great difficulties. He forecasts that after he has despatched Maṇi and Malla and is known as Mallārī she (Jayā) will be born as a daughter of the demon Bāṇa (Bāṇāsura) and thus will be called Bāṇā. When Malla was slain by Malhāri, Bāṇā was born after some time. She insisted on marrying nobody except Hara. Seeing his daughters's obstinacy Bāṇāsura consulted Nārada who said that she would become Śiva's wife after performing *tapas*. When Nārada saw the bhakti of Bāṇā he taught her the Malhāri-mantra. Bāṇā retired to the frightful forest equipped with the mantra. She practised excessively harsh *tapas* without avail. Thus she left the place and came to a village called Candanpur. There, on the bank of the river, she practised austere *tapas* with pleasure. She stood on the river bank under the Candana tree and recited the mantra remembering Nārada's feet. Mārtaṇḍa remembered the boon granted to Jayā. In the forest there was a shepherd's *vāḍā* (encampment) which was inhabited by Dhangars. Their headman was Ajāmeḷ, who was very rich and a great bhakta of Śiva. Mārtaṇḍa called the Minister and both speedly rode to Bāṇā. Malhāri swooned *(dehabhāna gelā visaroni)*. Then he ordered the Pradhān to tell that the aim of her *tapas* had been accomplished and that he whom she had seen in her mind was present in person. When Bāṇā saw Malhāri, her mind was shaken and she was overpowered by the eight feelings *(aṣṭabhāva)* of bhakti and her eyes filled with tears. On her request Ajāmeḷ, her fosterfather, was to come along for the marriage. Immediately elephants, horses, and palanquins appeared in the forest. Ajāmeḷ and all the Dhangars took a seat on the elephants etc. Malhāri took Bāṇā along on his horse and full of joy they all quickly reached Naḷdurg.

There, after an auspicious time *(muhūrta)* had been fixed, the marriage with Bāṇā was performed *(Bāṇesī lāvileṃ lagna)*. After 16 days the festival *(utsāha)* came to an end.

Jayā/Bāṇāī as the "third wife" of Mārtaṇḍa and daughter of Bāṇa seems to be an exceptional solution which just serves as an etymological aetiology for "Jayādri/Jayā" which is Jejurī. Bāṇāsura, however, himself figures occasionally in oral stories when Gaṅgā is to be "born" on earth as Bāṇāī. It is left to Bāṇāsura to deposit the little girl in the middle of the forest:

> Gaṅgā had fallen out of Śiva's matted hair during the war with demons and had become a rock. She had fallen near the place where the demons had turned into rocks after their defeat. Thus she had to be salvaged. Viṣṇu, Brahmā, and Maheś turned her into a three months' old girl. They made a box and kept her in it. They fixed a chain made out of nine jewels. They asked Bāṇāsura to place the box into the thick forest near Candanpur where it was found by the Dhangars. Because the box had been taken there by Bāṇāsura and she was Gaṅgā from Śiva's matted hair, the little girl was called Bāngaṅgā. Her father was a great bhakta of Śaṅkar, who worshipped him on the bank of the river. The girl would always follow him rather than do her work at home. When she was 15 or 16 years old she would go with father — where? To the Karhā-Gaṅgā. He had his bath (Ma. *aṃghol)* and then went ahead to visit the temple [of Khaṇḍobā in Jejurī]. She entered the Gaṅgā. Then she also [like her father] made 21 *liṅgs* of sand on the river bank.[22]

Some folk traditions make Bāṇāī one of the seven daughters of Indra.[23] She was expelled by Indra and left as the little girl in a box in the forest of Candanpur. There she was found by the Dhangars. When she grew up she became a worshipper of Śiva alias Khaṇḍobā

---

[22] Malhārī Sakhārām Vāḷke, Dhangar.

[23] In the *Bṛhatsaṃhitā* of Varāhamihira (42.39-40) Jayā und Vijayā are amongst the seven or five daughters of Indra (Raghavan 1979:142).

and eventually married him after staying with him in the forest for twelve years (Ḍhere 1961:52). According to another elaborate version, a childless, rich Dhangar called Khyāmū practised *tapas* in the forest for twelve years and worshipped Indra. Finally Indra sent the heavenly courtezan Raṃbhā in the shape of a net of flowers to the earth. Khyāmū had to retrieve it from the ocean and was nearly drowned. When he unfolded the net a little girl emerged, who was eventually called Bāṇāī.

She grew up and became the head of twelve Dhangar settlements. There is never any mention in this long and detailed version that Bāṇāī worshipped Khaṇḍobā before he appeared on the *vāḍā* (Sontheimer 1989:7-62).

Another story told by a Vāghyā shows how aspects of Bāṇāī proliferate, but also how she assumes the characteristics of her social and natural environment:

> A girl was born of Puṣpavantī and turmeric dust given to her by Nārada. She was called Bāṇu, that is Bāngaṅgā. She was put into a box and the box was immersed in the Gaṅgā. The box fell into the net of fishermen (Bhoīs). They tried to pull it out, but it was too heavy and they pushed it again into the river. Twelve boys of twelve castes were playing the stick game *(iṭhidaṇḍī)*. The stick fell into the river. They jumped into the river. The box came floating down the river. They pulled it out, but it smelled of *davṇā.*[24] "Damned," they said, "it stinks," and they threw it back. Meanwhile a Dhangar came with his flock to the bank of the river. He jumped into the river and pulled out the box. He tied it to the neck of his favourite sheep. It became the *ghāṭī* [the handbell of the Muraḷīs which they ring during their dances]. The sheep went into the field of the Māḷīs [traditionally "gardeners" and agriculturists], [the boys] untied the bell and kept it in a large sack. Her light spread from it. The light went to the field of the Māḷīs.

[24] Southernwood; it is a plant with a strong smell.

> The Māḷī women were stringing flowers. The light became Bāṇu. The Māḷī women put a flower garland around her neck. She went from the field of the Māḷīs to the Karhā river. She had a bath. She became Pāngaṅgā *[sic]*.[25]

In most stories Bāṇāī begins her career on earth in a river, for example, in the Bāṇgaṅgā which may be the tributary of the Godāvarī in the Nasik district, or, e.g. the Bāṇgaṅgā at Phaltan (Satara district). At times she is found in a hole or deep part of the river (Ma. *ḍoha)* where water stays even in the dry season, as, e.g. Indra's eldest daughter was found by Gāvḍās in a deep part of the River Girṇā (Nasik district).[26] Most of the sources make her a devotee of Śiva, and sometimes of the Sun and the Tuḷśī bush.[27] These twin traditions of the worship of Sūrya and Śiva in separate cults have their confluence in the Mārtaṇḍa-Bhairava cult. Sometimes the two are even taken as separate, and it is Bhairava and not Mārtaṇḍa who marries the Śaivite Liṅgāyat Mhāḷsā. The "identification" of the sun and the moon with Khaṇḍobā (according to Stanley 1977 *passim)* probably amounts rather to a subordination of the sun and the moon cult to that of the Khaṇḍobā cult. The *MM* (by Siddhapāl Kesarī) clearly states that Sūrya serves Śiva (5.30-31) and in the *MV* it is said that Mārtaṇḍa is of the *light* of the sun (28.138).

Bāṇāī's connection with the water and fertility is pervasive. Not only is she connected with the river, but as we have seen, she is also retrieved from the *ocean* by the Dhangar Khyāmū. When Khaṇḍobā goes on a hunt he invariably gets thirsty according to all versions known to us. Though probably the great magician could have quenched his thirst flinging a handful *bhaṇḍār* and thereby magically producing water, the oral sources agree that it is Bāṇāī who quenched his thirst. Thus we hear in a Dhangar epic *(ovī):*

---

[25] Bābū Bhaṃḍalkar, Vāghyā, caste: Dhangar.

[26] Mārtaṇḍa Candrabhān Thorve, caste: Vanjāri.

[27] For instance in the story of Nāmdev Vāghe: *Sūryācī ārādhīṇ, tuḷśicī mahāpujā.*

> "At Candanpur is Bāṇāī's *vāḍā*.| There you will get water."| Hegaḍe Pardhān [sic]| Took a pot| Went off| To Bānubāī's *vāḍā*.| "*Please* give us water| The god is thirsty| The god's throat is dry| He is very thirsty."| Hastily Bānubāī got up| Her own pot| She cleaned and | Filled with water.| "Hegaḍe Pardhān| Go to the god| Give him water."| Hegaḍe Pārdhān| Took the pot| Went to the god| The god drank the water| Became peaceful| The god looked at the pot| On the pot| Bānubāī's name| The god said:| "Alone I will go ahead."|[28]

Under Bāṇāī's leadership the cattle wealth of the Dhangars thrived. She herself is the owner of "the 900,000 sheep and goats." Her connection with fertility, vegetation and music is reflected in the strong fragrance of the *davṇā* plant which the boys of the 12 castes notice, the flower garlands of the Māḷī women, and the hand-bell of the Muraḷīs. She also provides food, which is typical of the pastoral area: On her *vāḍā* the disguised Lord is served tremendous amounts millet bread, buttermilk and 25 maunds of millet porridge (Sontheimer 1989a:33). Bāṇāī, though an *avatār* of Gaṅgā, is basically a goddess of the pastoral groups like the Gavḷīs, Dhangars, and the millet growing pastoral farmers. Her status is somewhat more stable than it seems to be in Andhra Pradesh where the traditionally pastoral Gollas worship the goddess Gaṅgā as the second wife of Śiva (Narayana Rao 1989:114). Bāṇāī's quarrels with Mhāḷsā are notorious, but her credentials as the "second wife" have become fully accepted, and on the level of the scriptural *Māhātmya* (*MV* 27.121), the unity of the two is even proclaimed. What Bāṇāī and the Gaṅgā of the Gollas have in common is their "watery nature" (Narayana Rao 1989:114). Besides, Khaṇḍobā's connection with the sun, which Bāṇāī worships, and her riverine and oceanic background suggest that she has some affiliation with the moon. For some ancient commentators on the Caṅkam literature Vaḷḷi is the lunar and female principle, closely connected with Murukaṉ, the

---

[28] Sakhārām Bābū Lakaḍe, caste: Haṭkar Dhangar. For the translation of the whole epic see Sontheimer (1989a).

sun (Zvelebil 1977:242). But we can suggest nothing except a vague possibility. At times the beautiful Bāṇāī reflects the beauty of the moon *(pad* 48):

> ... Her forehead glowed like the Full Moon's light
> Making the rising stars fade

Or *(pad* 29):

> ... She is beautiful as the Crescent Moon
> She makes Lord Malhār crazy.

And when Bāṇāī had to show herself to Mhāḷsā and to the whole court on the insistence of Mhāḷsā, the Vāghyā sings of it *(pad* 48):

> With hands joined in salutation Bāṇāī stood before them
> It was as though the Full Moon's light spread out
> When Mhāḷsā saw Bāṇāī she felt a stab of a
> dagger in her heart.

From a Vāghyā song recorded very recently we may cite two lines:

> The gem Bāṇāī is born
> As though the moon has risen.[29]

2. Khaṇḍobā's stay with the Dhangars and his marriage with Bāṇāī

The scriptural sources like the *MV* and some of the oral traditions influenced by them clearly point to a celestial prehistory of Bāṇāī and trace her origin to Gaṅgā or Indra's daughter. Moreover they often suggest that she performed *tapas* to obtain a husband who is equivalent to Śiva. Sometimes we hear that she wants a husband *(bhratār = bhartā)* who

> does not drown if he is thrown into water,

---

[29] Baban Bhāgujī Dheraṅge, caste: Marāṭhā.

who does not burn if he is thrown into fire,
and who does not get hurt by a stroke of an axe.[30]

As the seventh daughter of Indra she is relegated to the world of the mortals by a "curse" (Ma. *śāp)* which is countered by a boon (Ma. *aśāp):*

"It is very well that you leave me in the world of the mortals, but add a boon to the curse."
"There is the King of Jejurī. He will take you as a spouse and you will be his Queen of equal rank."[31]

Most versions of Bāṇāī's myth forego the "pretext" of the celestial credential or her purāṇic background is reduced at the most to epithets. They concentrate on the events on the earth. The horizontal cosmos on earth is divided into inside and outside, the *kṣetra* and the *vana.* Khaṇḍobā's encounter is then a thinly veiled love story at times. Bāṇāī has come into his dream and, maddened by love he leaves the town on a hunt and finds her in the forest. There are songs which describe him as a bully and a trickster, "a proud Paṭhāṇ" who resembles his royal demon predecessor with his waylaying habits and his sexual prowess. For example, we hear *(pad* 30):

All dressed-up Bāṇu
Pots of milk on her head
She was on her way to the weekly market
When she met the Lord.
"You are holding the loose end of my sari,"
Says Bāṇu,"Get out of my way
The Dhangars are ruffians
They will pick up a fight with you."
Bāṇu pushes the king away
Bāṇu pushes Mallāri away
"Hands off my sari, let me go home."

---

[30] For instance in the story of Nāmdev Vāghe, above.

[31] Mārtaṇḍa Candrabhān Thorve.

Hearing Bāṇu's rebuff
Says God Malhār,
"I charm you with a pinch of turmeric dust
And carry you off on my horse."
At this the beautiful Bāṇu
Began to tremble
"I report all this home
Hands off my sari, let me go home."

But the core of many versions about his stay in Bāṇāī's town or camp is essentially the same. It is striking that now it is not Bāṇāī who is practising *tapas* but it is the Lord who degrades himself and serves Bāṇāī in the disguise of an 'old man.' Some would tell us that Khaṇḍobā spent 12 years of *tapas* or *vanvās* (an unsettled life) in the *vāḍā* of Bāṇāī. We are reminded of Narasiṃha serving Ceñcūlakṣmī, and Murukaṉ "who walks on the thorns and rocks of Vaḷḷimallai seeking the golden hunter girl, massages her feet and brings sheaves of leaves for the royal hunter woman to fashion a dress for her" (Zvelebil 1977:244). Khaṇḍobā becomes Khaṇḍū Gāvḍā from Jejurī. Gāvḍās were (like in Karnāṭaka) farmers of the pastoral area owning cattle. Thus we hear *(pad* 45):

They call me Khaṇḍu Gāvḍā of Jejurī
Give me a chance to serve
So the Lord was employed as a servant in Bāṇu's house
Then in Bāṇu's house
He was given regular duties:
He grazed the 900,000 sheep
Just imagine — the Lord a herdsman!
He took the kids and lambs to suckle.
In the buttermilk gruel
The beautiful Bāṇāī served him some wool.

During his stay the Lord performed several tasks seemingly impossible to solve. The narrators and singers revel in describing the different miracles he performed and the final cathartic transformative sacrifice of the sheep. All versions nearly agree, as, for e.g. described in a song *(pad* 48):

"He, you servant," said Bāṇu.
"Go, wash my sheep in the 'Five Gaṅgās'."
The disguised Lord hearing Bāṇu's words,
Took charge of the nine lakh sheep
"I need no herdsman [to go] with me.
Just bring me my millet bread for the midday meal."
He drowned the nine lakh of sheep in the darkest
pool of the river deeps.
A bunch at a time he grabbed by their hind-legs
and smashed them on the rock.
The bank of the Gaṅgā was flooded with blood.
Their heads floating like lotuses.
The Gaṅgā rose wave after wave
Bursting into a bloody flow, rocks tumbled down.
There were mountainous heaps of sheep skin,
The god played his magic.
The god performed his tricks.
"Listen, O judges of merit! Nine lakh of sheep he slaughtered,
not one was left."

But Khaṇḍobā is ready to revive the sheep on the condition that Bāṇāī "first serves him food" (*pad* 48). Revealing his true nature he elopes with her on his horse to Jejurī. But that seems to have not been all that easy as we learn from the continuation of *pad* 48:

"A soldier has lifted Bāṇu."
They heard of the astounding deed.
Confounded, all the Dhangars gathered.
Their slings were ready for use, they wielded sticks.
There was a hail of stones which came down like a rainfall.
The god flung [turmeric dust], threw them into confusion.
They were beating each other [and] one another.
The son would not recognize his father and beat him with his stick,
The brother would not recognize his brother and hit him on the neck.
One would roll on the ground, shouting wildly.
Another would lisp or stammer in fear:
"Enough of punishment, now be merciful.
Let the birds of the forest live as their nature is."

A straightforward case of a marriage of elopement or, as the Dharmaśāstra would teach us, a mixture of a *gāndharva* and a *rākṣasa* marriage befitting royalty (Kane 1974:Vol. II, pt.1,522f.), is found in the traditions of the Māṅgs or Mātaṅgs. They are ardent devotees of the Khaṇḍobā of Pāli (Satara district) and attend the *jatrā* in the month of Pauṣ (Dec.-Jan.) on the Mṛganakṣatra after fullmoon. On that day the marriage of Khaṇḍobā to Mhāḷsā is celebrated by large numbers of devotees. A Mātaṅga devotee tells us:

> The Lord escaped with Goddess Bāṇu and came into this village. He had brought her from a Dhangar family. He stayed with her in the jungle on the bank of the river Taraḷī near the little village of Pāli. Goddess Bāṇu had gone with her father into the *jungle* for grazing the sheep. While the Lord was wandering in the forest on a hunt, he and the goddess met. He was attracted by the girl, but her father objected and so the Lord took her on his horse and eloped. All the Dhangars did not like the outrageous behaviour of the Lord. They pursued him in the narrow valley of the Tāraḷī river. He was hiding in the forest looking for a chance to escape with Bāṇu.
>
> At that time the Lord enlisted the help of the heroic and predatory Mātaṅgas and Rāmośīs, who keep their word once it is given. They supported the Lord. All of them took up their sticks and axes and told him: "Even if it meant our life, we will not let a hair of your head be touched." Thus, at that time, the Māṅg and Rāmośī people helped the Lord. For the sake of the Lord, they took up their sticks and axes and fought with the Dhangars. Therefore, to remember the bravery of that time the Māṅgs and Rāmośīs take part with sticks in the marriage procession as the vanguard, and only after them follow the other privileged notabilities *(mānkarīs)*.[32]

Most sources would say that before this happened Bāṇāī insisted on an actual marriage to be performed on the Dhangar *vāḍā*. It was done in a rather rustic manner (Sontheimer 1989:20,34). The *MV*,

[32] Pataṅgrāv Bhāū Avghaḍe.

however, suggests that there was a respectable *brāhmavivāha,* and that Bāṇāī, in the form of a *liṅg,* was married to the Lord Mārtaṇḍa on the 15th of the light half of the month of Śrāvaṇ (July-Aug.) (Khāḍe 1925:53). The whole affair retains the relished element of a scandal: Khaṇḍobā in Jejurī is said to visit Bāṇāī stealthily every midnight, or as we hear in a song *(pad* 29):

> The Lord has really mounted his horse
> Bravo! Bravo, O Bāṇu! Bravo!
> He took the beautiful Bāṇu along
> Brought her half-way up the Fort.
> A stealthy shower of turmeric dust for her
> See, my Lord, I lie at your feet
> I have come to sing
> Oh, the Lord has really gone crazy.

The scandal is cherished in the songs and narrations as if it were of a high value. The structured life in the settlement, in the pure *kṣetra,* has become barren and stagnant and needs the fresh wilderness. The story of Bāṇāī transgresses the regular bounds of society, but is a necessary complement to it. Bāṇaī's story is not only of entertainment value, because Bāṇāī also stands for fertility and beauty. The king or the royal god who goes for the hunt in the wilderness and meets the beautiful girl from the forest absorbs something of the nature and environment of the people she represents. Now Khaṇḍobā has become a Dhangar, too. He has enriched, so to say, his *sva* — his own self and properties. The myth of Bāṇaī binds the Dhangars to the Lord.

It is noteworthy how frequently the theme of the king and/or god, his hunt and the encounter with the girl from the "tribe" can be found in literature, myth and temple rituals, sometimes with detailed parallels (cp., for example, Obeyesekere 1978:470; L'Hernauld 1984: 257ff.).

VIII. *A commented description of the Somvatī Amāvāsyā festival.*

The festival which occurs twice or thrice a year depending on whether there is conjunction of the sun and moon on a Monday (see further Stanley 1977) attracts devotees from all over Maharashtra. Many devotees make vows which involve a promise for a request to be granted (Ma. *navas)* or they make an offering in return for a request granted (Ma. *navas pheḍṇe),* for instance by unloading sizeable sacks of turmeric dust (Ma. *bhaṇḍār)* on the *svāyaṃbhū piṇḍs* of Khaṇḍobā and Mhāḷsā in the temple of the Gaḍkoṭ. Many devotees come without a particular request to the god and simply feel that the participation in the festival lends strength, confidence and success (Ma. *yaś)* to their domestic and professional activities. Khaṇḍobā is primarily a family god (Ma. *kulsvāmī)* who looks after their life in the world (Ma. *prapañca).* Many will feel a sense of deprivation if they will not visit their god on this day diffused by the powers of the god. The *darśan,* the vision of Khaṇḍobā, and a previous bath in the river Karhā are the standard ritual expressions of this feeling and faith (Ma. *bhāv).* After the *darśan,* many devotees throw handfuls of turmeric powder mixed with coconut kernels, on behalf of the Lord, on the huge platform in front of the temple. Here Muraḷīs and Vāghyās might perform, devotees get possessed by the Lord, prostrate themselves, and many children try to catch the coconut kernels which are coloured yellow by turmeric dust. The coconut kernels are sometimes said to be the gold coins which King Mārtaṇḍa threw amongst the devotees, alas, in the Satyayuga. The importance of turmeric dust and the 'swinging' of the world in contradistinction to its standstill is demonstrated in another song of the Vāghyās *(pad* 32, 1st stanza):

See! The whole world is swinging
There is a scramble for turmeric dust
The magnanimous Mallukhān
Is giving away mountains of gold.
See! The whole world is swinging
There is a scramble for turmeric dust

The song expresses the turbulence throughout the festival, but the actual event starts with the preparation of the palanquin in the courtyard of the temple which is thronged by crowds. At a certain moment determined by a Brahman, who belongs to the "eight ministers" (Ma. *aṣṭa pradhān)* of Khaṇḍobā, the sign is given for the departure of the huge palanquin. The family name of the Brahman is Peśve, which suggests that it was originally a title, and that they are "ministers" of the King Khaṇḍobā (similar to the Peśvās who were prime ministers of the Marāṭhā kings before they rose to *de facto* rulers). We notice that the royal folk deity does not, even if only marginally, want to dispense with the Brahman's high knowledge of astrology and ritual. On the other hand, the Brahman, who from an "orthodox" point of view ought not to participate in folk festivals (Heesterman 1985:39), or get involved in the world, does not want to forego a limited, but important role in this festival. Not only he, but each of the "18 castes" have an honorary right or privilege (Ma. *mān)* which was acquired at one time by some ancestor on account of some special bhakti or heroic act and/or because of his occupation. He has the privilege of performing certain functions and assignments during this festival (and in the cult in general). The performance of these functions gives a structure to the festival which at first glance seems to be chaotic and uncontrolled.

Now the palanquin procession starts. It is carried by Rāmośīs and Kolhāṭīs at the rear, and by Marāṭhās in front. The Rāmośīs were a robber caste. One of them was the famous Sardār Umājī Naik who was defeated and hanged by the British in 1831. The privilege of the Rāmośīs to carry the palanquin at the rear is traced to this ancestor at times, but may, in fact, be older. The front of the palanquin faces east, like the god in the temple. The palanquin has to be turned 180 degrees so that the *pradakṣiṇā* around the temple complex can be correctly carried out. The turn causes tremendous "chaos" which is enacted precisely the same anew each time the festival takes place. The turn, as well as the whole procession around the temple, down the temple stairs and through the lanes of the town resembles an antagonistic game or a "tug-of-war" (Stanley 1977:36) between the two groups of palanquin bearers, the

Marāṭhās and Rāmośīs, or so it seems. There is incredible pushing and jostling. The swinging of the palanquin forward and backward, the semicircular turns at critical points, and the swaying descent down the "900,000" steps from the fort is said to be the "Lord's play." It is an expression of a folk-religious phenomenon which is, of course, not confined to the Khaṇḍobā cult. It is found in all such festivals. It reminds us of the "assault on the sense of equilibrium" of Bastar Muriyā youths when they dance with their (wooden) clan deity Aṅga.[33] The vehement movements initiated by the bearers of Khaṇḍobā's palanquin are multiplied by the inertial properties of the heavy wooden load. The movements seem to go counter to the intentionality of the individual bearers, and a rhythmicity is established, which is partially unwilled and originates in the inanimate mass of the palanquin. In other words the bearers are "outside themselves", because their physical equilibrium, the center of gravity is now lodged in the ponderous, but at the same time sensitive palanquin of the Lord. Or, we may say, the Lord "asserts his will" and generates his own forces (Gell 1980:222-224).

This extraordinary, "liminal" state of affairs is intensified, because the air is pervaded by *bhaṇḍār* (turmeric dust) and, at times, by flocks of wool thrown by Dhangars from the high wall surrounding the temple complex. Loud shouts resound in which all the devotees join: "Victory to King Khaṇḍobā, the leader of [or victor over] seven crores *(Khaṇḍerāyācā Yeḷkoṭ)*" or "The Seven Crores of eternal happiness *(Sadānandācā Yeḷkoṭ)*." The procession circumambulating the temple complex is led by musicians or Ghaḍśīs, who were formerly untouchables. The banner carriers are of the formerly untouchable Māṅg caste, who claim the hero Yeśvant Rāv, the *havildār* of the *khillā*, as their legendary ancestor. Now the "Hall of the Twelve Doors" or "Durbar Hall" has been reached. So far the god

---

[33] Gell 1980:219-248. I have adapted some of the observations and wordings of this author, but cannot dwell on his ideas because of the lack of space. Suffice it to say that his ideas correspond to my own experience of the festivals in Bastar. Note the description of the world as "swinging" during a Khaṇḍobā festival in *pad* 32, above.

and his wife or *śakti* Mhāḷsā have been invisibly present in the palanquin. Now the *utsav-mūrtis,* which embody the two deities in visible form, are carried from the "Treasury" to the Durbar Hall and are placed in the palanquin. The *mūrti* of Khaṇḍobā and of Mhāḷsā, respectively, are carried by members of two different families of Guravs, the (non-brahmanical) *pūjārīs* of Khaṇḍobā. In the mêlée inside the Durbar Hall a member of the barber caste manages to hold a mirror in front of the god. The palanquin leaves the Durbar Hall and is pushed through the two narrow gates of the wall of the fort which are connected by a steep staircase. The crowd, by now thoroughly coloured by *bhaṇḍār,* pushes down the "900,000" steps from the temple to the town. One wonders whether at times the individual bearer's feet have anything else than a fleeting contact with the ground. After a *pradakṣiṇā* of the cave temple of Bāṇāī the procession arrives at the foot of the hill and rolls through the narrow lanes of the town. The procession moves to a Śaivite *maṭh* and then proceeds for a halt at the Śiva temple built by Malhārāv Hoḷkar, a member of the blanket weaver subcaste (Khuṭekar) of the Dhangars. He rose to a position of a general of the Peśvās in the 18th cent. and founded the dynasty of the Mahārājās of Indore. His family god was Khaṇḍobā. Now the procession crosses the border of the town, beyond the town gate and moves in front of the goddess Marīāī, the cholera goddess. Here, as at other places, heavy iron chains are broken by devotees. At the border numerous nomadic Haṭkar Dhangars (shepherds) wait for the Lord. They wear red turbans, iron chains and carry "spears" which now have only ceremonial purposes. The spear (Ma. *jheṇḍā)* is also one of the many manifestations of Khaṇḍobā. He is said to have taken it along when he left for the forest after he had lost his kingdom to Mhāḷsā in a game of dice. The Dhangars also carry heavy iron chains over their shoulders. The god heads for the "wilderness," accompanied by his "hunters." A Marāṭhā tells about the hunt:

> After breaking the chain, the palanquin proceeds. From ancient times the *pālkhī* goes over the field of Sakhārām Thorat. The crop in the field will be extremely good. In former times the Lord would go for a good hunt on this path. They went hunting and hunting upto the foot of the

> Bhuleśvar temple [at the other side of the valley]. The god would hunt gazelles and tigers. But now the jungle has decreased, and so he will just hunt down a rabbit. Because of the *sattva* of the Lord *(devāce sattva)* they will hunt down a rabbit somewhere after he has left the Marīāī temple and before he reaches the Karhā river.

A Māḷī tells us in a similar vein:

> During the Somvatī Amāvāsyā which comes in the month of Śrāvaṇ the Lord comes to the Karhā. But when there is a hunt towards the river, it is excellent. So, if one comes across a rabbit or deer, a full-fledged hunt is on.

Other informants would remember that few drops of blood of the kill used to be offered to the palanquin of the Lord.

Meanwhile, the horse has left the Marīāī temple and is led far ahead of the procession. Some Dhangars try to touch his hoofs. The horse is led by a member of the Muslim family which is in charge of the care of the god's horses since many generations. The distance between the horse of the god and its invisible rider is striking, and may re-enact "the king breaking away... eluding all his horsemen." (See above *pad* 22). It also reminds us of the Vedic *aśvamedha*. The presence of the horse and the dramatic performances connected with the horse are ubiquitous in the Khaṇḍobā cult of Maharashtra and the Mailāra cult of Karnataka, in which festivals are called "festival of horses" (Ka. *kudureya habba;* Sontheimer 1989a:330). In the *aśvamedha* the horse of the king, embodying royal powers, roams through the "world" which is then claimed by the conquering king. Though the Vedic *aśvamedha* ritual is said to have become extinct, it was transformed and continued in the rituals of the traditional kingdoms, especially in the Durgā festival (Stein 1980:384ff; Sontheimer 1985:150ff.). In the Khaṇḍobā cult, devotees who beat themselves with special whips, get possessed by "the wind of the god," and trot like horses, or rather move up and down like riders on horses. These devotees appear in large numbers at the festival in Naldurg from the 1st to the 12th of the light half of the month of Pauṣ (Dec.-Jan.). Some of the "horses" (Ma. *vāru)* also turn up during the Somvatī excursion near the river, as we shall see.

Meanwhile, before the palanquin arrives, many families worship their ancestors, besides Khaṇḍobā and perhaps the Bhavānī of Tuḷsāpur, on the river bank. They are mostly represented by small plaques (Ma. *ṭāk)* which are otherwise enshrined at home. Khaṇḍobā, who is also presented by brass masks or brass figures showing him seated on a horse with Mhāḷsā, and the ancestors, who are depicted as heroes (Ma. *vīras)* on the plaques, are bathed in the river and worshipped. This is a ceremony of folk religion and not a *śrāddha* as prescribed in śāstric textbooks. In fact the *MV* following the *JM* is explicit that there can be no *śrāddha,* because Jejurī is the capital of the Lord.[34] The descendants eat together with the ancestors, engage the Muraḷīs, who dance for the ancestors, and the Vāghyās, who play and sing for them the deeds of the god and his wives. On this occasion songs are not coherent narratives and the lines are eclectic, but probably reflect what spontaneously comes into the mind of the singer in the context of the Somvatī Amāvāsyā festival. For instance:

> Bāṇu Mhāḷsā are the wives of the Lord
> The Lord went to Candanpur.
> To the house of Bāṇu, the Shepherdess
> He became thirsty in the wild forest
> On the sixth month's Somvatī
> The Lord came to the Lady Karhā.[35]

Some worshippers get possessed by the ancestors and Khaṇḍobā as soon as they hear the songs, the sound of the tabors played by the Vāghyās, and the handbells rung by the Muraḷīs. The devotees leave no doubt that participation in the Somvatī Festival in this way ensures the support of the ancestors and the Lord for their

---

[34] *MV* 36.62-63: Everywhere else in other *kṣetras* [the rituals of] *śrāddha-tīrtha, upavāsa,* and *muṇḍana* are performed. But this is not so in the *rājadhanī* of the Lord, famous in the three worlds by the name Jayā. There is no *tīrthaśrāddha, upavāsa* (fasting) or *muṇḍana* (tonsure) here.

[35] Khaṇḍu Vāghyā Jādhav.

domestic and professional life or for the coming months. Besides, the ancestors and the gods of the household shrines have been endowed with new powers.

The whole day, but especially before the procession arrives at the river, the Dhangars break their heavy chains. The chain is fixed in the hole of a boulder near the shrine of Raṃbhāī on the river bank. A pinch of *bhaṇḍār* is thrown on the chain and, calling upon the Lord, the devotees break it with a jerk. If the chain breaks, the *sattva,* the existence, nearness of the Lord is confirmed. It does not harm the credibility of the "miracle," if the chain, which on a superficial look appears to be unbreakable, has some thin places here and there. These may be treated with a hammer to make them even thinner, if the chain does not break at a second or third attempt.

The site on the river bank resembles a temporary encampment with small tea-shops and stalls where turmeric dust, coconut-kernel (Ma. *khobereṃ)* bananas etc. are sold. The Somvatī song of the Vāghyās describes eloquently the scene *(pad* 22):

> ... Yellow tents pitched all over the place
> The shrines cannot be counted
> Holy men crowd around them
> At this fascinating centre there are
> Shops set up in every direction
> The bazaar arrests the eye with its display
> One forgets hunger and thirst here
> Oh what a joyous *yātrā !*

Thus the family gods have left their domestic shrines and receive temporary shrines in the wilderness: They are worshipped on a strip of red cloth which is placed on a woolen blanket. The scene and the incidents of the festival *(jatrā)* on the river also suggest the temporary 'city' which comes into existence at the time of the *aśvamedha* according to the classical epics (Raghavan 1979:26ff.). There are the makeshift tents, the music and the dance of the Muraḷis and Vāghyās, their narration of the deeds of the god, the mention of the presence of the Ṛṣīs etc. (cp. Raghavan 1979:26ff.) The *jatrā* on the river may actually also be an echo of the ancient *sattra* which was performed by Ṛṣīs in the wilderness (Falk 1986:34). Meanwhile, most of the Dhangar 'hunters' running far ahead of the palanquin have arrived, have planted their *jheṇḍās* into the earth and wait like everybody else for the entry of the Lord. That the Lord is a "hunter" accompanied by "hunters" is also indicated by the fact that occasionally devotees bring a dog with a garland of marigold around its neck and the forehead heavily coated with *bhaṇḍār*. The Lord's arrival is announced by the sudden appearance of the horse. Then the palanquin of Khaṇḍobā arrives and before it dozens of devotees dance and trot as if they were to embody the "horses" of the god. They are seized by his power and have become as if a part of him. Like the Nandī and the horses made of stone facing the god as his *vāhanas* in the temple, the devotees as the horses now face the palanquin of the Lord. The day is, as Stanley (1976) has shown, full of the fluidity of the powers of the Lord. We may say that not only the motionless equine *vāhana* in the temple is now alive in the form of an actual horse, but also in the form of the devotees who act like live horses. The dogs of the Lord are worshipped and heavily coated with *bhaṇḍār*, and the human dog devotees of the god, the Vāghyās, who are the bards of the Lord, sing but are said to have growled and barked in a not so far-away past.

The palanquin is placed on a pedestal near the river.[36] With deafening shouts of 'Sadānandācā Yeḷkoṭ' the Lord and his *śakti* (Mhāḷsā) are taken out of the palanquin, and bathed shortly with the five nectareous substances *(pañcāmṛta)*, that is, milk, curds etc., a rite which is performed by Brahmans "and all."[37] Within seconds the *mūrtis* are carried into the river while the shouts praising the

---

[36] The venue has shifted several times after a new dam had been built down the river. Today the regular spot of the bath has to be shifted if the river is flooded.

[37] This is the view of a Dhangar informant. Śāmkākā Peśve, a Deshastha Brahman said that it was the privilege of the Peśves of Jejuri and was ceded to the Belsare family, who are also Deshastha Brahmans. Note that *amṛta* is distributed by the moon through his rays (Enthoven 1924:52; Gonda 1965:58). *Amṛta* consists of the milk of the cow etc. and rain (Gonda 1965:62).

Lord continue. Numerous Dhangars who carry a chain over their shoulder stand in the water and throw water on the Lord. That it is a privilege *(mān)* of the Dhangars to perform this chaotic play is spontaneously acknowledged by members of different castes, including Brahmans.[38] But there are also numerous Son-Koḷīs, the sea-fishermen from Bombay, who participate in the common bath, and other devotees as well, especially the "horses." After a few moments the *mūrtis* are carried back to the pedestal and placed into the palanquin. The Lord receives new clothes and a new turban brought by a washerman *(pariṭ)*. The new clothes are traditionally contributed by the Brahman Peśve family and one of them dresses the Lord. After this the Lord may look at himself in a mirror held by a member of the barber (Nhāvī) caste.

The folk religious mythological background of the cult and the observation of the dramatic performance of the ritual of the Somvatī Amāvāsyā festival let us discern more than just an astrological event and its polluting effects which are averted and turned into something "unambivalently auspicious" (Stanley 1977:42). The preponderantly horizontal view of the cosmos in folk religion leads to the enactment of the astrological event under the aegis of Khaṇḍobā. Rather than Khaṇḍobā identified with the sun, the powers of the sun are reflected in his *mūrti* and manifest in turmeric dust. On this day the fertile powers of the moon are said to dwell or rather are absorbed in the vegetative and aequous female nature including forests, rivers, which are parts of the forests (Feldhaus 1990:92), the deer of the forest and the wealth of the pastoral area in the form of sheep. Thus the *Śatapatha-brāhmaṇa* (1,6,4,5) declares, for example: "When the moon is not seen either in the east or in the west, then he visits this world, and here he enters the waters and the plants"[39] By his action the Lord reabsorbs these

---

[38] Everybody seems to agree:
Dhangar lok pāṇyāt ubhe rāhūn pāṇī siṃpadūn devalā āṅghoḷ ghāltāt. (Śāmkākā Peśve).

[39] Gonda 1965:45. The moon directs and governs the waters which sponsor the growth of living beings, Soma expresses or is in these waters: *Aitareya-brāhmaṇa*

powers of the sun and the moon and his powers become comparable to theirs. As King on earth Śiva has a role to play and he needs the loyalty, assistance or bhakti of his followers, whereas, they are in need of protection and deflect renewed strength from him. The followers are associationed with either the *kṣetra* or the *vana*. The claim to belong to the sun's powers or to him who conveys them may even be seen as dramatised by the antagonistic struggle of the palanquin bearers.[40] Others serve the Lord by showering cascades of turmeric dust. The people of the forest, or of the moon's powers, present themselves as "hunters," pastoralist Dhangars and ocean fishermen. The mingling of the substances of power may already be seen to begin when the Dhangars, in fulfillment of vows, rain flocks of sheepwool,[41] which mixes with the clouds of turmeric dust, on the Lord in the courtyard at the beginning of the excursion. But the climax is the throwing of turmeric dust and water in the ritual on the river. The mingling of the powers of the sun and the moon during which the Lord takes his bath in the river are also echoed in the *Somvatī Song (pad* 22) when it is said:

> When the Lord is bathed in milk
> It is as if the Karhā becomes as luminous as the sun
> pure as the Bhāgirathī
> The source of the Karhā is higher than the twenty-one heavens
> The pure water of the seventeenth part of the moon
> [or: The pure water of the glowing and blooming life].[42]

1,7,10. Gonda *ibidem:* 48. On the relationship between the moon, *soma*, and *amṛta* see Gonda *ibidem:* 38ff.

[40] Cp. the famous passage in the *Kaṭhā-saṃhitā* 34.5 and elsewhere, where in the Mahāvrata ritual an Ārya and a Śūdra fight for a skin representing the sun. Sontheimer 1981:2 and fn.5.

[41] The woolen wreath at the base of the blade of the *jheṇḍā* or spear made of wool and the sheep and cattle wealth are called *Lakṣumi* (Standard Ma. *Lakṣmī*). One may observe Dhangars who mix a little bit of wool in their food offerings during *jatrās* and afterwards eat these as *prasād*. See also *pad* 45 where Bāṇāī mixes some wool into the food of Khaṇḍobā.

[42] *pad* 22: ...
dudhī snāna hotī āṃgoḷa
ase suryāce teja karhe jaḷa

It would be tempting to straightaway identify the river Karhā which is the Bhāgirathī (= Gaṅgā), with Bāṇāī. Gaṅgā is reborn as Bāṇāī on earth according to most versions of her origin, or she is found in the ocean. But there is no confirmation that the Karhā is Bāṇāī. On the contrary: it is frequently said that the Lord crossed the Karhā during his hunt on his way to Bāṇāī's Candanpur which is now normally located in Khandesh (Malegaon district). The Dhangar informants, however, stress that it is because of Bāṇāī that they came into contact with Khaṇḍobā and received the privilege to participate in the bath in the river and throw water on the god. No informant from another caste would dispute this. Bāṇāī as the goddess from the forest has, as we have seen, riverine and pastoral associations. Like the Dhangars, their predecessors, the Gavḷīs, were frequently "discoverers" of a Śiva *liṅg* in forests and on mountains at the origin of the Śaivite cult. A Gavḷī and a Koḷī are often said to have been the first worshippers of a Śiva *liṅg* with the water of the river. Today Dhangars bring water from far away rivers to their male gods. The static temple custom in the *kṣetra* is to bring water from a local tank and let it drip from a pot *(gaṅgājaḷī)* suspended

---

śuddha bhāgirathīcī kevaḷa
ekavīsa svargāvara karhece mūḷa
śuddha satarāvīcem [sattravīcem] jaḷa.

The seventeenth digit of the moon is the root digit in which the 16 digits inhere. It is called *jīvabalā* that is, 'blooming and beaming of life.' (See *Mahārāṣṭra Śabdakośa*, pt. 7, p. 3007). The new-moon enters the plants and the waters with the moon's last, sixteenth part *(kalā)* (Meyer 1937:230 (part II)). According to the *Bṛhadaraṇyaka-upaniṣad* (1,5,14) it is Prajāpati who enters as the moon with his sixteenth *kalā* into everything which has life, and nothing should be injured on that day (Meyer 1937:*ibidem)*. The prohibition not to injure anything on this day would contradict Khaṇḍobā's violent hunt and the subsequent mythical slaughter of the sheep. But it may be that the killing of the *mṛgas* and boars may also echo the famous killing of Prajāpati disguised as a *mṛga* by Rudra (who is *mṛgavyādha)*. *Aitareya-brāhmaṇa* III.3.; Deppert 1977:90ff., 100; Hofstetter 1980:22ff.

The term *sattravī* also reveals the Vāghyā's (Mukindagiri) acquaintance with the yoga of the Nāths. In fact, the sacred geography of Jejurī can also be expressed in yogic cosmology. This is another component in the cult which cannot be pursued here.

over the *liṅg*. This is thus supplemented by the (earlier) folk custom to bring water from beyond the *kṣetra*. On certain occasions, however, the god - tired of ritual routine - goes himself into the forest and in folk myths it is often a Dhangar who directs him to Bāṇāī. She sends the pot of water to the thirsty god. In rituals and especially in the context of the Somvatī Amāvāsyā festival, the Dhangars are the mediators between the river goddess and the Lord who on this day comes, as if mobilised, from the mountain. On this day the Dhangars lead the Lord to the water and provide a cooling bath for him.

After he has received the five nectareous substances, his bath in the river, and his investiture with new clothes, the Lord moves in his palanquin to the goddess Raṃbhāī. She resides in a rough unhewn *mūrti* covered with read lead (Ma. *śendūr)* on a high platform covered with a tin-roof, but open on all sides. It looks like a temporary *maṇḍap* rather than a full-fledged temple. The Lord stays for a few moments with Raṃbhāī who had once come from Indra's heaven as a Devāṅganā (heavenly courtezan), but has become a deified Muraḷī of the Śimpī (tailor's) caste. In the songs of the Vāghyās she is famous for her spontaneous love for the Lord when for the first time he came circling in the air on his horse and descended on Jejurī. The gracious Lord settled her outside the town on the river Karhā and ever since visits her on Somvatī Amāvāsyā (Sontheimer 1991:24; *pad* 19):

> ... He brought her, the Beauty
> Kept her, "O Mālu!"
> On the bank of the Karhā River, "O Mālu!"
> Once every sixth month, on Monday
> The Lord goes to her temple.

In another song *(pad* 2) the scene after the bath is described:

> The Lord put on [new] clothes,
> Came to Raṃbhāī's palace.
> When he saw Raṃbhāī's faith,
> Khaṇḍerāv was pleased
> Accepting spontaneous faith,

He gave her a place at his feet.

The fleeting, though riotous halt at Raṃbhāī's shrine which includes an *āratī* ceremony for the Lord, doesn't suggest that according to oral traditions (*Somvatī pad* 22):

The God holds court in Raṃbhā's palace
Among those seated is Indra himself
Sakhyā, the barber, holding the mirror
Stands in front of the god
His mirror reflecting the dazzling sun
Anointed with fragrant Mailagiri sandelwood paste
A dot of musk on the forehead
On the decorated floor his ruby-encrusted plate is laid
With shining silver-bowls inside
Ṛddhi and Siddhi in person serve sweet rice porridge
Ṛṣīs eat Amboḷī[43]
As soon as they finish and rinse their mouth,
Raṃbhā offers them *pān*
It is a joyous *yātrā.*

After this halt the procession moves to the village Dhālavḍī. Some would tell that the Lord continues his hunt. Formerly, according to the *Somvatī Song* (*pad* 22), horse races seem to have taken place on the way to Dhālavḍī. Today the palanquin proceeds to Bābīr, the Gavḷī-Dhangar god in Dhālavḍī and the palanquin bearers are given a meal of millet bread by the villagers. Then the Lord returns. The procession stops at a hamlet inhabited by Māḷīs. From there the Lord proceeds to visit another 'wife' or Muraḷī, Phulāī Māḷīṇ of the Māḷī (gardener) caste at the outskirts of the town in the Davṇe Maḷ (Southernwood Field). Here the palanquin is kept for five minutes on the stone pedestal of Phulāī Māḷīṇ to allow the devotees to have a vision of the Lord. Because of Phulāī Māḷīṇ, reputed to be the first Muraḷī, the Māḷī women have a special privilege to sell *davṇā* (Southernwood), *jhenḍū* (marigold), and *bel* (Skt. *bilvā)* leaves at the Nandi Chowk in Jejurī. Here the

[43] Flour soured by exposure to the air and slightly parched upon a baking-plate (Molesworth 1857: 37).

"900,000" steps leading to the temple begin.

Then the Lord makes a triumphant entry into the town according to the *pads* describing the return from his sojourn in the wilderness. The epic song, especially, on the encounter with Bāṇāī *(pad* 49) gives a vivid picture of the huge army of the Lord as it arrives in Jejurī. The Lord is followed by Bāṇāī in her "green" chariot. We may wonder from where the huge army is supposed to come after the king has "eluded his horsemen" and stayed in the wilderness separated from his retinue. However, the song shows that he emerges enriched and powerful from the wilderness. Today the palanquin moves to the goddess Janāī, who is supposed to be the Lord's sister and senior to him. At this spot the women perform the *āratī*-ceremony to the palanquin welcoming the returning Lord. After a rest of 1 1/2 hours the palanquin is carried up the hill with a similar, but less violent display of competitive game as at the beginning of the excursion. Finally the palanquin is placed in the "Hall of the Twelve Doors." The Peśve, "one of the eight ministers," distributes what is called *rojmarā* (P. "wages") or *muśārā* (A. "pay" or "wages") to all devotees who served the Lord in this ritual, especially the musicians and the palanquin bearers. The *rojmarā* consists of *bhaṇḍār* and millet *(jovārī)* grains which have a special power and are sown into fields for a good crop or kept in the house shrine or "near one's business." The palanquin may return at any time depending on the time of conjunction of the sun and the moon. If the palanquin returns in the night, the description of the procession in the *Somvatī pad (pad* 48) is vivid, but these days perhaps no longer a reality:

> When the sun sets and there is the dark night of new moon
> then see!
> The torches, the rockets, the red display of fireworks
> As the king's procession meanders to the fort *[killā]*,
> the Assembly is seated in the
> "Hall of the Twelve Gates."

IX. *Conclusions*

The Khaṇḍobā cult has its mythical background in scriptural and oral traditions. Today oral texts and their interaction with ritual expressions and scriptural texts tend to become evanescent; as literacy increases, proliferation of temple pamphlets and booklets is widespread, and generally modern change has an accelerating effect. The oral myths of the King's hunt and the myth of Bāṇāī are not found in the scriptural texts *(MM, JM, and MV)*, but they had an important place in the cult and are complementary to the scriptural texts. The pervasive function of oral texts is seen in the Somvatī Amāvāsyā festival where they contribute to the mythical backgound of the festival. On the surface the festival may look like a simple ritual event just consisting of a purifying *snāna* of the god in the river Karhā, and this is also suggested by the texts *(JM, MV)*. This strand may even survive in a modernised world where the powers and goods of life will be sought elsewhere. Today the festival is still celebrated in a dramatic way which reflects a playful, folk-religious worship (Ma. *kheḷ)* of the Lord. According to this strand of expression Khaṇḍobā, who is King as God on earth, is on a hunt in the wilderness. The important role of the pastoralist Dhangars, who accompany the Lord on his hunt and throw water on him, is mythically connected with the story of Bāṇāī, the shepherdess. The royal Khaṇḍobā with the help of his followers negotiates a dramatic ritual (Ma./[Skt.] *utsāh[a], utsava[a])* which leads to the renewal of his reign and holds out the promise of renewal of life and success in the domestic affairs of all his followers participating in the festival. The festival also enlists the goodwill of the ancestors. With the help of his followers who have to perform different, actual or potential functions, Khaṇḍobā dramatically re-enacts the conjunction of the sun and the moon on a Monday by cojoining the moon's and the sun's powers which are subordinated to the Śaivite cult. The festival also echoes the ancient *aśvamedha* and *rājasūya* sacrifices in their non-classical (rather than "pre-classical"; Heesterman 1985: 5f. *et passim)* form, whereby the ultimate authority and legitimacy of the royal god may be presumably seen in the fact that Khaṇḍobā is also identical with Śiva. The festival also reflects the need for the periodical, dynamic interaction between "inside" *and* "outside", the static *and* the mobile, the settlement *and* the forest, or the *kṣetra and* the *vana* (Ma. *rāṇ* < Skt. *araṇya),* the daily ritual temple routine *and* the dramatic, playful performance of the ritual, the hierarchized, vertical *and* the earthbound, horizontal cosmos of the cult. The Somvatī Amāvāsyā festival, its mythology and performance then suggest many identifiable meanings. Many traditions are reflected in this complex cult, which simultaneously co-exist and present an open network. To assign one meaning to these traditions instead of leaving their meanings in abeyance might please the argumentative scholar, but may inadvertently amount to a reductionist, if not a fundamentalist approach.

Abbreviations

A.	Arabic
Ka.	Kannaḍa
JM	*Jayādri Māhātmya*
MM	*Mallāri Māhātmya*
MV	*Mārtaṇḍa-Vijaya*
Ma.	Marāṭhī
P.	Persian
Skt.	Sanskrit
Tel.	Telugu

References

Blackburn, Stuart H. 1978. Death and deification: Folk cults in Hinduism. In *History of Religion* 24, 255-74.

Brubaker, Richard 1977. *The ambivalent mistress: A study of South Indian village Goddesses and their meaning*. Ph.D. dissertation, University of Chicago.

Carman, John B. and Marglin, F.A. (eds.) 1985. Purity and auspiciousness in Indian society. In *Journal of Developing Societies* I.1 June.

Chhabra, B. 1955. The incised inscriptions. In G. Yazdani (ed.) *Ajanta* Vol. IV, 121-124. London: Oxford University Press.

Derrett, J. D. M. 1957. *The Hoysaḷas*. A medieval Indian royal family. Oxford: Oxford University Press.

Dhere, Ra. Cim. 1961. *Khaṇḍobā*. Puṇeṃ: Deśmukh āṇi kaṃpanī.

Elwin, Verrier 1947. *The Murias and their Ghotul*. London: Oxford University Press.

Enthoven, R. E. 1924. *The folklore of Bombay*. Oxford.

Falk, Harry. 1987. *Bruderschaft und Würfelspiel. Untersuchungen und Entwicklungsgeschichte des vedischen Opfers*. Freiburg.

Feldhaus, A. 1990. The image of the forest in the Māhātmyas of the rivers of the Deccan. In H. Bakker (ed.) *The history of sacred places in India as reflected in traditional literature*. Leiden: E. J. Brill, 90-102.

Gell, A. 1980. The gods at play: vertigo and possession in Muria religion. In *Man*, 15, 218-248.

Gonda, J. 1954. *Aspects of early Viṣṇuism*. Den Haag, Nordeinde 115a: Oriental Bookshop.

______, 1965. *Change and continuity in Indian religion*. The Hague:Mouton.

Heesterman, J. C. 1985. *The inner conflict of tradition. Essays in Indian ritual, kingship, and Society*. Chicago and London: The University of Chicago Press.

Hiltebeitel, Alf (ed.) 1989. *Criminal gods and demon devotees*.

Essays on the guardians of popular Hinduism. Albany: State University of New York Press.

Höfer, András. 1968. Randbemerkungen über die Jagdriten im nordwestlichen Hinterindien. In *Archiv für Völkerkunde* 22, 67-89.

Hofstetter, Erich 1980. *Der Herr der Tiere im alten Indien*. Wiesbaden (Freiburger Beiträge zur Indologie, 14).

Israel, Milton and Wagle, N.K. (eds.) 1987. *Religion and society in Maharashtra*. (South Asian Studies Papers, 1). Toronto: University of Toronto.

Jayādri Māhātmya Ms. (Sanskrit), dated śake 1678 (1756 A.D.) (in the possession of R.C. Dhere, Puṇe).

Kane, P.V. 1974. *History of Dharmaśāstra*, Vol. II, Part 1. Poona: Bhandarkar Oriental Institute.

Khāḍe, Bā. Khaṃ. 1925. *Śrīkṣetra Jejurīmāhātmya*. Puṇem: Law Priṃtiṃg Pres.

Khaṇḍobācīṃ padeṃ Śrī Sadguru Bhāūmahārāja yāṃcyā saṃgrahāṃtīl Śrī Khaṃḍobācīṃ padeṃ. Puṇeṃ 1963.

Khare, G.H. 1958. *Mahārāṣṭrācīṃ cār daivateṃ*. Puṇeṃ-2.

Kosambi, D.D. 1962. *Myth and Reality*. Studies in the formation of Indian culture. Bombay.

L'Hernauld, Francoise 1984. Subrahmaṇya as a supreme deity. In Meister, Michael W. (ed.) *Discourses on Śiva. Proceedings of a symposium on the nature of religious imagery*. Bombay: Vakils, Feffer & Simons Ltd., 257-270.

Malandru, Geri H. 1982. The date of the Ajaṇṭā Cave 27 inscription. In *Wiener Zeitschrift für die Kunde Südasiens* 26, 37-46.

Marglin, Frédérique 1985. *Wives of the god-king. The rituals of the Devadasis of* Puri. Delhi: Oxford University Press.

Marriott, McKim 1976. Interpreting Indian Society: A monistic alternative to Dumont's dualism. In *Journal of Asian Studies* 36. 1, 189-195.

Mārtaṇḍavijaya of Gaṃgādhara. Ed. by Rā. Ciṃ. Ḍhere, Puṇem: Varadā Buks, 1975.

Meyer, J. J. 1937. *Trilogie altindischer Mächte und Feste der Vegetation.* Zürich-Leipzig.

Molesworth, J.T. 1975. A Marathi English Dictionary. Poona: Shubhada Saraswat (reprint).

Narayan Rao, Velcheru 1989. Tricking the goddess: Cowherd Kāṭamarāju and goddess Gaṅgā in the Telugu folk epic. In Hiltebeitel, Alf (ed.), 105-121.

Potdār, Da. Vā. 1913. Jejurī yethīl śilālekh. In *Bhārat*

Itihās Saṃśodhak Maṃḍaḷ Vārṣik Itivṛtta, 235-271.

Obeyesekere, Gananath 1978. The fire-walkers of Katagarama: The rise of bhakti religiosity in Buddhist Sri Lanka. In *Journal of Asian Studies* 37.3, May, 457-476.

Oppitz, Michael 1983. The wild boar as a plough. In *Kailash* 10. 3-4, 187-226.

Raghavan, V. 1979. *Festivals, sports and pastimes in India*. Ahmedabad: B.J. Institute of Learning and Research.

Ruben, Walter 1962. *Waldabenteuer des indischen Helden*. Berlin: Akademie Verlag.

Sāvant, Kṛ. Rā. 1985. Āṃgaṇevādīcī jatrā. In Savitā Ṭāṃkasāḷe (ed.) *Utsava, Dīpāvaḷī*. Muṃbāī, Dādar: Śrīgaṃgādhar Primṭīmg Pres, 77-80.

Shulman, David Dean 1980a. *Tamil temple myths. Sacrifice and divine marriage in* South *Indian Śaiva tradition*. Princeton: Princeton University Press.

______, 1980b. On South Indian bandits and kings. In *The Indian Economic and Social History Review*, 17, 3, 283-306.

______, 1985. *The King and the clown in South Indian myth and poetry*. Princeton: Princeton University Press.

Sontheimer, Günther D. 1985. Folk deities in the Vijayanagara empire: Narasimha and Mallaṇṇa/Mailār. In Anna Libera Dallapiccola (ed.) *Vijayanagara - City and Empire. New Currents of Research.* Wiesbaden, 144-158.

_____, 1987. Rudra and Khaṇḍobā: Continuity in folk religion. In Israel, Milton and Wagle, N.K. (eds.), 1-32.

_____, 1989a. The myth of the god and his two wives: Two pastoral versions from Maharashtra. In Richard K. Barz and M. Thiel-Horstmann (eds.) *Living texts from India.* Wiesbaden.

_____,1989b. Between ghost and god: a folk deity of the Deccan. In Hiltebeitel, Alf (ed.), 299-337.

_____, 1989c. *Pastoral deities in western India.* (Transl. by Anne Feldhaus). New York: Oxford University Press.

_____, 1991a. The Rāmāyaṇa in contemporary folk traditions of Maharashtra. In M. Thiel-Horstmann (ed.) *Rāmāyaṇa and Rāmāyaṇas.* Wiesbaden, 115-137.

_____, 1991b. Bhākti in the Khaṇḍobā cult. In Diana L. Eck and Francoìse Mallison (eds.) *Devotion divine. Bhakti traditions from the regions of India.* Studies in honour of Charlotte Vaudeville. Groningen/Paris:

Groningen Oriental Studies 8, 231-253.

Śrīkṣetra-Jejurī-Māhātmya see Khāḍe 1925.

Sri Venkateswara Leela Mahathyamu see Subrahmanyam, N.

Stanley, John M. 1977. Special time, special power: fluidity of power in a popular Hindu festival. In *Journal of Asian Studies*, 37.1, 27-43.

______, 1987. Niṣkāma and sakāma bhakti: Pandharpur and Jejuri. In Israel, Milton, and Wagle N.K. (eds.), 51-67.

Subrahmanyam, N. 1962. *Sri Venkateswara Leela Mahathmyamu*. (Engl. transl.) *The glories and mysteries of Lord Venkateswara*. Tirumalai Hills.

Stein, Burton 1983. Mahānavamī: Medieval and modern kingly ritual. In Bardwell L. Smith (ed.) *Essays on Gupta Culture*. Delhi: Motilal Banarsidass, 67-90.

Verma, Onkar P. 1970. *The Yādavas and their times*. Nagpur: Vidharbha Samshodhan Mandal.

Thurston, Edgar, 1909. *Castes and tribes of Southern India*. Vol. IV. Delhi: Cosmo Publications (repr. 1975, 1st edn 1909).

Wilhelm, Friedrich 1991. Hunting and the concept of

dharma. In Julia Leslie (ed.) *Rules and remedies in classical Indian law.* Leiden: E.J. Brill, 7-16.

Zvelebil, Kamil 1977. Vaḻḻi and Murukaṉ - a Dravidian myth. In *Indo-Iranian Journal* 19, 227-246.

RITUAL RIVALRY IN KERALA

Gilles Tarabout

Temple festivals in the former Cochin and Travancore States frequently follow a similar pattern in their organisation: specified groups of devotees, sometimes from different castes, aggregate in two factions entering into ritual competition on (or near) the temple precincts. These factions have only a ritual purpose and should not be confused with political factions or other feuds which might occur in villages.

This specific kind of rivalry has to be distinguished from other kinds — quite widespread in South India — where many separate teams or individuals are competing during games, races, or fights.[1] We shall only be concerned with competitions between two factions. Out of some twenty festivals observed in the southern half of Kerala ten featured such a rivalry, most of them in the Trichur-Palghat region (in or near the former Cochin State) but some as far south as the Quilon area in former Travancore.

---

[1] See for instance: Beals 1964 (hand wrestling in Karnataka); Muthanna 1953: 340, and Srinivas 1952: 198, 240 (stick fencing and competition games in Coorg country); Dumont 1957:382ff (bull races in Tamil Nadu); Fawcett 1915: 294 (former archery competition in North Kerala); Kareem 1976: 182 (bull fights in the Palghat area of Kerala); Sreedhara Menon 1965: 295, 836ff, id. 1975: 152ff, 589ff, Devassy 1966: 165ff, and Kurup 1966: 9ff, 21ff (boat races in Central Kerala); Tarabout 1986: 139ff, 334 (competition of processions in South Kerala).

After a brief overview of traditional Kerala society, a few festivals will be presented.[2] The analysis will then try to outline the symbolic world within whose paramaters these rituals ought to be understood as well as the sociological terms of their organisation. This in turn suggests a comparison with two neighbouring areas of India (the Tulu and Coorg regions of Karnataka State) and with Sri Lanka.

The Social Setting

The rituals we will study are still linked in many respects to a traditional order of society in which caste distinctions are relevant. Festivals with competing factions are especially frequent in temples owned or frequented by upper-status castes although other castes might participate. Among castes of high status in Kerala we find the (patrilineal) *namputiri*[3] brahmins and the (matrilineal) *nāyar*, two well studied groups. In a kind of symbiosis, which included alliances with royal lineages, they exercised ritual, political and economic dominance in the region.[4]

---

[2] Examples are drawn from a field enquiry made in 1980-1983. They can receive only a cursory treatment here (details in Tarabout 1986 — except for unpublished material: "festival 3"). Field-work was made possible by a grant of the Government of India (Indo-French Cultural Exchange Programme). My thanks are especially due to Prof. V.I. Subramoniam, head of the International School of Dravidian Linguistics, Trivandrum, for providing constant support during my stay, and to all the friends in Kerala whose help was boundless.

[3] Transliterations will follow Malayalam spelling, whatever the origin of terms. In order to make the text more readable, "*nayar*" and "*namputiri*" will be further refered to without diacritical marks. Names of regions, places, and of gods, demons, and heroes too, have not been transliterated.

[4] Literature on the subject is too abundant to be detailed here. A very subjective selection of some of the main studies could include Ananthakrishna Iyer (1969), Dumont (1961), Fuller (1976), Gough (1952, 1961), Mencher (1965, 1966a), Mencher & Goldberg (1967), Moore (1985), Panikkar (1918), Thurston & Rangachari (1965).

What should be stressed here is the locality component of the social units of these castes. Take the *nayars* for instance. A *taṟavāṭu* ("authority in the *taṟa*" — the term will be explained later) is formed of the descendants in the female line of common ancestors (a woman and her brother), and has been variously termed as "lineage" or "clan". But the word means at the same time the dwelling house and its compound, which is not only a garden but also the place where important rituals are performed, including cremation of the dead and — at least in former times — burial of the charred remains. As Melinda A. Moore (1985) has aptly pointed out, the house-cum-compound unit is symbolically self-contained, like a small realm. Each *nayar* was known after his *taṟavād's* name — therefore also a locality name — which was supposed to be the only one of its kind in the whole of Kerala. The preservation of the *taṟavād's* name along with its agricultural and political rights and its possible ritual privileges was a principal concern, and whenever its perpetuity was at risk, adoptions were resorted to — a fact well supported by evidence and already stressed in the XVIth century by the Arab traveller Sheikh Zeen-ud-deen (Rowlandson 1833: 66). Matrilineal filiation was thus completed by adoptions as a means to preserve the system, a fact ignored in most of the literature on kinship in Kerala. The *taṟavād* was, thus, ideally perpetual with indivisible rights (though segmentation did in reality occur), and was deep-rooted in its locality; members who could number more than a hundred in big *taṟavāds* were under the authority of the senior-most male.

Even though *namputiri* brahmins were patrilineal and had quite a different way of preserving their rights undivided, similar remarks apply to them. Moreover, *namputiris* and *nayars* could enter (in past times) in hierarchically oriented matrimonial relationships — it was in fact a necessary condition of the equilibrium of the *namputiri* customs. Thus both castes (taken as exemplary cases of the higher castes in Kerala) can be viewed as forming two poles in a single system, whose characteristics and dynamics were determined by the interaction between conflicting tendencies: caste endogamy/across-the-caste hypergamy, patrilinearity/matrilinearity, "blood"/"soil" references[5] These tensions are characteristic of what C. Levi-Strauss (1979; 1984) has described as a society of Houses, referring to a mediaeval feature of European society. In this state of society, political and economic interests, in order to be preserved, tend to alter the traditional reference to blood relationships. This was quite explicitly the case in Kerala, regarding both the *nayars* and the *namputiris*. We shall therefore speak of Houses in their case rather than of "lineages".

In most parts of Kerala settlements are of a dispersed pattern, and typically occupy comparatively highland grounds bordered by the lowland paddy fields (for a comparison with Tamil Nadu, see Mencher 1966b). Namputiri Houses could be found separate or with others in a (dispersed) *grāmaṃ* ("troop", sometimes rendered as "village"). Nayar Houses were, as a rule, part of a (dispersed) neighbourhood called in the south *kara* ("embankment"), in the north *taṟa* ("ground, platform, altar, embankment"). The importance of the *nayar* neighbourhood was formerly far greater than it is nowadays — and has been somewhat underrated by social anthropologists. The neighbourhood used to be the place where local *nayar* affairs were discussed in an assembly of the different Houses, and where the youth was trained in martial arts (*nayars* were reputed for their fighting ability). It is used today as an organisational basis for the socio-politically powerful Nayar Service Society and is still the place where social and ritual cooperation is extended (for instance during funerals), and where issues of local life are regulated (caste authorisation for weddings, registration of births etc.). Each neighbourhood is known by a name and we shall see participants in festivals eager to defend that name. Neighbourhoods and settlements of other castes were under the authority of a chief of a *deśaṃ* (sometimes rendered as "village"), who was the leader of the local militia

---

[5] For an elaboration of these points and a discussion of their effect on the *nayar* and *namputiri* kinship terminologies see Tarabout, forthcoming.

and himself owed allegiance to a regional *(nāṭu)* ruler. In some places Houses still retain these titles which can still have a ritual relevance, but their power belongs to a bygone age.

The Sacrifice of Battle

The martial tradition of the *nayars* is well known. One should not forget, however, that such a tradition was widespread among many other communities in Kerala: among brahmins (one subcaste) as well as castes of lesser status, and among muslims and christians. In times of peace fights were regularly organised by chieftains in order to keep up the martial spirit of their men. They have been described from the XVIth century. There were also ritual occasions for such armed (and bloody) contests, which were extant until the XIXth century (Thurston & Rangachari 1965: II-60). Nowadays sham fights are still regularly held in many places, but in a more friendly way. Let us look at two such occurences. The festival of *ōṇaṃ* in the solar month of *ciṇṇaṃ* (mid-August, mid-September), the first month of the Malayalam calendar, is an occasion for general rejoicing, connected, according to popular Hindu belief with the celebration of the annual return of the "good king" Mahabali. People will discard used objects and buy new ones, they will receive and offer gifts, and many will practice games. In some "villages" (for instance in Palghat district) one of these games is the *ōṇattallụ ("ōṇaṃ's* blows"), a kind of boxing which includes slapping hands. Two factions are opposed, the actual fights being done by groups or by pairs (Kurup 1966: 22; Marar 1979: 7). It does not occur, as a rule, in connection with the local temple festival, though in some cases the fight might be held on temple grounds (see below the case of Pallassena).

Festival 1: The *ōcciṟa kaḷi*, "play of Occhira [locality]", in Travancore, is a sham fight specifically organised as a temple festival. The temple complex is presided over by Parabrahma, a form of Siva.

Three main festivals are celebrated during the year; the *ōcciṟa kaḷi* is the last one and falls on the first two days of the month of *mithunaṃ* (mid-June). It is thought that its celebration brings rain, a belief often verified since the time corresponds to the onset of the south-west monsoon in this region. Local newspapers regularly publish pictures of fencers with water up to their knees.

The festival is said to perpetuate the memory of an XVIIIth century battle in which a Rājā lost his life. It is held on the "battleground" *(paṭanilaṃ)* of the temple, specifically in a rectangular depression south of the shrines. People from two neighbourhoods,[6] East and West, trained and led by fencing masters *(kaḷari āśān,* "masters of gymnasium"), fight each other with small canes or sticks. Technically it is different from the style of fencing formerly practiced by *nayars (kaḷarippayaṟṟu,* "exercises of gymnasium"), and is more akin to the style termed by the latter as merely "warding off blows" *(aṭittoḷaṃ)*. Fighters will choose opponents of similar dexterity: beginners (often young children) against beginners, experts against experts. Blows are not given at full strength; the winner is the one who makes his opponent fall, or disarms the opponent, whose weapon he then takes. The best fighters can be seen at the end of the game parading with five or six sticks.

Why do wargames have significance in a religious festival ? Some interconnected reasons can be put forward: real battle is a sacrifice lead by the king, as is borne out both by Sanskrit speculations (Biardeau 1976: 131ff) and by old Tamil poetry (see Book III of *cilappatikāraṃ,* "The Lay of the Anklet"). In this sacrifice, the king puts his life at risk, loses some of his soldiers (abandoning therefore something of himself), and slays his enemies, who can be seen as

---

[6] In the Occhira festival the term kara is not used in its restricted meaning of "*nayar* neighbourhood," for nearly all castes, including lesser-status ones, participate (a fact noted already a century ago by the Rev. S. Mateer, 1883: 56). For a description of the ritual cycle in Occhira see Devassy 1966: 116-118.

substitutes for his own life (Biardeau 1976: 134). Through his victory, the king attains pre-eminence, and fame *(sri);* under his protection rituals are peacefully performed, rains are abundant, the kingdom obtains prosperity. From a different perspective, J.C. Heesterman (1967) has argued that Vedic ritualists, in order to attain a "pacified" form of ritual, tried to rationalize away an originally agonistic logic, which still permeates (other) actual religious practices. In a way, battles would have been the model for "classic" sacrifices — out of which real human death had to be eliminated. The author points out that in agonistic festivals "the basic pattern...is dualistic, in principle involving two parties: hosts and guests" (ibid., p.27); "the antagonist is not just an enemy, he is related to the conquering party in a dualistic pattern...the two parties, like the Pandavas and the Kauravas in the great epic, needed each other for the agonistic exchange in which life could only be rewon out of the other's death" (ibid., pp.40-41). Thus, playing war during mock-fight competitions is a way of performing sacrifices or at least — since direct rivalry can give place to more "diluted" forms of competition as we shall see — can be ascribed to a "sacrificial logic". Note in the case of *ōcciṟa kaḷi* the reference to a king's death and the belief that the fight brings rains.

There is a cosmic symbolism behind both, a "model" war such as the Mahabharata and many temple festivals: *praḷayaṃ*, the necessary resorption of the worlds between two *kalpaṃ* (cosmic periods).[7] The presence of this symbolism in festivals where different rituals refer, more or less explicitly, to this articulation between an old age and a new forthcoming (and better) one helps to mark the cyclical nature of time and the auspiciousness of the coming year. The time of *praḷayaṃ* is a time of wars, followed by a conflagration, which itself is followed by a deluge. According to orthodoxy it is also a time when there is no more order in society, high castes and elders

---

[7] For a discussion of the *praḷayaṃ* dimension in a Tamil temple festival, especially during the cart procession, see Reiniche 1979: 102ff.

are shown disrespect, all castes are mixed up. In Occhira "deluge" and caste mixing can be considered to allude to this cosmic dimension.

Glorifications

Festival 2: The Chinakkattur Puram festival is held in a locality some twenty miles west of Palghat in the middle of Kerala. It falls during the month of *kumbham* (mid-February, mid-March) when the moon is in line with the *makam* ("sacrifice") and *pūraṃ* ("abundance") constellations: a time well in agreement with the values previously stressed.

The temple has two main shrines side by side, sacred respectively to Siva and Kali Bhagavati, both facing south. For the ceremonies of this festival, the shrine of Siva is closed. The "trusteeship" belongs to a *namputiri* who has to assume all the temple expenses not covered by the devotees' gifts, and who receives a yearly contribution of paddy from surrounding neighbourhoods (collected in the name of the Goddess).

Here also a historic battle is said to be at the origin of the celebrations. Two factions, East ("local") and West ("enemy") compete, each comprising eight *nayar* neighbourhoods *(taṟa)*. On the *makam* day each neighbourhood brings in procession to the temple esplanade a huge fake stallion of rudimentary shape, its body stuffed with dry leaves, wrapped in clean white cloth, surmounted by a wooden sculpted head; ten to twelve feet in height, it might weigh nearly half a ton. The horses are offered by the *nayars*, but the bearers can be "any workers" (as a participant put it). When all the horses have reached the foreground of the temple, they are placed in two rows face to face. In the middle of each faction's row, a horse bigger than the others, with a palm umbrella attached to its neck, is named the "Rājā".

Low-status castes (washermen, basket or palm-umbrella makers, former agricultural bonded labourers) form their own groups, sometimes preceding closely a *ta̱ra* horse procession, or sometimes coming in completely distinct processions. Some present costumed or masked dances.

Twice during the festival, on the afternoon of *makam* day and on the morning of *pūraṃ* day, there will be a "play of horses" *(kutira kaḷi):* beginning with the Rājās of each faction (West first), each horse in turn is carried in front of the goddess where it is made to rush to and fro, then to jump vertically in movements of growing amplitude up to the point where the horse is thrown eight or ten feet above the ground and caught when falling down, then thrown up again — to the awe and enthusiasm of the spectators. After the first play the horses are put at each end of the esplanade.

Ce̱ruman (agricultural workers of low status), in some eight tumultuous processions, bring fake decorated bulls and cows — smaller than the *nayar* horses and palm-leaf umbrellas with long fringes (the umbrellas are held by both men and women). They make the umbrellas rotate very fast so that the fringes fly horizontally, or they dance around them holding the handle up to a point where some fall on the ground in a swoon. After this play they salute the goddess in her shrine and go to the eastern or western part of the esplanade, where they form three groups (one group in the East, two in the West — following an internal feud).

In the evening, East and West are completed by the coming of deities from the nearby sanctuaries, borne on fully caparisoned elephants and accompanied by big, traditional orchestras. They group at each end of the esplanade, then proceed in very slow and majestic motion toward the sanctuary to the sound of "war" music. Each orchestra is surrounded by enthusiastic supporters, jumping in excitement and waving their hands high to mark the complex rhythms. In front of the temple, elephants will salute the goddess

(East faction first), make a circumambulation and leave the esplanade. Then, in the middle of the night, two powerful fireworks, each sponsored by a faction, will be set ablaze in turn on each side of the esplanade.

At the end of the festival, when the second and last "play of the horses" is completed in the morning, the horses, stripped of their decoration and their wooden head, will be abandoned at each end of the esplanade; for a fortnight, nobody will dare touch them, for the *bhūta*, the dangerous and often malevolent spirits which form the goddess' turbulent army, are playing with them.

By comparison with the fight of *ōcci<u>r</u>a kaḷi*, this is a more symbolic way of enacting battles. Blows are replaced by mere competition and offering of emblems, so that an image of confrontation is conveyed through pacific means (but in a different way from what J.C. Heesterman has said about Vedic ritualists). Rivalry between the two parties will be expressed in the size and decoration of the horses, in the strength and abilities of their bearers, in the performance of the "play of horses", in the number and in the size of the elephants, in the richness of their decoration, in the volume of noise and rhythmic precision of orchestras, in the demonstrations of enthusiasm from supporters, and in the impressiveness of the fireworks — especially during the final deafening explosions (think again about the *praḷayaṃ*!). Fireworks should not be overlooked as much prestige is attached to them: factions will spend a great deal (Rs 100,000 each in another festival of similar size), so much so that some festivals will be reputed throughout Kerala mainly for this item thus bringing fame to the temple's locality.

Fame is the only prize the participants may obtain. But it is a powerful force bringing people to the festival.[8] It is a testimony of

---

[8] For instance hundreds of thousands will flock to Trichur town during its Puram celebration — supposed to be the grandest of its type. In this Puram the two factions

the deities' power through a reversal of the current logic: a "powerful place" (deity) attracts a lot of people and has a lot of rituals.[9] Then it gives wide public recognition to the factions' own power and good name and to their social components. In most festivals the core of the factions are *nayar* neighbourhoods, a fact which should remind us of the peculiarities of traditional society, in which Houses are "rooted" in locality: it was not mere fancy but a matter of crucial importance for the Houses to defend their name in front of other local Houses as well as outsiders, and for that purpose they could engage in very high expenses. Likewise, the name of the Houses' neighbourhood is at stake in festivals; to defend it a lot of money, physical exertion and participation of followers and dependents are deemed necessary. Also worth noticing is the fact that while the two factions in Chinakkattur are symbolically "local" and "enemy", that is like "hosts" and "guests" in Heesterman's terminology, together they constitute the actual cult unit of the festival — none being in that respect more "local" than the others. Dual factions, therefore, imply a wholeness at a higher level, found, here, in the deity on the religious plane, and on the social plane in its *namputiri* trustee — who does not take part in the outer rituals of the festival.

Stallions, bulls and umbrellas are offerings (and in some respects elephants, too). This is brought out by local evidence, since all these offerings are shown to the goddess, umbrellas are thrown in the sanctuary's yard and the *bhūta* play with the horses. Comparatively, similar festivals in Travancore — with hints to the Mahabharata war — are called *keṭṭukāḻca,* "built gifts", *kāḻca* being a traditional word

are made of different temples' deities along with their devotees.

[9] This is popular talk. Another instance is given in a myth of the Mammiyur Ambasivan temple: following ghost-infestation the *caitanyam* ("effulgence") of the deities is lessened so that they have no more rituals and no more festivals; only the main deity whose *caitanyam* is strong enough to resist the infestation retains a daily cult (Venni Vasupilla 1983a). For a brief discussion of the notion of *caitanyam* in Kerala temples see Tarabout 1990: 219ff.

for ceremonial offerings to a superior. These offerings have symbolic inferences. In Indian culture all have obvious connotations of kingship; the horses are specifically connected with kings and warriors; bulls, which in some other places are offered with new paddy spikes, can be seen as symbols of agricultural production, (just as the palm-leaf material out of which umbrellas are made); finally both horses and bulls are linked to fertility. Their manipulation is noteworthy: vertical agitation of the horses and bulls is akin to the characteristic jumping that takes place during masculine possession in Central Kerala *(tuḷḷal);* The quick rotation of the palm umbrellas with their flying fringes closely evokes the rotating movement of the head with loosened hair, characteristic of feminine possession in the region. In the same moment, it is an enthusiastic offering to the goddess and the visible sign of their being taken by her. This kind of agitated presentation of gifts has a name in other parts of Kerala: *kāppoli* (which can be understood as "increase in fruits, benefits"). In a locality of Travancore, reputed for its ritual masked dances (*paṭayaṇi,* "battle row" — another means of enacting mythic war), people say that in former times two competing neighbourhoods went too far during their respective *kāppoli:* one faction conceived of exhibiting a corpse whereas, the other, not be outdone, empaled a man alive on a stake and presented him to the deity; this put a definitive end to *kāppoli* as far as the locality was concerned, but the story shows that a sacrificial logic is still at work throughout all these rituals, even in seemingly subsidiary details.

Be it from the enactment of war or from offerings of emblems of the kingdom and its prosperity or from manipulations in a logic of possession/sacrifice, this kind of festival is popularly thought of as nourishing the deities, and is also seen as a contribution to the yearly renewal of their power (though according to orthodoxy only the tantric cult lead by the brahmin priest inside the sanctum is supposed to have that effect). Through competition, which brings fame, through symbolic sacrifices, which bring "food" and power, deities are glorified, as are the human rivals who glorify them, and the whole of the temple "realm" (the kingly dimension of the deity-in-temple is well-known) partakes of this effulgence.

A few other festivals will offer the opportunity to add some further remarks.

Whole and parts

Unlike most parts of Kerala, the Kollamkode area south of Palghat is grouped into villages. In that area there is also a tradition of enacting theatrical sketches during temple festivals (similar traditions can be found elsewhere of course). The village of Pallassena does this, with the peculiarity that the sketch takes the form of a competition between two factions.

The village is multicaste. In the *nayar* neighbourhood two temples, close to each other, are sacred, respectively, to the goddess Bhagavati and to a hunter god, Vettakkaruman (thought to be a form of Siva — his son in some other places, under the name Vettakkorumakan). A single, regular, oracle dances both deities.

The *nayars* take part in two main festivals during the year.[10] At the time of *ōṇaṃ*, together with two other castes, they engage in the traditional fight *ōṇattallu̧* (see above). The *nayar* neighbourhood splits into two halves *(muṟi)*, East and West, each forming with other castes, which are similarly divided, a multicaste faction. The ritual is said to commemorate a past battle in which a local ruler was (treacherously) slain: in reparation the overlord of the victorious party gave the Vettakaruman idol to the aggrieved House. *Ōṇattallu̧* is fought on its temple ground.

---

[10] For an overview, see Choondal 1978: 77-86. Some extracts of the theatrical sketches have been published (in Malayalam), for instance in Bharggavanpilla 1979 and Visvam 1979.

Festival 3: The second main festival is a theatrical competition which occurs in front of the same temple, beginning on the tenth of *mēṭaṃ* month (last week of April).[11] The participation is restricted to members of the *nayar* neighbourhood born there; another caste has a similar but separate theatrical competition ten days before in its own neighbourhood.

In order to acquire the necessary skills, rehearsals are held in each *muṟi* during the few weeks preceding the festival. Only men will play. The direction is assumed by senior masters *(āśān)* of three specified Houses, two in the West half, one in East; the overall authority belongs to the "master of the play" *(kaḷiyāśān)*, the seniormost *āśān:* each of the three aforesaid Houses may have to assume the charge in turn, seniority being the only rule — a fact which is not unlike the traditional former exercise of authority among the different branches of a same *nayar* House.

The festival is called *kaṇṇyārkaḷi* (*kaḷi:* "play, game"). It lasts four nights, each night having a specific name. Typically, the night begins with a procession of all the neighbourhood (supposed to correspond to "99 *nayars*", the 100th being the oracle who leads the way), starting from the Bhagavati temple and arriving in front of the Vettakaruman temple, where the game will be played. In the middle of the performing area are a lit oil-lamp, the sword of Bhagavati, and a stool, on which the oracle sits during the preliminary dances. The male members of the neighbourhood will execute these dances (*vaṭṭakaḷi*, "circle, wheel play") together, in a circle, around the lamp and the oracle, with devotional songs. This is the time of the first appearance of new young performers, garlanded and tonsured. The festival *kaṇṇyārkaḷi* is not just an entertainment —

[11] The date is called pattamudayam, "tenth dawn", when the sun is said to be at the zenith of Kerala; it is, throughout the region, an important event, associated with numerous festivals; it is an especially auspicious day for initiating agricultural operations.

though it is obviously a good one: it is the traditional, local form of offering to Bhagavati and Vettakkaruman, and many performers have to participate to fulfill their vows, thus making this an offering to the deities for past favours. When the circular dances are over, the oracle leaves the area and East and West go to their respective quarters, where they will get ready for the competition of theatrical plays *(poṟāṭṭukaḷi,* "farcical play"). Each night there will be some ten to twelve of them, alternating plays, with a single character, two, or a full group. They are supposed to portray the day-to-day life of tribals or low-caste people from the area or from Tamil Nad, through songs, dances and dialogues. By contrast, as characters in the plays, the *nayars* are conspicuous by their absence — the exception is a "learned man of the locality" who, as a link between the audience and the fiction enacted, asks the characters questions in order to make them declare their identity or their intentions. We shall thus see joyful tribals bringing the products of the forest or of their "gardens", happy agricultural labourers carrying spikes of corn, silk-clad Tamil leather workers, merchants, potters and so on. We shall witness disputes between pairs of washermen or of "gypsy" castes, with erotic if not obscene implications which provoke hearty laughter in the audience. In short, more than a realistic portrayal of humble life, that which is stressed through such idealized presentation of people engaged in agricultural production and harvest is fertility (sexual and agricultural) and abundance. The whole performance ends with the chanting of ritual verses *(tōṟṟaṃ),* more circular dances with the oracle and processions to both temples, then to the Houses of two former local rulers. A final salute takes place before Vettakaruman and sacrificial honoraries *(dakṣiṇa)* are given to the main master.

In this competition, as in the previous ones, no winner is proclaimed, no prize given. Mutual evaluation and public appraisal are based on the quality of the performance (technical perfection, beauty of songs and dances, wittiness of improvised parts, innovative details in costumes or accessories). What should be observed from our perspective, is the strict regulation of the competition: if West plays first on the first night, East will play second, then West, then East...the last to play on this night being East; the following night it is the opposite. Every male member has to participate; but the rivalry is organised through the channel of traditional hereditary rights of a few Houses; everyone, every House, will try to do the best to defend its name — but there is no scope for a modification of precedence, nor in the social order; even the most expert player will never become "master of the play," if he is not born in one of the three Houses whose hereditary right it is, and if he is not the seniormost in them.

This kind of regulation, especially apparent here, but not altogether unknown in other festivals, shows that such a rivalry between factions refers more or less explicitly to a superior unity (of which factions are but temporary parts). The *kaṇṇyārkaḷi* organisation in Pallassena underlines this superior level in many different ways: unity of cult and unity of neighbourhood, equally emphasised when the oracle is said to be the 100th (and ultimate) member of the neighbourhood (indicating that this is not a mere grouping of people, but a totality); a single "master of the play" and its mode of designation; ceremonial recognition of the "above-the-neighbourhood" (former) rule of two Houses — whose formal authorization is a prerequisite for performing the play. In fact there are no real competitive aims that would upset or simply modify the local order of society. In short, Houses in the neighbourhood do not gain pre-eminence through the competition, they just defend their name and position. It is at the level of the "whole" of the festival unit that preeminence or fame can be gained.

So far the factions we have encountered were obvious ones; more subtle forms of expression can also be found.

Assuming Charges

Instead of a competition between face-to-face factions, the rivalry can be fully sequentialized. For instance, in the Kartyayani temple of Shertallai, south of Cochin, the annual Puram festival is conducted by two neighbourhoods, North and South, each of them in turn being in charge of all the events in a day. In the nearby Krishna temple of Ambalappuzha two troups compete in a martial dance called *vēlakaḷi*. They dance together, alternating in the pole position according to the days of the festival. But ritual factionalism can also structure the repartition of charges in rituals — as the Kongan Pada festival in Chittur village (not far from Pallassena and Palghat) will demonstrate.

Festival 4: The Kongan Pada festival (*koṇṇappaṭa*, "war of the King of Kongu Nad") and the story to which it refers have been described by many authors.[12] For the present concern a few indications should be enough. The festival is supposed to re-enact a past war which opposed the king of neighbouring Kongu Nad and the people of the locality. At that time a warrior form of the benign goddess (or her sister, according to others) came forth to protect the villagers and in return asked for blood and alcohol. Now there are two shrines: one of Bhagavati, vegetarian and served by a brahmin; the other, east of the former and on higher ground, sacred to Chittur kavilamma (Lady of the *kāvu*, "small wood", a general term for some sanctuaries in Kerala). She gets vegetal substitutes for blood offerings, is served by a *nayar pūjāri*, and has a *nayar* oracle. Both of these men belong to specific Houses of the West *nayar* neighbourhood, adjacent to the sanctuaries: the *pūjāri* comes from a House which had previously the charge of the local gymnasium, from

---

[12] See for instance: Ananthakrishna Iyer (1969: II, 71-75), Devassy (1966: 348-351), Tarabout (1986: 170-174); in Malayalam: Venni Vasupilla (1983b), Kottarattil Sankunni (1974: 833-848); I was unable to obtain a Malayalam publication on the subject written by P.R. Menon.

whose shrine the Bhagavati temple is itself said to be an offshoot. The oracle is selected by Chitturkavilamma from among the male members of two other Houses.

There is also an East neighbourhood. Kongan Pada is said to be the festival of four main *nayar* Houses *(pramāṇakkār*, the "pre-eminent ones") other than the *pūjāri* and oracle's Houses. There are two "pre-eminent ones" in each neighbourhood. These Houses had the power to obtain, even through coercion, financial contributions and manpower from the different Houses of the two *nayar* neighbourhoods (an informant put forward the number of 108 Houses — a figure quite theoretical, but indicative here also of a "totality").

There are numerous and complex processions during Kongan Pada in which people from both neighbourhoods along with other castes take part. Many of these processions are costumed. If in the general participation there is no distinction along neighbourhood lines, yet some characters in the processions are played by members of specific Houses: the impersonation of the enemy king — supposed in the myth to be mounted on a buffalo and to look "like Yama" — is the hereditary privilege of a House belonging to East; a different House of the same neighbourhood has the task of providing a man who has to act as a corpse during a mock funeral; from East also a third House (one of the "pre-eminent ones") has to enact short costumed plays, especially an obscene parody of astrological calculation in front of the Bhagavati temple.

Thus we have *nayars* of both neighbourhoods participating equally in all processions, but a distinctive repartition of tasks held by a few Houses. Houses of West neighbourhood, which is close to the sanctuaries and said to be at their origin, assume all the *(nayar)* charges connected with the worship. Houses of East neighbourhood have the privilege to enact all the *(nayar)* costumed characters during processions, including the enemy king and the fake corpse. Such a polarisation can be seen as a variant of the "host-guest" agonistic relationship, but is not formulated at all by devotees, especially in its symbolic, hierarchical consequences; instead, the equality of both neighbourhoods is stressed. In a subsequent festival a few weeks later confrontation — on an equality basis — of the two neighbourhoods is explicit: during *karivēla* ("black procession") the youth of East and West, blackened with soot, forming two separate processions and accompanied by low-status *paṟayan* playing drums, will compete in wild exuberance; when these processions cross each other, it can degenerate into real blows.

Let us try to resume what we have seen. Participation in factions which have no existence outside festivals can be a duty, most of the time on a basis of neighbourhood membership: factions appear to be anchored in locality — as are neighbourhoods and Houses — and to partake of the same concern for prestige. There is often an internal organisation if not hierarchy, the rank of each component being well established by tradition: the rivalry does not bring out any change in the local social structure. Factions are therefore the result of a ritual partition of the cult unit thought of as a totality; placed on an equal footing, they are often symbolically polarized ("hosts/guests"). No winner is proclaimed, no prizes are won, only the "names" are held up. The whole of the festival celebration, the deity, the locality, attain fame — this can be considered as a certain idea of force. In this respect the competitions we have come across, based as they are on multiple references to the logic of sacrifice (even though people might speak in devotional terms of their relation to the deity), are certainly effective in nourishing and glorifying the gods. The importance of these forms of celebration seems to be connected with some features of Kerala society: locally rooted aristocratic Houses exert dominance and tend to constitute their relationships into traditional stable networks in which prestige is a crucial issue. Such a social morphology appears to have been a fertile ground for the development of factional forms of rituals. But, though frequent, the latter are by no means the only ones in Kerala, and the peculiar social morphology described should therefore be considered as essentially a fertile ground for their blossoming. It is rather tempting to ask the inverse question: can similar ritual factions develop in societies without "House" characteristics ?

Additional Remarks

Competitions and evocations of battle are not restricted to festivals of "carnivorous" deities: vegetarian divinities can also be worshipped in this manner. Factional organisation of rituals is not related to specific categories of gods. Brahmins and rulers are above the factions, they are at the level of the "whole", and have therefore no observed participation in the competition proper — though their agreement to proceed to the festival is often necessary (but not always: for example this is not the case for Kongan Pada, which is said to be the festival of the four "preeminent ones"; the local ruler's permission is not even sought). Though Kerala society has changed since the XIXth century, reference to neighbourhoods and former Houses has still some relevance in day-to-day rural life, and a lot during festivals. Modern small families, created by the partition of Houses, might well have their own cults, individuals might seek personal salvation through bhakti (devotion), the locality level of religious practice is mostly founded on references to the old order of society (except in some urban contexts) and is still the scene where social mutual evaluation is at its peak.

Let us conclude on a comparative note. Few similar cases have been reported from South India outside Kerala, except in the Tulu region (Biardeau 1981: 878ff). There are, however, well-known ritual factions in Buddhist Sri Lanka during festivals of the Pattini cult (Yalman 1965; Obeyesekere 1984: 381-423) — with the difference that a party must win. These similarities are part of other ritual resemblances (for instance religious masked dances) which can be observed from Tulu and Coorg regions, Kerala, to Sri Lanka — but not typically in nearby Tamil Nadu or in the northern parts of Karnataka (Tarabout 1986: 617-633). Factional competitions appear, in this general perspective, as an element in a wider common ritual complex, found along the south-western coast of India and in Sri Lanka. What about the societies concerned? Briefly put, it seems possible to consider the patrilineal Coorg *okka* as a House and to suggest that the Bants in the Tulu region might present some of the features earmarked for Kerala (Bhatt 1975: 149, uses in some contexts the term "manor-house"; Claus 1975: 91 underlines the importance of locality). In the Goyigama caste in Sri Lanka strong interference of a locality component in kin definitions has been stressed: "anyone who lived in the same garden or house (whether related or not) could use the same gedara [dwelling] name" (Yalman 1967: 269). The "kindred" (pavula) tends to be a neighbourhood (id., pp191ff). Locality is brought into evidence also by E. Leach (1961: 7): "it is locality rather than descent which forms the basis for corporate grouping"; the same author links the time-enduring kindred groups to the detention of agricultural rights (id., p.123).

Whatever the obvious contrasts between all these societies, we notice a distinctive importance of locality in the definition of social groups and loyalties. This is not to say that it is altogether absent in other parts of South Asia but, at least in most castes of the same level in neighbouring parts of India, we do not find such a systematic interference of locality with descent. That the south-western coast of India and Sri Lanka should possess similar social and ritual features, notwithstanding current differences in religious references, in languages, in history, leaves us in fact with more disconcerting questions than before — but provides also a stimulus for further research.

References

Ananthakrishna Iyer, L.K. 1969. *The Cochin tribes and castes,* 2 vols. New-York/London: Johnson Reprint Corp. (1st ed. 1909-1912, Madras: Higginbotham-Govt. of Cochin).

Beals, Alan R. 1964. Conflict and interlocal festivals in a South Indian region. In *Journal of Asian Studies,* XXIII: 99-114.

Bharggavanpilla, J. 1979. *Poṟaṭṭunāṭakavuṃ maṟṟuṃ.* The author/Kottayam: National Book Stall. [In Malayalam].

Bhatt, P. Gururaja. 1975. *Studies in Tuluva history and culture (from the prehistoric times up to the modern).* Kallianpur: The author.

Biardeau, Madeleine. 1976. Le Sacrifice dans l'Hindouisme. In M. Biardeau and C. Malamoud (eds.) *Le Sacrifice dans l'Inde ancienne.* Paris: PUF/Ecole Pratique des Hautes Etudes, pp. 7-154.

Id. 1981. The ball-game: Myth and rite. In *Ludwik Sternbach Felicitation Volume:* 875-881. Lucknow: Akhila Bharatiya Sanskrit Parishad.

Choondal, Chummar 1978. *Studies in the folklore of Kerala.*

Trivandrum: College Book House.

Claus, Peter J. 1975. Determinants of household oganization among tenants and landowners in the Bant caste. In *Contributions to Indian Sociology, N.S.* 9-1: 89-110.

Devassy, M.K. (ed.) 1966. *Fairs and festivals of Kerala,* 1. (Census 1961, vol. VII, part VII, B-1). Delhi: Census of India.

Dumont, Louis 1957. *Une sous-caste de l'Inde du Sud - Organisation sociale et religion des Pramalai Kallar.* Paris/ La Haye: Mouton/Ecole Pratique des Hautes Etudes.

Id. 1961. Les mariages Nayar comme faits indiens. *L'Homme,* I-1: 11-36.

Fawcett, F. 1915. Nāyars of Malabar. In *Madras Government Museum Bulletin* III-3: 185-323 (reprint ed. 1901).

Fuller, C.J. 1976. *The Nayars today.* Cambridge University Press.

Gough, E. Kathleen 1952. Changing kinship usages in the setting of political and economic change among the Nayars of Malabar. In *Journal of the Royal Anthropological Institute,* 82-1: 71-88.

Id. 1961. Nayar: Central Kerala; Nayar: North Kerala. In D.M. Schneider and K. Gough (eds.) *Matrilineal kinship*. University of California Press, pp.298-404.

Heesterman, J.C. 1967. The case of the severed head. In *Wiener Zeitschrift für die Kunde Süd und Ostasiens*, XI: 22-43.

Kareem, C.K. (ed.) 1976. *Kerala District Gazetteers*. Palghat. Trivandrum: Government Press.

Kottarattil Sankunni 1974. *Aitihyamāla*. Kottayam: Kottarattil Sankunni Memorial Committee/Current Books (1st publ. 1909-1934). [In Malayalam].

Kurup, A.M. (ed.) 1966. *Onam. A festival of Kerala*. (Census 1961, vol. I, part VII, B-2). Delhi: Census of India.

Leach, Edmund R. 1961. *Pul Eliya, a village in Ceylon. A study of land tenure and kinship*. Cambridge University Press.

Lévi-Strauss, Claude. 1979. *La voie des masques*. Paris: Plon.

Id. 1984. *Paroles données*. Paris: Plon.

Marar, T.K. 1979. Onam. The national festival of Kerala. In *Malayalam Literary Survey*, III-3: 2-10.

Mateer, Samuel. 1883. *Native life in Travancore*. London: Allen & Co.

Mencher, Joan P. and Goldberg, Helen 1967. Kinship and marriage regulations among the Namboodiri Brahmans of Kerala. In *Man N.S.*, 2-1: 87-106.

Mencher, Joan P. 1965. The Nayars of South Malabar. In M.F. Nimkoff (ed.) *Comparative family systems*. Boston: Houghton Mifflin Co., pp. 163-191.

Id. 1966a. Namboodiri Brahmins: An analysis of a traditional elite in Kerala. In *Journal of Asian and African Studies*, I-3: 183-196.

Id. 1966b. Kerala and Madras: A comparative study of ecology and social structure. In *Ethnology*, V-2: 135-171.

Moore, Melinda A. 1985. A new look at the Nayar Taravad. In *Man N.S.*, 20-3: 523-541.

Muthanna, I.M. 1953. *A tiny model state of South India*. Pollibetta: 'Tiny Spot'.

Obeyesekere, Gananath. 1984. *The cult of the goddess Pattini*. Chicago: University of Chicago Press.

Panikkar, K.M. 1918. Some aspects of Nayar life. In

Journal of the Royal Anthropological Institute, XLVIII:254-293.

Reiniche, M.-L. 1979. *Les Dieux et les Hommes. Etude des cultes d'un village du Tirunelveli - Inde du Sud.* Paris/ La Haye: Mouton/Ecole des Hautes Etudes en Sciences Sociales.

Rowlandson, M.J. (transl.) 1833. *Sheikh Zeen-ud-deen: Tohfut-ul-Mujahideen.* London: Oriental translation Fund of Great-Britain and Ireland.

Sreedhara Menon A. (ed.) 1965. *Kerala District Gazetteers.* Ernakulam. Trivandrum: Government Press.

Id. 1975. *Kerala District Gazetteers.* Alleppey. Trivandrum: Government Press.

Srinivas, M.N. 1952. *Religion and society among the Coorgs of South India.* London: Asia Publishing House.

Tarabout, Gilles. 1986. *Sacrifier et donner à voir en pays malabar. Les fêtes de temple au Kerala (Inde du Sud): étude anthropologique.* Paris: Ecole Francaise d'Extrême-Orient.

Id. 1990. Sacrifice et renoncement dans les

mythes de fondation de temples au Kérala. In M. Détienne (ed.) *Tracés de fondation*. Paris/Leuven: Ecole Pratique des Hautes Etudes/Peeters, pp.211-232.

Id. (forthcoming). Au 'royaume' des brahmanes, les guerriers sont rois. Souveraineté, pouvoir et statut au Kérala. In H. Stern and J. Pouchepadass (ed.) *Purusartha* 13: De la royauté à l'Etat, anthropologie et histoire du politique dans le monde indien. Paris: E.H.E.S.S.

Thurston, Edgar, and Rangachari, K. 1965. *Castes and tribes of Southern India*, 7 vols. New-York: Johnson Reprint Corp. (1st ed 1909, Madras Government Press).

Venni Vasupilla. 1983a. Aṃpalanaṭayil: mammiyūr śrī aṃbāśivan. In *Malayāḷanāṭu*, 14-49: 56-60. [In Malayalam].

Id. 1983b. Aṃpalanaṭayil: ciṟṟurkāvilamma. *Malayāḷanāṭu*, 14-43: 54-59. [In Malayalam].

Visvam, K. 1979. *Poṟāṭṭukaḷi*. Trivandrum: Kerala Grandhasala Sahakarana Sanghom. [In Malayalam].

Yalman, Nur 1965. Dual organization in Central Ceylon? or the goddess on the tree-top. In *Journal of Asian Studies*, XXIV-3: 441-457.

Id. 1967. *Under the Bo Tree. Studies in caste, kinship, and marriage in the interior of Ceylon*. Berkeley: University of California Press.

PERFORMING POSSESSION: RITUAL AND CONSCIOUSNESS IN THE TEYYAM COMPLEX OF NORTHERN KERALA*

J. Richardson Freeman

To the foreign observer, performers engaged in the worship of Northern Kerala's Teyyam deities appear perhaps deranged, as though in the grip of some potentially violent fantasy. Rattling ornaments and clattering weapons, their limbs tremble in the monstrous forms which costume their bodies. They glower menacingly from floridly painted faces, then suddenly burst into hoarse shrieks directed to unseen beings. They swagger, whirl, and lunge into the onlookers, who scatter before their brandished sabers. Elsewhere, priests reel in the ambit of a raging bonfire, their eyes fixed on the swords which dance in their hands and seem to jerk them spasmodically through their movements. Assistants restrain them from doing harm, while worshippers look on in glassy awe.

* The research for this paper was carried out in Kerala, India in 1987-88 under a grant from the Fulbright-Hays Doctoral Dissertation Abroad Program of the United States Department of Education. Much of the writing of a dissertation from which this paper is abstracted was supported by a Charlotte W. Newcombe Fellowship administered by the Woodrow Wilson National Fellowship Foundation. I wish to acknowledge a debt of gratitude to both these agencies for support of this work, as well as to Dr. K.K.N. Kurup, University of Calicut, for his initial assistance in my undertaking the project.

The indigenous perception is that these dancers and priests are "possessed" by their Teyyam deities.[1] As evidenced by the ancient Tamil literature, the reports of colonial missionaries, and modern ethnographic accounts, it is clear that such states of possession are a fundamental and perduring feature of South Indian religious belief and experience.[2] Yet despite the growing number of studies which address issues of possession in the region, either directly or in passing, there are few attempts at a cultural comprehension of the central phenomenon itself — of how possession is conceptually constituted, behaviorally induced, and morally evaluated by its actual practitioners. Instead, as has been noted (Claus 1979: 30ff.), anthropological analyses of possession complexes are generally hampered by two methodological problems: the overly hasty move to reduce possession to Western models of psychological pathology, on the one hand, and to those of social-structural function (or dysfunction), on the other. Such approaches are especially problematic to the extent that they pre-empt cultural expositions given by the informants themselves in favor of a prior commitment to some particular social-scientific paradigm.

By contrast, in the present treatment of Teyyam worship in Northern Kerala, I shall be concerned neither with sociological nor psychological "explanations" of the possession encountered there. I shall instead engage in a cultural interpretation of the possession rites, based on the activities I observed, the indigenous exegesis of their symbolic significance, descriptions of the psychological experiences, and the manifest content of the songs and vocalizations which precede and accompany possession. I make no assumptions

---

[1] The divine beings who possess these exclusively male specialists are both female and male. For stylistic purposes I use "deity" and "god" to cover beings of both genders. I use "goddess" only when I have a specifically female deity in mind, or where my informants have used the Malayalam equivalent (generally *dēvi*).

[2] See Hart 1975, Caldwell 1849, many articles in Thurston 1909, Whitehead 1921, Harper 1957, Dumont 1957, Claus 1973, Moffatt 1979, Obeyesekere 1981, and Blackburn 1988.

regarding my ability to infer psychological states (or assess their genuineness) from external behaviors, except for what informants have actually told me. The only significant theoretical presuppositions I make are the following: that possession beliefs and behaviors are culturally produced, symbolically instantiated, and socially transmitted. I thus take as my primary task in this paper the representation of how possession as a system of belief and practice is culturally constituted in Teyyam. In order to situate the specifics of the exposition, however, I wish to first make some general observations on the cultural context of Teyyam worship and practice.

Teyyam in its Cultural Context

Although designated in some of the literature as a "cult,"[3] it should be noted that virtually every caste and community in the region, from the ritually highest Nambūtiri Brahmans to the lowest Pulayan Untouchables, traditionally sponsor and participate in yearly Teyyam rites at their own and others' shrines. It should also be pointed out that before the temple entry legislation of the late 1940's took effect in Malabar,[4] Teyyam shrines were the only functional temples accessible to those "polluting" castes *(avarṇṇar)*, who in fact constituted the bulk of the Hindu agrarian population.

This is still reflected in the fact that many informants do not clearly differentiate between Teyyam as the costumed form of the deity which a dancer assumes in performances, and the divine being who is thereby represented. (Indeed, this accords well with the origin of the word Teyyam itself, which derives from the Sanskrit *daiva,* and means simply "god") (Gundert 1873: 480). Even an English-educated and widely travelled member of the high Potuvāḷ caste told me, "When we were children and came before the Teyyam

---

[3] E.g. Kurup 1973, Holloman and Ashley 1983.

[4] Menon 1980: 376.

[dancer], we weren't aware that this was something special called 'Teyyam'; to us this was simply god." Furthermore, the worship of Teyyams, as named divine beings, involves other specialists and vehicles of possession aside from the costumed dancers who lend the complex its name. I thus find it useful neither to regard Teyyam as a "folk art," nor as a "cult," but rather as a related set of religious beliefs and practices centered on the cultural proposition of divine possession.

At the most basic level, the possession complex is predicated on a widespread and general belief in the existence of invisible powers and beings, and their capacity to inhabit human beings' bodies. From the perspective of the person undergoing such inhabitation, the state may be brought on intentionally, or it may come of its own, involuntarily. The intentional possessions are effected by various ritual procedures, and such possessing agencies are ordinarily felt to be beneficial, or at least not harmful to the host whose body they occupy. The second type of possession takes the form of an assault, wherein the unseen being seizes the body of the host, without their consent, or often, even their knowledge.

While a terminological distinction could be made between these two types of possession for analytic purposes, it would be very difficult to establish a set of indigenous criteria by which we might dichotomize the different forms of possession in any absolute way.[5] These beings' natures are relative to the parties with whom they interact, and to the mode and situation of that interaction; the same being may be variously perceived as a blood-thirsty vampire *(yakṣi)* or a paramount goddess *(paradēvata)*, depending on context.[6] Lin-

[5] Claus notes that there is no linguistic evidence for making such distinctions in the closely cognate traditions of the Tulu country (1979: 29), though he goes ahead and makes the analytic distinction between possession (as involuntary) and mediumship (as voluntary) in his exposition (ibid., p. 35ff.). I find this distinction not very relevant for dealing with Teyyam, per se; Cp. notes 7 and 8, below.

[6] Unfortunately I cannot deal with the nature of the many supernatural beings and their relations with human beings in the space permitted, although this has been

guistically, this is substantiated by the fact that the same phrases are used for describing the onset of possession whether this comes about voluntarily, by beneficial beings, or involuntarily, by inimical and demonic beings.[7] Textually, the shifting nature of this distinction is likewise encountered in a number of the gods' narrative songs which depict them as vacillating from cases of spontaneous seizure to controlled invocation, and vice versa.

Even for purposes of an externally derived analytic framework, however, there would be little point in distinguishing voluntary from involuntary possession in a discussion of Teyyam, for its practice is almost entirely directed to possessions of the voluntary, ritual type, as confined to socially appointed specialists.[8] Accordingly, even those afflictions addressed in Teyyam worship which are attributed to involuntary possession prove to be for the most part purely attributional, in that they have been previously diagnosed as "possession" by diviners, with no manifest psychological symptoms on the part of the afflicted *(piṇiyāḷ)*.

There are two broad divisions of specialists who serve as possession vehicles in the religious complex of Teyyam worship. First,

---

treated at length in my recently completed dissertation.

[7] Whatever the type of being and circumstances may be, the onset of possession *(āvēśam)* is described as a "coming to" *(varuka)*, "joining" *(kūṭuka)*, or "mounting" *(kēruka)* of the body *(meyyal)*. In this state the host is said to be "illumined" *(veḷiccappeṭuka)*, "fixed," or "in-dwelt" *(uṟayuka)*, to be "internally moved" *(iḷakuka)*, and possessed of "spiritual vision" *(darśanam)* (Cp. Claus 1979, p. 50, note 2, for a comparison with Tulu cognates).

[8] Out of the more than fifty Teyyam celebrations I have attended, I observed instances of overt trance behavior among lay-worshippers at only two of them, restricted to a handful of individuals. On the basis of these observations and subsequent interviews, it is clear that these behaviors do not provide the models for the routinized, voluntary possession of the specialists which are encountered in Teyyam performance. A more complete treatment of the religion of this area would need to address these involuntary seizures as well, typically experienced by women and treated by rites of sorcery *(mantravādam)* at home, rather than in Teyyam performances, proper. (Cp. Claus 1975, for a case of public, mass treatment).

connected with most permanent shrines where Teyyam deities are established, there is a class of ecstatic priests known as *kōmarams* or *veḷiccappāṭus*. While there are differences between the two in certain of their costuming items and attributes, and while each caste group will generally have only one or the other serving at their shrine, the basic functional characteristics of both types of specialist are the same. On certain occasions of the year, and always in conjunction with Teyyam festivals, these individuals enter the small chamber of their shrines where Teyyam deities are installed (either as fixed images or swords), perform certain rites and incantations, and emerge from the shrine possessed by the particular deity to whom they are dedicated. They then dance with swords representing their respective deities, (occasionally hacking their heads and chests), speak in the voice of the gods, and receive offerings and give blessings to worshippers who have gathered on these occasions. *Veḷiccappāṭus* and *kōmarams* are dedicated to one particular god at one particular shrine, generally for life. While eligibility is determined by heredity within particular matrilineages, the actual election to the office usually comes about through spontaneous seizure by the specific deity, who thereby chooses the individual.[9]

The other kind of specialists are the Teyyam performers *(teyyakkār)*, proper. These professionals from certain lower castes (most often Vaṇān, Malayan, or Vēlan) are entitled by lineage rights to incarnate specific gods at a number of designated shrines in their region during the Teyyam season. Each shrine in a given region has its annual Teyyam festival on dates specified by tradition, so that the troupes of *teyyakār* know from year to year where they are expected to perform specifically designated deities at any given date in the season. Thus unlike the case of the *veḷiccappāṭus* and *kōmarams*, the *teyyakkār* travel from shrine to shrine, profes-

---

[9] The reputed spontaneity of this choice is obviously undercut by the requirement of inherited eligibility as well as by the further requirements imposed on the aspirant. Cp. p. 132f. of the text and the informant cited there in the translation of note 35 below.

sionally incarnating a variety of deities.

Each deity has its own elaborate costume and make-up which is donned by the performer with fixed ritual songs and incantations unique to that deity. The songs often tell the story of the deity's creation and events of its biography, its travels, its establishment at various shrines, and also descriptions of its physical appearance — the last somewhat loosely based on the appearance of the Teyyam itself. The songs may also in some cases consist simply of verses of praise with little narrative content. In the course of singing certain lines of the songs at the close of the costuming sequence, the dancer enters the state of possession *(uṟaccal)* by the deity. He then performs a well-rehearsed sequence of dancing and rituals, which culminates in his speaking in the voice of the god and interacting directly with the worshippers in receiving offerings, giving blessings, and granting boons. The possession ends with a general blessing to those assembled and a rite of returning the divine power *(śakti)* of the deity from the body of the dancer to the shrine from which it was received.

In addition to the central ritual sequence, performed in the fully elaborated form of the Teyyam, there is a phase of preliminary rites done in abbreviated costume and make-up. This phase takes one of two forms, depending on the particular deity, one known as *tōṟṟam*, the other, as *veḷḷāṭṭam*. (See plate I). With minor exceptions, the costumes of *tōṟṟams* and *veḷḷāṭṭams*, though different from each other, appear basically the same for all deities, in contrast to the full-fledged Teyyam forms which are highly differentiated. (See plate II). The same dancer who has been dedicated to perform a particular Teyyam that year at that shrine, performs the *veḷḷāṭṭam* or *tōṟṟam* over the preceding evening or evenings. Most of the structural phases of the possession, the dancing, and the rituals of the full-fledged Teyyam performance of the following day are performed in brief in these preliminary rites.

Between these two kinds of shrine priests (as *veḷiccappāṭu* and *kōmaram*) and the three forms of Teyyam costuming and rites (as the full-fledged Teyyam, *tōṟṟam*, and *veḷḷāṭṭam*) we thus have five morphological forms of human vehicles for possession. In all of these cases, however, it is the same god or goddess who may possess all five forms, (in the case of the priests and Teyyams, often simultaneously), and in all cases this power derives from the deity's main image and is transferred into the vehicle's body by a set of structured ritual actions. As a *kōṟāccan* (an elevated *kōmaram*) described the situation:

> The consciousness of the goddess has been deposited in a certain place; that is the temple at which we worship. At the time we get the spiritual vision of possession *(darśanam)*, all of that divine power *(śakti)* we get comes from that image which is installed in the shrine chamber... The possessed vision of all the Teyyam performers and *kōṟāccans* is one and the same, but it is only in the rites [by which they get it] that there are differences.[10]

Possession as Performative Act

What this clearly suggests is that possession in Teyyam is a fundamentally ritual activity, that is, it is characterized by a highly formalized set of behaviors and beliefs which owe little to individual motivations or dispositions. This is not to deny that the rituals do induce certain states and conditions in the performers, but we must also stress that these rites and their results have a verbally and symbolically defined content and interpretation prior to and independently of the performer as an individual agent. The performer is

---

[10] *Dēvīcaitanyam oriṭattu nikṣiptam āyiṭṭuṇḍu; atāṇu nammaḷ ārādhikkunna kṣetram. Darśanasamayattu kiṭṭunna śakti muḻuvanum ā paḷḷiyaṟayil pratiṣṭhicca vigrahattil ninnāṇu kiṭṭunnatu... Teyyakkāranṟeyum kōṟāccanṟeyum ellām darśanam onnum tanne, pakṣē karmmattil mātram vyatyāsam uṇḍāyirikkum.*

therefore embedded in a set of conventions which presuppose the constitution and effectiveness of the possession rituals to which he subjects himself through training, and by which he is himself turned into a ritual object. He is, therefore, acted upon far more than he acts; rather than him performing the Teyyam, we may say the Teyyam, as a collective representation, performs itself through him. In this light, I view Teyyam possession as a performative process (in the Austinian sense),[11] which by the very conventions of its constitution is socially defined as real and effective. Those conventions, however, consist not just of ritual acts, but of texts and interpretations which place those acts in the wider context of Teyyam possession as a source of divine power. It is my intention now to chart this process through the ritual acts which effect that possession, demonstrating the conventions of speech and belief in which they are situated.

We may first proceed by noting that the principal activity which is supposed to signify the transference of the god's power into the body of the dancer, is a simple ritual act. Wicks lit from a lamp burning within the shrine are handed over in a banana leaf to the partially costumed dancer.[12] The concept *(saṅkalpam)* behind this, I was told, "is that the actual divine power *(śakti)* is given to the dancer through that flame."[13] He receives the leaf and touches his hand to the wicks and his brow three times, thereby incorporating

---

[11] My use of "performative" in this paper is intended to access what I regard as the highly significant insights into linguistic pragmatics as expounded by J. L. Austin and others. Austin's departure point was the discovery that whole classes of sentences, when uttered under the force of certain social conventions, actually accomplish the acts they purport; these he called performatives or speech acts (Levinson 1983: 227ff.). It is these insights whose application I extend to ritual sequences (Cp. notes 16, 17 and 23, below and Tambiah 1985). I, in no way, mean to invoke "performance theory," as its proponents call their amalgam of "processual" anthropology and theatrics.

[12] Cp. Ashley 1979: 104.

[13] *Itinṟe saṅkalpam...yathārthadēvīkamāyiṭṭuḷḷa śakti ā dīpattilūṭe ayāḷkku koṭukkunnu.*

the divine power into his person.

This outward act, however, really only signifies a juncture in a process which has begun in the make-up room and will continue through the songs and ceremonies which follow. For certain major celebrations, the dancer undergoes a prolonged period of fasting and isolation prior to his performance, but even for the smaller Teyyam rites, he is supposed to observe certain dietary vows *(nōnbu)* and a partial fast. The purpose of this, I was told, is to begin turning his mind away from worldly concerns and towards the deity. Similarly, during the actual make-up and costuming sequence, he is supposed to be concentrating his mental energy *(manana śakti)* on the deity whose form is being built up by stages on his body. For certain Teyyams, there are formulae *(mantrams)* which the performer murmurs to himself at junctures in the costuming process to help fix the deity's power in his body.[14]

While there is considerable variation among the various full-fledged Teyyams, *tōṟṟams*, and *veḷḷāṭṭams* as to whether the bulk of the costuming is completed in the make-up room, before a special offering platform, or in front of the shrine itself, at some designated point during this process, the performer and his assistants begin to sing the initial verses addressed to the particular deity. These invocatory verses belong to the sections of songs known as *varaviḷi*, literally the "summons to come".

The length and content of this genre is generally short, and invariably includes the stock promptings and laudings to the god, "may you come," and "praised be you".[15] Sometimes, these sum-

[14] Cp. ibid., p. 105.

[15] The genre *varaviḷi*, whose purpose is the "call/invitation" *(viḷi)* "to come" *(vara)*, including its characteristic phrases "may you come" *(varuka* vēṇam), and "praised be you" *(vāḻka*, and its Sankritic equivalent *vandikkā)*, finds a remarkable parallel in the invocatory songs of the kōṭaṅki priests in Tamil Nadu, whom I read as equivalents of *kōmarams* or *veḷiccappāṭus* in Kerala. As reported by Diehl (1956: 227), these songs correspond to the *āvāhana* of āgamic *pūjā*, and are known as *vara-v-*

mons contain highly compressed versions of the deity's narrative, as well as promised results from its worship *(phalaśruti)*. In conformity with such opening speech acts[16] that invoke and praise the god, the representative content of the songs *actually indexes* the god's presence, either through references to a chain of places culminating in the present shrine, or through the god's sacred paraphernalia and offerings which are *actually present* in the rites.[17] The following short *varaviḷi* to the god Vēṭṭakkarumakan will provide an example:

> May you come, O Vēṭṭakkarumakan of
> Bāliśśēri!

---

vaḻaittal, thus combining in name exactly those two phrases and themes most characteristic of these Teyyam songs. Regarding my interpretation of these two phrases as true Austinian performatives, see the following note.

[16] I interpret the forms *varuka* and *vāḻka* as being explicitly performative verbs signifying illocutionary acts (Levinson: 236), for they formally possess the conventional force to effect what they say they do. To invoke or order the god to come is to have the power to do so, just as to praise the god is to simultaneously announce and establish its life and rule (literal meanings of the verb *vāḻ-)*. Formally, the Tamil/ Malayalam verbal ending *-ka* lends itself readily to performatives, for though called on analogy an "optative," its semantics slide between desire and command and it is found with all three persons (Agesthialingom 1979: 100); accordingly, it can frequently signify a wish with the force of a command.

[17] I follow here the synthesis of Jakobson's insights into indexicals with the semiotic of Peirce as formulated by Silverstein (1976) and applied to ritual analysis by Tambiah (1985). The basic idea derives from the linguistic phenomenon of deixis, wherein demonstratives, tenses, first and second person pronouns, adverbs of time and place, etc., rely for their semantic completion on the actual context of utterance, (e.g. the meaning of the utterance 'I' depends on who utters it). Such forms are often called indexicals in that they thereby link formal semantics into the actual pragmatics of natural language use. This situation can be seen to parallel Peirce's distinction between those signs he called icons which have merely formal similarities to what they signify, and those he called indexes, which are physically co-present or connected with what they signify (like a temperature gauge, or a pointing index finger). As Silverstein and Tambiah have pointed out, however, signs can take on both these functions, as both formally representing and simultaneously indicating application to their co-present objects. This is how I argue the Teyyam songs frequently function when they create verbal images which they then indexically link into the context of the actual performance.

The fort at Bāliśśēri and the fort of the
Lord of Kuṟumbranāṭu,
The shrine at Ceṟuvaḷḷiyūr, the steps at
Uḷḷiyūr, Mēnappuṟam and
Karippūram,
Veḷḷiśrīmānyamaṅgalam, and the shrine of Udayagiri
— these you saw!
Over the sword of Kāṟakūṟa Nāyar, and over his cloth,
Your splendor shines, O Vēṭṭakkarumakan.
As it was before, so now in this assembly,
For the feud and the battle and their tumult,
For the realm of Aḷḷaṭam and the Nāyar who serve its king,
May you come marching here to give your benediction!
O sacred prince of the King of Hunters,
O Vēṭṭakkarumakan![18]

The song marks a progression: from the founding shrine *(mūlasthānam)* at the Bāliśśēri fort, where the god is supposed to have secured the victory of those Nāyars who first worshipped him; along the route where he established various other shrines on his northward march; and up to the major regional shrine of Udayagiri, near the place of performance. Next, the frame shifts to the current shrine and the objects of the sword and the cloth that are actually used in the rites. These objects, however, are imagined to belong to the Nāyar who originally established the god's worship, thereby identifying the current shrine and its rituals with those of the deity's originary shrine. The operative logic here is that analogous rituals should yield analogous results: just as the god's original presence at

---

[18] *Varika vēṇam Vāriyēri (Bāliśśēri) Veṭṭakkarumakanē!*
Vāriyēri kōṭṭayum, Kuṟumbrātiri kōṭṭayum,
Ceṟuvaḷḷiyūr kāvum, Uḷḷiyūr paṭi, Mēnappuṟam, Karipūram,
Veḷḷiśrīmānyamaṅgalam, Udayagiri māṭam — kāṇum ceytu.
Kāṟakūṟa Nāyare vāḷin mēlum tukalin mēlum
Oḷi pakarnnu pōrunnoru Vāriyēri Vēṭṭakkarumakanē!
Annē nāḷāle innē yōgattināle,
Aṅkattinum, paṭakkum, aṅkam paṭa kalahattinum,
Aḷḷaṭasvarūpattinum, ādikōn ādarikkum
Nāyarkkum, nallatine colli koṭuppān eḻunnaḷḷi varika!
Vēṭarājāvu Tirumakan Vāriyērī Vēṭṭakkarumakan!

Bāliśśēri fort assured the Nāyar there of victory, so his presence in the current shrine will bring victory to this realm. But this is, of course, contingent on actually getting the god to manifest his presence here, which is what the Teyyam is concerned with demonstrating, and what the *varaviḷi* seeks to effect.

Following the *varaviḷi* come various hymns of praise *(stuti)* which describe the deity, its attributes, and activities. These then lead into the sections of song which give the narrative of the deity's origins and establishment on earth.[19] These songs are called, like one of the preliminary ritual phases itself, *tōṟṟam*, a term which is extended to cover the whole genre of Teyyam songs, generally.

The etymology of this word is highly significant for indicating the instrumentality by which possession is effected. The word is a nominal form of a transitive verb, from a normally intransitive root meaning "to spring up, to seem, appear, to come to mind" (Gundert 1873: 492). As a transitive, however, it means to imagine, but with a more creatively substantial force than most Western traditions would attribute to such mental activity. It means to bring something to mind which simultaneously takes on an actual existence, a notion for which there is no cognitive or lexical equivalent in English, unless perhaps we consider fusing the two meanings of the verb "conceive".[20] In Teyyam songs, this verbal form is used when

---

[19] The order of songs given here differs from that suggested by Holloman and Ashley (1983: 103-104, note 9). These authors quite properly noted there that their listing was provisional and subject to correction. Part of the problem is the great variation of song elements and their structuring across performing castes, lineages, and Teyyam deities. The other problem is the fact that there is no set and invariant taxonomy of indigenous terms for talking about the songs. Nevertheless, I am confident about the grosser stretches of song and their sequence as I have used them here, especially as they apply to performances of the Vaṇān caste.

[20] The semantics I present here are a synthesis of those meanings found in the standard dictionaries of Malayalam and Tamil, for the transitive forms of this word are not in common modern use and are restricted, in my experience, to these old songs. I believe my exposition is substantiated, however, by Dr. M.V. Viṣṇu Nambūtiri, undoubtedly the pre-eminent indigenous authority on Teyyam. He says in a note on

deities create other gods and beings, as for instance in the *tōṟṟam* song of Kuṇḍōṟa Cāmuṇḍi, when this goddess, having burst in flames from Śiva's third eye, asks him, "Why is it that you have created *(tōṟṟi)* me?"[21] In a revealing parallel, it is also the verb employed by the Teyyam dancer in the last line of invocation sung at the very onset of possession:

> Unfading, O Bhairavī of the fair breast and fine nose,
> By conceiving *(tōṟṟu)* you, come to this place, to me![22]

I would argue that such an employment of this verb *tōṟṟ-* is again performative, when uttered under the conditions of the ritual context. The meaning revealed in this word's usage clearly indicates that the same process by which the gods are created and create each other is that by which human beings conceptually recreate this divine presence in the physical locus of their own bodies. It is because the Teyyam songs participate in this act that they are called *tōṟṟams*. Such a process, to paraphrase the title of Austin's famous work, enables one to do things with thoughts, and constitutes a performative concept we might label as a "thought act."[23]

---

this verb's transitive usage that it signifies acts of "imagination" *(tōnnal)*, "birth" *(piṟavi)*, "resuscitation" *(punarujjīvanam)*, "spirit-possession" *(āvēśam)*, and "manifestation" *(veḷippāṭu)* (1981: 266).

[21] *Entināyik koṇḍenne Tōṟṟiccamaccitu?* (Viṣṇu Nambūtiri 1981: 345).
The creative and effectual aspect of the transitive usage of *tōṟṟ-* is confirmed and strengthened here by the addition of the auxiliary verb, *camekkuka*, meaning "to produce an effect" (Gundert 1872: 347).

[22] *Vāṭāte nalla stanam nalla nāsika*
Bairavī, tōṟṟu koṇḍīsthalam varika mē! (Viṣṇu Nambūtiri 1981, p. 266). The final word *mē* might indeed be construed as I have taken it, meaning "to me", as the Sanskrit clitic form of the first-person pronoun, since this particular song is a highly Sanskritized piece. On the other hand, it may be construed as an expletive or vocative abbreviation from the Dravidian full-form, *ammē*, "Oh Mother!"

[23] While such usages of *tōṟṟ-*, when spoken under the conventional force of ritual conditions, constitute clear examples of Austin's speech acts, (since as utterances they simultaneously accomplish what they purport), the semantics of the verb and the performative context suggest a province which is more than simply verbal. Such

The old usages of the verb *tōṟṟ-* encountered in the songs are taken over in modern Malayalam by the Sanskritically derived *saṅkalpam* (with its verbal forms), commonly used to mean simply "imagination," but retaining for use in religious contexts, the older meaning of a mentally effected yet substantial creation. Its usage is continually evoked whenever one seeks exegesis of ritual, for it is this power of *saṅkalpam* which asserts that symbols which we would regard as merely iconically representative, here indexically create the actual presence of the object to which they refer. Such substantial "conceptions" may further be manipulated and aggregated from smaller symbolic constituents into larger complexes. This is exactly what happens in Teyyam, as the various elements of the costume and ritual implements are built up and each reflected upon in song as representing parts, activities, or attributes of the deity being conceived. Some of these elements may be actually present, such as the goddess' sword (with which she is imagined to slay demons), some may be altogether absent (such as the demon which serves as her mount), and some may be based on an object which is transformed by the song's conception (such as the flower garland around the dancer's neck, said to be the intestines of a demon she has disemboweled). Indeed, I was told that all of these separate symbolic associations *(saṅkalpam)* contribute to the larger realized belief *(viśvāsam)* that the performer's body is actually inhabited by the deity.

The central importance of effecting possession *(uṟaccal)* in the Teyyam performance is clearly shown by the fact that there exist songs explicitly addressed by name to that purpose *(uṟaccal tōṟṟam)*. These mark the culmination of the singing of the *tōṟṟam*, after which the performer is expected to stomp and shake, showing

---

utterances in fact signify the culmination of a protracted internal process of mental visualization, an act which is believed to tap the universal force of creativity itself, a force which is the power of mind *(manana śakti)*, focused and controlled. Such structured chains of thinking, executed under the force of ritual conventions, are mental performatives, which I am calling, somewhat playfully, "thought-acts."

the onset of possession. Paralleling the fact that these gestures and signs of possession are themselves learned, at the level of content, these *uṟaccal tōṟṟams* are fixed, stereotypical, and formulaically constructed. This shows that the specific vision of the deity is not left to the individual performer to fashion; just as the outward form of the costume is fixed by tradition, so the mental imaging of the deity's form, history, and behavioral attributes, is dictated by the songs.

Thematically, there are at least three major strands, generally standing individually, though sometimes combined, which inform this class of possession songs. One theme identifies the parents of the god, tells of the deity's birth and the rites of the first month of the child's life, culminating in the bestowal of a name. Another theme simply lists the places where the deity has been previously established, culminating with the current shrine, exactly as in the *varaviḷi* or "summons" described earlier. A final theme is an abbreviated description of the deity's physical appearance, in part following the actual Teyyam costume and what it is imagined to represent. What do these three kinds of theme have in common? I would argue that they are all directed to substantially constructing the god's presence according to three convergent modalities: social person, geographical place, and physical form.

In the first instance, it should be obvious that reciting the god's former circumstances of birth and construction as a social person through rites of passage, culminating in the fixing of a name, is intended as a symbolic re-enactment of conceiving and giving birth to the god anew in the dancer's mind and body.[24] Similarly, in the second instance, the same attempt is broached in the idiom of place. The power of the foundational place *(mūlasthānam)* and the original divine birth is invoked, and then a syntagmatic chain of subsequent sites of manifestation of the god's power is accessed, culmi-

---

[24] On the importance of ritual naming as opening into and accessing narrative in the cognate tradition of the Tamil bow song *(vil pāṭṭu)*, see Blackburn 1988: 220-21.

nating in a phrase of the general formula: as it was then and there, so may it be here and now. This chain of places map out what is conceived of as the god's domain or realm *(svarūpam)* over which it rules, yet, as the word implies, this territory in which the god dwells is literally its "selfsame form" *(sva-rūpam)*, imputing an immanent personal substance to the political realm. Therefore, as part of the logic of possession, this territory which instantiates the god's power is symbolically mapped into the dancer's mind. Finally, in the recitation of the god's physical form, the possession song indexes and recapitulates the entire ritual process which the dancer has actually been undergoing through the costuming, and fixes the constructed form and its significance in the dancer's mind.

The possession song's intention to fix the god's image internally as a parallel to the external process of constructing the god's form in costuming and make-up is shown by the rite which immediately follows: the mirror-gazing. As he completes the possession song, the dancer takes a small hand mirror and gazes fixedly into it for a few moments. The eyes grow round and he trembles, seeing his own visage which has been transformed into the god's by the make-up.[25] The ritual process is complete; he is the god. A performer explained the mirror-gazing rite to me as follows:

> Before putting on the Teyyam, the Teyyam performer will know which Teyyam it is that he is donning. Accordingly, when he looks into the mirror, the conception will arise, "This is not my form — this is the actual form of the goddess that I am seeing." The act here is the seeing of the sacred face by the sacred face, a divine occasion in which they are fused through seeing each other. In that manner, he receives an invigorating stimulus directly from the actual goddess.[26]

---

[25] Cp. Ashley 1979: 107.

[26] *Teyyam keṭṭunnatinu mumbu ñān ētu teyyam āṇu keṭṭunnatennu teyyakkāran aṟiññirikkum. Aṅṅane ayāḷ kaṇāṭiyil nōkkumbōḷ, "itu enṟe rūpam alla, yathārtha*

Rather than possession deriving from psychogenetic factors in the individual, it could not be more clear that both the form and thematic content of the deity's person have their genesis as external cultural productions which are only subsequently internalized through ritual and song. The sense of *communitas* is clearly brought on here by the individual performer, his supporting troupe, and the worshippers all participating in the same shared pool of cultural symbols which actually constitute the larger person of the deity. I frequently heard it said that Teyyam worship required the intense belief *(viśvāsam)* of both the performer and the audience, a fusion of persons in a single conception *(saṅkalpam)* of the deity, "in the manner of the self witnessing itself."[27] This is a phrase reportedly used by all Teyyams, which was explained as meaning, "When it comes about that two selves are brought into the state of witnessing each other as one, in that place a divine power is created."[28]

The collective nature of this representation is manifest in the following performer's account of a shrine compound thronging with expectant devotees at the time of the Teyyam's procession:

> In that atmosphere, thick with devotion *(bhakti)* — in one direction stands the Teyyam, with his costuming items in place; in another the women are sounding their ritual ululation, and in yet another the Vaṇṇāns are beating out a powerful rhythm on the drums and singing the *tōṟṟam* songs. Seeing all this, anyone with devotion will perceive *(tōnnum)* that a great power *(śakti)* is proceeding through this vast assembly... Accordingly, the devotion which is in the spectators and the power which the Teyyam dancer

dēviyuṭe rūpam āṇu kāṇunnatu" ennu tōnnal uṇḍāvum. Itinu tirumukhattōṭu tirumukham kāṇukayāṇu ceyyunnatu, daivīkam āyiṭṭu tammil kūṭi kūṭikāṇukayāṇu ī avasaram ceyyunnatu. Aṅṅane ayāḷkku yathārtha dēviyil ninnu oru uttējanam kiṭṭunnu.

27 *Ātmāvōṭu ātmāvu sākṣiyām prakāram.*

28 *Raṇḍu ātmāvu onnilēkku sākṣitvam varikkuka iṅṅane varumbōḷ aviṭe oru daivīka śakti uṇḍākunnu.*

> has received are blended with each other on that occasion and they receive a power which has become divine.[29]

It should be clear from the foregoing that the actual onset of possession is culturally scripted, is protracted in time, and is dispersed over several registers of song and ritual. If I might extend Austin's concept of the speech act to such ritual sequences, I would say possession itself is a performative act whose constituent ritual and verbal sequences, as performed by the various personnel of the Teyyam troupe, the shrine officials, and the laity, are the conditions which establish its effectiveness.[30]

But what of the activities following the onset of possession? We may answer this in a summary fashion by stating that after possession is achieved, the performance is even more rigidly structured. For then the Teyyam commences its series of dance steps, each carefully rehearsed and executed to the sets of changing rhythms kept by the drummers. These are further interspersed with set rituals to be performed by the dancer in a quasi-priestly role, carried out with ritual exactitude according to the traditions *(ācāram)* of the particular shrine.

Following these activities, the Teyyam utters a series of vocalizations in the first person, as the deity itself. While it is strongly

---

[29] *Bhakti sāndram āya antarīkṣattil — teyyam oru bhāgattu ninnu vēṣavidhānaṅṅaḷ veccu keṭṭumbōḷ, oru bhāgattu ninnu strīkaḷ pūram taḷikkukayum, oru bhāgattu ninnu Vaṇṇānmār uṣāṟ āyi ceṇḍa koṭṭukayum tōṟṟam pāṭukayum ceyyunnu. itellām kāṇṇumbōḷ, ī mahāsadassilēkku ētō oru valiya śakti el̲unnaḷḷunnuṇḍennu bhaktiyuḷḷa ētōrāḷkkum tōnnum... Aṅṅane kāl̲cakkāruṭe uḷḷil oru bhaktiyum teyyakkāranu kiṭṭiyiṭṭuḷḷa śaktiyum tammil sammiśram ākunna avasarattil daivīkam āyiṭṭuḷḷa śakti kiṭṭunnu.*

[30] These effectuating conditions Austin called "felicity conditions," for it is their existence and satisfaction which give speech acts their conventional force to accomplish deeds. Given the even greater degree of conventional structuring which governs the speech-activity matrix of ritual, I propose that a set of conventions may similarly operate in this sphere to render such acts effective.

asserted that these are not the dancer's words at all, but the deity spontaneously speaking through him, these phrases are, for the most part, highly structured as well. Whole stretches of these divinely inspired words are in fact memorized. When, for instance, the god Ūrpaḻacci begins his speech, his Teyyam dancer places his foot on the threshold of the shrine entrance and screams into it the following introduction:

> Praise to my Udayamānūr Ūrpaḻacci shrine, to the Udayasthamānam Mēlūr fortress, to the western shrine at Mēkkalūr, to the eastern shrine at Kīkkalūr — After this, I have to find an ally, a mighty swordsman with a strong arm, and pledge true friendship...[31]

Though voiced in a hoarse cry which makes them barely intelligible, the performer takes these lines verbatim, though in random stretches, from a long piece of prose which marks the penultimate phase of a Teyyam performance.[32] If one is familiar with the set pieces of a given Teyyam, it is apparent that many such spoken pronouncements are simply taken from other songs or fixed recitations and rendered as spontaneous acts of speech.

When it comes time to actually engage worshippers for the distribution of blessings *(anugraham)*, the dancer is required to be more spontaneous and address individuals as to their specific needs. In

---

[31] *Vāḻka enṟe Udayamānūr Ūrpaḻacci kāvum, Udayastamānam Mēlūr kōṭṭayum, Mēkkalūr mēl māṭavum, Kīkkalūr kīḻmāṭavum — Iniyō vāḷum kaiyum ghanam uḷḷa caṅṅātine kaṇḍu nēr caṅṅāyttam paṟaññē mati pōrum...*

[32] This prose piece is known as the *mumpusthānam*, the recitation of previous shrines of the god's establishment. In the above cry, the first lines recite the founding shrines of the deity, following the text of the *mumpusthānam*, but then there is an abrupt jump to a point later in the text where the deity seeks as an ally his divine companion and over-lord, Vēṭṭakkarumakan. In the *mumpusthānam* itself, this second phrase is reported in indirect discourse as a thought having occured to the god, but here it is just blurted out by the performer as though it were occuring to him spontaneously and he were thinking aloud.

special cases this indeed occurs, and sometimes there are even quarrels between parties, or between the performing troupe and the sponsors, which the dancer as deity may be called upon to settle. Yet for the most part, the performer simply gives out turmeric powder *(kuṟi)* for the worshippers to put on their brows with stock blessings. He must, however, be fully alert in the conduct of these rites, for the blessings must be given out to worshippers in a pre-defined order, based on their status in the shrine, caste identity, and age. Oversights may offend participants and sponsors resulting in their withholding patronage from that particular dancer in the future.

This absence of spontaneity on the part of the possessed is shown in the content of the blessings themselves, characterized by special forms of address and set lines appropriate to each office and caste. For instance, the Nāyar are called "Akambaṭi," (the title of royal attendants and bodyguards), as in the following:

> O Akambaṭis! Your status is called Akambaṭi, your Veda is manliness, your standing orders are the Śūdra's Oath — for your manliness, your code of vengeance, your oath, and your orders — for you who are repositories of victory and heroic might — your submission to deity, your agricultural holdings, residence rights, your war stipend, your son and your sister's son — such are your traditions and authority. With your status at the royal gate, your copper-plate grant, and your military leadership, you have no need of the paddy wage of hirelings. In such a manner have all your honors been established, haven't they?[33]

[33] *Akambaṭimārē! Akambaṭi ennōru paṭi, ucitam ennoru Vēdam, Śūdrāṇa ennoru ājña — ucitattinum, uttarattinum, āṇakkum, ājñakkum — balavīrya parakrama śālikaḷ āya niṅṅaḷkku — daivādhīnavum, kottuvāḻccayum, kuṭiyirippum, kūliśēṣavum, makanum, marumakanum — ennirikkunna ācāravum adhikāravum. Cēramān kaṭṭilayum, cembōla maryādayum, nāyma talayum, mūnnāḻi aḷavum, mūḻakkum ennu vēṇḍa. Iṅṅane sarvva aucityaṅṅaḷum nila nirttiyiṭṭuṇḍallō, alle?*

A performance manuscript I have consulted contains nearly forty such prose passages which are memorized and used in a variety of contexts. Many performers do a good deal of improvizing, but the stock of these rote pieces is always there to fall back on for standard situations of blessings. If indeed, as a few performers claim, their memories of what they do or say during possession are either dim or altogether absent, the high degree of stereotypy and rote recitation which they actually display should caution us against the assumption that their words are therefore emerging from some "deeper" than normal, spontaneous psychological state. Indeed, following this segment of interactive blessings, this "divine speech" *(dēva vākku)* phase itself reverts to rote recitations directed to the shrine assembly in a conclusion of general blessings.

The Cognitive Style of Possession: Ritual Exactitude

I trust my analysis of Teyyam thus far has shown that the attributed state of possession and the beliefs and behaviors surrounding it exhibit a high degree of culturally structured determinacy. The extent of this formalization, indeed, accords well with anthropological notions of how behaviors are recognized as being "ritual," cross-culturally. But more importantly for my analysis, this formalization reflects an indigenous concern with focus, structure, and the control of action, which proves to be central to religious conceptions of the effectiveness of ritual.

To examine this principle more closely, let us look at a considerably less visual and performatively extravagant form of possessed religious behavior exhibited by those permanent shrine priests, the aforementioned *kōmarams* or *veḷiccappāṭus.* From the viewpoint of the religion of this region, they can in no way be separated from the larger complex of possessed ritual specialists. They are possessed by the same Teyyam deities as the costumed dancers, perform equivalent rituals, and are considered by all worshippers I interviewed, and by themselves, to be virtually identical, in all significant respects, to the full-fledged Teyyams.

Like the Teyyams, their primary functions are to become possessed by the power of the deity who resides in the shrine, to dance or jump about *(tuḷḷuka)* under a state of possession, to utter words in the god's own voice, to receive offerings, and to give out grace in the form of turmeric powder. The principal difference in their rites is that these priests actually enter the shrine chamber (instead of sitting outside as do the Teyyams), then close the door and perform recitations and rites to transfer the divine power from the image to their bodies. Despite these differences, however, they explicitly equate what they do and say in the shrine with the process of costuming and recitation of the "summons" *(varaviḷi)* on the part of the Teyyam.

This emphasis on the performance of rituals in both the onset of the possession state and what is done and experienced after that onset is similar to that encountered in the case of the full-blown Teyyam. In dealing with these specialists, there is evidence from several contexts which makes it additionally clear that possession entails no loss of consciousness, or "dissociation" in psychological terms, but rather a *heightened* sense of consciousness and performative acuity with regard to the rituals. This was revealed incidentally when I enquired of them whether they had any memory of the rites they did in this state.

> We should give our mind over to the Dēvi only. At the time when we come there from our bath, nothing else whatsoever is in our mind. We know nothing of the coming of that power. But after it has come upon us, there is no experience of a loss of memory [or consciousness]. For the god has created and bestowed on us the ability, the power to do the respective rites...
>
> At the time when the *veḷiccappāṭus* get the divine power, they are fully conscious *(bōdhavānmār)*. Otherwise they might run off somewhere else. They would never remain standing where they should... Each and every rite has an ordered mode of con-

> duct... So there will be memory of the ceremonies performed at this time.[34]

There is evidence from other genres of folk songs that such states were routinely invoked in the martial arts, and that certain Nāyar *veḷiccappāṭus* were actually war leaders, conditions in which an abstracted or dissociated state of consciousness would hardly be appropriate. This substantiates my argument here that what is indicated is a heightened, rather than a diminished state of consciousness. This is perhaps also in consonance with the indigenous perception that one's consciousness has not travelled somewhere else, shaman-like, but that instead, one's own body and mind are taken over and animated by a higher and more powerful form of consciousness.

The holders of these priestly offices are said to be chosen by the gods themselves as their representatives, although almost always from the same lineage as the former office holder. Yet despite the apparently spontaneous and divine election, we can see from the passage above that an ecstatic who will "run off somewhere else" (as the deranged do) is hardly suitable for the job. Instead, note how the nature of the test imposed on the aspirant for the office reflects the concerns of ritual control:

> He should have a spiritual vision of the god. When this happens, he should come here (to the shrine). When he arrives, there are certain rites he must perform and there are rules governing those rites. We examine the one who has thus experienced spiritual

---

[34] *Nammuṭe manassu Dēviyil tanne koṭukkaṇam. Vēṟe onnum ā samayattu kuḷiccu vannāl ñaṅṅaḷile manassil uṇḍāvukayilla. Ā śakti varunnatonnum ñaṅṅaḷ aṟiyukayilla. Vannu kaḻiññāl, ōrmmaśakti onnum naṣṭam saṃbhavikkunnilla. Atātu karmmaṅṅaḷ ceyyān uḷḷa kaḻivu (śēṣi) ñaṅṅaḷkku daivam uṇḍākki tarum...*
Dēvīkam āyiṭṭuḷḷa śakti kiṭṭunna samayattu veḷiccappāṭanmār śarikku bōdhaṅmār āyirikkum. Illeṅkil, avar eviṭeyeṅkilum ōṭippōkum. Nilkēṇḍiṭattu ninnennum varukayilla... Ceyyēṇḍunnatāya kāryaṅṅaḷ ellām tanne oru naṭapaṭikramam āyiṭṭu natannu pōkunnu... Ī samayattuḷḷa caṭaṅṅukaḷ caṭaṅṅukaḷkku ōrmmayuṇḍāyirikkum.

> vision to see whether he does the rites according to the rules.[35]

This state of possession, frequently said to be brought about through a mental focusedness *(ekāgram)*, is thus exhibited behaviorally in characteristics of ritual exactitude *(kṛtyam)*. This latter is indeed elevated to the status of a general religious value, as reflected in the word *kṛtyam* itself. Derived from the Sanskrit gerundive meaning "a thing which should be done," it has the common meaning of ritual; yet as an abstract noun it also signifies a mode of doing things — correctly, precisely, and mindfully. While this mode is perhaps most characteristic of the performance of rituals in a sacred context, it is generalized to a principle of exactitude which is supposed to inform one's entire life. One's very existence becomes a single, focused rite, for this effort towards exactitude and integrity is the power of mind, of being, and of deity itself.

> It is only through focusing the three powers of the mind, speech, and body that the *kōṟāccan*, Teyyam performer, or temple priest get their actual and effective divine power. It is only through concentrating with our minds that our acting and speaking become effective. If this activity is not correct, nothing else will come out right. We will not be able to enlighten others by what we do. That will only come about if we act with exceeding correctness *(kṛtyam)*. By correctness, we mean the very truth of being, and by this truth of being, we mean correctness. By this truth of being, we mean god *(Īśvaran)* himself. Whatever one's faith may be, these are all one and the same.[36]

---

[35] *Daivattinṟe darśanam uṇḍākaṇam. Darśanam uṇḍāyi iviṭe varaṇam. Vannāl avar iviṭe ceyyēṇḍunna karmmaṅṅaḷ ceyyunnatinu oru ciṭṭayuṇḍu. Ā ciṭṭaprakāram darśanappeṭṭayāḷ karmmaṅṅaḷ ceyyunnuṇḍō ennu ñaṅṅaḷ pariśōdhikkum.*

[36] *Manassu, vākku, karmmam ennī mūnnu kriyakaḷ ēkīkariccāl mātramē kōṟāccan alla, teyyakkāranum tantrikaḷkkum ellām avaruṭe yathārtha śakti kiṭṭukayuḷḷu. Manassu koṇḍu nammaḷ cintikkunnatu tanne pravartikkukayum paṟayukayum ceytāl mātramē atu koṇḍu kāryam uḷḷu. Ī pravṛtti śariyalleṇkil maṟṟuḷḷa kāryaṅṅaḷum śariyāvukayilla. Nammaḷ ceyyunnatu maṟṟuḷḷavare bōdhyappeṭuttān alla. Atu vaḷare kṛtyam āyi ceyyaṇam ennu mātramēyuḷḷu. Kṛtyam ennu paṟaññāl satyam āṇu, satyam ennu paṟaññāl kṛtyam. Satyam ennu paṟaññālum Īśvaran tanneyāṇu. Ētu*

Conclusion

One common social-scientific approach to the behaviors described in the opening paragraph of this paper would treat them as maladies, as either psychopathologies, or as desperate strategies of the socially oppressed. Such assessments, I would argue, represent the misapplication of standard Western models, which could only attribute such beliefs and behaviors to the delusions of psychologically diseased or socially maladjusted individuals. From the indigenous perspective, however, the experience of possession by Teyyams is not an affliction, but a divine blessing, a source of great power, both for the specialist and for his fellows. Such events are therefore not matters left to individuals and their psyches. Rather, as I have shown through tracing the rituals which create and instantiate it, possession is a collective venture, culturally scripted and socially actualized.

Viewed in this light, possession itself *is* ritual, a formalized set of physical, verbal, and mental activities whose very performance constitutes its authenticity. To be possessed means to perform the possession rituals correctly and manifest possession behaviors. Privatist notions of a Western individual psychology are, I feel, misplaced in this case. The line between the operations of an unseen human psyche and the equally unseen collective representation of a divine or demonic will is not one this South Indian culture readily demarcates.

I have further suggested that the performative effectiveness of possession is informed by a substantializing power which this culture attributes to focused consciousness. To conceive of something under the proper ritual conditions is to actualize its presence. It is in this way that the component conceptions *(saṅkalpam)* of Teyyam rituals and recitations are substantially aggregated into the larger and encompassing presence of the deity. The control and

---

matakkārkkum itu oru pōle tanneyāṇu.

focused power of the mind is thus conceived of as the very source of divine power, and the archetypical manifestation of this control is ritual. This is how possession is viewed — not as a state of mental dissociation, but as a state of ritually induced, superconscious acuity. And the ritual exactitude *(kṛtyam)* through which this state is achieved and expressed, is none other than the general principle of deity itself, that divine consciousness which informs all human life. As an eminent *kōmaram* summarized this relationship in an etymology, "It is because we possess the divine power of mind *(manana śakti)*, that we are called human *(manuṣyan)*."[37]

[37] *Manana śakti manuṣyan uḷḷatu koṇḍāṇu manuṣyan enna pēru nammakuṇḍākān kāraṇam.*

References

Agesthialingom, S. 1979. *A grammar of Old Tamil with special reference to Patirruppattu.* Annamalainagar: Annamalai.

Ashley, Wayne 1979. The Teyyam Kettu of Northern Kerala. In *Drama Review* 23 (T82).

Austin, J.L. 1962. *How to do things with words.* Oxford: Clarendon Press.

Blackburn, S.H. 1988. *Singing of birth and death: Texts in performance.* Philadelphia: University of Pennsylvania Press.

Caldwell, Rev. Robert 1849. *The Tinnevelley Shanar, a sketch of their religion, and their moral condition and characteristics as a caste.* Madras: Christian Knowledge Society.

Claus, Peter 1973. Possession, protection and punishment as attributes of the deities in a South Indian village. In *Man in India* 53: 231-242.

Id. 1975. The Siri myth and ritual: A mass possession cult of South India. In *Ethnology* 14.1: 47-58.

Id. 1979. Spirit possession and mediumship from the perspective of Tulu oral literature. In *Culture, Medicine and Psychiatry* 3: 29-52.

Diehl, Carl Gustav 1956. *Instrument and purpose: Studies on rites and rituals in South India*. Lund: C W K Gleerup.

Dumont, Louis 1957. *Une sous-caste de l'Inde du sud. Organisation sociale et religion des Pramalai Kallar*. The Hague: Mouton.

Gundert, Rev. Herman 1872. *A Malayalam and English dictionary*. Mangalore: C. Stolz, Basel Mission Book and Tract Depository.

Harper, Edward 1957. Shamanism in South India. In *Southwestern Journal of Anthropology* 13.3: 267-287.

Hart, George 1975. *The poems of ancient Tamil: Their milieu and their Sanskrit counterparts*. Berkeley: University of California Press.

Holloman, Regina and W. Ashley 1983. Caste and cult in Kerala. In *South Asian Anthropologist* 4.2: 93-104.

Kurup, K. K. N. 1973. *The cult of Teyyam and hero worship in Kerala*. Indian Folklore Series, no. 21. Calcutta: Indian Publications.

Levinson, Stephen 1983. *Pragmatics*. Cambridge: Cambridge University Press.

Menon, Sreedhara 1980. *A survey of Kerala history*. Kottayam: National Book Stall.

Moffatt, Michael 1979. *An Untouchable community in South*

India: Structure and consensus. Princeton: Princeton University Press.

Obeyesekere, Gananath 1981. *Medusa's hair: An essay on personal symbols and religious experience.* Chicago and London: Chicago University Press.

Silverstein, Michael 1976. Shifters, linguistic categories, and cultural descriptions. In K. H. Basso and H. A. Selby (eds.) *Meaning in anthropology.* Albequerque: University of New Mexico Press.

Tambiah, Stanley 1979. A performative approach to ritual. In *Proceedings of the British Academy* 65: 113-169.

Thurston, Edgar 1909. *Castes and tribes of Southern India.* 7 Vols. Madras: Madras Government Press.

Viṣṇu Nambudiri, E.M. 1981. *Uttarakēraḷattile Tōṟṟampāṭṭukaḷ* (Malayalam Folk Songs). Trichur: Kerala Sahitya Akademi.

Whitehead, Henry 1921. *The village gods of South India.* Calcutta: Oxford University Press.

TĀI PARADĒVATA: RITUAL IMPERSONATION IN THE TEYYAM TRADITION OF KERALA

Balan Nambiar

I

Kerala and its northern neighbouring region in the West Coast have unique geographical and cultural characteristics. This stretch of land, between high mountains in the east and the Arabian sea in the west, is the most densely populated region in India. The mountains are covered by thick, evergreen, tropical forests full of herbal and medicinal plants and wild animals, while in the plains there are mainly rice fields, coconut groves and banana plantations. Several rivers flow from the mountains, through the plains and join the sea. The nature of the land, its flora and fauna, play an important role in the rituals connected with the life of the people of Kerala.

By and large, the indigenous art of this region has a great deal in common with that of Sri Lanka, Indonesia (particularly Bali Island) and the South Sea Islands. Aryan Hinduism appears to have reached the West Coast much later than other parts of South India. Although different religions have had their impact, the ethnic culture has remained intact while subsuming aspects of these varied influences. It is not a dead culture. It lives in and around homes and villages with vigorous participation from people of every age group, caste and class.

Teyyams (etymologically derived from Skt. *daiva* - "deity") are deities impersonated in ritual dances of the Cannanore and Kasargode districts of Kerala.[1] After the harvest season, the work in the fields is reduced and the skies are clear. From then, until the onset of the monsoon, people have a lot of leisure time. They gather around shrines, many in forest groves, to celebrate the festival of Teyyam. The performer of the Teyyam invokes the spirit, gets possessed and becomes a medium. In a state of identification with the divinity the performer bestows his grace and manifold blessings on the worshippers. The translation of emotional reactions into ceremonial representations give Teyyam rituals a stability they would not otherwise possess. The rituals are rigidly observed by the people and have become time-honoured conventions. In the attempts to explain and justify established customs the mythological setting may vary as new revelations of reality become explicit, and receive sanctions of people involved. Thus, the ancient rites are given a new significance and made to fulfill a new function.

Some Teyyams are performed every year, some every alternate year, some once in a while, some once in three, seven, twelve or twenty-four years. In 1982 there was a festival of thirty-nine Teyyams at Kannamangalam near Payyannur, after a gap of sixty years. These kinds of festivals are called *perumkaḷiyāṭṭam,* or grand festival.

People belonging to all classes and communities worship the Teyyams and participate in the Teyyam festivals. During such festivals the participants shed caste considerations and conduct the festivities for the general prosperity of the village. The festivals incorporate religious sentiments which develop from an initial obeisance to an increasingly fascinating blend of ritual and entertainment, involving the performer as well as spectators, in brahmanical temples dedicated to goddesses, most of which are run by non-brah-

---

[1] Cf. Nambiar 1982.

mins. Even in those shrines where regular daily *pūjas* are conducted by non-brahmins, once a month, on the day of the *saṃkrama,* or once a year, the brahmins are engaged to conduct *puṇyāha,* or purificatory rituals. Where *madhyama pūjas* (see below p. 143) are conducted daily, they are forbidden on the day of the *puṇyāha.* Brahmins, who were immigrants to Kerala, eventually integrated themselves so that they too claimed their share of responsibilities in the overall celebrations. In some shrines, the brahmanical *pūjas* are held as a part of other ritualistic worship of non-brahmanical groups. Both groups, brahmanical as well non-brahmanical, mutually respect each other, without in any way interfering in each other's exclusive sphere of rituals.

A feature unique to Teyyam is that although the festival is conducted by a particular caste or community, it is, as already mentioned, performed for the prosperity of the entire village. Also, on the occasion of the festival, the performer, even though he belongs to a so-called lower caste, becomes a medium between the audience and the divinity and assumes a superior status in his role as a Teyyam.

There are many communities performing Teyyam, but five are particularly prominent. Among these, the Vaṇṇān community performs over 60% of Teyyams. Other communities are Malayan, Vēlan, Kōppāḷan and Pulayan. There are families in the performing communities who have, by tradition, the exclusive right and privilege to perform specific Teyyams. Nobody dare encroach on the right of such families.

The various castes and communities, as well as particular families, have their own *iṣṭadēvata* (patron deity). The artisan community has its own deities, called Bāli and Ghaṇṭakarṇa; the community of oil makers, called Vāṇiyan, has Mucculōṭṭu Bhagavati; the potter community, called Kuśavan, worships Kōṭṭattamma and Puḷḷivēṭṭakarumakan; Nayars generally worship Tāi Paradēvata,

Rakta Cāmuṇḍi, Ūrpēśi, Vēṭṭakkaran etc.; Mūvāḷamkuḻi Cāmuṇḍi is the patron deity of the Cāliyan (weavers); Pañcuruḷi, that of the Maṇiyāṇi community (masons) and Bhairava is the patron deity of the Cōi[2] community. Perumpuḻa Accan is the *kuladaiva* of Vaḷḷuvas or Mukhaviras (fishermen) and Poṭṭan is the patron deity of Pulayans etc. However, the demarcation is not clear; often the same Teyyam is worshipped as a patron deity by more than one community.

Grāmadēvata or village goddesses are the most widely worshipped deities in Kerala. The stories of these *grāmadēvata* are sung at the beginning of the performances. However glorious these narrations are, they consist, in most cases, of local legends which have no sanctions in *purāṇas.* At the end of the story, the heroine dies and her spirit is identified with *śakti.* This spirit is deified and worshipped.

The worship of goddesses in connection with fertility cults was in existence long before the influence of Brahmanical gods and goddesses. Some of the names of goddesses referred to in Teyyam rituals are Amma, Tāi, Bhagavati, Srīpōti or Pōti, Dēvi, Paradēvata, Kāḷarātri, Kāḷi and Bhadrakāḷi.[3] Some of these terms, such as

---

[2] *Cōi,* (Skt. *yōgi,)* refers to the community of Śākteyas, the followers of Gōraknāth Panth. There are about 500 families of this community in Cannanore and Kasargod district of Kerala.

[3] Kāḷi and Bhadrakāḷi:

a. According to Devī-Māhātmya, Kāḷi is said to have emanated from the brow of Durgā during one of the battles between the divine and anti-divine forces. In this context Kāḷi is considered the forceful form of the great goddess Durgā.
b. The name Bhadrakāḷi is supposedly first mentioned in the *Gṛhya-sūtra.*
c. Bhadrakāḷi is one of the nine names of the goddess Kālī mentioned in the *Mahākāḷasaṃhitā.* The other eight Kāḷis are Dakṣiṇakāḷi, Smaśānakāḷi, Guhyakāḷi, Kāḷakāḷi, Kāmakālakāḷi, Dhanakāḷi, Siddhikāḷi and Caṇḍikakāḷi. Abhinavagupta wrote a *Krama-stōtra* in praise of the twelve Kāḷis. These twelve Kāḷis are: Sṛṣṭhikāḷi, Raktakāḷi, Sthitināśakakāḷi, Yamakāḷi, Saṃhārakāḷi, Mṛtyukāḷi, Rudrakāḷi or Bhadrakāḷi, Mārtaṇḍakāḷi,

Amma and Tāi, mostly used in compound with names of local goddesses, stress their 'mother' aspect.

Wherever a large number of shrines of Teyyam exist in the same location the goddess has a special shrine. Most of the goddesses are Śaivite and are manifestations of Kāḷi or Bhadrakāḷi, no matter what story is depicted. During my field survey of Teyyam, I noticed that the priest of the goddess was the most important functionary in the *perumkaḷiyāṭṭam* ('grand festival') and that he considered it beneath his dignity to conduct *pūja* in the Vaiṣṇavite shrine which was located outside the courtyard or compound wall of the shrine of the goddess.

There are several *śāktēya* temples in Northern Kerala. The goddess is the main deity in all these shrines. The Saptamātrikas, Brāhmi, Mahēśvari, Kaumāri, Vaiṣṇavi, Varāhi, Indrāṇi and Cāmuṇḍi as well as Gaṇeśa and Bhairava are worshipped in these *śāktēya* shrines.[4] By and large, the *pūja* at the *śāktēya* temples is conducted by a community called Piṭarer or Moosat. This priestly community, members of which wear the holy thread, is lower in status than Brahmins because of practicing *madhyama pūja*. The *madhyama pūja* involves *māṃsa, matsya* and *madya* (meat, fish and liquor) which are offered to the deity, the goddess, during the *pūja*. All the *śāktēya* shrines were patronized formerly by local rulers.

Paramārkakāḷi, Kālānalarudrakāḷi, Mahākālakāḷi and Mahābhairavacaṇḍograghorakāḷi. See Mookerjee 1988.

d. Lord Śiva, on hearing about the self-immolation of his wife, Sati, at the famous *yajña* conducted by Dakṣa, rushed in anger to the spot, and struck the earth with his matted hair. There ensued two forces, Vīrabhadra and Bhadrakāḷi. This Bhadrakāḷi was really Sati or Parvati in another form.

e. Tamil *purāṇas* aver that Laṅkalakṣmi, who was the first to prevent Hanuman from entering the city of Laṅka, was an incarnation of Bhadrakāḷi.

f. According to *Bhāgavata, daśama* skandha, Bhadrakāḷi was created by Śiva from his third eye and she killed the *asura* Dāruka. See Vettam Mani 1982.

[4] This group of nine deities can be seen depicted symbolically in many temples in Kerala. They are located on the southern side in the courtyard next to the *srikovil*.

Though no Teyyam is performed in the temple in Kodungallur, this temple is one of the most important *śāktēya* shrines in Kerala. Kaṇṇaki, the heroine of the Tamil classic *Cilapadikāram* ("The lay of the anklet"), is believed to be deified as a goddess at this shrine (Kurup 1973). In the northern part of Kerala, Kodungallur-Amma is called Cīrmma or Sri Kurumba and there are special shrines for this goddess, called Cīrmmakāvu. (Chandera 1973). The impersonators of this mother goddess, Cīrmma, are called Āyattans.[5] Cīrmma is a patron deity of the Tiya community.

II

Having described the Teyyam cult in general, let me narrate, in chronological order, the rituals of one of the main Teyyams, Tāi Paradēvata. Tāi Paradēvata, the goddess, is a widely performed Teyyam. (See plate III). She is the Teyyam of Bhadrakāḷi, who was created by Śiva from his third eye to kill the *asura* Dāruka (Dārika). The goddess is referred to by several names some of which are associated with the name of the shrine or sacred places: Thus we have Tiruvarkāṭṭu Bhagavati, Aṣṭimiccāl Bhagavati, Erinhikkal Pōti, Kāḷakāṭṭu Acci, Kaṇṇangat Bhagavati etc. Some other names used for Tāi Paradēvata are Sripōrkāḷi, Kōlasvarūpattiṅkal Tāi and Sarvēśvari Amma. The original centre where Tāi Paradēvata was deified and made a Teyyam is Tiruvarkāṭṭu Kāvu at Madai in Cannanore district. This is a *śāktēya* shrine patronised by the erstwhile Kōlathiri Rājas of Chirakkal. Images of Śiva, Durgā, Kṣētrapālan and Śaśta are installed in Madayi Kāvu. The main deity Bhadrakāḷi faces westward, on the south-east of Śiva's shrine, which is in the centre and faces east. The statues of the Saptamātrikas, Gaṇēś and Bhairava are installed in the hall in front of the shrine of Bhadrakāḷi. These nine statues and the main image of Bhadrakāḷi are made of *khaṭiśaṛkara*, a medium for sculpture composed of lime, mortar, jaggery, carbon of coconut shell etc. It is because of the

[5] Cīrmma is not depicted as Teyyam.

composition of the material that no *abhiṣēka* is performed for the image. Instead, *abhiṣēka* is done on an *utsavamūrti*,[6] a small *pañcalōha* image, which is normally kept at the base of the main idol. Though there is an idol of Bhadrakāḷi at the shrine at Madayi Kāvu, in most other shrines of Tāi Paradēvata an object such as a *vālkaṇṇāṭi*[7] or *kaṇṇaṭi bimbam*[8] is placed on a pedestal covered with *virāḷi paṭṭu*.[9] There are several shrines dedicated to Tāi Paradēvata in Northern Kerala. Though all the castes in the region worship Tāi Paradēvata, it is the Nayars who are the main patrons of this Teyyam. Wherever *mantramūrtis*[10] are worshipped Tāi Paradēvata is an essential deity.

The Teyyam of Tāi Paradēvata is performed by the Vaṇṇān community. Invariably the right to perform at a particular shrine is hereditary and only one who is the recipient of the title Peruvaṇṇān'[11] for having proved his proficiency in performing

---

[6] An *utsavamūrti*, normally made of *pañcalōha* (five metals), is the replica or representative smaller version of a main image, which, because of its weight or permanently installed state, cannot be taken out for procession. The *utsavamūrti* is taken out for procession during festivals.

[7] *Vālkaṇṇāṭi* is a metallic mirror, flat, oval or circular in shape and with a handle. It is made of a specific composition of bronze alloy - the technique of the composition of the metal is kept secret by the family who traditionally make the mirrors. An imitation, made of brass, is very often used by the Teyyam performers. *Vālkuṇṇāṭi* is one of the nine auspicious objects used in *pūjas*. It is carried by girls during the puberty ceremony. The most famous place where the *vālkaṇṇāṭi* is made is the Aranmula in Pathanamthitta Dist., Kerala.

[8] *Kaṇṇāṭi bimbam* is a bronze mirror with a *prabhāvalī*, standing on a pedestal and used in place of the image.

[9] *Virāḷi paṭṭu* is a special woven silk textile. See Nambiar/Fischer 1987.

[10] *Mantramūrtis* are Rakta Cāmuṇḍi, Ucciṭṭa, Karuval, Bhairavan, Kuṭṭiccāttan, Ghaṇṭakarṇan, Pañcuruḷi etc. All these Teyyams are performed by the Malayan community.

[11] Receiving a title such as Peruvaṇṇān, Karṇamūrti, Maṇakkaṭan or Neṇikkam is a landmark in the life of a Teyyam performer of the Vaṇṇān community. Formerly this title was given by the local Rājas. In the recent past the title is given by the priest of a prominent temple. On the occasion of the title presentation ceremony, a silk cloth (formerly *virāḷi paṭṭu*) and a golden bangle *(paṭṭum vaḷayum)* are presented to

Teyyam is entitled to perform the Tāi Paradēvata.

Like some other important Teyyams, the Tāi Paradēvata has three stages of performance. The first stage of Tāi Paradēvata's performance is called *tiṭaṅṅal* (beginning). The second stage is Eḷamkōlam and the final one is Tāi Paradēvata. The *tiṭaṅṅal* is a prelude to the main performance. This is the occasion when the legends of the Teyyam are sung in elaborate detail. The performer pays obeisance to the elders present and seeks the blessings of *māta, pitā, guru,*and *daivam* - mother, father, teacher, and God, in that order — for the success of the proceedings. Eḷamkōlam is a junior version of the main performance of Tāi Paradēvata. Almost all the rituals are conducted during the performance of Eḷamkōlam. The dance movements are vigorous and more spectacular at this stage. Eḷamkōlam is usually performed in the evening before the final or third stage of Tāi Paradēvata. It is during Eḷamkōlam that the performer goes into a trance and personifies the goddess for the first time. Tāi Paradēvata, the next day, is personified as Bhadrakāḷi in her complete form. Because of the heavy head gear the dancer's movements are slow and restricted compared to those of Eḷamkōlam.

Tiṭaṅṅal

The *tiṭaṅṅal* is held before the Eḷamkōlam performance either on the same day or earlier. The timing depends upon the convention of the particular shrine. During the *tiṭaṅṅal*, the *tōṟṟam* describes the story of Bhadrakāḷi killing the *asura* Dāruka. The *kōlakkāran*, the performer, goes through *vrata*, or penance, for a minimum of three days before the *tiṭaṅṅal*. He refrains from eating meat and from contact with women; however, there is no restriction on his drinking

---

the awardee. The golden bangle is not supposed to be sold or exchanged by the recipient. Quite often one can see title holders wearing gold bangles at the place of Teyyam performances.

toddy. He takes a bath early in the morning, prays, and only then eats. The food is very simple, normally a porridge or *kañji* made of rice or tina and vegetables. All functionaries connected with the actual performance of the rituals must have a bath and put on freshly washed clothes.

The greenroom or the place where the performers get ready, is an improvised one, normally an area enclosed on three sides with dry coconut thatch, leaving the top open to the sky. For Tāi Paradēvata, such an area is called *kuccil* or *aṇiyaṛa*. Normally it is situated on the southern side of the courtyard, in front of the shrine.

The *tiṭaṅṅal* begins only after the completion of the *kāḷi-pūja* at the shrine. At many well-known shrines of Tāi Paradēvata the *pūja* is conducted by brahmins. A *kaiviḷakku* (oil lamp) is lit and placed in the *kuccil*. The performer dresses up with *kāṇimuṇḍu, mēlāppu, cukappu,* and *talaccuttu.*[12] He prays at the *aṇiyaṛa*, and reverently touches the *talappāḷi, talataṇṭa, talappāḷi-paṭṭam* — decorative items meant for adorning the performer's head later on. These are kept on the floor next to the *kaiviḷakku*. He then pays his respects to those helping him and those who are present in the *kuccil* according to their age, status and position. Then, holding a *vālkaṇṇaṭi* in his hand, he proceeds slowly to the courtyard accompanied by an *akambaṭi*, a companion, who holds a *kaiviḷakku*. He pays obeisance to the *nāgastāna* (Skt. *nāgasthāna*, serpent shrine), the *kalasataṛa,*[13] and the other shrines and finally reaches the *naṭa* (door) of the shrine of Tāi Paradēvata. He bows three times with an *añjali*[14]

---

[12] *Kāṇimuṇḍu, mēlāppu, cukappu* and *talacuttu* are items of clothing. These simple garments are worn one over the other.

[13] The *Kalasataṛa* is a masonry altar in the courtyard, the location and size of which is decided by the *vāstu śilpi*, the village architect, who builds the shrine.

[14] An *añjali* is a formal folding of hands together in a stylized manner. Different communities have slightly different, but distinct, hand movements associated with this way of greeting.

towards the shrine and then greets the important people connected with the shrine. By this time, the *kōmaram*[15] comes in front of the performer with water in a *kindi* (bronze vessel), sandal paste, turmeric powder etc. He offers water first to the *kalaśakkāran*,[16] then to the performer. They receive the water in the right hand holding the left hand below the right. They sip some of the water, and then throw the remaining water around their head, symbolically purifying their body. Then the sandal paste and turmeric powder are also given to the *kalaśakkāran* and the performer. They apply the sandal paste to their foreheads, chests and arms, and make spots or lines of turmeric on top of the sandal paste marks.[17] The performer turns to the north and, with the help of assistants, ties the red *mēlappu* on his head and decorates it with *talappāḷi*, *talataṇṭa* and *talapaṭṭam*. *Talappāḷi* is a square, red cloth, while the *talataṇṭa* and *talapaṭṭam* are silver ornaments. After that the *ūrāḷan*, the owner or main representative of the shrine, gives the *kainittam* first to the *kalaśakkāran* and then to the performer, his assistants and the drummers in that order. The *kainiṭṭam* consists of three betel leaves and three pieces of areca nut. The performer, from what he receives, gives one betel leaf and a piece of areca nut to the drummer, who then places a small drum *(eṭantala ceṇṭa)* on the *pīṭham* (pedestal) in front of the performer.

---

[15] The *kōmaram* is the person who is delegated to conduct intermediary activities between the brahmin priest and the Teyyam. However, in the absence of a brahmin priest, the *kōmaram* functions as a priest. He is also called *nōttirikkunnāl*, 'the dedicated person,' and *tiruvāyudhakkāran*, 'the one who holds the holy weapon.' Probably because of the rigidity of the conventions related to the rituals, dedicated newcomers, especially those who train as *kōmaram* and the oracles, are becoming rare.

[16] The *Kalaśakkāran* belongs to Tiyan community. His responsibilities include arranging the *kalaśam* (decorated waterpot) and providing materials that are required for the rituals in the courtyard.

[17] Application of these marks with sandal paste and turmeric powder differs for different Teyyams, for different castes of performers as well as for the different functionaries in the ritual festivals.

The performer greets the shrine with an *añjali*, and when he begins to play on the *eṭantala ceṇṭa*, the drummers begin drumming. The group of drummers consists of men playing the *ceṇṭa*[18] (normal drum), *vīkku ceṇṭa* (base drum), *kuḻal* (flute), *elattāḷam* (cymbals) and *maddaḷam* (finger drum). While the drumming is going on in a special rhythm, the *kōmaram* brings a *koṭiyila* (banana leaf) containing rice, betel leaves and pieces of areca nut and hands it over to the performer. The performer picks up three betel leaves from the *koṭiyila*, places them on the *pīṭham* in a row and drops rice and pieces of areca nut on each leaf. This ritual is called '*pīṭham* mutirka'. The performer then collects some rice from the banana leaf in his hand and the banana leaf with the remaining rice is returned to the *kōmaram*, who takes it back to the altar where the insignia of Tāi Paradēvata are kept. The drummers play a special *tāḷavrittam*,[19] at the end of which the performer throws rice towards the shrine and recites the '*varavu viḷi*'. The *varavu viḷi* is in alliterative and rhythmic Malayalam prose which is recited in a sing-song style. This benedictory or eulogistic composition is a prayer to seek blessings for prosperity, auspiciousness and for a successful performance of the Teyyam. The drummers play another specific *tālam* and when it stops the performer recites the second *varavu viḷi*. The second *varavu viḷi* is an invocation, more elaborate than the first, inviting the deity to be present at the auspicious occasion to listen to the prayer, to bless the village, its ruler, the performer, the auspicious silver *pīṭham*, the shrine, the locality, cattle, women and children, and so on.

At the end of the second *varavu viḷi*, too, the drums are played. After doing a *tāḷavrittam* for a while the drummers stop and with-

---

[18] The *ceṇṭa* is often referred to by the performers as *asura* vādyam. The present writer has been familiar with this expression from his childhood. See also Menon (1974).

[19] The *tālavrittam* is a system or composition of *tālam* (beat). *Tālavrittam* is also the name of a composition or song *(tōṟṟam)* based on the legend of Tāi Paradēvata.

draw from the scene. The performer and one or two of his assistants remain. One of them, at least, holds a *maddaḷam* (drum) and joins in the *tōṟṟam* singing.[20] *Tōṟṟam* is a word used with reference to songs which are in general connected with the Teyyam performance.

The performer begins the *tōṟṟam*. Normally, a few lines of the song are sung alternately by the performer and by the *maddaḷakkāran* (the assistant who uses the *maddaḷam*). At times one or two others may also join them in the singing. The first portion of the *tōṟṟam* is called *koṭṭiyaṭakkam*, and has only four lines. Then the *tāḷavrittam* is sung. This has eight lines. Both are prayers. Then comes the *stuti* or *gadyam*. It takes nearly four hours to sing the main body of the story of Bhadrakāḷi killing Dāruka. This portion of the *tōṟṟam* contains the important *valiya gadyam* and *ceriya gadyam*. Other *gadyams* are *Tiruvarkāṭṭu stuti, Eriyum kanalkaṇṇil*[21] and *'om namo jaya Bhagavati'*. A couple of other *stutis* are sung depending upon time. Then *añjaṭi tōṟṟams* are sung. The *añjaṭi tōṟṟams* are the *Kaḷariyil añjaṭi*, the *Tiruvarkāṭṭu añjaṭi* and the *Kālināṭakam*. The last item in *tōṟṟam* singing is the *policcupāṭṭu* (glorifying song). Eleven important shrines connected with Tāi Paradēvata are mentioned in the *policcupāṭṭu*.[22] Apart from these main shrines, Tāi Paradēvata, it is mentioned, had 108 incarnations and was dominant in six regions.

Along with the *policcupāṭṭu* the drumming begins again; it stops after the song is finished. Then the performer throws rice towards the altar, holds his hands in an *añjali*, pays obeisance to the shrine

---

[20] *Tōṟṟam* has dravidian *mātras*, meters, counted by syllabes. These are recited in a free rhythm, creating a fusion of syllabic and melismatic styles. The performance at *tiṭaṅṅal* too, in many cases, is referred to as a *tōṟṟam* performance.

[21] Literally, 'eyes that are like glowing cinders'.

[22] They are Tiruvarkaṭṭu kavu, Sriporkali kavu, Vellarkulangara kavu, Srimanattana, Ammakunnu, Mamanikottam, Kalarivatukkal, Tekkumpatam perumkulom, Ramanthuruti perumkulom, Pattuvathu perumkulom and Kizhara perumkulom.

and then removes his *talappāḷi.* He then pays respect to the people present and returns to the *kuccil* with his assistants. There are no dance steps for the *tiṭaṅṅal* if it is performed the day before Eḷamkōlam. The procedure of the *tiṭaṅṅal* lasts well over five hours.[23]

While the *tiṭaṅṅal tōṟṟam* singing is going on, the *kalaśakkāran,* facing north, makes a *kalaśataṭṭu* on the *kalaśatara.* The *kalaśataṭṭu* has a square framework, with three layers made up of eight strips of banana trunk each, dividing the square into nine equal smaller squares. The joints of the frame work are fixed with 16 *kōltiris* (torches) made of bamboo sticks, the tops of which are covered with pieces of cloth soaked in oil, which are to be lit later. The *kalaśakkāran* places the banana leaves in the nine squares and fills the leaves with raw rice, beaten rice, puffed rice, and paddy, and then places bananas and jaggery on these items. Paddy is placed in the centre square. Tender coconuts are laid on the rice and the puffed rice. A mud pot decorated with tender coconut leaves, containing either toddy or tender-coconut-water, is taken by the *kalaśakkāran* three times around the *kalaśatara.* Then, facing south, he reverently places the *kalaśam* in the middle square of the paddy, and then comes back to the original place, on the southern side, of the *kalaśatara,* and faces the north. Here he throws rice and pays obeisance. The *kōltiris* are lit while *añjaṭi tōṟṟam* is being sung.

If the *tiṭaṅṅal* is on the day of the Eḷamkōlam performance, immediately after the *policcupāṭṭu* is sung, a *koṭiyila* containing lighted wicks is brought from the shrine by the *kōmaram* and given to the performer. At that time the *tālam* of the drumming is changed. Receiving the *koṭiyila,* the performer pays his obeisance to the shrine and walks toward other shrines with special steps.

---

[23] In the recent past, the writer noticed that there is a tendency to condense the rituals. This tendency is noticeable in the *tōṟṟam* singing and in the spectacular dance movements, although the latter have been retained to some extent.

The performer throws rice at the *nāgastāna* and other shrines and pays respect. Then he returns to Tāi Paradēvata's shrine. Again he throws rice and pays obeisance, removes his head dress and then returns to the *kuccil* with his assistants. The drumming stops.

Eḷamkōlam

Eḷamkōlam, which can be considered as a junior form of Tāi Paradēvata, is performed invariably in the evening before the performance of Tāi Paradēvata.

An oil lamp burns in the *kuccil.* The facial make-up as well as the costuming for the performance are done with solemn reverence. The performer lies on his back for the facial make-up. Red, orange, yellow and black are the colours commonly used to paint the face. *Cāyilyam* (red ochre), turmeric, lamp black, *kumkum* etc., are mixed in coconut oil and used to achieve the pigments. These colours are applied on the face with fingers, but the stem of coconut leaf is used, almost in the place of a brush, to draw thin and delicate lines. It takes nearly two hours to do the facial make-up, which has to be done in precise patterns. This time seems to be a period of contemplation for the performer. The facial make-up of Eḷamkōlam is called *'Saṅkum Vairidaḷam'.* When the facial make-up is completed, the performer gets up and begins donning his costume. A couple of assistants help him put on the costume. The performer wears a very tight waist-band, ties the dress below the waist and tightens it behind by taking it between the legs. Then *kaikudu* (sleeves) are placed on the arms, then wrist bangles called *cūṭakam, kaṭakam* and *kaitaṇṭa* (made of *cekki* flowers). On the head *talappāḷi, talappāvu* and *paṭṭam* are worn. The performer puts on *ekiṟu* (fangs) made of silver. In front of the ears *ōlakkātu* and *ceṇṭāritaṇḍi* (which are round metal pieces) are fixed. The head gear of Eḷamkōlam is called *eḷamkōla-caṭṭa* ; it is triangular with a convex front, right above the head.

During the process of decoration one of the Vaṇṇān men goes to the *naṭa*, in front of the shrine, and sings the *tōṟṟam, koṭṭipāṭal*, with the accompaniment of a *ceṇṭa* or a *maddaḷam*. This *tōṟṟam* is generally an abridged form of the original *tōṟṟam*.

After putting on the *ōlakkātu*, which is the last piece of the costume, the performer greets the men who are in the *kuccil* and comes out accompanied by the man with a *kaiviḷakku*. By this time a new *kalaśataṭṭu* is made, the *kōltiris* are lit and the drumming begins. The performer sits on the *pīṭham* facing eastwards in front of the shrine of Tāi Paradēvata. Immediately the *muṭi* (head decoration) is placed on the head and fastened. Then the attendant puts *cāyilyam* (red powder) onto the lips of the performer. Thereafter the performer looks into the mirror and goes into a trance. This is the point at which the performer becomes the Teyyam, Eḷamkōlam. She gets up from the *pīṭham* and goes rapidly with dance steps and turns around many times. She turns around in four different places in the courtyard and returns in front of the shrine, *naṭa*, and twirls around again. The *kōmaram* who brings the weapons, *tiruvāyudham* and *cētakam*,[24] gives rice first to the Eḷamkōlam, who throws the rice onto the weapons, and then the weapons are given to the Teyyam. She turns around again. By the time she finishes turning and faces north, the *kalaśakkāran* is ready, facing her with the *kalaśam* in his hand. Two Vaṇṇāns hold the hands of the Eḷamkōlam for support. These people go around the *kalaśataṛha* slowly three times. The Eḷamkōlam walks forward with very slow steps, whereas the *kalaśakkāran*, facing the Eḷamkōlam, walks backward. After three circumambulations, the *kalaśakkāran* reaches the northern side of the *kalaśataṛha* and, facing south, places the *kalaśam* on the *kalaśataṛha* and throws rice on the Eḷamkōlam.

---

[24] *Cētakam* and *tiruvāyudham:* These are swords and a shield made of bronze (or steel); there are tiny bells attached to the weapons, which make a jingling sound when the performer moves the weapons.

The Eḷamkōlam blesses the *kalaśakkāran* with a gesture of the sword. After this the Eḷamkōlam goes round the *kalaśataṛha* quickly and comes back to the courtyard. This movement is called *eḷamkōlappāccil*. Then she goes to the other shrines and dances, and if there is any other Teyyam on the scene, she dances with the other Teyyam, too, exchanges weapons, and continues dancing for some time. After the *eḷamkōlappāccil*, she dances two *kalāśams*,[25] specific dance movements, namely *'kuḷurma kalāśam'* and *'ariyeriña kalāśam'*. Drumming and dancing continue for a while. The Teyyam, then, goes in front of the drummers and, facing them, dances *'vēlakkalāśam'*; the drummers drum vigorously as if mutually respecting and acknowledging each other. By then, a banana tree laden with raw fruits and a flower is brought by the *kalaśakkāran* and held vertically near the *kalaśataṛha*. The Teyyam goes around the banana tree three times in different dance steps and then she cuts off the banana flower with a knife. This might be a symbolic act of sacrificing something else, possibly a *narabali*[26] in the olden days. Next a cock is sacrificed. The Teyyam holding the head of the cock, cuts its neck with a knife.

---

[25] In Kathakali several *kalāśams* are danced by the performers: *Aṣṭakalāśam, murikkalāśam, itakkalāśam, vattam vecca kalāśam*. K.P.S. Menon (1963: XVIII - XIX) and id. (1966: XIX) mentions the names of different *kalāśams* used in Kathakali.

[26] The former existence of the practice of *narabali:* (human sacrifice) is indicated by one of the songs called *'kōḻistōtram,'* sung during Cīrmma's festival. A portion of *Kōḻistōtram* runs as follows: "To propitiate you, formerly a human being was sacrificed. When a human being was not available, an elephant was sacrificed. When a human being or an elephant were not available, a sheep was sacrificed. In the absence of human being, elephant or sheep let me sacrifice this cock and offer its blood to you." (Chandera 1973).

A ritual performance called *'uccērikūttu'* is another indication of the former existence of the *narabali*. During this ritual, the performer pierces his hand with a sharp needle *(nārāyam)* and sheds his blood. Further proceedings are a sort of mock death ceremony staged by the performer. Originally this could have been a *narabali*. This performance is held for the long life of the owner-conductor of the performance. By sacrificing one man, the life span of another is expected to be extended. *Uccērikūttu* is a very rare performance these days.

Before the cock's head is cut, a few drops of water and a few grains of rice are put in its mouth, probably to symbolise that the sacrifice is not done as a punishment to the cock. After the cock sacrifice the drumming stops. The Teyyam goes in front of the *naṭa*. The *kōmaram* hands over three betel leaves, three pieces of areca nut and a coconut to the Teyyam, who throws these items one by one on the floor, to see the omen. This ritual is called *camanam kāṇuka*, i.e. to see the omen. The next ritualistic item is *mukham tuṛakka*, literally meaning "open the face." For this a silver coin or a golden flower from the shrine is fixed on the forehead of the Teyyam, who looks into a mirror to see her own reflection. Then she throws the rice received from the *kōmaram* towards the shrine and begins saying *mumbustānam*. This is a narration of her own legendary origins. She then addresses the *mummoḻi*, benedictory verses, first to the brahmin priest, then to the *kōmaram*, and finally to the important functionaries of the shrine and the devotees. She receives *kaṇikke*, the offerings of money, cock, coconut etc., from the devotees and in return gives them *prasādam* of *cekki* flower or *mañjal-kuṛi* (turmeric powder). After receiving the offerings and giving blessings to all the devotees, she goes to the *naṭa*. Again, a silver coin taken from the shrine is fixed on the forehead of the Teyyam and, looking into the mirror, she says *mummoḻi*, this time to the important functionaries of the shrine. She throws rice towards the shrine and turns around, and when the drumming begins, she dances in special steps. Thereafter, she returns the weapons to the *kōmaram* and turning around a few times sits on the *pīṭham*. The assistants immediately untie the head dress, the *eḷamkōlacaṭṭa*. This is the point at which the power of the divinity departs from the *kōlakkāran* and he emerges from the trance.

The *kōlakkāran* throws rice towards the shrine and pays respects to all. The *kōmaram* gives him three betel leaves, three pieces of areca nut and one coconut. The performer returns to the *kuccil* with the *kaiviḷakkukāran* and other assistants. With a special concluding *tāḷa*-session, the drumming stops. When the performer reaches the *kuccil*, he greets all the elders present there.

During Eḷamkōlam the performer shows his stamina and proficieny in dancing and his ability as a Teyyam performer. The conical head gear and the other costumes make the performer execute very brisk movements and special dance steps. Turning, jumping and bending in all directions are possible during Eḷamkōlam performance, whereas they are impossible during the performance of Tāi Paradēvata.

Tāi Paradēvata

The facial make-up of the Tāi Paradēvata is called *prākkeḻuttu.* Her head decoration, called *tirumuṭi,* is very tall. The height of the *tirumuṭi,* the frame of which is made of strips of bamboo or areca trees, varies approximately from 5 to 15 meters.[27] The front of the *tirumuṭi* is covered with black, white and red cloth strips. At the bottom, in front and just above the position of the head the *tirumuṭi* is about 2 meters wide and convex in shape and at the top the width is only about 25 cm. The convex area of the *tirumuṭi* is elaborately decorated with peacock feathers, *cekki* flowers, red cloth and golden, coloured motifs of snakes. At the back, the *tirumuṭi,* up to the half its height will be covered by the projected flat form of red cloth. On the waist of the performer *ceṇṭavāḷam* is tied. *Ceṇṭavāḷam* is a decorative item made of cloth, metal and wood. On the body of the performer *ēvukaram* is worn, on the neck *kaḻuttukeṭṭu,* and on the arms *kaikūṭu, muṅkaivāl, cūṭakam, kaṭakam* and *kaitaṇṭa.*[28] On the legs are *paṭṭum, kaṭakkam, maṇikai* and *cilambu.* The head is decorated with *talappāvu, talapāḷi* and *talapaṭṭam.* The Tāi

---

[27] The *tirumuṭi* of Kaṇṇaṅgāttu Bhagavati is made of one areca tree. The *tirumuṭi* of Kalarivātukkal Bhagavati is the tallest the present writer has seen. It might be over 15 m in height. The balance of the taller *tirumuṭis* is maintained by a scissors-cross support, made of bamboo, which is held by the devotees.

[28] These are ornaments made of wood and metal. Wooden items are invariably covered with gold foils and all of them are decorated with *cekki* flowers.

Paradēvata's costume also includes *ekiru* (fangs) made of silver. Two sticks, called *uṭakkol,* are tied at the waist line.

The performer, after greeting those present at the *kuccil,* goes with his assistants to the *naṭa,* and pays respect with *añjali.* The *kōmaram* brings a *koṭiyila* with lighted wicks and gives it to the performer. The performer takes the *koṭiyila* through the frame of the *arayuṭa* and puts it on the *pīṭham.* This is a purificatory rite for the *arayuṭa.* He puts on the *arayuṭa,* which stands supported by the *uṭakkol* at his waist. He sits on the *pīṭham.* Then the *tirumuṭi* is put on the performer's head. Three people are needed to lift the *tirumuṭi* and to put it on the head of the performer. Though the *tirumuṭi* rests on his head, it is in fact tied to the *arayuṭa* so that the weight of the *tirumuṭi* is distributed.

Because of the weight and height of the *tirumuṭi* the movements of the Tāi Paradēvata are very restricted. All the movements and dance steps are done in an upright position; most of the time the performer is supported by assistants who hold his arms as well as the *tirumuṭi.* From the time the performer is being dressed at the *kuccil* the *koṭṭi-pāṭal* goes on in front of the *naṭa.*

The *koṭṭi-pāṭal,* at this stage, consists of a *gadyam, añjaṭi* and *policcupaṭṭu,* all the three in an abridged form. Red powder is applied to the lips of the performer. The main drumming begins and the *koṭṭi-pāṭal* stops. The performer looks into the mirror, meditates, identifies himself with the deity, returns the mirror to the assistants, then stands up on the *pīṭham.* The Teyyam turns toward the shrine and goes to the *naṭa.* She makes a particular dancing step, *kalāśam,* turns around a few times and receives the holy weapons. By this time the *kalaśakkāran* with the *kalaśam* (the decorated vessel) in his hand stands at the *kalaśataṛha,* where a new *kalaśataṭṭu* has been made and lit, and faces the Teyyam. They go round the *kalaśataṛha* in the same way as the Eḷamkōlam did. After three circumambulations *(pradakṣiṇam)* the *kalaśakkāran* places the *kalaśam* on the altar and then goes to the courtyard. The Teyyam blesses him. The Tāi Paradēvata blesses the audience with the sword by way of a gesture. The next ritual is a cock sacrifice. Further rituals are the same as those for the Eḷamkōlam.

Just before the end of the performance the owners of the shrine and other devotees go to the Tāi Paradēvata and listen to her oracular blessings. Thereafter the Teyyam dances a while, turns around several times to drumming, and then returns the holy weapons to the *kōmaram*. He sits on the *pīṭham* and the head decoration *(tirumuṭi)* is removed by the assistants. The *kōlakkāran* throws rice towards the shrine, does obeisance and returns to the *kuccil*.

There are local variations of the rituals at different shrines. For example, in some shrines the Teyyam goes around the shrine with the *veḷiccappāṭu*[29] *(kōmaram)*, who is dressed up, and with the functionaries of the shrine.

During the circumambulation, devotees, particularly women, throw rice to the Teyyam as a way of greeting. At the shrine of Tāi Paradēvata, two types of *pūjas* and rituals are conducted: inside the shrine (in many places) where brahmins conduct the *pūjas* and other rituals, no offering of animal sacrifice or alcohol can be used. But at the courtyard, where the actual Teyyam performance is conducted, animal sacrifices are common, as well as the use of toddy. At some shrines Tāi Paradēvata has in her hand a metallic head called *koccu-śirasu* (small head) while dancing. This represents the head of Dāruka and depicts Bhadrakāḷi's *kapālāmṛtam* (drinking of nectar from the skull). The *tōṟṟam* songs of Tāi Paradēvata are descriptive

[29] The *veḷiccappāṭu*, who functions as a priest, but occasionally gets into a trance and makes oracular statements, belongs normally to the Tiyan or another community lower in status than the Nayars. The one who takes the role of *veḷiccappāṭu* (the word meaning 'the enlightened one') has to go through austerities and dedicate himself to the ritualistic duties connected with the Teyyam festival. The status of the goddess's *veḷiccappāṭu* is an exalted one. In most cases his role, too, is hereditary.

and full of imagery and symbols.

The *asura* Dāruka,[30] after having secured a boon from Brahmā that he could not be killed by any man, either on earth or in the sky, began to harass all people in the world and the *devas* in heaven. When his depredations became unbearable, the *devas* went first to Viṣṇu and then to Śiva. Śiva, on hearing the complaint from the *devas*, created Bhadrakāḷi from his third eye and instructed her to kill the *asura* Dāruka. The goddess is described in the *tōṟṟam* as follows:

> Wearing the moon as decoration
> With eyes sparkling with fire
> Wearing wild elephants as earrings
> With fangs like curved swords
> Holding *nāndakam* (sword) in hand
> She rushes forward to fight the *asura*.

In another *tōṟṟam* she is described in this way:

> She who is wearing wild elephants as earrings,
> Wearing snakes as rings and bangles,
> Holding a handsword, *vaṭṭakam* and trident,
> Screaming like the sound of the stormy sea
> She charges forward to kill the angry *asura*.

---

30 a. According to *Dēvibhāgavatam, pañcama skanda,* Dāruka (Darika) was a charioteer of Mahiṣāsura. See Vettam Mani (1982).

b. One text sung at Cīrmma-kāvu during the annual festival is the story of Dāruka, who is described as a proud tribal king:

> When there was a drought, Dāruka and the kings of the Cēra, Cōla and Pāṇḍya kingdoms jointly decided to present offerings to Kāveriyappan (Śiva) to please him so that he would bring rains. The offerings were accepted by Kāveriyappan and the devotees were blessed with rain. Dāruka, however, entered the *mantrasāla* of Kāveriyappan and plundered it. This infuriated the other kings, who began treating him as an *asura*. Thus Dāruka, the tribal king, was depicted as an *asura* king. See Chandera (1973).

Bhadrakāḷi created a mythical animal called 'Vēṭāla' and, sitting on the animal, went to the battle field and challenged Dāruka. The war cry of Bhadrakāḷi was like thunder. During the ensuing fight she caught hold of the tuft of Dāruka and, placing him on the tongue of Vētāḷa, chopped off his head with her *nāndakam*.[31]

It is interesting to note that not only Bhadrakāḷi has been deified as the Teyyam, Tāi Paradēvata, but also Manōdari and the *rākṣasa* who have been deified as Vasūrimāla and Ghaṇṭakarṇa respectively.

The story of Dāruka and other stories connected with Tāi Paradēvata clearly indicate the hierarchy in which the gods and goddesses were held. *Asuras* invariably did penance, approached Brahmā or Viṣṇu and obtained boons from them. However, when the *asuras* misused these boons against the people or the *devas*, it was Śiva who came to their rescue. When Dāruka was intolerant, people and *devas* went to Viṣṇu first, and when Viṣṇu could not solve their problem, they, along with Viṣṇu, went to Śiva for a solution. For all of them Siva is the most powerful of the gods!

---

[31] The story goes on as follows: Dāruka's wife Manōdari, the daughter of Maya-asura, was sunk in grief at the death of her husband. She began to do *tapas* (austerities), praying to Śiva. Śiva was in his *yōganidra*. He woke up agitated, sweating profusely. He gave the sweat from his body to Manōdari saying that the person on whom she sprinkled the drops of sweat would suffer from smallpox and such patients would deify her and worship her by lighting *antitiri*, an oil lamp, at her shrine in the evening and providing offerings. Manōdari rushed to Bhadrakāḷi and threw the drops of sweat on her. Immediately Bhadrakāḷi fell down, suffering from smallpox. Hearing the mishap, Śiva created from his ear a *rākṣasa* and instructed him to lick the smallpox off the body of Bhadrakāḷi. And when he tried to lick the smallpox off the face of Bhadrakāḷi, she prevented him, saying that she and he were sister and brother, as both of them had been created by Śiva, and that it was improper for a brother to lick the face of his sister. Thus the smallpox marks on the face of Bhadrakāḷi remain as decorative spots. The *rākṣasa* is called Ghaṇṭakarṇa. In the beginning he was an enemy of Viṣṇu. He could not even tolerate hearing the sound of Viṣṇu and in order to ward off the sound he wore *ghaṇṭa* (bells) in his *karṇa* (ears). Hence the name Ghaṇṭakarṇa. Eventually, however, he becomes a devotee of Viṣṇu. (Vettam Mani 1982).

The most powerful among the goddesses is Bhadrakāḷi who, though ferocious, is a widely worshipped goddess in Kerala. Different types of performing arts have divergent visualisations of Bhadrakāḷi's forms. In *Bhagavati Pāṭṭu*, for example, she is depicted in *kaḷam* (floor drawing) with 18 arms, with different weapons in each of them and wearing garlands of skulls. (See plate IV). In *Kāḷiyūṭṭu*, she is personified as the black goddess. In *Muṭiyēttu*, *Tiṟa* and *Paṭayaṇi*, she has her own specific forms and attributes.

The artistic forms of Tāi Paradēvata and Eḷamkōlam must have evolved to the present state of sophistication from very primitive originals, traces of which can be noticed in the Teyyams performed by Pulayar, Vēlan and Kōppāḷar. The costumes, drummings, dance steps and even the oracular blessings bestowed on the devotees by the Teyyams of these communities still preserve a rugged and unadulteratedly earthy aesthetic quality.

The dance has specific choreography, leaving sufficient scope for the performer to show his proficiency. The sequences of the performances, incorporating rituals, lead to a marvellous climax. They appear to be based on ancient conventions of dramaturgy. In spite of variation in the chronology of rituals, in dance steps and in the style of singing according to different performance traditions, the underlying dedication of the performers and their belief in the ritual are in each case absolute.

The widely prevalent worship of goddesses in connection with fertility began, in the course of cultural evolution, to incorporate elements of current incidents, legends and episodes of epics according to its own requirements. During this process, the resurrected myths and the ritualistic performances connected with them, became a medium through which the moods of people are reflected. Thus the response and the reaction to Sanskritic Hinduism and its eventual integration can be noticed in the story of Bhadrakāḷi. As an art form, the performance of the Teyyam of Bhadrakāḷi (Tāi Paradēvata) combines all aspects of art such as singing, acting, dancing, choreography, craftsmanship, painting and design. The mystic power attributed to the performance transforms it into a superior art form, glorifying Bhadrakāḷi as a supreme goddess of Kerala.

References

Chandera, C.M.S. 1973. *Kaṇṇakiyum Cīrmma Kāvum*. Kottayam: SPCS Ltd. [in Malayāḷam].

Kurup, K.K.N. 1973. *The cult of Teyyam and hero worship in Kerala*. Calcutta: Indian Publications.

Menon, K.G. 1974. Pañcavādyam, pañcārivādyam and pāndivādyam. In *Margi annual* 3: 30.

Menon, K.P.S. 1963. *Kathakali-yāttaprakāram*, vol. I. Ahmedabad: Darpana.

Id. 1966. *Kathakali-yāttaprakāram*, vol. II. Quilon: V.V. Press.

Mookerjee, A. 1988. *Kali. The feminine force*. London: Thames and Hudson.

Nambiar, Balan 1982. Teyyam and Bhuta rituals. In *The Performing Arts* 64-73. Bombay: Marg Publications.

Id. and Fischer, E. 1987. Patōla/Virāḷi Paṭṭu from Gujarat to Kerala. In *Asiatische Studien* XLI.2. Publ. by Peter Lang. Bern, Frankfurt, New York, Paris.

Vettam Mani. 1982. *Puranic Encyclopedia*. Kottayam: SPCS Ltd. [in Malayāḷam].

ŚIVA UNDER REFUSE
THE HIDDEN MAHĀDEVA (LUKUMAHĀDYAḤ) AND PROTECTIVE STONES IN NEPAL

Axel Michaels

Introduction

The main concern of this paper is the tradition of covering seats of deities with food, leftovers or household waste, particularly with regard to rituals and myths associated with the Nepalese folk deity Lukumahādyaḥ. My aim here is to demonstrate how even a small and specific object of veneration is related to so many different deities that it becomes almost impossible to identify it clearly. Since this is by no means a singular case in Hinduism, I shall also draw some general conclusions from the material presented here, pointing out how the deity, to a certain extent, resists the influence of the great tradition.

Who is Lukumahādyaḥ? He is a deity worshipped by Newars on the dark 14th of Caitra, a day when a number of Newar festivities and rituals can be observed in the Kathmandu Valley. The day is called *piśācacaturdaśī* ("goblin's fourteenth") or, rarely, *preta-caturdaśī* ("the fourteenth of the deceased persons") or in Nevārī *pācāre* (also spelt *pāsācahre*, *pahāṃcahre* etc.). For most Newars (and scholars of Newar culture) "Lukumahādyaḥ" (also spelt *Lukmādyaḥ*, *Lukumāḥdyaḥ* etc.) means "hidden or hiding Mahādeva," linking the Nevārī verbal prefix *luku-* with the Nepālī verb *luknu* ("to hide, conceal oneself") and combining it with

Nev./Skt. *mahā* "great", Nev. *dyaḥ* < Skt. *deva* "god". However, the prefix *luku-* has more meanings, which have to be taken into consideration for the etymology of "Lukumahādyaḥ" (see below).

On this day Śiva himself is supposed to become a demon, ghost or goblin (*piśāca*),[1] depicted in a small stone, only rarely shaped as a *liṅga*, which is "kept hidden in filthy 'unclean' places such as the neighbourhood garbage dump. (...) This is the day when these insanitary disposal places must be cleaned and Luku Mahadev is removed from his stone-covered hole to be washed, anointed, and worshipped with offerings of flowers, smoking incense and foods which include meat, garlic and alcoholic drink, otherwise abhorred by Shiva.[2] A votive oil wick lamp is kept flickering all through the night[3] at Luku Mahadev's hiding place and the lampblack collected therefrom is especially effective, when painted around the eyes of women and children, in curing eye disease and improving eyesight." (Anderson 1971: 264). (See plate V).[4]

---

[1] In the context I am referring to, *piśāca* means a class of malevolent, but rather unspecific ghosts whose existence is (similar to *bhūta/preta)* often explained by impure or unpacified death. Despite the findings of, for example, Crooke 1894: 145-184 or Penzer 1927: 205-6, the differences between *piśāca, bhūta, preta, vetāla, rākṣasa* etc.;with regard to their function or origin, have not yet received a satisfactory explanation, for mostly these terms remain untranslated or are vaguely explained as "a kind of demon" while, interestingly, the different terms for female ghosts or demons (*ḍākinī, yoginī, śākinī*, etc. or Nep. *bhokṣī)* are generally translated by "witch."

[2] In fact, sometimes just flowers of radish and mustard plants are offered, cp. Vajrācārya V.S. 2036: 114.

[3] Cp. Bhāṣāvaṃśāvali I: 83: *deśamadhye mahādeva sthānaprati akhaṇḍa rātribhara agni jagāi*, or — almost a translation of this chronicle — the chronicle of Padmagiri: "while fires are kindled before images of Mahādeva throughout the city" (Padmagiri's Chronicle, p. 41; similarly Wright Chronicle, p. 126).

[4] The lampblack (Nep. *gājal)* too is regarded as such a means of protection; it is, however, not only painted around the eyes but also on the forehead as the so-called *mohinīṭikā*.

Among the various offerings garlic plays a major role. The day of Piśācacaturdaśī is, in fact, also known as Nev. *lābhā nakhaḥ*, "the festival of garlic" (Śreṣṭha and Juju N.S. 1108: 55). Similar to the widespread Western belief that garlic is a useful device against vampires, Newars sometimes carry a garlic clove with them to protect themselves against ghosts. The extensive use of garlic on Piśācacaturdaśī is explained in the context of the demon Bhasmāsura's terror against Śiva (see below). After Piśācacaturdaśī, many Jyāpu (a Newar farming caste) do not eat the green leaves or the clove of garlic anymore since they consider it to have become too hot or foul-smelling. Moreover, at the festival of the local goddess Kaṅkeśvarī, to be held on the same day, participants often sing a Nevārī song with the refrain *kahnaseṃ neseṃ vayeke makhu, lābhā tarkāri nayeke makhu* "From tomorrow we don't come [and] we don't eat garlic vegetable." (Śreṣṭha and Juju, ibid.) The period following Piśācacaturdaśī is considered to be extremely dangerous, due to infections and diseases caused by ghosts and demons. The worship of Mahādeva with garlic, as well as many other festivities on that day, which also include offerings and feasts with garlic, are explicitly celebrated in order to protect oneself against these dangers.

In the last and only Hindu kingdom of the world, as Nepal likes to declare herself, it is quite bewildering to see Śiva being worshipped in a hole or stone covered with refuse, which is dumped by Newars in the courtyards of their private homes until it gets collected by special cleaning castes (e.g. the Poḍe). However, if we leave aside for a moment the aspect of unclean garbage, it looks as if a popular theme of high tradition has manifested itself: Śiva being hidden somewhere and being discovered, more or less accidentally, for e.g. by a cow, or coming into existence by himself (*svayambhū*), is a major topic of Śaivite mythology as well as of legends of origin at Śaivite temples.[5]

---

[5] Cp. Eichinger Ferro-Luzzi 1987 for a collection of such myths and legends.

According to the Gopālarājavaṃśāvalī (fol. 17a-b) and modern chronicles[6] the *liṅga* of the Paśupatinātha Temple too was discovered by a cow in a (covered) hole:

> *srī paśupatiko aghiko liṅgako devālaya bhatkī chopī rahâdā kīrtipur dekhī kailī gāī nitya āī dūdh caḍāī gayākī goṭhālāle dekhyā ra herdā śrī paśupatinātha prakāś bhayā.* (Rājavaṃśāvalī I:8)
>
> While the temple of Śrī Paśupatinātha's first *liṅga* was broken and covered, a greyish cow came daily from Kīrtipur offering (her) milk; after she was seen and observed by a herdsman Śrī Paśupatinātha was made known (i.e. literally dis-covered).

We find a similar topic in the Śivarātri myth of the Great Tradition handed down to us principally in its paurāṇik sources, especially in the Śiva-, Padma- and Skandapurāṇas.[7] In nearly all the versions it is a hunter (*vyādha, lubdhaka, kirāta* etc.) who gets lost in the jungle and — frightened at nightfall by wild animals — ends up climbing a *bilva* tree. There, he stays awake the whole night, dropping from time to time some water and some *bilva* leaves, which both fall upon a hidden *liṅga* on the ground. Unwittingly, he thus worships Śiva through fasting (*upavāsa*), a night vigil (*jāgara*), *bilva* leaves — much favoured by Śiva — and water (*sparśana*). Śiva, therefore, grants the hunter — who in the social sphere stands at the bottom of the brahmanical hierarchy because his profession involves the killing of animals — salvation (*mukti*) or a place near to Śiva (*Śivaloka, - purī, - gaṇa* etc.). He also exculpates the hunter from his sinful way of life (by granting *pāpahīna, nirdagdha* etc.).

Although there are parallels between the myths and rituals of Śivarātri and Lukumahādyaḥ such as the hidden *liṅga*, the dark

---

[6] Bhāṣāvaṃśāvalī I: 2-3 and 6; Devamālā, pp. 2-3; Wright Chronicle, p. 107; Padmagiri's Chronicle, p. 33.

[7] See, for details, Michaels (in press) and id. (forthcoming).

14th and the night vigil, the myths of Lukumahādyaḥ present a different picture. To the best of my knowledge, there are basically two popular myths of Lukumahādyaḥ: one has to do with Śiva and the Goddess, the other with Śiva fleeing in fear from a figure called, variously Virūpākṣa, or the Buddhists, or a demon called Bhasmāsura.

I have, however, noted two more myths told by a single Rājopādhyāya informant and not known to other Newars who were asked about it: a) Bhīmasena tried hard but without success to sing a pleasing song. He asked Śiva-Mahādeva how he liked it. Śiva didn't fancy at all the roaring sounds produced by Bhīmasena. This enraged Bhīmasena, who lost all control and beat Śiva heavily on the head. As a result only the small top portion of Śiva (in his *liṅga* form) can now be seen, the rest having been knocked into the earth by the mighty Bhīmasena. b) Śiva-Mahādeva had contracted leprosy in India and was expelled from the country and disregarded by the other gods. In order to rescue him Gaṇeśa took him via Cobār to Nepal carrying him on his back or shoulders.

Both myths could be important for the etymology of "Lukumahā-dyaḥ". Thus the carrying on one's back is expressed in Nevārī by the transitive verb *luku* (var. *lukũ*) *chiye* (var. *chine*) [*haḥgu*]. The verbal prefix *luku(ṃ)* also appears in verbs, which express the disappearing of something: *luku(ṃ) biye* (var. *bile*) means for instance "to set (of the sun)", referring mostly to the half circle at sunset seen on the horizon, or "to dive, to plunge into" (e.g. a person, who dives into water so that just the crown of his head is visible). Both meanings imply not necessarily, that something is completely hidden but rather that there is still a little bit left of it which can be seen. Since this describes, to a certain extent, the actual shapes of Lukumahādyaḥ stones, the common but unusual (and linguistically uncertain) derivation of *luku-* from Nep. *luknu* ("to hide, conceal oneself") must perhaps be revised. It remains, however, for the Nevārī specialists to supply historical evidence for a more definitive etymology of this name. For my purpose, the fact that most Newars do understand Lukumahādyaḥ as "hiddden or hiding Śiva" is the more important point.

Interestingly, no mythological identification of Rudra with Lukumahādyaḥ is known, although this vedic god lends himself easily to such an identification, since he received the leftovers from the sacrifice. This almost certainly implies that the local deity called Lukumahādyaḥ was not a *liṅga* which, due to reasons unknown, had to be covered. In such a case one could also expect the deity to have a Sanskrit name such as "Gupteśvara", which I have, however, never heard in this context.[8]

Śiva hiding with Pārvatī

The myth which connects Lukumahādyaḥ with the Goddess is handed down orally, although it centres around a common topic, namely the conflict between Śiva and (his) Śakti. The following is the version recorded by Puṇyaratna Vajrācārya, who was among the first to publish on Nepalese festivals:

> *dherai dherai samaya-agāḍi satyayugamā ekapalṭa pārvatī jasale āvaśyaka pareko samayamā kālī ra bhagavatīko rūpa dhāraṇa garī madya, māṃsa ādi bhakṣaṇa garne gardathin unale mahādevalāī bhanin: 'he maheśa, deva devamā pani mahādeva kahalāunubhaekā tapāīṃko ardhāliṅginī bhaera ma sāhrai saubhāgyavatī bhaekī chu, malāī yasamā*

---

[8] See, for instance, Himavatkhaṇḍa, *adhyāya* 99, dealing with a Gupteśvara-Māhātmya which refers to a *liṅga* at Phūlcokī. Although the myths of this *liṅga* speak about a demon called "Vṛṣāsura" (99.7) and a fallen *brāhmaṇa* who became a *brahmarākṣasa* (99.14) who both — like Virūpākṣa (see *infra)* — oppress Śiva, although this Gupateśvara is among the replica of 64 *liṅgas* which Virūpākṣa has to worship within the so-called Catuḥṣaṣṭi-liṅgayātrā (Himavatakhaṇḍa, pp. 197-332; cp. Devatā-tīrthādimālā, *ibid.* Pariśiṣṭa, p. 81; Bhāṣāvaṃśāvalī I: 6-8) in order to get rid of his sin, although there is another *liṅga* called "Gupteśvara" east of the Paśupatinātha Temple above the Āryaghāṭ (cp. Wright Chronicle, p. 112), — no mythological or ritual parallel has been drawn in the texts or by the local inhabitants to Lukumahādyaḥ.

ṭhūlo harṣa cha. tara tapāīṃ ra mamā eka kuramā samāna nabhaekole malāī ali kheda lāgcha. tyo samāna nabhaeko kurā ke ho bhane maile bakhata bakhatamā aneka rūpa dhāraṇa garī madya, māṃsa ādi bhakṣaṇa gardachu tara tapāīṃle ukta padārthaharū bhakṣaṇa garnubhaeko kahile pani dekhinaṃ. tyasa kāraṇa malāī kehī apṭhyāro jasto lāgirahecha.' pārvatīko yo kurā sunī mahāde- vale bhannubhayo: 'gaurī, timī bhramamā parekī rahichyau. timīle mātrai aneka rūpa dhāraṇa garera samaya samayamā madya, māṃsa bhakṣaṇa garekī hoina, maile pani gareko chu.' mahādevako yasa vacanalāī sunepachi pārvatīle āgraha garīkana mahādevale madya, māṃsa bhakṣaṇa gareko herne manasāya prakaṭa garin. unako icchā-anusāra mahādevale piśāca rūpa dhāraṇa garī rāyoko ra mūlāko sāga umriraheko khetamā jānubhaī, kasaile nadekhne prakārale khālḍomā basnubhaī madya, māṃsa, lasuna khāera dekhāī pārvatīko citta śānta garidinubhayo. tyasakāraṇa tyastai velādekhi phālguna [sic!] kṛṣṇa caturdaśīko dinalāī piśāca caturdaśī bhanī uparyukta prakārale mahādevako pūjā garī cāḍa manāune garī āeko ho. (Vajrācārya V.S. 42036: 114-5)[9]

A long, long time ago, still in the Satyayuga, Pārvatī used to take the form of Kālī and Bhagavatī after she had accepted alcohol, meat etc. Once she spoke to Mahādeva: 'Great Lord (Maheśa), who is called even among all gods the Great God (Mahādeva), since I am your half, I am always full of happiness and I feel great pleasure about it. However, since between you and me one thing is not on an even keel, I feel a little bit distressed. It is because of this: I take from time to time another form and consume alcohol, meat etc., but I have never seen you eating these things. Therefore I feel somehow uneasy.' After Mahādeva had listened to Pārvatī's speech, he said: 'Gaurī, you seem to have got things wrong! It's not only you who from time to time, after taking another form, consumes alcohol, meat etc. I have also done it!' After Pārvatī had heard this speech of Mahādeva she forcefully expressed her desire to see him

---

[9] Cp. Anderson 1971: 264 for a similar version of the myth.

> taking alcohol, meat etc. [in front of her]. According to her wish Mahādeva took the form of a demon (*piśāca*), went into a field in which mustard and radish plants were growing [and] where he could not be seen, sat down in a hole and gormandized on alcohol, meat [and] garlic. By showing all this to Pārvatī he set her mind at ease. Thus, since that time, the day on the dark fourteenth of Phālguna [sic! correct is Caitra] is called 'Goblin's Fourteenth', and the festival is celebrated by worshipping Mahādeva in that manner.

This myth of Śiva questioned by Pārvatī regarding his refusal of alcohol and meat is not — as in the myth of Śivarātri — a peaceful story of the accidental discovery of the hidden Śiva, but a conflict between two religious and ritual traditions: the (tantrik) cult of the Goddess along with godlings (*piśāca*) accompanying her and the brahmanical tradition of the pure, vegetarian Śiva/Mahādeva refusing unclean food. Moreover, Śiva is inferior to the Goddess, it is he who has to suffer under her and to eat foods usually abhorred by him. In other words, it is not a myth of the hidden Śiva but of the hiding Śiva, and not one in which leftovers are offered to Śiva, but unclean food stuff.

However, Devī mocking Śiva is another common theme of the Great Tradition, and in order to understand its local implications better one must compare it with other rituals performed on the same day.

The Goblin's Fourteenth

Any fourteenth night in the dark half of a lunar month is *caturdaśī*, the day of spirits (*bhūtadina*) and the night of Śiva as the lord of the night (*niśāpati*). The date of Lukumahādyaḥ's ritual, the Piśācacaturdaśī, in the month of Caitra, falls in a period which is very much concerned with the "chthonic forces and the indigenous 'root' manifestations of deity in the [Kathmandu] Valley" (Slusser 1982: 343). Moreover, there are many clues to suggest that Goblin's Fourteenth was a special time for appeasing the *piśācas* and Goddesses with human sacrifices.

It is on Piśācacaturdaśī that the cannibal ogres Gurumāpā (see Slusser 1982: 364) and Tuṇḍi (see Anderson 1971: 266-8) are worshipped, two insatiable demons who seize and eat mainly children. It is on Piśācacaturdaśī that, "men masked and costumed to represent twelve different divinities, dominated by Neta Ajima[10] herself, come to Nar Devi Tole near Neta's temple. They perform ceremonial dances all through the night and into the following morning. Animals, essentially buffaloes and lambs, are sacrificed to all these dancing deities, and when the blood is drunk by the performers they dance in fiendish glee, possessed thereby with the spirit of the god or goddess they represent" (Anderson 1971: 266). Finally, it is on the same day that the local goddess Vatsalā from Deopatan is made an offering to, again with many traces of human sacrifice. Since this festival demonstrates, perhaps, best the virulent conflict between Śiva and Śakti, it should be outlined here in a bit more detail:[11]

The Vatsalājātrā takes place in the city of Deopatan (situated 3 km northeast of Kathmandu), a city better known by the name of its main sanctum: the temple of Paśupatinātha, Nepal's tutelary deity and a favoured place of pilgrimage throughout the country. The *jātrā* commences with a series of animal sacrifices: a cock on the *pratipad* day of Caitra, a goat on *dvādaśī*, and a buffalo in the night of the *trayodaśī*, the day which marks the beginning of the actual Vatsalājātrā since, from then on, the head of the buffalo is kept for four days until the end of the procession.

In the same night the seat (*pīṭha*) of Vatsalā is covered with cooked rice (Nev. *jā-pyāvanegu-pūjā*, Skt. *annaprāśanna*). This ritual

---

[10] Netā-ajimā alias Naradevī is a grandmother goddess in Kathmandu who used to demand human sacrifices and still requires regular blood sacrifices (cp. Slusser 1982: 344).

[11] For a more detailed description of this festival see Michaels 1984, id. 1989: 51ff. and id. (forthcoming).

is repeated one more time since there are mainly two *guthis*[12] or religious communities involved: Cva (lit. "Upper") Guthi and Kva (lit. "Lower") Guthi. Both terms are related to the topography of Deopatan, to the upper and lower parts of the city, but they are also associated with the dominance of Śakti over Śiva, for during the festival, the Cva Guthi is responsible for Vatsalā, while the Kva Guthi takes care of Śiva. Another important deity is a so-called Dhvā̃dyaḥ, lit. "jackal-god". He is cared for during the rituals by a member of the Śresṭha caste who becomes the so-called Dhvā̃juju, lit. "jackal's king", and thus exercises semi-priestly functions.

In the following night — which is Piśācacaturdaśī, when Śiva is also worshipped as Lukumahādyaḥ — icons of Vatsalā and Śiva are brought from their god-houses (Nev. *dyaḥchẽ*) to a public place east of the Vatsalā temple. The icon of Vatsalā is a silver statue surrounded by copper or silver garlands which depict, among accompanying deities, the Eight Mothers (Aṣṭamātṛkā) and Eight Bhairavas. Śiva is represented by a small *liṅga*, which is, however, mostly covered. He also gets decorated with the garlands of Vatsalā during the night. Both icons are placed on two separate seats with a distance of approximately 8-9 meters between them. During the whole night both deities are worshipped in a great number of rituals, of which I shall sketch out only two, in order to demonstrate the way in which Śiva is threatened by Vatsalā.

Around midnight, members of a special *guthi*, for instance, build a pyre between Śiva and Vatsalā. This is a clear and recognised symbol of human sacrifice, for which Vatsalā is famous: not only do the local chronicles, the Vaṃśāvalīs written in the 19th century either in Nepālī or Nevārī, mention this fact,[13] there are also frescoes on the outer, eastern wall of the Vatsalā temple in which jack-

---

[12] Since the Vatsalājātrā is a Newar festival, I prefer the Nevārī spelling instead of Nep. *guṭhī*.

[13] Bhāṣāvaṃśāvalī I: 83; Wright Chronicle, p. 130; Padmagiri's Chronicle, p. 41.

als are depicted with human limbs sticking out of their mouths. I have also collected several oral myths relating that Vatsalā used to kill inhabitants of Deopatan and that it was only by the courageous Karmācārya priest named Bandhudatta Ācājū[14] that she was forced to give up her cruel claims. However, she agreed only on the condition that she would be given a permanent seat in a temple at the Bāgmatī River, which should not have any closable windows or doors, so that she could always inhale the smoke of the funeral pyres from the cremation grounds nearby. Indeed, the Vatsalā temple is the only one in Deopatan which cannot be closed.

This portrayal of Vatsalā differs greatly from her benevolent, peaceful image, as described in the Nepālamāhātmya of the Himavatkhaṇḍa ascribed to the Skandapurāṇa, where Vatsalā is the sweet, obedient and subordinate wife of Paśupati:

> *mama vātsalyato yasmāt sthātum icchasi pārvatī /*
> *tasmāt te vatsalā nāma bhaviṣyati varānane //*
> *mamāgneyyāṃ sadā tiṣṭha mamājñāto maheśvarī /*
> *vāgmatyāḥ payasi snātvā dṛṣṭvā tvāṃ vatsalām śive //*
> *drakṣyanti māṃ narā ye vai te syuḥ kailāsagāminaḥ /*
> (NepM I.39-41ab)
>
> Since you, Pārvatī, whose face is so beautiful, wish, due to your affection, to remain (with me), your name will be 'Vatsalā' (the devoted one, the tender one, also: small calf). Maheśvarī, remain by my command forever to the southeast of me.[15] Those people who behold me after having bathed in the waters of the Vāgmatī River and seen you, Śivā, as Vatsalā, shall in truth be such as shall go to the Kailāsa Mountain.

---

[14] A common figure in Nepalese mythology, especially in the popular Matsyendranātha festival.

[15] The Vatsalā Temple is indeed located southeast of the Paśupatinātha Temple.

At the end of the long night of Piśācacaturdaśī the *pīṭha* of Vatsalā is showered with rice beer (Nev. *thvã*, Nep. *jāḍ*). It is remarkable that before this orgiastic part of the ritual takes place both icons are tied together on the *pīṭha*. When, however, the alcohol is brought in five huge jars (Nev. *thvãtepa*, Nep. *ghyāmpo*), the icons are taken out of the temple again. Then the rice-beer is poured through three extremely large buffalo horns (donated V.S. 1852 by Rānā Bahādura Śāha) onto the *pīṭha* of Vatsalā until it rises up to the ankles of four tantrik Karmācārya priests. At that moment, the Dhvãjuju howls like a jackal and this is the sign to open three pipes leading into the Bāgmatī River where participants in the ritual then take a shower in the beer.

It is, of course, mainly Vatsalā who eats and drinks unclean food in this ritual, but Śiva is made a witness to the scene and has to tolerate it. That Śiva is opposed to this ritual enacted on his consort is demonstrated by the procession of the Vatsalā festival which follows in the next three days. Vatsalā and Śiva are first tied together on a processional litter (Nev. *khaḥ*, Nep. *khaṭ*), with Vatsalā on top of Śiva, who is now represented by a bigger wooden *liṅga*. In the first night Vatsalā is carried to the Paśupatinātha temple nearby. Paśupati, however, who does not want her to enter the temple, directs his temple priests, the so-called Bhaṭṭas (see Michaels 1988) – who are vegetarian South Indian Brahmins in contradistinction to the Newar Karmācārya priests responsible for the festival -, to close the temple doors. Vatsalā, outraged and disappointed, threatens Śiva/Paśupati that she will leave the town: she is carried through the western city gate where she rams the city walls. Śiva, then, feels sorry and has his priests call her back. For two days Vatsalā is carried through the whole city and worshipped with lots of ritually pure gifts: *sindūra*, flowers, umbrellas, fruits etc. As a sign of reconciliation the main temple priest finally presents her with a piece of red cloth, symbol for a sari.

Vegetarian and meat-eating deities

In the Vatsalā festival there is a clear conflict between Śiva and Śakti or between vegetarian and meat eating (female) deities and their traditions. The same conflict was solved more peacefully in the myth of Lukumahādyaḥ, although the ritual on Piśācacaturdaśī involves unclean food given to Śiva. This is no doubt a fundamental opposition in South Asia, and one could summarize the differences involved in the following way:

	Vegetarian deities	**Meat-eating deities**
forms of worship	*pūjā*, homa, prayer *(bhakti)*; personal esoteric elements; communicative, isolating	(animal) sacrifice; technico-ritualistic elements; communal, compelling, integrating
time of worship	related to personal horoscope and individual motives *(vrata)*; optional	related to calendrically fixed days in connection with the harvest cycle and seasons; obligatory
food	*naivedya*, fruits, cooked food	*bali*, alcohol, blood, eggs, animals
location	inside settlements, temple	beyond settlements, open shrine
type	*mūrti*, iconic	*pīṭha*, aniconic
"elements"	water *(tīrtha)*, air, "vertical"	soil *(pīṭha)*, "horizontal"
mobility	movable, can manifest itself almost anywhere, pilgrims move to the gods	immovable, rooted in the soil, pilgrims move with icons of the gods in processions
festivals	individualistic, related to ego, clan or lineage	collective, related to community of different castes

kinship	patrilineal, married, related to forefathers	matrilineal, unmarried, related to sisters, mothers and grandmothers, demons
participants	service, merchants (brain-worker); few participants in rituals	peasants (hand-worker); many participants in rituals
priests	Brahmin, "Vedic"; priesthood hereditary, priest — *yajamāna* relationship	local, sectarian, "tantrik"; priesthood not always hereditary, sharing of priestly functions
functions	individual "aims": *(puṇya):* personal welfare, wealth and health, sons, — ... death, salvation	common "aims": welfare of the village, harvest, rain, — ... life, prosperity (creation and recreation)
	protection against personal diseases and danger	protection against epidemic/diseases, misharvest, earthquakes, evil demons and spirits
	protection through cosmic harmony	protection through "magic" harmony (*maṇḍala, yantra*)
categories	purity; male patriarchal; raised, superior deities; city deities; peaceful; positive; benevolent; pure; high; supralocal	power; female, subordinate; fallen deities; village deities; angry, fierce; desacralizing, negative; malevolent; impure; low; local

Despite arguable entries in this table, despite disputable concepts, isolating entities which, perhaps, cannot be separated in this way, and despite overlapping categories on both sides, we *can* distinguish these two traditions no matter whether we call them "great/little", "supralocal/local", "pan-Indian/regional", "Sanskritic/folk", "Vedic/ Tantrik" etc. This is certainly facilitated if one focusses on ritual actions and the participants involved, and it is made more complicated if one focusses on myths and the belief system.

Taking this into consideration one is tempted to conclude that Piśācacaturdaśī is a day when Śiva comes under heavy oppression from the Goddess, and, roughly speaking, that the day expresses the old tension between Folk and/or Tantra and Veda. Three main justifications for such a hypothesis have been suggested so far: a) the name "Lukumahādyaḥ" denoting a Śiva who, for reasons of purity, has to hide himself; b) the myths, including their dramatic expression in the festivals of this day (e.g. Vatsalā-jātrā), which centre around a conflict between Śiva and the Goddess; c) the rituals in which Śiva is covered with either leftovers or unclean food.

As regards social groups, one is further tempted to see behind all this a kind of protest of the Newars against the brahmanical tradition and its Smārta rules for a pure conduct of life, or *vice versa* the expression of triumph of Śiva-Mahādeva over a lower, i.e. more public, level of religious practice. After all, only the indigenous Newars celebrate the festivals of Piśācacaturdaśī and not the Indo-Nepalese Parbatiyās. Perhaps, we might continue to argue, this has to do with a region at the periphery of Hinduism, or with a comparatively late or weak influence of Indo-Nepalese Brahmins in this part of the Himalayas.

Śiva oppressed by Virūpākṣa, Buddhists or a demon

Such ideas get support from another group of myths in which Śiva is exposed to great danger because he is attacked by a figure named Virūpākṣa, a demon called Bhasmāsura or by the Buddhamārgīs. Who are these figures and how are they related to Lukumahādyaḥ?

In the Himavatkhaṇḍa, Virūpākṣa is a *brāhmaṇa* who, through unintentional incest with his mother, leads a sinful life (*pāpācāra*): He just eats meat, neglects the study of the Veda, hunts after prostitutes etc. As a consequence, he loses his caste status and contracts leprosy. Tortured by this disease, he seeks relief in the Himalayas where Nemuni, the legendary founder of Nepāla, advises him to go on a long pilgrimage to 64 *liṅga-tīrthas* located mostly in the Kathmandu Valley. If Virūpākṣa bathes by these *tīrthas* and completes the Catuḥṣaṣṭiliṅgayātrā at the Paśupatinātha temple, his sins will be washed away and he will reach heaven.[16]

This is the brahmanical Sanskrit version of Virūpākṣa,[17] which provides the background for a statue of Virūpākṣa being embedded in the floor of a little shrine east of the Paśupatinātha temple. This image (cp. Bangdel 1987: fig. 45), which is related to Lukumahādyaḥ (see below), depicts a man with a third eye on his

---

[16] *pūrvokto yo dvijo 'gastya virūpākṣo 'bhidhānakaḥ /*
antarvedyāṃ nagaryāṃ sa kule mahaty ajāyata //
pūrvajanmavipākena pāpācāro 'bhavad dhi saḥ /
mātṛgamanasambhūtaṃ kaścit surāpānarato 'niśam //
māṃsāhārī tv anācārī veśyāgamanatatparaḥ /
jātibhraṣṭo 'nvayais tyakto vedaśāstravivarjitaḥ //
kiṃcitkālāntare 'sau hi deśād viniryayau mune /
tyaktvā priyām priyaṃ gotraṃ vrīḍayā vyathito dvijaḥ //
bhramati sma kṣitideśān nirjanaḥ kuṣṭhapīḍitaḥ /
himādriṃ prāptavān laṅgya deśād deśaṃ vanād vanam //
(Himavatkhaṇḍa 89.11-15)

[17] See for similar versions in Nepālī: Rājāvaṃśāvalī IV: 4 and Bhāṣāvaṃśāvalī I: 29.

forehead, so that tradition declares it to be a form of Śiva. Art historians, however, concentrating on the tribal features of the sculpture (flat nose, broad lips, curly hair) prefer to see in the face an "ethnic type, quite unlike the more 'Aryan' faces of other figures" (Pal 1974: 52). J.C. Regmi (V.S. 2039: 16) declares that it is without doubt of Kirāti origin. The statue is indeed known among the Rai-Limbus or Kiratis from East Nepal as Kirāteśvara or Kirātsor although the Kirāteśvara-liṅga in the Mṛgasthalī forest near the Paśupatinātha temple is not known to them.[18] Moreover, Virūpākṣa is claimed by some Hindu movements among the Kiratis as proof of their long Hindu tradition.[19] It is this figure which is on the cover page of the first issue of the journal *Kirāteśvara Sandeśa* — a special number published when on Śivarātri V.S. 2041 a Śivajyotisiddha Kirāteśvara Temple was established at Sītapurī in Jhāpā District.

Only the upper part of the Virūpākṣa statue at Deopatan can be seen: the lower half is embedded in a hole of muddy water. As the water level of the Bāgmatī River changes, the statue moves up and down but people insist that it just emerges, very slowly, a few millimeters every year. As a reason for this, they say that pilgrims worshipping Paśupati share with Virūpākṣa half of their religious merit (*puṇya*),[20] and, therefore, the extremely popular worship of this deity is thus called *ādhādharmapūjā* (Nep. *ādhā* < Skt. *ardha*, "half"). Is Virūpākṣa attractive for most devotees of Paśupati because his features as well as his myths reflect somebody who does not fulfil the standards and values of brahmanical Smārta-Hinduism?

---

[18] I am grateful to Martin Gänszle for this information.

[19] See, for instance, the article of Bulu Mukāruṅga Bāntava titled "Kirātaharūko Parama Iṣṭadeva Śiva ra Śaivadharma," in Kirāteśvara-Sandeśa I: 125-6.

[20] See, however, for a different version Vaidya 1986: 293: "The more it [Virūpākṣa] rises, the greater will be the sins and crimes in this age of Kali (Yuga)."

This assumption is, to a certain extent, supported by the story of Virūpākṣa as told in the Buddhist Vaṃśāvalī in Nevārī known as the Wright Chronicle:[21]

> Birūpāksha, when twelve years of age, saw it written in his horoscope that he would commit incest with his mother. He was so disgusted at this that he left his home and became a devotee. His mother, however, did the same, and after several years they met, without knowing each other, and the incest was committed. Afterwards Birūpāksha, becoming aware of his sin, went to Siva to enquire how he was to purify himself. Siva told him to drink twelve loads of melted copper. Seeing that he would lose his life by following this advice, he next went to a bhikshū, who gave him a rosary, and told him to recite certain holy names while counting it, and that when the thread of it was worn out he would be pure. Birūpāksha for a time followed this advice, but, finding the occupation very tiresome, he gave it up and went on travel. During his journey, he saw a man cutting down a tree with a needle, and on asking why he did not cut it with a hatchet, the man replied that that would be too laborious a work. This brought him to his senses, and he returned to his rosary, but soon left it again. Then he saw a bird taking water with its bill from a tank full of water, and dropping it into an empty one to fill it. This again brought him to his senses, and he returned to his rosary. Once more, however, he forsook it, but on seeing a man attempting to make a mountain and a plain level with a few handfuls of dust, he returned to his rosary and completed his task. After this he saw an emblem of Siva (the Linga), and saying, 'It was you who advised me to lose my life,' he began to break every emblem of Siva he met with. At last he came to Pashupati, who prayed

[21] This Buddhist Vaṃśāvalī was translated into English by two Vajrācārya pandits employed by Daniel Wright, a resident surgeon at the British Residency in Kathmandu, who edited the translation in 1877. I have not studied the original manuscript (kept in the Cambridge University Library, No. Add. 1952A), but David Gellner, who had used it, remarks: "In a number of places the translation glosses over or omits vital information." (Gellner 1987: 367 fn.)

> to Buddh to save him, and through his blessing, and being provided with a head-dress of Buddh, Birūpāksha, instead of breaking him, worshipped him. For this reason every emblem of Siva is a little bent to one side, except the one at Pashupati. Then, as Buddhists do not eat when the sun has gone down, he requested the sun, whom he caught hold of with one hand, not to set until he had taken his meal; and in this posture he died at Pashupati. (Wright Chronicle, p. 91f.)[22]

Besides its almost oedipal connotations, which, although astonishingly rare in the vast field of Indian mythology, are not of immediate interest here, this myth confronts us again not only with a conflict between two different religious traditions, this time Buddhists versus Śaivas, but also with the theme of covering Śiva or his *liṅga*. Here it is called a head-dress, and the background to this myth is a famous Nepalese ritual, famous for its syncretistic implications: On each *mukhāṣṭamī*, i.e. the 8th day of the bright half in Kārttika, the main *liṅga* in the Paśupatinātha temple is supposedly worshipped as Avalokiteśvara and is covered for this purpose with a crown of the Bodhisattva.[23]

In the Hindu *vaṃśāvalīs* written in Nepālī, the Buddhists are, however, accused of throwing their leftovers onto Paśupatiṇātha.

> ... the Buddhists became very powerful and built a Vihār called Punya-Vihār which was inhabited by their class, who used to throw leavings of their food and drink on Paśupatināth every evening and next morning remove it from his image and worship it. (...) While they were going on in their own manner the Śivamārgīs made an unsuccessful attempt to prevent their throwing the *ucchiṣṭa* or leavings of food on

[22] See for a long oral version of this myth Vaidya 1986: 290-292.

[23] Lévi 1905/I: 361, Nepali 1965: 331, Slusser 1982: 227-8, Vaidya 1986: 290. There are, however, strong doubts wheter this ritual was ever really practised in the Paśupathināthа temple or whether it was just claimed to be the case.

Paśupatināth. (Padmagiri's Chronicle, p. 38)[24]

According to these chronicles, it was only through Śaṅkarācārya that the Bauddhamārgīs were defeated and the Śivamārgīs obtained power again over the Paśupatinātha. The covering of the *liṅga* was, thus, not an inclusivistic act by which Paśupatinātha was made a follower of Buddha but, on the contrary, he became a victim of the Buddhists and could only become pure again through Śaṅkara.[25]

Both the Hindu and the Buddhist *vaṃśāvalīs* are brought together with the myth of Lukumahādyaḥ in a third myth which has been orally handed down in, basically, two variants: (a) one focussing on Virūpākṣa, (b) the other on a demon called Bhasmāsura:

> a) ... Virūpākṣa, angered at Śiva's recommended penance, tried to destroy the god. Fleeing in terror, Śiva sought refuge in the interior of a domestic rubbish heap. He was undetected in this unlikely spot, and the chase was at last terminated by the Buddha's clever intervention at Paśupati's shrine. Śiva emerged, by chance, at the time of Piśācacaturdaśī in honor of the Mother Goddesses; the startled family invited the divine guest to share the meal, albeit one traditionally not to his taste. (Slusser 1982: 232)

> b) Shiva était ému du zèle d'un démon appelé Basmasur qui priait sans cesse et il décida de lui accorder la réalisation d'un voeu. Basmasur demanda le pouvoir réduire en cendres tout être qu'il touchera sur la tête. A peine Shiva eut-il accordé cette faculté qu'il s'aperçut que le démon voulait vérifier sur lui-même si son don était efficace, Shiva s'enfuit alors à travers le monde pour lui échapper. Vishnou se réveillant d'un de ses longs sommeils se rendit compte qu'il devait intervenir pour le sauver. Il apparut sur terre sous la forme d'une jeune femme attractive qui

[24] Cp. Bhāṣāvaṃśāvalī II: 18, Wright Chronicle, pp. 118-121.

[25] On this famous conflict between Śaṅkara (or one of his followers) and the Buddhists in Nepal see Lienhard 1978: 148f., Ṭaṇḍan V.S. 2043, Nepāla V.S. 2043: 17.

> arrêta Basmasur et lui proposa de danser. Le démon un peu timide, lui avoua qu'il ne savait pas comment s'y prendre mais il se laissa convaincre par la merveilleuse créature à répéter les gestes que Vishnou lui montrerait. C'est ainsi qu'il mit la main sur son front et provoqua sa propre perte. Shiva sortit alors d'un fossé, où à bout de souffle, il avait dû se cacher. (Vézies 1981: 79f., cp. Anderson 1971: 264f., Nepali 1965: 293-4)

All these myths indicate that Śiva hides himself on Piśācacaturdaśī because he is mocked by the goddesses, or attacked by Buddhists, the demon Bhasmāsura or an infuriated Virūpākṣa — an exponent of somebody who lost his brahmanical status. He hides in a hole under garbage, unclean food or leftovers. In his myths, Lukumahādyaḥ, thus, is clearly identified with Śiva, proposing various reasons why Śiva is worshipped (and named) in a "hidden manifestation". Either Devī is mocking Śiva or Śiva is endangered by Virūpākṣa or the Buddhists.

Lukumahādyaḥ and protective stones

In his rituals, however, another identity of Lukumahādyaḥ is suggested. First of all, it is surprising that the ritual of Lukumahādyaḥ is mainly celebrated in Kathmandu but far less in other cities of the Kathmandu Valley. In Kathmandu it is one of the main days in the festival calendar because it happens to fall together with the many festivities of the grandmother goddesses (*ajimā̃*) and with the Ghoḍejātrā, a crowded and spectacular horse festival in the Tuṇḍikhel area the following day (new moon). In Pāṭan, however, Lukumahādyaḥ is much less known and worshipped since there are Lukumahādyaḥ stones worshipped only in the courtyards of some private houses, but not, for instance, in the monasteries. In other cities with a majority Newar population there are either none or only very few deities called Lukumahādyaḥ. Thus, in Deopatan there is no Lukumahādyaḥ stone, in Bhaktapur there are only one or two stones called by this name, and the same is true for Pharpiṅg. In Kīrtipur and Dhulikhel there are several Lukumahādyaḥ stones but apparently they have different functions and identities (e.g. Gaṇeśa, Kumāra, Aju-Aji: see Devkota 1984: 14f.). In Dhulikhel, for instance, these stones are not (or not only) worshipped on Piśācacaturdaśī but (also) on all kinds of occasions (e.g. marriage, Dasaĩ, Śivarātri, any kind of religious feast etc.).[26] Given the overall situation in the Kathmandu valley it seems that many different stones are declared to be Lukumahādyaḥ. To mention just a few examples:

a) *Pikhā- lakhu* (var. *pikā lakhi*, *°-lukhā*, *°-luku)* means (according to Lienhard 1986: 136, fn. 24) "das außerhalb (*pikhā*) des Hauses Verborgene (*lakhu*)" (what is hidden outside the house). Although *lakhu-* means probably just "door",[27] the function of the *pikhā-lakhu* is clear (and also thoroughly described by Lienhard, ibid.). It denotes "1. common entrance of a courtyard. 2. guardian stone in front of a threshold (syn *chetrapāla*)" (Gutschow et al. 1987: *s.v.*). It is a stone or a part of the street in front of any Newar house sometimes marked with a cult object in lotus- or *maṇḍala*-like form. Herdick (1987: 261f.) calls it "an integrative 'contact point' between the house and its inhabitants and the transcendental world of the dead and the deities". All kinds of ritual material brought in or out of the house or passing it (e.g., at processions) is placed on this stone: any kind of *pūjā* material for the rites of passage; the firepot with whose help the funeral pyre is lit later on; food for the deities at Māpūjā, Pitṛpūjā etc.; the bier before being carried to the cremation ground; the Dhaludyaḥ or lamp deity, kept in a clay pot, is smashed on this stone when the cremation is completed; etc. Moreover, during processions the litter (Nev. *khaḥ*) stops on the *pikhā-lakhu*. In Kīrtipur the *pikhā lukhā* of the Cīlāco Stūpa is the

---

[26] From the fact that the cult of Lukumahādyaḥ is strongest in Kathmandu one can assume that other cities imitated it. Unfortunately, the chronicles and other texts or documents do not mention any historical event which could explain this concentration on Kathmandu.

[27] Cp. Manandhar 1986: *s.v.*: "the area outside the main entrance of a house, the portion of the street or road just in front of the house."

easternmost of altogether four or five such Lukumahādyaḥs.[28] All these stones represent Śiva who is believed to reside under the city of Kīrtipur (Herdick 1988: 100).

b) This idea of a deity which lives underneath the city and manifests itself in stones is current also in Bhaktapur and practically all Newar towns. There is, for instance, the concept of the *chvāsa lhvã* which is a "stone in the street (for the disposal of objects exerting a magical threat, such as clothes of the dead, umbilical cords, ashes of the torch used to exorcise evil spirits from a house; furthermore, the place for pacifying the ajimā [grandmother goddess])." (Gutschow et al. 1987: *s.v.*).[29] *Chvāsas* are basically connecting points to *bhūtas* and *pretas*, i.e. those dead persons who have not (yet) become pacified ancestors (*pitṛ*), for whom the funeral rituals (*śrāddha*) have not been properly performed or who died a violent, untimely or accidental death and are thus determinded to become *bhūtas*. As Niels Gutschow informed me, the only Lukumahādyaḥ stone iṇ Bhaktapur is also called *chvāsa*, and on Piśācacaturdaśī many people in this town worship these *chvāsa* stones.

c) As in the case of the *chvāsa lhvã*, it is commonly believed among Newars that dangerous deities hide in the earth and endanger the settlements from there unless they are pacified. Thus it is said of the Navasāgara Bhagavatī of Bisālnagara, that "the original image of this Devī, made by Viswa-karmā, was so frightful, that no one would pass that way. The people therefore buried it, and covered

---

[28] Herdick 1988: 100, 105 mentions only four Lukumahādyaḥs; he kindly informed me, however, that he recently discovered a fifth Lukumahādyaḥ in front of the old palace.

[29] See also Pieper 1975: 68-9: "It is believed that a goddess Chowasa Ajima, who takes everything unclean and spoiled, dwells under the city and is manifest in the pavement. Black stone slabs with various ornamentations are placed in the brickwork of the street surface to mark her body, and people take their leftovers and household waste as sacrifices to these stones," and Herdick (1987: 247), for a distinction between favourably disposed *(bhī̃chvāsā)* and unfavourably disposed *(mabhī̃chvāsā)* deities.

the place with stones." (Wright Chronicle, p. 160). Very often, the seat (Nev. *pīth* < Skt. *pīṭha*) of a deity, mainly a manifestation of Durgā, Bhairava or Gaṇeśa, is represented aniconically, i.e. it consists of just a simple unhewn stone, mostly located in the fields or in the streets.

d) Stones, often called *dvakā*, also symbolize the evil spirits of the crossroads (see Gutschow et al. 1987: fig. 15). The so-called *bvasāla* ("fleeing horse stone") in Deopatan, which is actually an upright water gargoyle, is, for example, said to have become a horse ridden by the goddess Pīgāmāī at midnight in order to catch victims; it is used during the main festival of this goddess, which also takes place at Piśācacaturdaśī, as a pole for tying animals to, which are to be sacrificed later on.

These stone deities, which represent mainly demons, ghosts and ancestral spirits, are either directly identified with Śiva-Lukumahādyaḥ or they show features very similar to those of Lukumahādyaḥ. Ritually too, it is to these stones that refuse or garbage is offered, or to the deities who are believed to reside in garbage dumps.[30] It is, on the other hand, not necessarily garbage which covers the seats of such godlings and spirits but simply dust or soil, since their stones are located just under the earth or in the form of a stone on the pavement. The same is true for Lukumahādyaḥ stones in Kathmandu: they, too, can be hidden among and covered by extremely filthy garbage,[31] but they can also

---

[30] "The Chwāsa is a socially accepted place where people can throw household rubbish." (Devkota 1984: 12). "Kaladeo, the spirit, is believed to reside at a place where garbage from the area is deposited." (id. p. 14). "[...] it is to these beings [*bhūt, pret*,etc.] that refuse or inedible parts (beak, feathers, etc.) of a sacrificial animal are offered (while edible parts are dedicated to the gods)." (Höfer and Shrestha 1973: 75). "Witches control evil spirits and some deities by invoking them with spells, [...] and feeding them with refuse (N[ep.] *putali)*, ideally consisting of nail and hair clippings of their victims." (Durkin-Longley 1982: 67).

[31] Strolling through the courtyards of Kathmandu I have seen (besides the usual household rubbish) human excrements, or even decaying rats and cats on

be a flat open stone on the pavement. What is surprising is that even if the Lukumahādyaḥ stones have the shape of a *liṅga*, they never have the typical ring-stone (*yonī* or *jaladroṇī*).

Conclusion

When one takes these protective stones into consideration, another feature of the religious background of Lukumahādyaḥ literally sticks its head out of the ground. One could perhaps describe it as a kind of network of religious forces, gods or godlings, spirits and ancestors underlying the city and connecting individual households with these forces, in order to protect the inhabitants. Very often, the connecting points are just stones in the streets or in the fields covered by dust and filth, neglected for most of the year. Only for certain ritual purposes are they cleaned and regarded as seats or places of various deities.

What remains essential in the cult of Lukumahādyaḥ is a more or less simple stone with various religious identities and mythological explanations ranging from low to high, simple to complex, local to supralocal, specific to common etc. It remains an open question whether a *piśāca* became Śiva or Śiva a *piśāca*, whether the deity was raised or degraded, whether it was related to the Goddess from its origin or whether this was an aspect added later, through Indian influence.

However, one could perhaps suggest the following scheme of layers in the historical development: First there is nothing other than a simple, unhewn and uncarved stone representing an indigenous, pre-Hinduistic, possibly not anthropomorphic deity, most likely a dangerous demon. No matter whether it had the shape of a *liṅga* or not, this stone was associated with Śiva-Mahādeva and it was declared to be a *liṅga;* sometimes the original stone was even

---

Lukumahādyaḥ stones.

replaced by a modelled or carved *liṅga*, sometimes not. Why was the stone identified with Śiva? A possible answer could be that the demon had no name or that it was dangerous to call him by his original name lest his power be provoked. I have, of course, no proof for this hypothesis but it is surprising that often highly localized deities in Nepal are called by a collective name (e.g. Pīgādyaḥ or -māī, Gaṇeś, etc.), although their function is extremely specialized, for example, helping only in the case of toothache.

From this level onwards it is not clear anymore whether a highly localized deity is raised to a Great God or whether the High Tradition incorporates a local deity in order to extend its influence. It seems to be yet another case where it is almost impossible to determine the direction of religious developements: We simply don't know whether it was an upward movement (Sanskritization) or a downward one (Marriott's parochialization). If, however, the stone was identified with Śiva, why was this Great God not strong enough to overcome the demonic deity in the stone? Why was the stone/*liṅga* instead of Gupteśvara still called Lukumahādeva, "Hiding or Hidden Mahādeva"? Apparently there were counterforces; as such the myths mention a demon (*piśāca*), the Goddesses, the Buddhists and Virūpākṣa, but there are many instances where these opponents of Śiva were incorporated into his mythology without making him hide. Thus, Lukumahādyaḥ must still be more than just Mahādeva hiding himself. He resists, to a certain extent, the influence of the Great Tradition.

However, we must not forget that all this happens in a world which we have left with Empedokles or Plato at the latest, in a world which has no clear boundaries between man and nature, matter and soul, one's own and foreign gods, — a world in which everything mixes because forces, substances, winds and breath flow into bodies or objects and flow out again so that a bodiless self, truth without sensation and thoughts without feelings become literally senseless, a world which is so open, so porous, so oceanic, so coalescent and unlimited that all our attempts to understand it by drawing boundaries and limitations, or by separating and differentiating, might be useful for us, might give us insight into possible historical developments, and might please us with its different layers and levels, but will never make us see the point.

If, on the other hand, we do not want to get lost in piecemeal- and fragmentary studies of Hinduism, if we still — besides its many diversifications and alterations — want to get an idea of what it all means we must focus on the determining principle itself. India and Nepal have always been open to a multitude of religious forces, to new gods and it has always been risky to exclude gods, ideas or beliefs.

It is this principle of, as I would call it, unlimited and reciprocal substitutions that make valid definitions in Hinduism not only difficult but, in the last analysis, even impossible, for to understand a rule implies, according to Wittgenstein, the capability to carry on with it independently. "The story is often told of the foreigner visiting the Kathmandu Valley who asks a Newar whether he is a Hindu or a Buddhist, and gets the simple but confusing reply 'Yes!'." (Gellner 1988: 41) It is not the Newar who is confused, it is our dilemma that, at least in the academic field, this rule cannot be continued.

Acknowledgements

Thanks are due to the following friends for letters and oral information on Lukumahādyaḥ in their special fields: Martin Gänszle on Rais (or Kirātis), David Gellner on Pāṭan, Niels Gutschow on Bhaktapur and Reinhard Herdick on Kīrtipur. I would also like to thank Nutan Dhar Sharma for discussions and assistance in the field work. Moreover, I gratefully acknowledge the support given by the *Deutsche Forschungsgemeinschaft* in the past years for my work on the Paśupatinātha Temple upon which this paper is based. Last but not least I thank Philip Pierce and Katrina Kelsey for revising my English. Parts of this paper have also been read at a "Seminar on German Research on Nepal - Results and Problems: The DFG Nepal Research Programme 1980-1990" (March 12-15, 1990 in Kathmandu). A summary and some new findings on the rituals of Lukumahādyaḥ, along with comments by G. Tandon, will be edited shortly by B. Kölver in the proceedings of this conference.

References

I. Texts

Bhāṣāvaṃśāvalī	[Pt.1:] ed. Nayanātha Pauḍela. Kathmandu: Nepāla Rāṣṭriya Pustakālaya, V.S. 2020.
	bhāga 2: ed. Devīprasāda Laṃsāla. Kathmandu: Nepāla Rāṣṭriya Pustakālaya, V.S. 2033.
Devamālā (-Vaṃśāvalī)	comp. Yogī Devīnātha, ed. Sūra Śaṃśer J.B. Rāṇā. Mṛgasthalī [Deopatan]: Gorakṣapīṭha, V.S. 2013.
Gopālarājavaṃśāvalī	ed. and trans. Dhanavajra Vajrācārya and Kamal P. Malla. Stuttgart: Franz Steiner, 1985 (Nepal Research Centre Publications, 9).
Hasrat, Bikram Jit (transl.)	*History of Nepal as told by its own and contemporary chroniclers.* Hoshiarpur 1970.
Himavatkhaṇḍa	*(Skandapurāṇamadhye)*, [with Pariśiṣṭa]. Kāśī: Gorakṣaṭillākāśī, V.S. 2013 (Gorakṣagranthamālā, 69).
Nepālamāhātmya	Ed. et transl. H. Uebach. München: Fink Verlag, 1970.
Padmagiri	see: Hasrat, Bikram Jit.

[*Rājavaṃśāvalī*] *Kāṭhmāṇḍu-Upatyakāko ek Rājavaṃśāvalī*, ed. Bālacandra Śarmā. *Prācīna Nepāla*, vol. 4 (July 1968) - vol. 6 (Jan. 1969).

Wright, Daniel (ed.) *History of Nepal - translated from the Parbatiyā by Munshi Shew Shunker Singh* and Pandit Shrī Gunānand. Cambridge: University Press, 1877.

II. Books, articles etc.

Anderson, Mary M. 1971. *The festivals of Nepal.* London: Allen & Unwin.

Bangdel, Lain Singh 1987. *Nepal - Zweitausendfünfhundert Jahre nepalische Kunst.* München: List Verlag.

Crooke, W. 1894. *An introduction to the popular religion and folklore of Northern India.* Allahabad: Government Press.

Devkota, Padam Lal 1984. Illness interpretation and modes of treatment in Kirtipur. In *Contributions to Nepalese Studies* XI.2:11-20.

Durkin-Longley, Maureen Suzanne 1982. *Ayurveda in Nepal: A medical belief system in action.* Phil. Diss. (Univ. of Wisconsin- Madison) Ann Arbor: University Microfilms International.

Eichinger Ferro-Luzzi, Gabriella 1987. *The self-milking cow and the bleeding Liṅgam - criss-cross of motifs in Indian temple legends.* Wiesbaden: Harrassowitz.

Gellner, David N. 1987. The Newar Buddhist Monastery - an anthropological and historical typology. In N. Gutschow and A. Michaels (eds.) *Heritage of the Kathmandu Valley - Proceedings of an International Conference in Lübeck,* June 1985. Sankt Augustin: VGH Wissenschaftsverlag, pp. 365-414.

Id. 1988. *Monk, householder and priest: Newar Buddhism and its hierarchy of ritual.* Unpubl. D.Phil thesis Oxford (xerox).

Gutschow, N., B. Kölver and I. Shresthacarya 1987. *Newar towns and buildings - An illustrated dictionary Newārī - English.* Sankt Augustin: VGH Wissenschaftsverlag.

Herdick, Reiṇhard 1987. Death ritual in Kīrtipur in relation to urban space - on the evolution of a complex ritual. In N. Gutschow and A. Michaels (eds.) *Heritage of the Kathmandu Valley - Proceedings of an International Conference in Lübeck,* June 1985. Sankt Augustin: VGH Wissenschaftsverlag, pp. 235-276.

Id. 1988. *Kirtipur - Stadtgestalt, Prinzipien*

der Raumordnung und gesellschaftliche Funktionen einer Newar-Stadt. München/Köln/London: Weltforum Verlag.

Höfer, András and B.P. Shrestha 1973. Ghost exorcism among Brahmans of Central Nepal. In *Central Asiatic Journal* 17.1: 51-77.

Lévi, Sylvain 1905. *Le Népal - Étude historique d'un Royaume Hindou.* 3 vols. Paris: Ernest Leroux.

Lienhard, Siegfried 1978. Religionssynkretismus in Nepal. In H. Bechert (ed.) *Buddhism in Ceylon and studies on religious syncretism in Buddhist countries.* Göttingen: Vandenhoeck & Ruprecht, pp. 146-177.

Id. 1987. Dreimal Unreinheit: Riten und Gebräuche der Newars bei Geburt, Menstruation und Tod. In B. Kölver (ed.) *Formen kulturellen Wandels und andere Beiträge zur Erforschung des Himālaya.* Sankt Augustin: VGH Wissenschaftsverlag, pp. 127-154.

Manandhar, Th. L. 1986. *Newari-English Dictionary.* Delhi: Agam Kala Prakashan.

Michaels, Axel 1984. Śiva's wild and wayward calf - The goddess Vatsalā, her temple and Yātrā. In *Kailash* XI.3-4: 105-147.

Id. 1989. Paśupati's holy field and the temple priests' authority in Deopatan. In V. Bouillier et G. Toffin (eds.), *Colléction Puruṣārtha* 12, pp. 41-60: *Prêtrise, Pouvoirs et Autorité en Himalaya.*

Id. (in press). Śivarātri at Deopatan. In S. Lienhard (ed.) *Change and continuity - studies in the Nepalese culture of the Kathmandu valley.* Torino: Centre Piemontese di Studi sul Medio ed Estremo Oriente.

Id. (forthcoming). *Tīrtha und Pīṭha - Der nepalische Paśupatinātha-Tempel und sein rituelles Umfeld.* Ms. XX,562 pp.

Nepāla, Jñānamaṇi V.S. 2043. *Paśupatināṭhako Darśana Sparśana Pūjanasambandhamā Samīkṣā.* Kathmandu: Mahes Raj Pant.

Nepali, Gopal Singh 1965. *The Newars - An ethno-sociological study of a Himalayan community.* Bombay: United Asia Publications.

Padmagiri see: I. Texts: Hasrat, Bikram Jit (transl.).

Pal, Pratapaditya 1974. *The arts of Nepal.* Part 1: Sculpture. Leiden: E.J. Brill.

Penzer, N.M. 1927 Mythical beings. In *The Ocean of Story being C.H. Tawney's translation of Somadeva's Kathā Sarit Sāgara*. Vol. I, Appendix I, pp. 197-207. (Reprint) Delhi: Motilal Banarsidass.

Pieper, Jan 1975. Three cities of Nepal. In P. Oliver (ed.) *Shelter, sign and symbol*. London: Barrie and Jenkins, pp. 52-69.

Regmi, Jagadīśacandra V.S. 2039. *Nepālako Dhārmika Itihāsa*. Kathmandu: Ratna Pustaka Bhaṇḍāra.

Slusser, M. Sh. 1982. *Nepal Mandala - A cultural study of the Kathmandu valley*. 2 vols., Princeton: Princeton University Press.

Śreṣṭha, Surendra Māna, and Baladeva Juju N. S. 1108. *Kāntipura* [in Nevārī]. Yẽ (Thāyamaru): Pāsāpiṃ Jnāpa Presa.

Ṭaṇḍan, Govinda V.S. 2043. Devapāṭanako Śaṅkarācārya Maṭha. *Viśrānti* 2.2: 1-11.

Vaidya, Karunakar 1986. *Buddhist traditions and culture of the Kathmandu valley (Nepal)*. Kathmandu: Sajha Prakashan.

Vajrācārya, Puṇyaratna V.S. 2036. *Hāmro Cāḍa-parva*. (4th ed.) Kathmandu: Ratna Pustaka Bhaṇḍāra. [1st ed. V.S. 2020].

Vézies, J.-F. 1981. *Les fêtes magiques du Népal.* Paris: Editions Cesare Rancilio.
Wright, Daniel see: I. Texts.

ON HIMALAYAN BALL GAMES, HEADHUNTING, AND RELATED MATTERS

Claus Peter Zoller

Indigenous ball games (handball, football and hockey) are presently dying out in the Western and Central Himalayas. The tradition has survived in just a few villages in and around the upper Ṭons and Yamunā valleys, in a few places in southern Garhvāl and in Kumaõ.[1]

They were noticed for the first time more than 70 years ago by Gairola and Barker in a Garhvālī village. The gist of their report is:

The game is played during the festival of *makar saṁkrānti* (mid January) "between the inhabitants of the neighbouring paths.[2] The object of each side is to carry the ball over the wall at one or the other end of the ground and to obtain possession of it there. Until this possession is attained neither party can win, however far they may have carried the ball into the territory of their opponents. The ball itself is a, more or less, spherical bag of leather stuffed with odds and ends of cloth, and weighing a few pounds"(p.165). Around 50 men, bare except for loin cloth, gather on each side of the field (the number increases as the game progresses). They then assemble

---

[1] In the latter area according to Prof. M.P. Joshi, Kumaon University, Almora.

[2] 'path' in Garhvālī means a dry or a square measure. Perhaps it is a printing mistake for *paṭṭī* 'boundaries'.

in the middle of the field and fight to grab the ball. "Fainting players are dragged from the seething mass, are laid on their backs and flapped vigorously with cloths by the attendant spectators; but in a few minutes they are back again to the scrum"(p.166). "At length and none too soon, for the day is almost done, one of the winning side gets hold of the ball and the game is over. The time is 6 p.m."(p.167). The game seems to have lasted for 3 to 4 hours.

The remarkable thing about this play is that it has no apparent rules: the number of players is not fixed, nor is the length of the game. From the above report it appears that there was no score-keeping and the notion of a final victory was only vaguely defined.

Majumdar (p.270) gives us a similar description for Jaunsār. There the game is called 'pheeta' and it is played on the first three days of the month of Māgh (January-February). The first two days are intra-village games where one party is formed of the elder brothers of the families ('jethingya') and the other of the younger ones ('nanchhingya').[3] "The third day's game is more important because the hitherto intra-village sport becomes an inter-village contest..."(ibid.). "The two parties defend their sides against the ball being thrown into their respective 'goal', which not infrequently is limitless"(ibid.). "To start the game, the ball is dropped from a place of worship, and then the two parties run to catch and carry it"(ibid.).

Nand and Kumar inform us (p.141) that football ('genda') and hockey ('hindoda') are played on *makar saṁkrānti* in village Deora (upper Ṭons valley).[4] They say that the whole *paṭṭī* participates in the game.

---

[3] As for the rules of how elder and younger brothers are distributed, see Majumdar ibid.

[4] In Deora there is a regionally important temple of the god Karṇa.

Tārā Cand Ṭhākur of Manālī (Himachal Pradesh)[5] says that a kind of hockey was played in this region till a few decades ago. The players (male) would try to drive the ball of rags towards the opposing side. The number of players and the duration of the game was not determined. Nor is it clear what constituted a goal or which was the winning team. The men were fond of playing the game in the evening, after work. At certain festivals teams from different villages participated and victory meant "blessing and fertility for that village during the following year".

Another informant, Gabi Jettmar-Ṭhākur[6] on interviewing Ghiru Devi, a 90-year-old woman of village Vaśiṣṭ said the game was called 'hal gindi'[7] or 'gindu khelna'(to play ball). It was played by boys up to about 15-20 years ago in the upper Beas valley. During the festivals it was played both in the morning and evening: in village Vaśiṣṭ on 'Bost Birshu', the birthday of the sage Vasiṣṭh (April 13), in Old Manālī at 'Phagli' in January, and in the villages Gośal, Śanag, and Burua in August. The hockey gradually yielded to 'rassa-kassi', a kind of tug of war, which has been in vogue for about 35 years now.

Though we have three forms of ball games and various designations for them, the similar patterns of play are obvious. There are, however, two authors reporting somewhat deviating patterns. The first is Bahuguna (1932: 51f.), who writes about Ravaĩ (upper Yamunā valley) where the ball game 'indoro' is played on the last day of Māgh: "Two persons stand at some distance from each other and the ball is put in the middle. A third person whistles, both of

---

5 A mountain guide living in village Vaśiṣṭ near Manālī . I was able to meet and interview him in July 1989.

6 Mrs. Jettmar-Ṭhākur lives in village Vaśiṣṭ. She kindly gave me the information in a letter in August 1989.

7 This probably means a back and forth movement (see Turner 14001) with a ball, *giṇḍi*.

them run towards the ball and each tries to drag it on his side ... In this way the game is repeated again and again between different persons." Thus, in Ravaī it is important to get the ball on to one's own side.

The same fact, to get the ball on to one's own side, is also reported by Nautiyal (1981: 305-307) for village Ḍāḍāmaṇḍī and a place at the river Thal (both in Garhvāl).[8] He presents a somewhat lengthy depiction of a handball match played on *makar saṁkrānti*. I will only reproduce the most noteworthy points here. It is a game characterized by rivalry, *'pratisparddhā'* (ibid., 305). The players of the one team hail from villages to the right side of a river and the players of the other team from villages to its left. In the month of Pauṣ, Harijans of one village are told to manufacture the leather ball. This ball receives *pūjā* together with Devī or Bhairava. The guests bring along with them a banner of Devī or Bhairava into the host village, where it is sunk into the playground. Those villagers who win the game[9] take the ball together with their banner and return home, dancing the whole way.[10] After their arrival in the village, ball and deity receive *pūjā* and the whole night is spent with merry-making. Early next morning again both receive *pūjā*. Then the ball is buried in front of the temple. Long ago, all the captured balls were stored up in a room adjacent to the temple of the deity.[11]

---

[8] *jab gẽd khelnī shurū ho jātī hai to apnī-apnī taraph gẽd ko le jāne ke liye khilāṛī bahut zor lagāte hãĩ.*

[9] Formerly the players who had won the game were highly respected: *gẽd jītne vāle khilāṛī kā bahut baṛā sammān kiyā jātā thā* (ibid., 306).

[10] Unfortunately, the author does not explain whether the ball now 'belongs' to a single village or to the whole area to one side of the river.

[11] To my knowledge the only rooms that can be adjacent to a temple in the Garhvāl hills are the vestibule and (at the backside) the kitchen of the priests. Thus, it is highly probable that the balls were stored in the vestibule. Later on I will show (p.212) that these are very important details, and therefore I would like to quote the original Hindī here (ibid., 306): *dūsre din prātaḥ-kāl punaḥ devtā-viśeṣ va us gẽd kī pūjā hotī hai aur usko devtā ke mandir ke āge gāṛ diyā jātā hai. bahut pahle devtā ke mandir ke kināre vāle kamre mẽ in gẽdõ ko sãbhāl kar rakhā jātā thā.*

Before turning to my own text material, which was gathered recently in Baṅgāṇ (North-Western Garhvāl between the rivers Ṭons and Pābar)[12] I would like to, briefly, present information that I had collected on previous visits to the area. This will give the reader an impression of the present state of disintegration of this custom.

There the game is a kind of football. It is called *iṇḍuaṛɔ khēlṇɔ*[13] 'to play the (ball called) *iṇḍuaṛɔ*'. Men, young and old, used to play it almost in the manner described above. It gained special importance when played by teams from different villages on *saj̈ɔ* (meaning 'fresh' or 'the fresh month or year') which corresponds to *makar saṁkrānti*. However, only a few villages in the whole of Baṅgāṇ and Baur (the latter in Western Garhvāl) played it on this day. Why this was so will be explained presently. A new ball was used every year and was made by an outcaste Koḷṭa from the skin of a he-goat and filled with wet cowdung or moist earth. The animal was slaughtered during the *tiār* festival, which starts a month before *makar saṁkrānti* (called *pośe ri mɔsi* or 'the maternal aunt of (the month) *Pauṣ*') and ends with the *śiuriāt* festival in February. The soil is derived from a *bɔ̀stua* field, of which there are four, considered sacred, in every village. Their location changes every year. The ball, I was told, was bigger than a standard football.

The game began late in the morning after a Brāhmaṇ sprinkled consecrated rice, called *j̈indaɔ*[14] on the ball. Only male Rājpūts, dressed as usual, but barefooted, participated in the game. The ball was placed in the middle of the village square near the temple with the teams standing opposite each other. The number of players were

---

[12] I had my first chance to see a traditional ball game in January 1990 only.

[13] Probably from Old Indo-Aryan *iṇḍva-* 'two coverings made of muñja grass to protect the hands from fire' (Turner 1969).

[14] Translated literally: 'make alive'! Note also that j̈ represents a voiced affricate [dz] and ċ a voiceless dental affricate [ts].

not fixed. The game ended at the latest by *pūja*, half an hour before sunset. The winning team was the one that kept the ball longest in the opponents' side. There could be a time limit also, in which case the ball stayed longer with the side of the losing team during an *ēk tɔmakhu ri bēr* 'time of one tobacco' or in which time a hubble-bubble is smoken. Besides, it was also necessary to kick the opponents in their calves or bite into their hands.[15] However, it was not allowed to push or beat with the arms. When the game ended a he-goat was sacrificed to the presiding deity (Mahāsu). The winners kept the ball for some time before handing it over to the Koḷṭas for destruction.

Though ball games of other regions are basically similar there are also regional differences: the inter-village game is played in Garhvāl on *makar saṁkrānti* (however not in Himachal Pradesh and in Ravaī), the number of players and the duration varies, and usually, but not always, the winner-to-be must keep the ball longer in the territory of the rival side.

I had a chance to see the *iṇḍuaṛɔ* game in January 1990 in village Ciũa in Baṅgāṇ. The same day it was also played at another Baṅgāṇi village, in Bhutāṇu. Compared with the descriptions of the game as it was played in the past, I observed the following differences: it was not played on *sajɔ* but one day earlier on *ɔdɔkhɔ*. It was not an agonistic play as it used to be, with one team from the right side of the river Khɔṇiaṭɔ and the other team from its left side.[16] At the morning of *ɔdɔkhɔ* professional singers were sent from Ciũa to the villages at the other side of the valley to invite people. However, the invitation was rejected and only people from

---

[15] The motif of biting into the hand appears also in the Baṅgāṇi song 'Child-of the Sun'(see p.14).

[16] Old rivalries between Baṅgāṇi villages are at least partially identifiable with geographical demarcations like: rivers, ridges, and conceptual opposites like 'high'-'low', 'hot'-'cold', etc.

village Jāgṭa, situated at the same side as Ciũa, joined the game. There was no he-goat to be sacrificed. The game started early afternoon and lasted about 90 minutes. The size of the ball was that of a coconut. All the other details remained unchanged.

After the game the guests were invited into the houses and were served snow mixed with apricot compote, tea, brandy and snacks. I was told by several people that the game was only still played because of fear of punishment from the gods. But now the Baṅgāṇi game calls for further explanations.

First, I shall present my conclusions so that the details will be understood better. The Baṅgāṇis regard the ball as a 'head'. The game is a striving for this 'head' and winning it means capturing the rival village's 'head'.[17] If we assume that the ball games were an ancient institution — and this thesis has enough arguments in its favour — the question arises whether the villages in Garhvāl always played them on or around *makar saṁkrānti.* I believe they were always played at this astronomical point, i.e. in olden times at the winter solstice.

The reason for claiming that the game is played on this day only in a few villages in the upper Ṭons valley (see p.203) is related to the dominant god, Mahāsu. Though referred to in the singular, he includes four brothers: Boṭhɔ, Pɔvasi, Baśik and Caḷda.[18] Boṭhɔ, the eldest, is a resident of the village Hanol on the river Ṭons and never leaves his temple. Unlike Bothɔ, the other three are mobile, staying in different villages, according to a complex pattern. Pɔvasi

---

[17] The conclusions I draw in this paper are based on repeated observations and conversations in Baṅgāṇ over a period of more than five years. I am aware that a number of the motifs discussed in the following pages have their parallels in other cultures and have been pointed out by Eliade, Sontheimer, and Heesterman, only to mention a few. I intent to discuss such parallels in depth in a comprehensive study on Baṅgāṇi culture, which is now in its initial phase.

[18] For a general introduction to Mahāsu see Rose, pp.151-173 and 290-299.

and Baśik usually never cross the Ṭons. (At times Pɔvasi does so when visiting Boṭhɔ on the left of the Ṭons).[19] Ċaḷda stays 12 years each on either side. The game, so I was told, was played in all places except Boṭhɔ's place in Hanoḷ. The games were an obligation, called *khirɔ* 'duty towards a god'. Its non-observance incited the threat of *dōś* or 'divine punishment'.

It is significant that the ball was fabricated by Koḷṭas (outcastes) as the games had an agonistic dimension: the fight for the 'head'.[20] Though a Koḷṭa could be a warrior and a hero, his basic function was to help his Rājpūt master. Thus, he made and kept in hand arrows for his master for use in fight or during archery contests. The Koḷṭa activity at ball games should be seen in this context.

Consecrated rice was formerly sprinkled on the ball probably to neutralise it, since it was made by the host village Koḷṭas and was not yet neutral. By hitting the temple wall during play,[21] the leather ball contaminates it, thus making a goat sacrifice necessary. This seems contradictory because the ball was considered holy. The contradiction may be explained in this way: the game could be played either on *sajɔ̃*, that is the first day of the month of Māgh or on *ɔdɔkhɔ*, the last day of Pauṣ. The last five days of Pauṣ are distinctly named and each 'belongs' to different groups in society. Thus *ɔdɔkhɔ* is associated with certain subgroups of the Rājpūts (called *khūnd*). And *sajɔ̃*, the first day of the Māgh month, 'belongs' to the Brāhmaṇs. Mahāsu's advent in the region was probably later than the ball game and he was only subsequently associated with it.

---

[19] In April 1989 Pɔvasi undertook for the first time a yātrā to Uttarkāśi in the Yamunā valley.

[20] The homology of the ball and head is not the result of the author's analysis of cultural deep-structures. Whenever I asked a Baṅgāṇi about this identity I got an emphatic affirmation.

[21] This is usually unavoidable when the ground was limited on one side by the temple wall.

Thus, we may assume that the game was originally played on *ɔdɔkhɔ* only. Due to the influence of Mahāsu and his Brāhmaṇs it was later sometimes played on *sajɔ*, the day of the Brāhmaṇs, and brought into the local vicinity of Mahāsu's temple. We may term such a development as Folk-brahmanisation. This does not mean a brahmanisation in ways known to other parts of India, but a result of the intrusion of a regional folk-god, who is, however, dealt with by Brāhmaṇs, themselves of a highly regional character.

The players either kicked the ball or kicked the calves of opponents. This is because head and calf are regarded as homologous. This can be illustrated with the bow and arrow festival of *biśu* in April. Here, a male Rājpūt shoots a blunt arrow at the padded calves of another (kin or otherwise) who must avoid it by jumping while supporting himself with a stick. In case of a miss another chance is given. In olden days, if the archer would hit his target elsewhere than on the calves, and if both players were not of the same clan or ancestry, the "target" could behead the archer with a battle-axe. In case the arrow finds its mark, the game and accompanying music stop and the archer swaggers about the ground praising himself with a short song. It is spontaneously composed but must contain the traditional phrases. For example:[22]

> 'Straight (is the life in) my (village) Gamri
> — the glittering sand of the river —
> when the arrow hit,
> the head convulsed in pain'.

There the archer boastfully regards a shot on the calf as one on the head. Similarly, in a ball game the players by kicking the calves, symbolically behead their opponents. The use of hands and arms is disallowed as that would give cause for a duel.

---

[22] This song has been published in Choice India Vol.IV, No.8, August 1988.

The winners hold the ball for some time because they have conquered 'the head of the opposing village(s)'. The winners never tell the losers that their 'head' is conquered. This is understood. A wrong remark could lead to a fight.

Now, what does it mean for the Baṅgāṇis to contend for a 'head'? The answer is rather complex because there are four spheres of competition for it:

1. The *iṇḍuaṛɔ* game
2. Mythical (oral) literature
3. Headhunting
4. Wife-capture

It is clear that, when dealing with the 'head' in the Baṅgāṇi tradition, we find a concrete meaning and several metaphorical connotations. The meaning is concrete in the case of the harsh practice of headhunting, but has metaphorical allusions when it comes to the ball game or wife-capture where it is said that ball or woman is a 'head.' In folk-literature, the concrete meaning is found in heroic songs (*aruḷ*) and the metaphorical one in a popular lullaby (see pp.217ff.) and the local version of the Mahābhārata (see pp.214ff.). The lullaby and a scene in the Mahābhārata depict agonistic ball games.

The 'head' is a metaphor of prestige. The winner of the 'head' gains prestige while the loser earns ridicule and shame. In the case of wife-capture, for instance, the following equations are found: the *woman* is the captured *'head'* of her village and the *'head'* is its *prestige* or honour.

The 'head' whether in a concrete (e.g. headhunting) or metaphorical (e.g. wife-capture) sense, in play or war, among humans or gods, symbolises the martial counterpart to the peaceful Baṅgāṇi cultural activity of exchange of women.

An important aim of this paper is to prove that traditional Baṅgāṇi society knows two complementary forms of social exchange: the peaceful exchange of women, associated with sexuality and procreation, and the belligerent exchange of 'heads', associated with aggression and destruction.

It would be quite appropriate to start with a description of traditional headhunting, called *kerɔ aṇṇɔ* 'to bring a neck' in Baṅgāṇ. Once the practice was spread at least over Eastern Himachal Pradesh, Garhvāl and Kumaõ.[23] The warrior would try to chop off an enemy's head in a duel or group combat, which would be offered to the village 'deity', *j̈aga,* which name refers to the sacred precincts.

A typical example of group combat would be the fight for grazing grounds for sheep. Such an event could take place in the following way: assuming the winning party has conquered three or four heads. The heads were subsequently fixed with cords onto a wooden pole. Pole and heads were called *ceri.* Thereafter the *ceri* was carried towards the victorious village. Midway the warriors were received by other warriors of the village and when reaching the village boundary they were welcomed by rejoicing villagers and (if available) a music band. The heads were offered to the *j̈aga,* then there followed festivity with singing, eating and drinking.

A *j̈aga*[24] (see plate VI) is a square area lined with four stone walls, about 4 metres long and between a half and 2 metres high, covered with four logs called *lās.* In the middle is a hole, about half a metre deep, usually covered with an erect stone, about half a metre high. This hole, called *mũ* is said to be the *j̈aga*'s mouth.

---

[23] Cases of headhunting or decapitation of an enemy are reported from Eastern Himachal Pradesh (Hendriksen, p.35, sub 'khu:nd'), Jaunsār (Grierson, pp.408-412) and Garhvāl and Kumaõ (Oakley and Gairola 1935, in most of the heroic stories).

[24] j̈aga basically means 'place'.

A *j̈aga* is a female numinous being. She is associated with a particular clan and resides with them. Hence Baṅgāṇis do not call her *debi* or goddess, who can manifest herself everywhere and can be the *kuladevatā* (family-deity) of many clans, unlike a *j̈aga*, who is unique to a village.[25] She can assume occasionally the form of a hill woman. She has two basic functions: to protect a village, especially the women and children and to incite her warriors into a martial frenzy.

This frenzy or battle-intoxication is called *gerɔ*. *gerɔ* is evoked by the martial power of the *j̈aga*, called *mīr*. The *mīr* power of the *j̈aga* slowly enters a warrior and gets stored in the middle of his neck, called *j̈iān*. In a fight the *mīr* is released and leaves the body through his face by way of a complex 'physio-psychic' process. Moments before the fight the hostile *mīrs* would have clashed with each other and decided the battle.[26] The conquered head is supposed to contain some *mīr* and is placed into the 'mouth' of the *j̈aga* to strengthen her. This will give her an advantage in the face of revenge and raises the prestige of the victorious village.[27] When a head was conquered for the first time, the practice was to select a young tree, which could be a *čīl* or pine tree, and fashion a knot from its twig. This was repeated whenever another head was brought. The practice shows a relation between tree and head.

The presence of *mīr* within a warrior before and during a fight makes him *niḍɔrɔ* 'free from anxiety', evokes in him *gerɔ* 'battle-in-

---

[25] According to local traditions all villages (except those down in the big river valleys) are originally one-clan-settlements. The same is reported from Ravaĩ by Bahuguna (1932b: 305).

[26] There exist different ideas regarding the predestination of warriors in fights. According to one tradition the so-called old soul of the warrior predestined to die is taken away by a little owl the night before the fight.

[27] Usually, the head was removed from the hole the next day. It was then buried at a secret place under a boulder in the forest. This was done to prevent a recapturing of the head by the enemies. Even today, such places receive veneration. Whenever I passed-by such a boulder I found it decorated with flowers or bundles of grass.

toxication' and also stirs up a terrible anger *rōś*. Moreover, he experiences heat, *tāp*, that mainly concentrates in his ears.

mīr is the essence of (or in) the head, and the head is a trophy to be conquered. The captured *mīr* strengthens one's own *jaga* and thus one's combat strength, and possession of the conquered head augments the village prestige.

The *iṇḍuaṛɔ* ball game works accordingly. The leather ball becomes a container of enemy *mīrs* collected by the opposing parties' kicking. It is not the physical strength of the players but the power of the *mīrs*, which decides on which side the ball predominantly remains. That is why the ball is kept by the winning team for some time after the game: they have conquered the enemy *mīr* and take it into their possession.

Meanwhile, most parts of Garhvāl outside the upper Ṭons valley appear less original than Baṅgāṇ. This is mainly the result of immigrations from the plains and the impact of mainstream Hinduism. Nevertheless, even these areas are not completely bare of indigenous and archaic cultural features. Above (p.202) it was pointed out that the leather ball is worshipped together with a deity and that the deity of the guest village is present at the game in the form of a banner. The relations between deities of different villages in Ravaĩ are characterised by Bahuguna (1932b: 281) in the following words:

> Leaving aside the *Parchādhāri devatās*[28] and the gods who are commonly worshipped in the villages, generally people do not worship the gods of other villages. They think that the gods of a particular village is (sic) partial to its own village-people and and (sic) drives away all bad spirits towards other villages. It is believed that one village god is envious of others. So they are antagonistic to each other and the god of

---

[28] These are deities who are regarded as especially powerful. They do not govern clear-cut geographical areas (Zoller 1990).

> one village will not do good to the people of a second village.[29]

This information makes it very likely that the rivalry between (groups of) different villages at the time of the ball games are (or perhaps better: were) everywhere in Garhvāl connected with the powers of antagonistic deities, and that in fact the ball was a receptacle of these energies.

Its homology with the 'head' is evident when we recall the custom of worshipping and burying the ball in front of the village temple or of storing captured balls in the vestibule of the temple (see p.202f.). This resembles the past custom of the Baṅgāṇi warriors of placing the heads of vanquished enemies into the 'mouth' of their *jagas* and consequently burying them at a secret place. It also resembles the past custom, once common in other parts of Garhvāl, to bury the heads of slain enemies before the doorways of the houses[30] and in courtyards of fortresses.[31]

In the story "Bhagdeo the Warrior"[32] it is depicted how Bhagdeo's father Koku is beheaded by his enemy Gauria. Gauria then buries the head in the courtyard of his fortress. Many years

---

[29] Similar observations were also made by Ibbetson (quoted in Rose, p. 328, n.2): "There is one curious difference between the gods of the hills and those of the plains and that is, that many of the former are purely territorial, each little state or group of villages having its own deity, and the boundaries between their jurisdictions being very clearly defined."

[30] In one case, namely in the story "Adhapati Chauhan and Damdeo Chauhan" (Oakley and Gairola 1935, pp. 146-148) it is described how warriors of the Pundir clan had hung the head of their enemy Adhapati Chauhan from the lintel of their front door.

[31] In the stories, from which the following quotations are taken, Oakley and Gairola usually use the word "palaces." This is, in my opinion, a rather euphemistic translation of Garhvālī *gaṛh*.

[32] ibid., pp. 63-69.

later the head is reconquered by Bhagdeo: "Bhagdeo then dug up the head of his father and brought it home in a triumphant procession" (p. 68f.). A similar incident occurs in the story "Kunji Pal and Kirti Pal."[33] At the instigation of Guru Gyan Chand, king of Champawatgarh, Kirti Pal kills his brother, the hero Kunji Pal. Many years later this fratricide is revenged by Kunji Pal's son Khetra Pal: "Khetra Pal then asked Gyan Chand to give back his (Khetra Pal's) father's head to him. As soon as Kunji Pal's head was dug up, it flew up in the sky and immediately bullets showered down on Gyan Chand's palace, destroying it completely, and killing all the inmates. Then Khetra Pal, with his queen, brought Kunji Pal's head on a palanquin in a triumphant procession to his home" (p. 117f.). The third and last example is from the story "Ranu Rawat and Supia Rawat."[34] The hero Hinwa Rawat and his son Bhinwa are killed by the Airwals, a 'tribe' living in the Doon valley. The revenge for this evil deed is carried out by Ranu, son of Bhinwa. We read (p.162): "The Airwals had buried the heads of Hinwa and Bhinwa in a drain of their house. Ranu dug up the heads and brought them home in a triumphant procession."

Here we thus have conquered heads buried before front doors of houses or in the courtyards of fortresses,[35] the heads being prestigious trophies and containing tremendous energies which occasionally can drive them up, towards the sky. Apart from the identicality of burying charged balls and powerful heads at central places, we will later on also learn of balls that fly up to the sky (p.215) or to the centre of the world (p.216).

But this is not all. In Baṅgāṇ not only the ball gets homologised with the head but the head can also be homologous with the ball.

---

[33] ibid., pp. 105-118.

[34] ibid., pp. 159-166.

[35] Usually a fortress in the hills had to house a temple of the *kuladevī*.

In the heroic song *jitu jɔṛiāṇ*[36] it is described how the great Baṅgāṇi hero *dɔlu jɔṛiāṇ* decapitates two enemies, brings their heads into his village Sɔrās and then "he dances in (village) Sɔrās (and) plays football with the heads". The same performance is later repeated by *dɔlu*'s arch-enemy *nagdeu phɔdaṭɔ*. Out of revenge he and his family members treacherously kill nine men from *dɔlu*'s village. They bring the nine heads to their village Nɔkoṭ where "they play football" (with the heads).

It is not neccessary to quote here more examples from heroic songs where historical fights for the head are eulogized. But I think it is useful to present two examples from Baṅgāṇi mythology. They will introduce yet another variant of the ball games. The first is an episode of the local version of the Mahābhārata, called *pɔṇḍuāṇ* (Pa.).[37] Bhīma goes into a forest to get material for a ball. This is the text:

> "Before the night was over Bhīmseṇ had reached (the valley called) *gorɔ gaṭi* ('the awful valley'). (There) was a crippled stump of a tree. He thought: "Why should I (go on) searching, isn't that all right"? From the upper (portion above the earth) he made the ball, and from the roots the stuffing. He went to (lit.: into) Kurukṣetra, my dear. He started to throw (the ball up in the air). He threw it with one hand and caught it with a leg. But the Kauravas say: "Bhīmseṇ has gone (to Kurukṣetra), let's follow him". They entered (the valley where one could see): seats borne on palanquins, horseback, and on elephants, all (i.e. also other people) arrived in the 'awful valley' (which is on the way to Kurukṣetra). He (Bhīmseṇ) had placed branches (as a barricade). Nobody could cross (the barricade). All turned back. The palanquins belonged to the king of locusts (a king of the underworld). (The Kauravas) cut the branches and

---

[36] The song was taped in November 1989 in village Naiṭvāṛ.

[37] The epic was taped in 1987 in village Mahendrath. A few words of the text have not been translated because they will be explained after the text. In order to give a reasonably smooth translation some words have not been translated precisely. However, this does not affect the contents of the text.

> crossed (the barricade). The Hundred Kauravas arrived in Kurukṣetra. Bhīmseṇ saw that they had arrived. He placed the ball atop the cosmic tree, on its very top".[38]

I shall skip the next ten-odd sentences which mainly deal with Bhīma's immoderate appetite. Then Bhīma says:

> "You are the Hundred Kauravas, we are the Five Pāṇḍavas. Let us mix and play then". Duryodhana thinks, "You are just five, we are a hundred brothers" (and says), "How shall we proceed? You five (go) on one side, we shall (go) to the other". Bhīmseṇ thinks, "I couldn't say it (i.e. make this suggestion). Be praised"! They began to play. What did Bhīmseṇ Pāṇḍava do? He put on the 'iron glove' onto his right finger.[39] The others, my dear, continue to play. Bhīmseṇ 'identifies' the lower parts of the legs (i.e. the calves; see p.207). He gets down to making the lower parts of their legs 'crooked'. Then evening comes. Pāṇḍava Bhīmseṇ says, "Hey brother (Duryodhana), let us play the *kudbudūṛi* for a short while. Since you have always yielded the ball, let me shoot today". (Duryodhana says), "Throw with all the strength your mother's milk has given you. Make the *paṛɔā-ball* your slave". (Bhīma says to the ball), "O my *pāṛā-ball*, if you fall into their hands I will beat you into pulp! Stay up as long as they look at you. When they are tired come (into the crown) on the cosmic tree. Don't fall into their hands"! He shot (it away) with the hand. It (the ball) climbed higher and higher and reached the sky. When they (i.e. the Kauravas) got tired of looking at it, it fell on the Cosmic Tree. Bhīmseṇ calmed down everything (because everybody was agitated by his performance). "Let's go home now," he said to the Five Pāṇḍavas. He said to King Duryodhana, "(If) the ball does not come by next morning I will beat you 'thin'"! He (Duryodhana) says, "Sir, you have always brought

---

[38] The most common expression for this 'cosmic tree' is *bɔṛi rɔ būṭ*, deriving from Old Indo-Aryan *vaṭa-* 'the banyan Ficus indica' (Turner 11211) and **būṭṭa-* 'bush, plant' (Turner 9297). In reality, however, this tree is identified by the Baṅgāṇis with the tree Ficus religiosa.

[39] This 'iron glove', called *nɔkśotri*, provides its bearer with supernatural powers.

the ball back, although (you) are (only) five. We are a hundred brothers, the Kauravas. We'll bring it for sure"! The Hundred Kauravas started to search, (in): the north, the east, (on) every stalk, (in) every place, (in) the principal place,[40] (in) *gɔṛi-Gujarāt,*[41] (in) *indōḷ-sindōḷ* (?), (in) Śrīnagar-Saraī,[42] (at Lake) Mānasarovar-*mānsɔrai* (?), in 'Hari'-Haridvār, (in) Badrināth-Kedarnāth, (in) *śobnāth-tiləknāth* (?), (in) Gayā-Benares. They came to search for it at all (places) but did not find the *paṛɔā-ball.* One (of them) spent the night there (a few came back), a few returned in the morning, some came (back) before noon. In the morning time Bhīmseṇ says: "Hey brothers, let us play". (Duryodhana says), "Well then, let's go". The Five Pāṇḍavas (and) the Hundred Kauravas arrived in Kurukṣetra. (The Kauravas) whisper among themselves: "Have you found the ball"? Out of fear they do not talk loudly. They do thus.[43] Bhīmseṇ says, "What are you doing? Have you found it or not"? They say, "(We) have not found it". He says, "Shame on you! How could you find it. You who have (descended) some from cattle, some from sheep.[44] See it up (there), on the cosmic tree. Go, bring it down"! As the Hundred Kauravas climb up the ball comes down (simultaneously). As they climb down, the ball climbs up. (The ball) then makes them swing. Bhīmseṇ said, "What are you doing, Duryodhana, go and bring it down"! (Duryodhana answers), "What to do, it cannot be brought down". Duryodhana goes after the ball and every branch and every leaf is full of Kauravas. But they cannot fetch the ball. Then Bhīmseṇ says, "Hey brother Duryodhana, let me fetch the ball". The one had aches, the other had shooting (terrible) pains, when Bhīmseṇ kicked the cosmic tree he shook it by the roots. He only kicked (once) with one leg. Like the apricots in August: bump, bump,

---

[40] *muḷathān.* Or could it be the town Multan?

[41] Probably a place in Kumaõ. In Oakley and Gairola (1935, p. 135) the Kumaonī place name "Gauri Gujrant" is mentioned.

[42] A place in Himachal Pradesh.

[43] The singer mimes whisper.

[44] The four principal Kauravas have, according to local tradition, four animal-fathers.

roll, roll. Duryodhana fell with his backbone down powerfully".

I would like to emphasize the important points and make some preliminary remarks on the text.

Bhīma uses wood for the ball. Also, in the following example (pp.218ff.), we find the ball is not made in the usual way (cp. p.203). Moreover, this ball is sacred. Though not explained in this part of the text, it is said elsewhere that the ball is made from the wood of the sacred *thūn* tree. In Kurukṣetra Bhīma places the ball on the cosmic tree. It seems that the ball and the cosmic tree are interrelated.

Bhīma first suggests politely a non-agonistic football play by saying that both parties should mix. It is the Kaurava Duryodhana who insists on the agonistic variant. Though the singer does not say it explicitly it is clear that the Pāṇḍavas won the game and, thus, the 'head' of the Kauravas.

Then a new variant of the game is introduced: the *kudbudūṛi*. Its rules are simple. It is a duel, where one person throws the ball as far as possible for the other to find. It is fairly clear that the ball gets charged with *mīr* power. If the Kauravas had found the ball the Pāṇḍavas would have lost their 'head'. But since the Kauravas could not find the ball they had lost their 'head'. More explanations will follow.

I shall discuss the whole scene again in more detail after presenting the text of the song called *baḷɔ sunaia* 'Child-of-the-Sun'. It is a popular lullaby, sung only by males (e.g. father, grandfather) for children and during certain festivals. The 'Child-of-the-Sun' is actually part of an epic regarded by the Baṅgāṇis as their oldest and most glorious one, 'belonging' only to them (and to their immediate neighbours in Parbat, north of Baṅgāṇ). The epic has four parts and describes four generations of the semi-divine Indu clan: *buṛɔ induāṇ* 'the Old Indu', *ãsɔ induāṇ* 'God Indu', *ogauria* '(the twin-brothers)

Oga (and) Aria', and *baḷɔ sunaia* 'Child-of-the-Sun'. The following song deals with a small episode out of the epical story of the Child-of-the-Sun.[45] Every line ends with *gogōti* 'hush baby'. The first line also starts with the same word. The translation omits it.

> 1. "This is the Child-of-the-Sun, // 2. It goes over there to the cobbler, // 3. (It says) to the son of the cobbler, // 4. "Make a ball of copper," // 5. (It says) to the son of the goldsmith, // 6. "Affix (on it) a band of gold,"// 7. That Child-of-the-Sun set out on the way home, 8. It came nearer and nearer// 9. The *saj'ɔ* day in Pauṣ-Māgh,// 10. That Child-of-the-Sun// 11. Began to play with the ball,// 12. That Child-of-the-Sun// 13. Bit into (its) hand (out of excitement?),// 14. That Child-of-the-Sun// 15. 'Hit' (i.e. threw) with the hand (the ball),// 16. That copper ball// 17. 'Goes' (i.e. flies) to the *irɛṇi* bush, //[46] 18. That Child-of-the-Sun// 19. Started to search for the ball (as no one else could find it),// 20. That Child-of-the-Sun// 21. Goes to the *erɛṇi* bush,// 22. Near the *erɛṇi* bush// 23. Slept king leopard,// 24. That Child-of-the-Sun// 25. Started to challenge the leopard,// 26. Some time elapsed,// 27. That God Induāṇ// 28. Started to get worried,// 29. "Hey, children of the village// 30. Have you seen the Child-of-the-Sun"?// 31. "Your (Child-)of-the Sun// 32. We have not seen with (our) eyes"// 33. "Hey, cowherds and goatherds,// 34. Hey, have you seen the Child-of-the-Sun"?// 35. "Hey, your (Child-)of-the-Sun// 36. We have not seen with (our) eyes"// 37. He took up the bow (named) *sãga,* // 38. He took up the five arrows,// 39. That God Induāṇ// 40. Goes to the *eṛi* bush,// 41. That *eṛi* bush// 42. Next to it slept king leopard,// 43. Hey, that God Induāṇ// 44. Started to challenge the leopard,// 45. "If you are the child of a leopardess,// 46. O leopard, roar and come near!// 47. (And) if you are the child of a fox,// 48. O

---

[45] Taped in 1987 in village Dagoli.

[46] This word *irɛṇi*, with its various pronounciations in the lines below, seems to be a Baṅgāṇi 'Hapax legomenon' insofar as this song is, to my knowledge, the only case where this word appears. Apparently, the *irɛṇi* bush is sacred.

> leopard, (then) go and hide yourself"!// 49. Hey, that veritable king leopard// 50. Thereupon roared and came (near),// 51. (God Induāṇ) took up the bow (named) *sāka,*// 52. Took up the five arrows,// 53. Six thumbs (long) he stretched (the bow, that showed then towards the ground),// 54. (Having stretched the bow) nine (thumbs long) he 'shot' (actually: he held the bow) towards the sky,// 55. He shot into the mouth,// 56. (The arrow) pierced through the tail,// 57. That sleeping king leopard// 58. Set out to kill// 59. That God Induāṇ //[47] 60. He began to rip open the belly (of the leopard),// 61. That God Induāṇ// 62. Started to take the ball out (of the belly),// 63. (The God put) 'laughing leaves'// 64. (And) the 'speaking-mouth-living-rice' (upon the wound),// 65. (And put) 'immortality-splashes' (i.e. he sprayed drops of ambrosia upon the wound),// 66. (He) made the (leopard-)of-the-Sun (again) alive// 67. That God Induāṇ //[48] 68. They set out on the way home,// 69. Drums and tam-tam// 70. Started then to play,// 71. In the village and around// 72. They made music according to the custom".

Here, as in the Pa., the ball is not made of leather. It is made of copper with a golden band. In Baṅgāṇ, among all metals, copper is considered the purest. It is clear that the Child-of-the-Sun actually does not go to a cobbler (lines 2 and 3) but to a copper-smith. The confusion is due to the words for cobbler (*ċɔmār*) and copper (*cā̃mbɔ*) which sound quite similar. And there is no modern Baṅgāṇi equivalent to an Old Indo-Aryan *tāmrakāra* 'copper-smith'.

The Child-of-the-Sun plays the ball game on the *saj̈ɔ* day, when the agonistic ball game may be played in the hills (cf.p.203). The Baṅgāṇis believe that the Pāṇḍavas and Kauravas also played on the same day.

---

[47] Line 59 is grammatically subject, 57 is object. Thus, the normal sequence would be line 59, then 58, then 57.

[48] Grammatically subject.

The Child-of-the-Sun plays just like Bhīma did: He throws the ball as far as possible with the help of the *mīr* power and it can be found by no one other than the Child.

Ā̃sɔ Induāṇ is the Child-of-the-Sun's grandfather. When he prepares himself to kill the leopard he first directs his stretched bow towards the earth (line 53) and then towards the sky (line 54). This gesture can be seen even now during the Biśu festival (see p.207f.) before the archer tries to shoot at the calf of his target. From his manner it is clear that he thinks he is second to none — that his arrow can touch the sky or pierce the earth's bowels.

The leopard is the animal of the Induāṇs, but since the epic has not yet been translated it is difficult to determine its exact function. Probably, it protects and advises them and acts as a guardian of the world. Its most conspicuous feature, however, is its connection with the centre of the world and with the cosmic tree. Locals say that when the Child-of-the-Sun was led by the missing ball to the *irɛṇi* bush the leopard was there and they played together.[49] Ā̃sɔ Induāṇ might have killed the leopard for two reasons: the leopard could prove its identity only when attacked, and it had swallowed the copper ball.

A leopard also appears in a Baṅgāṇi song in which a crucial scene of the Pa. is depicted.[50] The important lines are:

> "Hey, in *othna* (the future capital of the Kauravas) live two Ṭhākurs,
> Hey, the Kauravas (and) the Pāṇḍavas, the heroic brothers
> Hey, the leopard 'opened' the cosmic tree (from the earth),
> Hey, (under) a good omen (the tree) is pulled up, (it is like) strained milk,

---

[49] The lines 24 and 25 do not make much sense.

[50] A longer section of this song has been published in Zoller 1990, p.155f. For a shorter version from Ravaĩ see Nautiyal, p. 138f.

Hey, the tree became big,
Hey, for this tree the fight was fought".

I have pointed out (1990: 156) that the leopard is the divine counterpart of the demonic dogs associated with the Kauravas. It is the leopard that pulls up the cosmic tree out of the earth. Thus we find the leopard connected with the Cosmic Tree that stands in the centre of the world and which, in turn, is either the setting for the ball game between the Pāṇḍavas and Kauravas or, in case of the Child-of-the-Sun, the destination of the ball. Thus, the ball and the cosmic tree seem to be related.

The quotation above from the Pa. does not contain some important details. From the text we learn, indirectly, that Duryodhana struck many times before Bhīma did. The text fails to mention that before he sent the ball flying straight up, he also sent it across. An omission also noted in the 'Child-of-the-Sun' song. The following line should have appeared somewhere near line 15: "From the north it (the Child) struck the ball (and) sent it flying to the east".

Such a feat is not possible if the cardinal points are arranged in this manner:

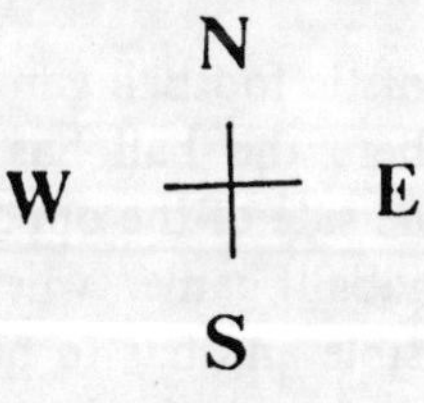

but when they are ordered as below the possibility becomes self-evident:

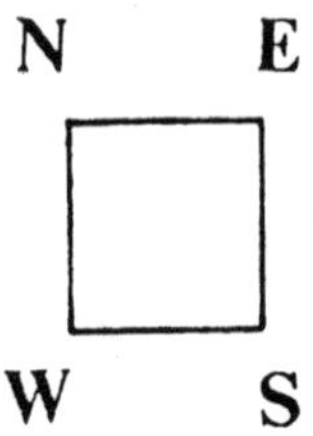

Both patterns differ in that the first one is abstract 'open', the second, concrete 'closed'. The latter probably indicates the conception of earth as a square. The Baṅgāṇis call the cardinal points *ċār khuṇṭɛ*,[51] which corroborates my assumption.[52] *khuṇṭɔ* has two meanings in Baṅgāṇi: 'corner' and 'tent peg'. *ċār khuṇṭɛ* thus indicates not only that the world has four corners but also that the vault of heaven is fixed at the four corners. However, one should not literally take it that the ball was thrown from one end of the world to the other. Again, one should be wary of a literal interpretation because the ball thrown by the Child-of-the-Sun lands in the centre of the earth. But the centre of the earth is also an extreme end.

A short summary on the ball games of Baṅgāṇ will be useful here. There are two ways of playing ball:

> a) a cyclical and agonistic football game between two opposing groups, where the ball has to remain as long as possible on the side of the opposing party;
> b) an agonistic handball game, where the ball is thrown as far as possible and has to be found by the antagonist.

---

[51] Turner 3893, sub. 2.

[52] Though I asked the Baṅgāṇis many times about the form of sky and earth I never got a clear answer.

I. The full *teyyam* of Ūrpalacci being taken in procession. (Freeman)

II. Tai Paradēvata. (Nambiar)

III. The introductory *veḷḷāṭṭam* form of Urpalacci. (Freeman)

IV. Kalam of Bhagavati. (Nambiar)

V. Worship of Lukumahādyaḥ who is covered with food plates, garlic, eggs, flowers etc. The locality is situated in a courtyard in Kathmandu (near Indracok). (Michaels)

VI. The *jaga* of village Kiroli a few days after the performance of *pūja* in January 1990. The bent branch and the four upright sticks are the remainders of the sacrifice. The four sticks mark the 'mouth' of the *jaga* which is usually covered with an upright stone. In former times the heads of slain hostile warriors were placed into this 'mouth.' (Zoller)

VII. The stone-shring (*māḍa*) of Kannalāye at Upper Agari. (Brückner)

VIII. The same stone-shring showing sacrificial offerings. (Brückner)

IX. Jumādī and Kannalāye take leave of each other while their media cross swords. Jumadi's *muga* ('face' or facial mask) is kept facing the scene (right foreground). In the foreground one can see the torch bearers of the gods. (Brückner)

X. Playing Cenne at the Siri Jātre at Urmibitota in February 1987. (Claus)

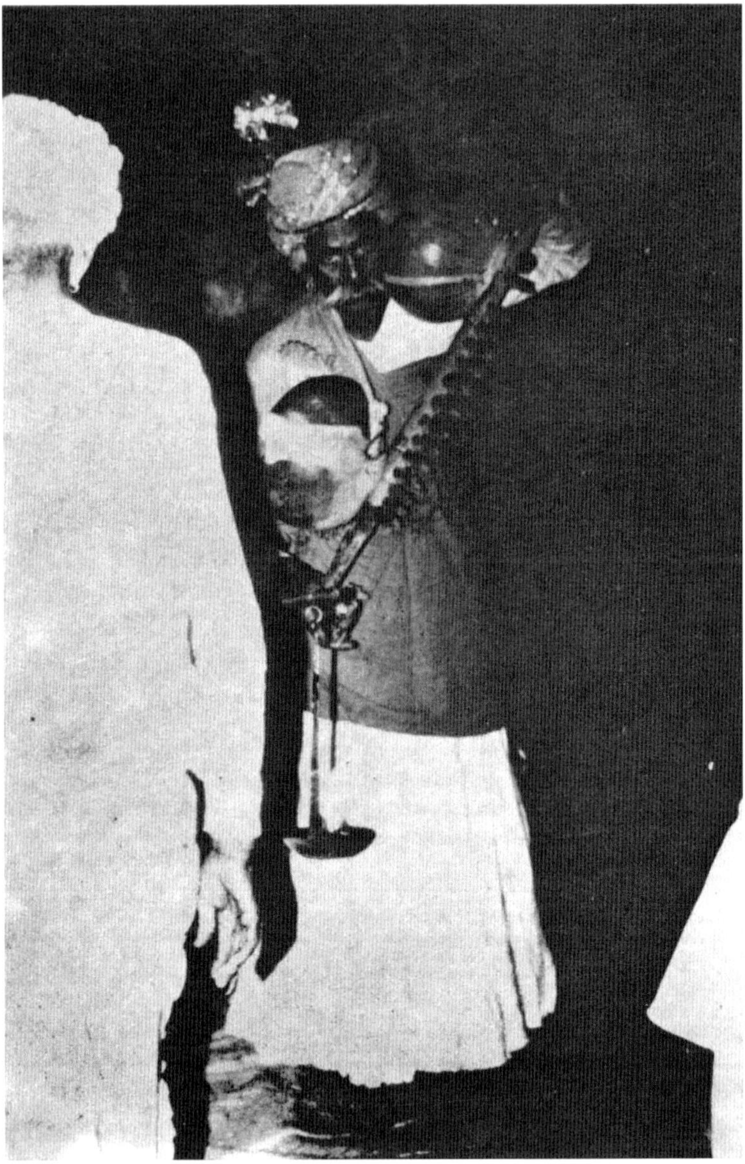

XI. Bhopa of Devnārāyaṇ, during a nocturnal performance of the epic. The peacock feather functions as a pointer for the illustrations on the *par*. The double-gourd string instrument used by the Bhopa is called *bīṇ* or *jantar*. (Malik)

XII. Detail from a *paṛ* of Devnārāyaṇ, showing the golden image of Śiva. (Singh; photo: Cornelia Mallebrein)

XIII. Detail from a *paṛ* of Devnārāyaṇ, showing Devnārāyaṇ and his four brothers in the center. (Singh; photo: Cornelia Mallebrein)

In fact, it is right to speak in the first case of opposing groups and in the second case of antagonists. In the first cyclical variant there can never be a final winner or loser whereas, in the second case a 'finality' is assured, in the sense that it strongly resembles actual headhunting (see below). Bhīma throwing the ball denotes two things: a) its infusion with his *mīr* only and b) its symbolism as a 'head'. If it is found by the other(s), they have conquered the 'head' of their opponents and gained prestige; if not, they have lost both. This is demonstrated more clearly by the Child-of-the-Sun who only threw once. There was no one to challenge him. In the first variant the ball contains the *mīrs* of both parties, and only in the end does it become clear who has (temporarily) lost his 'head' and his prestige.

These examples are mythological. Was there a complement on the level of social structures? To my knowledge the ball was never thrown and searched for on *sajɔ̃* or *ɔdɔkhɔ*. But this action existed, namely, in the form of a ritual gesture.

As an introduction I should like to quote a passage from the Pa. When Bhīma kills Duryodhana, Arjuna is moved to tears. Bhīmseṇ says, "You, Arjuna, are weeping, but it was he (Duryodhana) who carried on the war." With (his) foot (and) iron rod he (Bhīmseṇ) then strikes Duryodhana on his face.

A similar scene is described in Mahābhārata IX 59,3311 and 3330, where Bhīma strikes dying Duryodhana's head twice with his (left) foot. But this act is criticised in sections 59 and 60 as incompatible with the ethics of a warrior. And it is here that the Mahābhārata differs from the Pa. In the Pa. Bhīma's act of kicking Duryodhana's head is meaningful — if such a detached manner of expression can be allowed here.

A parallel to this drastic gesture is found at the level of social structures in the traditional warfare of Western Garhvāl. In an armed conflict it was custom to kick the felled enemy on his face.

And, if circumstance permitted, then, the foot would be circled thrice around the head of the fallen enemy. The significance of this latter act is not clear but there are two reasons for the kicking of the head:

pp a) To make it 'worthless' for the enemy group when the warrior feared there was no chance of snatching it himself. Besides making the enemy head 'worthless' an 'own' head could be 'saved' by the fallen warrior's fellow combatants, by throwing a battle-axe, coin, or a little earth from their *j̈aga* on the head. Also this would render the head 'worthless' for the enemy.

b) As a symbolic act that actualised the mythical throwing of the ball. Which meant: 'I kick away the head of your comrade, filled with my *mīr*. If you want to have it back, take revenge'.

The first, cyclical variant of ball games concerns the whole community,[53] while the second one is rather like a duel. Likewise, wife-capture and headhunting did not so much concern the community as it did individuals or the kinship system. This relationship will be the theme of the second part of this paper.

*

There are many clans, clan-segments, and lineages, all called *āḷ* among the Baṅgāṇi Rājpūts.[54] Among the *āḷs* there is an endogamous group of lineages called *khundāḷ*. These latter are traditionally exogamous in the sense that each *khundāḷ* can give and take women from two other *khundāḷs* only:[55]

→ ←A→ ←B→ ←C→ ←D→ ←

[53] In Baṅgāṇ only male Rājpūts could participate, but in most other areas members of other castes were allowed to play. See, for instance, Majumdar 1962, p. 270.

[54] The exact meanings and functions of Baṅgāṇi kinship terms and related notions are not discussed in this paper.

[55] Presently, this rule is hardly followed anymore. But the Baṅgāṇis are still aware of its former general validity, and that is the relevant point in our context.

As there are about 10 to 15 *khundāḷs* these exchanges can be graphically represented as a circle. Two counter-rotating circles, in fact. For when a girl is given in marriage, say, by the Ṭholiāṇ to the Yũāṇ, she retains her family name. She will be called Ṭholianṭi by her affines. Her daughters who are the nieces of the Ṭholiāṇ cannot be given back to them in marriage. The daughters will carry the name of the Yũāṇ and will be given in marriage in the same 'direction' as their mother. Thus there exists a clockwise and an anti-clockwise circle and there is, basically, not an oscillation but a rotation. A rotation in two 'directions'.

The exchange of women in the two 'directions' is restricted by the following rules: female descendants of the own *āḷ* can marry male descendants of a given-away woman of a present generation only after a gap of three generations, and female descendants of the given-away woman of a present generation can marry 'back' into one's own *āḷ* only in the fourth generation. However, this is an idealised description and there can be many exceptions. For instance, when a second *āḷ* splits off from one's own *āḷ* the rule of three respectively four generations is applied less rigidly with members of the new split-off *āḷ*.

The *āḷs* in Baṅgāṇ are named after historical or fictitious male founder-ancestors, after places from where the families had migrated and after other criteria.[56] However the founder-ancestors of the *khundāḷs* who take their name from them must have been decapitated in a fight and, usually, the head must have been 'saved' by their own people.[57] The sons of Ṭholi could call themselves his *khundāḷ* from the day he was beheaded.[58] Since this *āḷ* exists even today we can conclude that from the times of Ṭholi up to now there

[56] Similar conditions are described for Kāṅgṛā (Himachal Pradesh) by Parry 1979, p.137.

[57] I was told that a man could also become a founder-ancestor even if his head was not saved in case he had already proven before to have been an outstanding hero.

[58] There are indications in the folk literatures of Garhvāl and Eastern Himachal Pradesh that the motif, which I may call 'beheading for the sake of creating a lineage or dynasty,' was once more widespread. I will discuss this in a separate article.

were active *khūnds* (warriors) in every generation in that lineage.

Historically, any of the following could happen to a *khundāḷ*. It could become extinct when there were no *khūnds* in a given generation (i.e. men who devoted themselves to war and not, for instance, to rearing sheep). It could also become extinct (which seemingly took a longer period) when a *khūnd* or *khūnds* of a given lineage settled in another village. It probably took a few generations for them to be regarded as the *khūnds* of the *khundāḷ* of that village. Thirdly, a *khundāḷ* could survive when there were *khūnds* in every successive generation who never suffered death through decapitation. Fourthly, a *khūnd* could be decapitated but his head 'saved'. He would then become the founder of a new *khundāḷ* which was named after him.

Headhunting thus served the maintenance of the 'circles' that were formed of *khūnd* lineages. This is because a *khundāḷ* lost its status as a 'warrior-lineage' from the moment there were no more warriors in a given generation. This threat was compensated by the institution of decapitated founder-ancestors, through which new 'warrior-lineages' could come into existence.

The plural 'circles' indicates the existence of circles in Parbat, Baur and Jaunsār, and perhaps, other areas, in addition to the 'circle' of *khundāḷs* in Baṅgāṇ. Killing to live is indeed paradoxical but it was meant to preserve the system from reduction and final disintegration.

One must distinguish here between endopractical and exopractical forms of headhunting. A *khūnd* could conquer a head from another *khundāḷ* of his own 'circle' (endopractice) and earn great prestige or from a *khundāḷ* of another 'circle' (exopractice), which again was of high value. Or he could conquer that of a non-*khundāḷ* man (exopractice), which was of lesser value, and earn for himself insults.

An example for the latter case is found in the aforementioned Baṅgāṇi heroic song *jitu jɔṛiāṇ. dɔlu,* the great hero, is once strongly rebuked by his wife when he abducts a wezir.[59] She says to him, "But this is the wezir! I burn your beard, I scorch your head! You should have fought with a *khūnd,...but you (just) fought with an (ordinary)* Rāvat"! *dɔlu's* wife is 'not upset that her husband abducted an important office-holder but that he occupied himself with a "weak" man.[60]

There were many occasions for headhunting. One *khūnd* may have insulted and provoked another. In olden days, for instance, the *khūnds* of Baṅgāṇ and Parbat would meet occasionally at the border village of Duṇi in the valley of the Rupaṇ river or those of Baṅgāṇ and Baur in village Hanoḷ by the river Ṭons. At a place like Hanoḷ a *khūnd* could ask provocative questions, like, "Shall the accounts of Caḷda (the youngest of the Mahāsu brothers) be managed by someone from the area to the right of river Ṭons or from the area to the left?" Frequently, this would be answered with a fight.[61] Other possibilities were: punishment to a *khūnd* for breaking traditional law, or in answer to a *j̈aga*'s call for a fight with a certain *khūnd* after prolonged martial inactivity, when her *mīr* was in danger of 'drying out'. At such times she would speak through a medium when receiving sacrifices, usually every three, six, or nine years.[62] There could be challenges also when a group of warriors secretly covered the spring of an enemy village or stealthily removed the staircase (made of a log) of a house or fenced the path to the forest of an enemy village. In such cases, the deeds were announced aloud from a distance and then the culprits ran for their lives. If their provocation was accepted, they were pursued by the villagers, who tried to take on the challengers.

---

[59] A wezir in Baṅgāṇ means minister of a god — not of a king.

[60] Rāvats (Old Indo-Aryan *rājaputra*) are also Rājpūts, but only *khūnds* are reputed to be strong.

[61] The folk literature is full of cases where slightest provocation causes murderous actions. For instance, see Oakley and Gairola 1935, p.55 where the accidental fall of a piece of soil into the field of a neighbour leads to a bloody feud. A number of times I could witness the survival of this very exciteable spirit.

[62] The length of these three spaces of time corresponds to three increasingly powerful types of *j̈agas*.

A few decades ago it so happened that some Baur warriors assaulted a Deogār shepherd and herded him together with his flock deep into Baur. A few days later he was released along with the sheep. This deed was answered with the abduction of a married woman (called *rɔiṇ*) from Baur to Deogār. Such transactions always involve — besides honour and prestige — conquering or exchange of *mīr*, which to some extent also resides in all plants, animals, and human beings (in addition to a *jaga*'s warriors) belonging to a village. So much so that every village has a 'special *mīr* scent.'[63]

Generally, every conquered head from a *khundāḷ* was regarded as valuable. But some were more valuable on account of the notion of *lɔi-lūṅg*.

Morphologically *lɔi-lūṅg* is a typical Dvandva; there are probably hundreds of these formations in Baṅgāṇi. Literally, *lɔi* means 'creeper' and *lūṅg*, 'a prime cultivated plant given by God to man'. All cultivated plants in Baṅgāṇ are said to stem from these primary plants.

---

[63] *Mīr* can be translated with 'earth power' or 'power of one's natal place.' The importance of the natal place, which is thought to influence the character of its inhabitants, has been observed in Garhvāl independently by Sax 1990 (see especially p. 496). I cannot fully share, however, one of his theses regarding what happens when a bride has to shift to her husband's place after marriage: "Men... tend to assert complete transformation of the bride... Women, on the other hand, tend to believe that the bride changes only gradually...(p.491)". These differences of opinion are not, at least not exclusively, an expression of disputes between the sexes. They have, rather, something to do with what Sax himself calls "the implicit and the explicit". My own experience is that men, especially when they are office-holders, tend to relate 'explicit knowledge' to the researcher (in case of Sax's research-theme, knowledge that reflects the positions of 'official' Hinduism). "Tacit knowledge" (Sax ibid.) is often very difficult to obtain - this at least is my experience. Therefore, I think that Sax's male informants tended to relate to him 'explicit knowledge' and his female informants "tacit knowledge." An outmarried Baṅgāṇi woman always remains connected with her natal place through the invisible presence of her *jaga* (or the *mīr* of her *jaga)* within her. On the other hand, the *mīr* power from the head of a hostile warrior or from a captured woman has its 'roots' cut-off, as it were, from its place of origin, and gets completely assimilated to the *jaga* of the captors.

I would like to translate the notion *lɔi-lūṅg* as 'horizontal matrilinearity'. *lūṅg* 'prime cultivated plant' is the symbolic designation of the first woman of an *āḷ* X who has been given away for marriage. And *lɔi* 'creeper' is the symbolic designation of the 'matrilinear lineage' that started with her. This 'creeper' grows, as it were, in one 'direction' with the female descendants of each generation, who are given from one *khundāḷ* to the next, along the 'circle' of *khundāḷs*. *lɔi-lūṅg* is thus the complementary notion to *āḷ*. An *āḷ* refers to a dead male ancestor of the past, while *lɔi-lūṅg* refers to a present female descendant living in a locally distant *khundāḷ*. *āḷ* refers to a past time and is therefore 'vertical', *lɔi-lūṅg* to a present distance and therefore 'horizontal'.

The paternal features and characteristics inherited by a child are called *lō* 'blood' and those of the mother *dūd* or 'milk'. Both notions are also used symbolically to designate the two types of lineages: *lɔi-lūṅg* is also to be said to be the 'milk-lineage' and *āḷ* the 'blood-lineage' (a fairly fitting designation for *khundāḷs*, I think). The prestige of a *khundāḷ* depended also on the 'length' it could claim for its 'milk-' and 'blood-lineages' and references to 'blood-lineages' could be used as a challenge as when a *khūnd* provoked another.

What is the connection between the value of a head and *lɔi-lūṅg*? A head captured from a *khundāḷ* connected with one's *lɔi-lūṅg* was considered more valuable than a head from a *khundāḷ* outside one's 'milk-lineage'. This is an indication that headhunting was the martial complement to peacetime marriages. The head had its highest value when it was not only one of a *khundāḷ* but one with whose *khundāḷ* one had a 'matrilinear' affiliation.

The above-described system of woman rotation has a serious disadvantage. Traditionally, a *khundāḷ* in Baṅgāṇ could give and take women only from two other *khundāḷs*, which created an imbalance — there were either too many brides or a surplus of grooms. Wife-capture, I feel, may have served to offset this imbalance.

The Baṅgāṇi word for 'to capture a woman' is *bɔgāṇɔ*. A woman captured from another *khundāḷ* (a few such women are known to me) enjoys in her 'marital' village a higher status than a woman married into the village. This is because a captured woman is a 'head'. And a trophy is better than a bartering object (see below). A trophy reduces the prestige of the other village and enhances one's own, but not so a bartering object. A captured woman can be explicitly called *muṇḍ* 'head' and the act of capturing her was an invitation to her consanguineous males to take revenge by headhunting. Both headhunting and wife-capture were expected to be performed by a *khūnd*. In the words of a Baṅgāṇi informant: "The *khūnd* is one who should take the wife with force in a fight, without asking the parents and the relatives of the girl".

Wife-capture occured not only between *khundāḷs* but also when a *khundāḷ* member captured a woman from another *āḷ* outside the 'circle'. Here the woman was usually detained for a few days only. In case the other *āḷ* refused to pick up the challenge and fight back, the woman was returned. The *āḷ* then was doubly humiliated. We thus find a certain correspondence between the value system of heads and of captured women. This is also illustrated by the above mentioned sheep raid and consequent wife-capture. Theoretically, the reaction could also have been the severing of a head.[64] A homology of woman and severed head is possibly also contained in the aforementioned story "Kunji Pal and Kirti Pal" (see p.213). When Khetra Pal gets down to reconquer the head of his father, Gyan Chand, now fearing for his life, offers to give his daughter in marriage to him (at the end Gyan Chand is dead and Khetra Pal returns home with wife and head).[65]

The homology of headhunting and woman exchange becomes more lucid when we recall that the *mīr* power in the warrior's head is a female energy. Equally important, I believe, is the fact that the people of these hills regard marriage — contrary to 'normal' Hindu

---

[64] It is difficult to estimate when, in terms of years, the last beheading took place in the area. However, it is interesting that I was repeatedly told by various people that the last case happened "only a few years back."

[65] I am not aware of the institution of wergild in the area, but this scene could almost be compared with it.

tradition — as a 'secular' transaction.[66] Traditionally, women are bought and sold like other objects.[67] Repeatedly, Baṅgāṇi women are called *dinu* 'cows'. Peaceful exchange of women ('cows') and martial exchange of heads serve the common purpose of exchange of *mīr*. *mīr* originates in the *j̃agas*.

A *j̃aga* is found in all older Baṅgāṇi villages, though not in all more recent settlements. Every *j̃aga* has a peaceful and protective aspect and a martial aspect (see p.210). She protects the village, the fields, mothers and children. And she infuses the warrior with her *mīr*.

When a woman marries into another village Y, she not only retains the lineal name of her father, but also carries within her the presence of her native *j̃aga* X. Her daughters will bear the name of the *āḷ* of their father into village Z plus the invisible presence of X and Y village *j̃agas*. Thus a *j̃aga* extends along the two 'creepers' or 'milk-lineages' maximally till the two next but one *āḷs*. However, this depends on the consent of the maternal uncle *māma*. Should he stay in village X, then his niece to-be-married will stay in village Y (with her mother) and should be married to village Z. Now, at the time of marriage, the maternal uncle has to consent (or refuse, if he wishes to) that the so-called *poḷi* will be distributed by his family members also among village Z members, with whom the marriage is going to take place. If he declines, then the *j̃aga* of village X will extend only to village Y and the girl has to live in village Z without the presence of her *j̃aga* within her.

poḷi refers to a custom observed at the beginning of the Māgh month (January/February). Male family members bring presents of bread and liquor to their married sisters, daughters, and nieces. Important in our context is the fact that the extent of the distribution of *poḷi* among other *khundāḷs* is usually identical with the extent of the *j̃aga* of the distributors.

---

[66] Joshi 1929, pp. 60,123,316-17.

[67] ibid., p.114. However, one should be aware, that this legal transaction has nothing to do with the affectionate relationship between Baṅgāṇi men and women.

One's own *jaga* and a hypothetical hostile *jaga* are now rated in an opposite manner: there is a wish that one's own *jaga* should not extend too far along the 'creeper' lines as this would give rise to a twofold danger: decrease in her power and a chance of 'contamination' (as the sort of social intercourse far-off *āḷs* may indulge in cannot be controlled by her *āḷā)*. On the other hand, it is held that the value of a head to be conquered is higher the 'further' away the hostile *jaga* (and its warrior) is along the 'creeper line'.

It is striking that in Baṅgāṇ marriage was possible only with two *khundāḷs* whereas heads could be exchanged with many. This 'rule-of-two-families' was not valid everywhere outside Baṅgāṇ. For instance, in Deogār (southwest to Baṅgāṇ) there existed a 'rule-of-three-families'. Nevertheless, it seems that in those areas of the Western and Central Himalayas where headhunting was practiced with the aim of exchange of powers *(mīr)*, legal exchange of women was always limited to a very small number of possible clans. In fact, this is what has to be expected. If the number would be high, the *jagas* would be overstrained, as it were, no 'creeper lines' could develop as the 'matrilinear' descendencies would peter out very quickly. As a result, the closed system of ordered exchange of *mīr* would change into an open system that would end with a levelling of the *mīr*-'fluxes' and, consequently, with a breakdown of the whole system of twofold social exchange. On the other hand, it is also clear now that the 'rule-of-two-families' must be the minimum. Below this figure no 'creeper lines' could come into existence.

To recapitulate: Some important segments of traditional Baṅgāṇi society were organised in two interdependent layers for peace and war, life and death. The opposition of life and death unfolded within a coordinate system with a 'vertical' or diachronic axis of patrilinear linkages, called 'blood' and a 'horizontal', 'matrilinear' or synchronic axis called 'milk'. Indeed, a sort of two-dimensional 'space' of relations and exchange existed, insofar as the Baṅgāṇi Ego, to determine itself, can refer to its most distant male relative *in time* (the ancient apical ancestor who signifies death and exchange of heads) and to its most distant female relative *in space* (*lɔi-lūṅg*, associated with life and exchange of women).

Ball games and headhunting, marrying and wife-capture meant always an exchange of *mīr* powers. Exchange of *mīr* was not limited to these four activities — sheep raiding, for instance, also involved the acquisition of others' *mīr* — but their basic homology, perceived in the shape of 'heads', was motivated by an insight into the final identity of sexuality and aggression. That both originate in the 'head', or, in other words, that the 'head' is a receptacle of an energy that manifests two-foldedly, is not unknown at other places and times of Indian civilisation. But this will be described elsewhere.

Note

Among the Baṅgāṇis who supported me in my work, I would like to name the following with a feeling of great gratitude: Gabar Singh Chauhan, Roshan Singh Chauhan, Dalip Singh Panvar and Jval Das. I am grateful to Dr. Hugh van Skyhawk, Heidelberg, for correcting the English of large parts of this paper.

References

Bahuguna, S. D. 1932a. Festivals among the Rawaltas. In *Man in India*. Vol.XII. Ranchi, pp. 45-58.

Id. 1932b. Marriage and Marital Life amongst the Rawaltas. Ibid., pp. 301-319.

Gairola, Tara Dutt and Barker, D.A. 1917. Games and festivals of Garhwal. In *The Journal of the United Provinces Historical Society*. Vol.I, part 1. Lukhnow, pp.160-167.

Grierson, G.A. 1916. *Linguistic survey of India*. Vol. IX, part 4. Calcutta.

Hendriksen, Hans 1976. *Himachali studies*. I. Vocabulary. Kobnhavn: Det Kongelige Danske Videnskabernes Selskab, Historisk-filosofiske Meddelelser 48,1.

Joshi, L.D. 1929. *The Khasa family law in the Himalayan districts of the United Provinces of India*. Allahabad: Superintendent, Government Press, U.P.

Majumdar, D.N. 1962. *Himalayan polyandry. Structure, functioning and culture change. A field-study of Jaunsar-Bawar*. Bombay: Asia Publishing House.

Nand, Nitya and Kumar Kamlesh 1989. *The holy Himalaya. A geographical interpretation of Garhwal*. Delhi: Daya Publishing House.

Nautiyal, S. 1981. *Garhvāl ke loknṛtya-gīt*. Prayāg:

Hindī Sāhitya Sammelan.

Oakley, E.S. and Gairola, Tara Dutt 1935. *Himalayan folklore*. Allahabad: Superintendent, Printing and Stationery, U.P.

Parry, Jonathan P. 1979. *Caste and kinship in Kangra*. New Delhi: Vikas Publishing House.

Rose, H.A. 1986. *Hindu gods and goddesses*. Delhi: Amar Prakashan.

Sax, W.S. 1990. Village daughter, village goddess: residence, gender, and politics in a Himalayan pilgrimage. In *American Ethnologist* 17.3: 491-512.

Turner, R.L. 1969. *A comparative dictionary of the Indo-Aryan languages*. London: Oxford University Press.

Zoller, Claus Peter 1990. A preliminary investigation into the internal building up of the numerals 4 and 5 in mythology and folk religion of Western Garhwal. In Maheshwar P. Joshi, Allen C. Fanger and Charles W. Brown *Himalaya: Past and present*. Almora: Shree Almora Book Depot.

GODS, GHOSTS AND DEMONS: POSSESSION IN SOUTH ASIA*

Elisabeth Schoembucher

Introduction

The study of possession in South Asia has a fairly long tradition. As early as 1713 Bartholomaeus Ziegenbalg, the first Danish protestant missionary in India, mentioned "devil dancers" in his "Genealogy of the Malabar Gods".[1] Since then "devil dancers" are almost indispensable in the writings of missionaries, and one could quote many more examples of "devil worship". The first anthropological writings about possession date back to 1911, when the Seligmanns' published a rather detailed description of spirit mediumship (or shamanism) among the Veddas of Ceylon. This was followed by a number of more analytical publications on the subject of possession from the fifties onwards.[2] All these early writings have in common a fairly high degree of fascination for experiences belonging to the realm of the 'unreal', the 'inexplicable', or the 'irrational'. Yet whereas missionaries, such as Ziegenbalg, apparently had no diffi-

---

* I would like to thank Richard Burghart and András Höfer for their critical comments and my colleagues and friends of the department of Indology, South Asia Institute, Heidelberg University, for their stimulating discussions on the topic.

[1] Edited and published by Rev. Germann Wilhelm, 1867, Christian Knowledge Society's Press, Madras.

[2] Cf. Harper (1957; 1963), Freed and Freed (1964), Srinivas (1952), Dumont (1959), to mention just a few.

culty in seeing possession as an ecstatic religious experience (although condemning it as superstitious and pagan), Western social scientists have had a much more ambiguous attitude. Their search for a deeper meaning has resulted in a series of different interpretations, in which the fact that possession is seen as an ecstatic religious experience by the people themselves is almost forgotten.

Starting with a rational Western world view, most anthropologists think that a person cannot really become possessed by a divine or demonic being, and that phenomena such as possession have to be regarded as an expression of other events or conditions, for which more rational explanations have to be found. For a long time the most important question behind the anthropological analysis of possession was: what really happens when a person claims to be possessed? On these premises, a number of models came into being, with which anthropologists have interpreted possession in very different ways.

In this paper I am going to present the most important interpretive models of possession.[3] Lack of space does not permit me to give a complete overview of the entire literature on possession in South Asia. Rather I attempt to show the main issues behind the various concepts and their limitations. An overview of the various models of possession shows four different ways in which possession is analyzed. They can be termed psychological, sociological, cosmological and performative.[4] A comparative analysis of these four models will show different attitudes towards possession, different methodological approaches and different epistemologies. If one is

---

[3] I shall not take into consideration so-called physiological theories which reduce possession to calcium-deficiency syndromes (Kehoe and Giletti 1981) or which connect possession with extreme geographic and climatic conditions by which the human organism is more stressed than elsewhere, which therefore suggests that persons tend to be exhausted more often, resulting in "arctic hysteria".

[4] The psychological interpretation includes medical and psychoanalytic paradigms and is often referred to as the "medical interpretation".

dissatisfied with the existing interpretive approaches and in search of a new, less reductionistic one, it would be helpful to look back and analyze the various theoretical orientations in order to show their limitations and to look for a more comprehensive alternative. It should be noted, however, that some of these thoughts are still tentative. They are part of a larger research project on possession in South India and should be seen as an attempt to understand how social scientists deal with such an "irrational" phenomenon as possession.

Possession: The term, the person and the entities

The term

The term 'possession' is not at all as simple and unambiguous as it appears to be. Various experiences are described by this term and a phenomenology of possession in South Asia would show a vast number of different forms, ranging from possession by spirits and demons to different forms of oracular possession, to possession in ritual drama and finally possession in bhakti cults.[5] One element common to all forms of possession is the altered state of consciousness which the possessed person experiences. For historians of religion, therefore, possession is one of the basic forms of religious experience in which transcendental powers are felt by human beings in one way or the other.[6] The transcendental can be experienced either as a personal power or it can appear in impersonated form. The German historian of religion Benz (1972) distinguishes between two categories of possession, "Ergriffenheit" and "Besessenheit", in

[5] For an overview of the different forms of possession see Hitchcock and Jones (1976), Diehl (1956), Jones (1967/68) and Sontheimer (forthcoming).

[6] See Eliade (1951), who in his famous book on "Le chamanisme et les techniques archaïque de l'extase" takes the ecstatic experience as the most basic feature in shamanism and possession. Here, the more general term "altered state of consciousness" is used instead of "ecstasy" and "trance".

accordance with the manifestation of the possessing entity. Benz speaks of "Ergriffenheit" when transcendent powers interfere with human beings in a blessing, healing and renewing way; in contrast "Besessenheit" denotes possession by a demonic or malevolent entity which is perceived by the human being as being destructive.

Anthropologists also distinguish between two categories of possession. In the literature on possession we read about controlled and uncontrolled possession, induced and spontaneous possession, central and peripheral possession cults, desired and undesired, divine and demonic possession and, finally, spirit possession and spirit mediumship. All these categories have their origin in a distinction made by the afflicted persons themselves, a distinction of two different categories of supernatural entities: those who are benevolent and helpful for human beings and those who are malevolent and harmful. Despite the similar sort of distinction made by historians of religion and anthropologists, nonetheless, historians of religion see any form of possession as a religious experience and stress the passivity of the human being and the interference or the suffering of the transcendent, whereas anthropologists emphasize the active behaviour of the individual. Possession in the first instance is not seen as an ecstatic religious experience, but as a symbolic expression of other experiences. And, as we shall see, anthropological interpretations try to find either psychological, medical or social causes which lie behind possession.[7]

Rather than the terms mentioned above, I shall use the terms spirit possession' and 'spirit mediumship', as suggested by Claus (1979: 29). The term 'spirit mediumship' denotes possession of a ritual specialist by an entity, such as a deity, a demon, a ghost or ancestor. This form of possession takes place in a ritual setting, it is

---

[7] See also Claus 1984. In this article, Claus especially criticizes the "medical approach" to phenomena such as possession: focusing on only one aspect of possession, such as disease and healing, leads us to a rather narrow and reductionistic view of a phenomenon which is much more complex (Claus 1984: 60,61).

formally induced and it is controlled by a ritual specialist. These specialists may be known as oracles, media, shamans, ecstatic priests or exorcists.[8] The term 'spirit possession' is used when a person gets possessed by an undesired, harmful and malevolent entity. This form of possession appears to be uncontrolled and persons who are possessed by such spirits are often referred to as 'patients' or 'victims'. In the anthropological interpretation of possession the disparity between the two forms is often overstressed (see also Claus 1979: 48), and there is a strong correlation between the categories of possession on the one hand and the modes of interpretation on the other, which means that a certain interpretation "fits" either spirit possession or spirit mediumship.[9]

In the following pages I should like to show that an interpretation of possession which stresses psychological and sociological aspects results in a polarisation of the two forms of possession and reduces them to either "illness" or "ritual". By contrast, cosmological and performative approaches to possession allow the phenomenon to be viewed not only under functional aspects but also as an ecstatic religious experience, which reveals that there are no absolute but only relative, gradual differences between these two categories.

The possessed person

Three elements are central to anthropological interpretations of possession, each of which will be considered in some detail below.

---

[8] In a wider sense, the term spirit mediumship also refers to persons who impersonate divine entities in rituals and mythological dramas (see Brückner 1987 and this volume and Freeman, this volume). For the sake of brevity, these impersonators will not be specially categorized, but referred to generally as mediums.

[9] Sometimes the distinction leads to confusion as for instance in the case of Freeman (this volume, p. 134). To my knowledge, an approach which sees possession as "psychopathology" or as "desperate strategies of the socially oppressed" has only been applied to "spirit possession" and never to "spirit mediumship," which includes Teyyam rituals.

These are: the possessed person, the possessing entities and the performance of possession. All three elements are equally important for an interpretation of possession. An overview, however, of the literature on possession shows that each interpretation puts different stress upon each of the elements.

In the past, attention was paid mostly to the possessed person, with the possessing entities and performative aspects having only secondary interest. If we assume that a person cannot become possessed by someone other than his or her usual personality, it is only logical to take into consideration the psychic or social condition of the individual in order to determine the probable causes of this so-called "irrational" or at best "symbolic" behaviour. Thus, if a person gets possessed by a malevolent spirit, it is assumed without fail that the causes of possession will be found in the individual's psychic condition or social situation. From this perspective spirit possession gets reduced to the symptom of a psychic illness, such as hysteria (Freed and Freed 1964); or it is seen as a manifestation of suppressed sexual longings (Kakar 1983 and Obeyesekere 1981); or it is seen as an expression of psychic stress, which occurs and recurs in the life cycle of an individual (Obeyesekere 1977).

In this way we get a plausible explanation for the fact that all over the world, and also in South Asia, the majority of persons who get possessed by spirits are women (Lewis 1989 and Kehoe and Giletti 1981). It is argued that women in South Asia are of low social status, having no access to social prestige and power. Young women specially are exposed to stress due to marrying a stranger and living as a stranger in the household of their affines. In drawing attention to their precarious situation, these women have few alternatives. They can refuse to eat (and everybody will try to console them and try to fulfill their wishes and demands), they can commit suicide (an ultimate solution), or they can get possessed by a ghost (Harper 1963: 174). Of these three alternatives, Harper sees the third to be the most attractive strategy for women; in the words of Lewis (1989: 105) it becomes their "oblique strategy of attack." If a woman gets possessed by a malevolent spirit or demon, then suddenly attention is focused on her. An exorcist has to be summoned to get rid of the ghost, and the demands of the ghost have to be fulfilled. She has to be sent on a pilgrimage; offerings have to be made; her strange behavior, which is against all social norms, is tolerated, for it is ascribed to the ghost or demon. The woman herself can not be made responsible for demonic behavior.

But there are also men who get possessed by malevolent spirits, young as well as old men (Kakar 1983), and in these cases it is also the personal situation of the individual which provides a plausible explanation. Furthermore, the question why only some persons get possessed by malevolent spirits, while others, in similar situations, don't show any signs of spirit possession can be answered by looking at the person. Thus, Obeyesekere (1977 and 1981), Kakar (1983) and Freed and Freed (1964) agree that all possessed individuals are characterized by a so-called "hysterical personality".[10]

In the study of possession mediumship, it is also the person who has been at the center of interest for a long time. However, in this case, it is not the psychic condition of the individual which is taken as a basis for possession, but the course of the argument is completely different. Since possession mediumship is not regarded as socially abnormal it is not necessary to look for causes, but only for its function. In this case sociological aspects are more important, especially regarding the status and function of possessed mediums in society.

Dumont (1959) and Berreman (1964) have pointed out the complementary relationship between Brahman priests, on the one hand,

---

[10] A "hysterical personality" is characterized by a fear of sexuality accompanied often by a strong but hidden interest in it, an unresolved Oedipal conflict, by dramatized and exaggerated behavior and a capacity for multiple identifications (Kakar 1983: 75). It is especially the last two features by which such personalities are predisposed for states of possession.

and possessed media, on the other. The difference in the communication with divinities is a matter of worshipping the gods versus hearing them. While brahmanic priests communicate with the deity through temple rituals and offerings and in this way represent the connecting link between human beings and the deity, media act in the reversed way. The deity communicates through the medium with human beings, announces its wishes and claims and tells the cause of problems which are of supernatural origin. Both the medium and the Brahman priest use ecstasy as a distance-reducing technique between her- or himself and the deity. The medium who is often of low caste status achieves a state of trance, whereas the Brahman priest uses another form of ecstasy, meditation, as a distance-reducing technique between himself and the deity.[11]

Berreman (1964: 55ff) argues that North Indian Pahari media (whom he calls shamans) play a creative and innovative role in the religion of their people, whereas Brahman priests are to be seen as technicians, who exercise rituals in a stereotypical way. In Berreman's analysis it is not the supernatural which talks through a human being, but the medium him- or herself who decides which goddess is becoming influential for the time being, how costly the rituals should be, etc. A successful medium has to convince its audience by its rhetorical and performative qualities; it has to have originality, phantasy and knowledge of human nature and, of course, the ability to enter altered states of consciousness.

The altered state of consciousness, a general term for trance or ecstasy, is an important aspect in the study of possession. Both media and persons who get possessed involuntarily by malevolent spirits claim to have amnesia during their possessed state. They cannot recall what the supernatural had been talking about and, of course, they have no remembrance of their own behaviour, which is very often rather wild and under normal circumstances socially

[11] See Höfer 1974:162.

unacceptable. Since an altered state of consciousness is in itself a rather unusual event, all the incidents which happen in such a state of mind can be classified as irregular, unusual, extraordinary, creative, or hysterical as in the case of spirit possession. What seems to be a matter of creativity, innovation and other individual qualities according to Berreman (or a matter of hysteria in spirit possession), turns out to be also stereotypical and culturally determined, if seen from a different perspective. Freeman (this volume, p. 116, 118ff.) points out that the media, as well, are acting in a stereotypical way. He shows that there is a structure behind the divine utterances, long passages of which are memorized, whereas, only smaller parts of the recitations leave room for personal style and improvization. Furthermore, Stanley (1988: 55) shows that not only media but also persons possessed by a spirit act in a culturally determined way.

An interpretation with the possessed person as the main subject of analysis starts from the premises of Western rationality, according to which a person cannot get possessed by something other than his or her usual personality. On this basis, it is plausible to take into consideration only the individual, her/his personality structure and psychic state of mind in order to find the "real" causes for this "symbolic" behavior. However, this approach takes into account a specific (Western) concept of the person. Kjaerholm (1982) has shown that the concept of the person which is applied by Western social scientists to the analysis of possession in India might not be the same as that of the indigenous people. He suggests that we relate personhood in Indian culture to the philosophical concept of substance, according to which, "the phenomenal world is in general 'possessed' by subtle matter."[12] This would not only explain the notion that any person can get possessed by a divinity, but also the existence of different forms of possession. Furthermore, it would relate these forms to each other, and would also explain the fact that in India not only persons but also things can get possessed,

[12] See Kjaerholm 1982: 195.

since, "the reality of subtle matter may manifest itself anywhere and any time".[13] On the contrary, the assumption that nobody *"really"* can get possessed by demons, ghosts, gods, etc. results in a functional interpretation, which does not show any commonalities between spirit mediumship and spirit possession (if we set aside amnesia and certain performative abilities of both individuals). A spirit medium is seen as a kind of ritual specialist, whereas, involuntary possession by spirits is interpreted as illness or as an expression of stress. The passive component of possession which emphasizes the interference of a transcendental power is not taken into consideration. Possession is not seen as a religious experience in which the supernatural takes possession of a human being in one form or the other, but rather individuals on their part take over the supernatural and use it for their aims. Thus they become effective actors, whereas, they see themselves as passive sufferers or media of the supernatural.

It goes without saying that an understanding of the person is important for the analysis of possession. An interpretation of possession on the basis of the Western concept of a person, however, reduces the phenomena to Western categories, as for instance illness, or psychic disorder (Claus 1984:61). But the possessed individual is only one element in possession. Equally important for an interpretation are the possessing entities and the cosmological concepts about the status and character of these entities. This is shown by Obeyesekere (1977) in the case of Somavati whom he knew and observed for a long period of time. A rather detailed summary of her history is necessary for the understanding of the influence of the different entities on the pattern of possession.

---

[13] id. 1982: 195. Kjaerholm's "philosophical" approach to the study of possession (1982: 179) has to be criticized for major shortcomings. For instance, it is not clear which "philosophical concept" he is referring to. However, his preliminary "thoughts" concerning the concept of person are valuable and should be further elaborated.

The possessing entities

Obeyesekere met Somavati for the first time in 1969 at a local shrine where she was to be exorcised by the priest.[14] She was at that time 29 years old, and during the previous two years had been possessed by several prētaṣ and demons. Obeyesekere recounts in detail the social and personal background, which he thinks led to her possession.[15] Somavati was the eldest daughter of a poor farmer. Her father owned no land, so he left his natal village and earned his livelihood as a day labourer. In this economically unstable situation Somavati was given to her maternal grandmother for adoption when she was just a few months old. After getting over the shock of being separated from her mother, Somavati came to love her grandmother very much. At the age of seven she was taken home by her parents, where she was to take care of a number of smaller siblings. The separation from her grandmother was the second trauma in her young life. At the age of 18 years she married a 25 year old mason despite the initial objection of her parents. Her third traumatic experience occured one week after her marriage when she realized that she had married an alcoholic. In the coming years Somavati gave birth to two children, but was so frequently beaten by her husband that she finally went back to her parents and got divorced.

Back in her parents home, her situation became eventually unbearable. She had no income of her own and depended completely on her parents. In this situation she became possessed for the first time. This first possession by a prēta did not occur arbitrarily, but during an exorcistic ritual, in which the prēta had been exorcised from another woman. It is considered extremely dangerous to attend such a ritual, since it is well known that an exorcised spirit tries to find another victim immediately. Somavati, however, had been asked to be present by her father's employer and could

[14] For a detailed account see Obeyesekere 1977: 240ff.

[15] Note the terminology: Obeyesekere calls Somavati "patient" (240), he talks about possession as "illness" (240).

hardly object. According to Obeyesekere, Somavati's "hysterical personality traits" (1977: 250) and her "unconscious wish" to get possessed formed the basis of her possession.[16] Thus, Somavati becomes the actor who looks for a culturally accepted strategy to deal with her psychological problems. Obeyesekere views possession as a way of expressing psychic disorder in terms of illness; but, in doing so, he reduces spirit possession to Western categories. If we see possession as a religious experience - or at least as a state in which certain experiences are framed in a religious idiom, we have to look at the whole story in a different way: spirits are entities of low status in the cosmic hierarchy and are looking for potential victims, whom they can possess only under specific circumstances. Somavati's situation is indeed perfect for the attack of a spirit. Her state of mind seems to be extremely unbalanced. In terms of social status she is in a liminal state (divorced, a mother of two children but still dependent on her parents); moreover, she is asked to go out at dusk (a favourable time for malevolent spirits) and, in this condition, attend an exorcistic ritual. Thus she predisposes herself to become the victim of a spirit's attack.

In the following two years other prētas take possession of Somavati and various exorcists try to free her of them, but they succeed only for short periods of time. Somavati was eventually possessed not only by prētas but also by demons, such as Riri Yaka, the Blood Demon, and Mahasona, the Great Demon of the Graveyard (Obeyesekere 1977: 256). Demons are more powerful than prētas. They are permanent members of the pantheon, whereas prētas, who are the souls of dead persons, come and go. Simple exorcistic rituals, as for instance tying a charmed thread, are no longer effective. Demons have to be exorcised by more powerful deities. It was decided that the demons and all the prētas should be exorcised at a temple. An exorcistic ritual was arranged for Somavati and another woman at a local temple. It lasted the whole night and attracted a

---

[16] "It is not a psychotic or a nervous breakdown in the Western sense; the breakdown was culturally 'timed' and expressed in a prescribed demonic idiom." (Obeyesekere 1977:251).

fairly large audience, who had come to witness the struggle between the prētas and demons, impersonated by Somavati on the one side and various gods and goddesses impersonated by two priestly media on the other side. The prētas and demons turned out to be rather unwilling to leave and fights with several gods and goddesses were necessary to convince them. The two priestly media impersonated, successively, Skanda (the first medium), Dadimunda (second medium), Kali (first medium, who changed dress), again Dadimunda, and finally Kali, who succeeded in convincing the demons to leave.

In Obeyesekere's terms, Somavati was completely "cured" after the night-long ritual, for she wasn't bothered by demons any more. The whole anthropological story of her affliction could come to an end as yet another example of the subordinated South Asian woman, whose hysterical personality results in spirit possession, by which she draws attention to her unbearable condition. Once a sufficient amount of attention has been secured, the symptoms (i.e. spirit possession) vanish and the patient is cured. Somavati's story of possession, however, does not end at this point. One week after the exorcism, the goddess Pattini announces through the priestly medium at the same temple that she will take possession of Somavati. Pattini also announces the exact date, and four months after the exorcism Somavati is initiated into the Pattini cult, becoming possessed by Pattini during the ritual. This enables Somavati to become possessed regularly by Pattini. She is also entitled to have her own shrine in the temple compound and to act as a priestly medium and oracle of the goddess Pattini. This brings Somavati high social prestige but obliges her to lead a somewhat ascetic way of life. In point of fact, Obeyesekere notes that in the four years following her initiation Somavati became irregularly possessed by Pattini. She worshiped her as her protective deity, but did not develop medial and divinatory abilities.[17]

---

[17] According to Obeyesekere, this is due to the lack of intelligence and also due to Somavati's worldly orientation. (1977:291).

Somavati's story, which is unusually long when compared with other anthropological case studies, shows several important things. First, the dichotomy between spirit possession and spirit mediumship, which is stressed by other social scientists (Freed and Freed 1964, Harper 1957 and 1963, Kakar 1983), seems overemphasized. There is, of course, a distinction between the two forms of possession which is also made by the people themselves, but in the case of Somavati, we can see that there is a continuity rather than a dichotomy between the two forms. Somavati was first "patient" or "victim" and then became medium or priestess. She was occasionally possessed by spirits and demons for a long time (which was also a difficult, unbalanced and liminal period in her life), but the spirits and demons could be removed by higher divinities and finally Pattini, a regional goddess of great power, came to dwell in her body. What looked at first like illness, protest or oblique strategy turned out to be a potential for ecstatic religious experience that could be developed into divine possession. Obeyesekere is able to confirm this development of medial abilities with many other examples. In interviews with several ascetic priestesses, he shows that there is an initial period of pain and suffering in which the possessed person is considered a patient. But after some time she recovers and the spirit who tormented her earlier now becomes a positive being, a protector and mediator, who leads her to the gods (1981: 61). Thus, the same ancestor spirits, appearing as malevolent entities, can be transformed into benevolent beings, who act as intermediaries, in cases where a person does not become possessed by the gods directly (1981: 32; 70). From other descriptions about the development of medial abilities in individuals, we know that this process doesn't always proceed smoothly, but can be difficult, tedious, full of contradictions and drawbacks.[18] There are cases, in which mediumship is quasi-hereditary as, for instance, among the

---

[18] In studies on shamanism the transformational stage in the life of a prospective shaman is a well-documented feature. Frequently, in the beginning, the person doesn't know what happens after he or she fell seriously ill and is about to die. Even after the initial crisis is overcome and it is obvious that it was a transformational illness, the development of ecstatic abilities takes a long time.

Saora and Oraon in Central India (Elwin 1955: 133 and Kakar 1983: 94), but even then the development of these abilities is rather wearisome, and the result is not always predictable.

Aside from this, the different motivations of various concerned persons in defining the possessing entities are involved. At the first occurence of possession, the identity of the possessing entity is often obscure. Relatives of the possessed individual might have different opinions because the entity does not reveal its identity, or the possessing spirit deliberately announces a wrong name. For example, if among the Vāḍabalija, a South Indian fishing caste, a young woman gets possessed for the first time, an experienced medium has to confirm the identity of the possessing entity. If it is a malevolent spirit or demon it will be exorcised, but if it is really a deity then the girl or young woman has the potential to become a medium. But in this case it will still take several years until the medial and divinatory skills of the girl are fully developed and can be controlled. In the meantime, possessions may occur, but they are irregular, spontaneous and a cause for fear, because one never knows which cosmic entities are involved (Schoembucher 1986: 161).

Another example which points to a continuity rather than a strict dichotomy between the two forms of possession is the possession by Siri, a benevolent local goddess in Karnataka. Claus (1979: 39) shows that possession by Siri, initially, is a frightening and unwanted experience. The main reason for this is that the possessed person, usually a young woman shortly before or after her marriage, is not prepared to become a vessel of the goddess. It is mainly ritual impurity, which causes problems for Siri and to which she draws attention through causing troubles. Once Siri's identity is determined and it is promised that the person chosen by her will be initiated at the next yearly temple ritual, possession changes from being an unwanted to a welcomed condition. The initial danger becomes a blessing for the whole family.[19]

---

[19] This means that possession is not seen as "illness" which has to be cured, but rather that the appropriate preconditions have to be provided in order to make it a

These examples show that we shouldn't reduce one form of possession (spirit possession) to illness and the other form (spirit mediumship) to ritual, but that we should see possession primarily as a religious experience (as it is seen by the concerned persons themselves) which differs mainly in terms of the possessing entities and in the way it is perceived by the persons. This fact becomes even more evident if we take the cosmological concepts into greater consideration.

The Cosmic Hierarchy

In their studies on possession Obeyesekere (1977) and Kapferer (1983) emphazise the possessing entities and their status in the cosmic hierarchy. The nature of the entity and its place in the cosmic hierarchy has great influence on the way possession takes place. The cosmic order includes entities of different rank: besides human beings, there are ghosts and spirits of low status, ancestor spirits, demons and deities who all form a hierarchy. With respect to cosmological concepts there are, of course, considerable regional differences in South Asia but there are also points in common. The relation between human beings and those entities who can possess them lies in their common origin. All the entities who can possess a person have come into being either through deification or through transformation into spirits, which means that they themselves have been human beings. An intrusion of one of these supernatural beings can be experienced either in a positive or negative way, depending on their respective character. But in this case, as well, it is not a pattern with a clear-cut opposition, because the same supernatural being can manifest itself in its malevolent or benevolent aspect.

The supernatural entities form a hierarchy in the cosmic order. On the lowest level there are spirits who are the souls of dead per-

---

positive event.

sons who couldn't fully live their lives and are, therefore, too attached to life, those who died a premature or violent death or who have led an immoral life. Such ancestor spirits are named after the dead person, and they are not permanent members of the pantheon, but come and go (Obeyesekere 1977: 258). They come into being after the death of a certain individual and usually possess persons who are closely related to the deceased. These spirits are only existent as long as the deceased are remembered. After a few generations when the living memory of the ancestor fades, it is unlikely that her/his soul will possess a living being. Not only do these spirits have the lowest rank in the cosmic hierarchy, but they are also closest to human beings and not as powerful as higher spiritual beings. Therefore, the procedures adopted to deal with these spirits after they have taken possession of a human being are comparatively simple. They can be exorcised with mantras, amulets or charmed threads. In the case of Somavati we have seen that they can be rather obstinate, being subsequently replaced by demons who had finally to be exorcised by the powerful goddess Kali.

But there are also ancestral spirits of ambivalent character. They can either protect their descendants or punish them if they feel neglected. Ambivalent ancestors are the souls of persons who died after a fulfilled life in which they had an important social position (as the lineage of elders for instance). Since they can either protect or harm human beings, they have to be asked about their demands or the compensation they require for being thus neglected by their descendants. Contact with these more powerful ambivalent beings is established through a priestly medium who is possessed by a deity and who communicates directly with the spiritual being possessing the person.

Low spirits and demons are always looking for potential victims and for an opportunity to destroy the cosmic order. They cannot, however, possess their victims (or vehicles) arbitrarily. Rather - and in this respect like higher beings - they can do so only under certain circumstances. Thus, persons in liminal periods of life are especially in danger of attracting negative cosmic forces, such as malevolent spirits and demons. A good opportunity also exists for the malevolent spirits to act when positive cosmic forces cannot exercise their influence any more because they have become too weak or annoyed by the deficiences in the worship accorded to them. From this perspective the fact that women are often possessed by evil spirits can be explained in a different way. As Claus (1979: 37) suggests, the fact that many young women in the most important liminal period of their life (marriage until the birth of the first child) become possessed by Siri can be explained by the cosmological concepts of their culture, and not just by the assumption that women in psycho-social situations of stress take to the strategy of possession to draw attention to their situation. Additionally, Kapferer (1983: 100) has shown that women are more vulnerable to attack by malign spirits and ghosts because they are more frequently subject to pollution (menstruation, childbirth). That they are generally viewed as more attached to worldly matters, also explains why many ghosts are deceased kinswomen.

Supernatural beings on the lowest level of the hierarchy do not possess persons arbitrarily, though nevertheless unwanted, whereas supernatural beings of a higher order possess a person upon request, after the necessary ritual arrangements and preparations have been made, as for instance in spirit mediumship. The same deities, however, can also take possession of human beings without being invited, should they become angry over their neglect by human beings. In such cases contact with the divinity is felt to be highly threatening for mankind. As an example we may consider the notion that certain deities can manifest themselves in the human body in the form of smallpox or other diseases. The deities, who should and can protect human beings from these diseases, can also inflict the very same epidemic upon them. In such situations the sick person is perceived as a vessel of the deity, and the room of the patient becomes a temporary temple in which the deity is worshipped in this specific manifestation (Kolenda 1982: 235f).

Hearing the Gods: The Divine Performance

Until now I have tried to show that an interpretation of possession which takes into consideration indigenous conceptions will draw different conclusions concerning the meaning of possession than an interpretation in which only the psychosocial situation of the possessed person is taken as relevant. Psychological and sociological modes of interpretation reduce spirit possession to illness, exorcism to healing rituals and possession mediumship to divination. By contrast, an interpretive mode, which stresses the performative aspects of possession, avoids reductionism and attains a more comprehensive understanding. Performance theory attempts to understand the whole of the event (Claus 1985). It recognizes that possession is just one part of the performance. It is, of course, central to the performance, but it must nonetheless be understood in relation to the performance as a whole. For instance, besides the person who experiences possession, we always have an audience and a text. In a performative approach to possession the elements of the action and their structural interrelationships are shown, and then conclusions are drawn about the concepts which have been converted into practice by ritual action. The elements of the performance may be seen as attributes for structuring this transformation. In possession mediumship, ritual drama and exorcism the performative aspects can be seen very clearly, especially when the rituals are accompanied by music, dance or the recitation of texts.[20] There is a specific setting, characterized by certain elements which have to be present. These are: a fixed space, the "stage" as it were, a fixed time, performers, audience and sequence of events. The sequence of events in possession mediumship is precisely fixed. The medium as well as the "stage" have to be prepared by ritual purification. The space where possession is to take place, i.e. the stage, can be a temple, a house, or at least a place inside the village — that is, a place not associated with wilderness which can be purified comparatively easily. The time is fixed beforehand, preferably in the late afternoon

---

[20] See Brückner (1987 and this volume), Freeman (this volume) and Kapferer (1983).

or in the evening, to secure a large audience. The performers on stage are the oracles or the exorcist but, as is shown by Kapferer, there are also many others who take part in the preparations for the ritual (1983: 71f). After the space and the medium have been ritually purified, the evocation begins: the deity has to be asked to come into the body of the medium. The evocation ends, when the deity has entered the body of the medium. During the evocative stage not only the possessed person, but also the audience, are prepared for the events to come. In the following sequence, the divination, the deity speaks through the medium. The divine speech is completely different from ordinary speech, even though in many instances it is acquired without formal training.[21] The audience listen to the voice of the divinity, ask questions and also express their dissatisfaction with what the deity says. The performance ends when the deity leaves the body of the medium.

In spirit possession the performative aspects are not as evident, but we shall see that they are, nonetheless, present.[22] In this case as well, there have to exist certain preconditions in order for a malevolent spirit or ghost to possess a person. The sequence of events is not as clear as in spirit mediumship, but if we consider the performative aspects of this kind of possession, we find the same elements present, although in a reversed analogy. We have seen that possession by a spirit or demon cannot occur arbitrarily, but that it also depends on particular space and time. The best times for such an encroachment are the liminal stages in the life cycle of an individual, or situations in which the positive cosmic forces are weakened. Con-

---

[21] The text of the divine words which is sometimes hard to understand even for the audience is only rarely translated by anthropologists. However, it constitutes the central part of a performative approach. A notable exception are the works of Brückner (1987 and this volume) and Freeman (this volume) which provide a large corpus of translated texts.

[22] One reason why the performative aspects in spirit possession are not as obvious, lies in the fact that this form of possession is often described summarily and stress is laid on the spontaneity, individuality and arbitrariness of the events. But if we consider the performative aspects of possession, we will also tend to find elements by which the action is structured.

venient spatial preconditions will be for instance outside the village, at crossroads, underneath trees or in the vicinity of graveyards. Space and "medium" are, in some way or the other, polluted. The time, concerning both the period in the individual life cycle and the time of day is inauspicious. In spirit possession we also have performers and an audience. Possession by a malevolent spirit will not take place without a public. Otherwise the spirit would not be able to enforce its demands (we must remember that the victims claim amnesia). The spirit, like the deity, communicates with the public through its media. The relatives of the possessed person as well as the exorcist have to come to terms with the spirit and fulfil its demands. Thus, in spirit possession the "stage" is also the most important element of the performance, besides the words uttered by the demonic entity. In accordance with the character of the beings of a lower cosmic order, ghosts and demons need not be evoked, but come all of a sudden (though not arbitrarily) and unasked for. Once they are present (in the body of their medium), they make their demands known to the audience.

In both forms of possession the voice of the entities is not always immediately understood by the whole audience, but has to be further "translated" by a mediator, i.e. an exorcist or any person with enough knowledge and authority for her or his voice to be heard. As Kapferer (1983: 64ff) has shown there might be no immediate consensus as to the meaning of the words of the supernatural. Frequently it is a question of trial and error until finally the spiritual being can be identified and appropriate action for its removal can be undertaken.

Even though there is an outer sequence of events in every performance of possession, it might still be argued that the actor is acting in a rather unstructured fashion. After all, the actors claim to have been in a trance and to have no memory of that which has happened. An altered state of consciousness suggests, indeed, extraordinary, individualistic and innovative behaviour. A closer look at the phenomenon shows, however, that not only are the outer circumstances also well defined, but that the actors also act in a prescribed and stereotypical way (as for example Freeman shows for Teyyam dancers). Stanley, who explicitly analyzes all forms of possession in terms of a religious experience, shows that regarding personal experience, the two forms of possession (either by spirits or by deities) can clearly be seen as polar opposites. Persons who are possessed by the divine enjoy their state of trance and speak of it as an experience of great happiness (1988: 42). The ability to perform extraordinary acts, such as walking or dancing on fire as well as divination is seen as a gift from their god, obtained by sincere devotion (ibid., p. 46, 51).

On the other hand, persons who are possessed by malevolent spirits experience this as "wrongness", chaos and disorder (ibid., p.50, 57). The behaviour of the spirit victims is not just strange and unpredictable, but they are also identified with the traditional agents of disorder and chaos, in which case they act out the role of the rebellious agent, rebelling against the power of the priest or exorcist and creating chaos. Shouting, threatening, abusing, groveling in dirt, crawling in an abnormal manner cannot be interpreted merely as "hysterical behaviour" it has to be seen rather as an enactment of negative and chaotic cosmic forces.

Looking at possession in this way reveals that spirit possession is not just illness, exorcism not just a healing ritual and spirit mediumship not just divination, but that they are also ways of encompassing different cosmic forces for the depiction of various problems that may occur in everyday life. Persons who act in these performances should not be simply seen as patients or healers, but as impersonators or interpreters of different cosmic forces.

Conclusions

In this article I have attempted to present the various approaches by which possession has been interpreted by anthropologists. To understand the meaning of possession the phenomenon has to be examined from several perspectives. Claus (1984: 68f) has rightly argued that an approach to possession through problem-oriented

Western paradigms such as the medical paradigm will result in an oversimplistic interpretation of a complex phenomenon. Illness and protest might be one aspect of spirit possession, just as divination and healing might be one aspect of spirit mediumship, but an interpretation of possession should not restrict itself to this. It is not only the case that the problem-oriented approach results in a simplistic view of possession. Rather the rational Western world view, according to which a person cannot get possessed by supernatural beings, provides a set of premises which lead one to interpret signs of "abnormality" in a person's life, in terms of medical, psychic or social causes.

This overlooks the fact that possession may also be perceived as a religious experience by the people themselves. Most anthropologists obviously do not believe in such ecstatic experiences, and since scientific knowledge is based on empirical experience, a religious experience such as possession which cannot be rationally understood, gets reduced to "symbols", "projections" or "illusions". In this way, the reality of possession as a religious experience is ignored by many anthropologists.

Recent anthropological research, however, has shown that an ethnography which considers both the indigenous concepts and the performative aspects of possession results in a more comprehensive understanding. We need not refer to "paranormal" paradigms in order to understand what is happening when a person experiences possession. It might be sufficient for the time being to have a closer look at the ethnographic process of possession. Considering the performance of possession as a text or as a source for interpretation enables one to draw a different set of conclusions. An examination of the sequential nature of possession and the texts which are spoken during possession shows that possession is not as improvisational and spontaneous as one might expect. There is, of course, room for spontaneous acts of speech and improvisation, but there is also a stock of standard texts and long stretches of memorized but divinely inspired words. The possessed person not only recites the words of the entity but also assumes its character which is marked mostly by chaos and malevolence in the case of a ghost or demon and benevolence in the case of a deity. Thus, trance in possession cannot be seen as dissociation in psychological terms when the individual cannot control her/his actions any more, but, rather, has to be seen as a kind of "heightened consciousness" (Freeman, this volume p. 131) through which the individual is enabled to perform actions which would be impossible in an ordinary state of mind - such as impersonating supernatural entities, walking on fire, etc.

This critical review of the literature on possession in South Asia remains programmatic in its commitment to the interpretation of possession as cultural performance. This is necessarily so, for field research on the performative aspects of possession is not yet extensive and much of the existing literature only hints at the insights to be gained from this new approach. It is clear, though, that any ethnographic attempt to describe possession in all its complexity requires complex methods of observation and of textual construction, translation and interpretation. Despite the difficulties that lie before the ethnographer, the resultant ethnographic text will bring the description closer to the events experienced by the people themselves with fewer European presuppositions about the reality of the experience. The gains to our understanding will be immense.

References

Benz, Ernst 1972. Ergriffenheit und Besessenheit als Grundformen religiöser Erfahrung. In Jürg Zutt (ed.) *Ergriffenheit und Besessenheit*. Bern und München: Francke Verlag. pp.125-148.

Berreman, G.D. 1964. Brahmins and shamans in Pahari Religion. In E.B. Harper (ed.) *Religion in South Asia*. Seattle: University of Washington Press, pp. 53-70.

Brückner, Heidrun 1987. Bhūta-Worship in Coastal Karnāṭaka: An oral Tuḷu myth and festival ritual of Jumādi. In *Studien zur Indologie und Iranistik*. 13/14: 17-38.

Claus, Peter J. 1979. Spirit possession and spirit mediumship from the perspective of Tulu oral traditions. In *Culture, Medicine and Psychiatry* 3(1):29-52.

Id. 1984. Medical Anthropology and the Ethnography of Spirit Possession. In *Contributions to Asian Studies* 18: 60-72.

Id. 1985. *Possession as performance*. Paper presented at the Southwestern Anthropological Association Meetings. Chico, CA.

Diehl, Carl Gustav 1956. *Instrument and purpose. Studies on rites and rituals in South India*. Lund.

Dumont, L. 1959. Possession and priesthood. In *Contributions to Indian Sociology* 3: 55-74.

Eliade, Mircea 1951. *Le chamanisme et les techniques archaïques de l'extase*. Paris: Editions Payot.

Elwin, V. 1955. *The religion of an Indian tribe*. London.

Freed, S.A. and R.S. Freed 1964. Spirit possession as illness in a North Indian village. In *Ethnology* 3: 152-171.

Harper, E.B. 1957. Shamanism in South India. In *Southwestern Journal of Anthropology* 13: 267-287.

Harper, E.B. 1963. Spirit possession and social structure. In Bala Ratnam (ed.) *Anthropology on the march. Recent studies of Indian beliefs, attitudes and social institutions*. Madras. pp. 165-177.

Hitchcock, J.T. and R.L. Jones (eds.) 1976. *Spirit possession in the Nepal Himalayas*. Warminster: Aris and Phillips.

Höfer, András 1974. A Note on possession in South Asia. In Fürer-Haimendorf,C.v. (ed.): *Contributions to the Anthropology of Nepal*. Warminster. Aris and Phillips. pp. 159-167.

Jones Rex L. 1967/68. Shamanism in South Asia: A preliminary survey. In *History of Religions* 7: 330-347.

Kakar, Sudhir 1983. *Shamans, mystics and doctors. A psychological enquiry into India and its healing traditions.* Boston: Beacon Press.

Kapferer, Bruce 1983. *A celebration of demons. Exorcism and the aesthetics of healing in Sri Lanka.* Bloomington. Indiana University Press.

Kehoe, A.B. and Giletti, D.H. 1981. Women's preponderance in possession cults: The calcium-defiency hypothesis extended. In *American Anthropologist* 83: 549-61.

Kjaerholm, L. 1982. Possession and substance in Indian civilization. Thoughts emanating from field-work in South India. In *Folk* 24: 179-196.

Kolenda, Pauline 1982 Pox and the terror of childlessness: Images and ideas of the smallpox goddess in a North Indian village. In James J. Preston (ed.) *Mother worship: Theme and variations.* Chapel Hill, N.C.: University of North Carolina Press.

Lewis, I.M. 1989. *Ecstatic religion. A study of shamanism and spirit possession.* Second Edition. Routledge. London and New York.

Obeyesekere, Gananath 1977. Psychocultural exegesis of a case of spirit possession in Sri Lanka. In Crapanzano, V. and Garrison V. (eds.) *Case studies in spirit possession*. New York. Wiley. pp. 235-295.

Id. 1981. *Medusa's hair. An essay on personal symbols and religious experience*. The University of Chicago Press. Chicago and London.

Schoembucher, E. 1986. *Die Vāḍabalija in Andhra Pradesh und in Orissa. Aspekte der wirtschaftlichen und sozialen Organisation einer maritimen Gesellschaft*. Wiesbaden: Franz Steiner Verlag.

Seligmann, C.G. and Brenda Seligmann 1911. *The Veddas*. Cambrige: University Press.

Sontheimer, Günther D. 1991. Bhakti in the Khaṇḍobā cult. In Diana L. Eck and Francoise Mallison (eds.) *Devotion divine. Bhakti traditions from the regions of India*. Studies in honour of Charlotte Vaudeville. Groningen/Paris: Groningen Oriental Studies 8, 231-253.

Srinivas, M.N. 1952. *Religion and society among the Coorgs of South India*. Oxford: Clarendon Press.

Stanley, J.M. 1988. Gods, ghosts and possession. In E. Zelliot and M. Berntsen (eds.): *The experience of Hinduism. Essays on religion in Maharashtra*. State University of New York Press. pp. 26-59.

II *Textual Networks*

THE GENRES OF TUḶU FOLK-POETRY: AN INTRODUCTION

B.A. Viveka Rai

Tuḷu is the language spoken in Dakṣiṇa Kannaḍa, the coastal region of Karnataka, which is also traditionally known as Tuḷunāḍu (the Tuḷuva region). Since the Tuḷu language functions as a powerful medium of folk expression in this region, folk literature in Tuḷu is abundant and varied, and is also an integral part of the dynamic processes of oral tradition. Tuḷu folk literature comprises many genres which could be viewed as parallels to those identified by the folklorists as universal ones. The classification of a 'regional folklore' into different folk-categories, and identification of them as belonging to different genres comparable to those with international folklore, is a highly problematic and challenging task for modern folklorists. An attempt is made in this paper to discuss this problem and to view 'generic folkloristics' from new perspectives. Tuḷu folk poetry[1] is taken as a model for such study. It consists, to a large extent, of oral texts referred to as *pāḍdanas*.

Pāḍdana scholars have discussed the etymology, form, content, structure, context, performance and meaning of *pāḍdanas*. (Rai 1982, id. 1985, id. 1986, Claus 1975, id. 1978, id. 1979, id. 1987, id. this volume, Brückner 1987, id. this volume, Rao 1986, and Upad-

[1] The term 'folk-poetry' is used here only in the conventional sense. Actually, according to performance theory any folklore item is a performance, and cannot be distinguished from the other items whether they are in verbal form or not.

hyaya and Upadhyaya 1986). These texts as a group fall into different universal genres of folklore, and simply cannot be equated with any single folklore genre.

Pāḍdanas can be viewed as ballads or folk epics considering their oral formulaic form. Rai 1986 discusses *pāḍdanas* as folk epics: '*Pāḍdanas*, which form the major part of Tuḷu folk poetry, because of their narrative quality can be called ballads, in a limited sense.' The same paper posits that *pāḍdanas*, as a genre, can be seen from the point of view of 'single-epic type' (e.g.: Kōṭi-Cennaya and Siri) and 'ballad-cycle type' (e.g.: *būta pāḍdanas*). The paper offers three important conclusions: 1. The different narratives on a common theme, person or *būta* can be considered one single unit, called ballad cycle, in the form of a 'folk epic'. 2. In the diffusion cycle of *būta pāḍdanas*, one can discern a formulaic framework. 3. The overall structure of such ballad cycles, or folk epics, as far as Tuḷu *pāḍdanas* are concerned, consists of the formation and resolution of oppositions.

In his early papers (Claus 1975, 1978), Claus has equated *pāḍdanas* with legends: 'The cult is not a village group but a regional one, and the interactional structure is provided largely by the formal legend, the *Siri Pāḍdana*' (1975: 47). 'The legend of Siri or *Siri Pāḍdana*, is not the property of any single cult or caste... The legend is normally sung in formal *pāḍdana* style only by cult members in the context of ritual' (1975: 47). Speaking of Tuḷu *pāḍdanas*, he states: 'Much of this body of tradition consists of legends of the local spirits and deities, *būtas* and *daivas*' (1978: 2). 'The legend of Kōṭi and Cennaya is another *pāḍdana* in which Bermeru plays a central role' (1978: 7). In the earlier article, Claus also identifies the Tuḷu *pāḍdanas* as myths from the structural point of view: 'The Siri myth serves as more than a charter for these social institutions and customs' (1975: 51). 'The Siri myth revolves around more abstract emotions and morality principles. The myth concerns kinship and position of women' (1975: 56). In his recent paper (this volume)

Claus discusses *pāḍdanas* by taking into account text variability and context-and-performance variations. It is an interesting development in the study of Tuḷu folk genres like *pāḍdanas* to have more than one universal generic term to explain a particular type.

Rai (1985 *passim),* analysing the nature of *pāḍdanas,* also identifies them as 'folk myths' when considering their content and structure. Brückner, too, identifies *pāḍdanas* as myths: 'He (the performer) performs ecstatic dances which sometimes reflect or enact events referred to in the myth. These myths are called *pāḍdana* in Tuḷu.' Brückner (1987: 18-19) further observes: 'The *pāḍdanas* make up a mythological, linguistic, and poetic corpus which strengthens the cultural identity of major sections of the non-brahmin Tuḷu speaking population' (1987: 19). Rao in his paper on 'Folk-poem as epic' studies the folk-epic model with reference to Tuḷu *pāḍdanas.* According to him, 'most of the Tuḷu *pāḍdanas* have a geo-historical, legendary or mythical base. In turn, they animate the landscape, the history, legend, or myth that sustains the folk tradition (Rao 1986: 14) The *pāḍdanas* call for a modified aesthetic, a different creative critical model which might facilitate a more precise understanding of the creative factors at work in the Tuḷu folk imagination'. (Rao 1986: 22)

The reason for all such diverse opinions about *pāḍdanas* is that *pāḍdanas* belong to different categories. Every one views them from the angle of one particular folklore genre, and identifies them accordingly. In this sense, the *'pāḍdana'* genre is like the elephant of the well-known parable which is identified differently by different blind men.

At this point it will be helpful if I briefly introduce the general characteristics of *pāḍdanas* as a folk category in terms of their form and content, structure, and performance context. The word *'pāḍdana'* can be derived from the Dravidian root *'pāḍu'/'pāṭu',* meaning 'to sing'. The text can be called a *pāḍdana* only when it is sung or recited. The prose form with the same content would be called a *'katE'*, i.e. a story. (Cp. also Brückner 1987: 19)

The Kōṭi-Cennaya *pāḍdana* is popularly known as *banṭere sandi* (*sandi* of *banṭs*, i.e. warriors) — the term referring here to Kōṭi-Cennaya. The Siri *pāḍdana* is popularly known as *siri sandi*. Likewise, *abbage-dāraga sandi* and *sonne-giṇḍe sandi* illustrate that the word *sandi* is used as frequently as *pāḍdana*.

But even such usage has exceptions, folk terminology being dependent on other factors such as context and region. The term *'sandi'*, corresponds to the Sanskrit word *sandhi*, which means 'union', 'combination', 'connection' and also 'a division (in drama)'. In medieval Kannaḍa poetry (*e.g.* Kumāra Vyāsa Bhārata, 15th century A.D.), the chapters or the different divisions of texts were called *sandhis*. Ordinary people often use the terms *'pāḍdana'* and *'sandi'* as synonyms and there seems to be no specific distinction between *pāḍdana* and *sandi*. Genre classification according to ordinary people, which might be different from the scholars' classification, is worth studying, but may not be of much help in discussions of genre. The reason is that the generic terms which ordinary people use change from place to place, context to context, and also from person to person.

A large number of *pāḍdanas* deal with the origin and dissemination of *būtas*. Such *pāḍdanas* are normally recited in the context of *būta* performances like *kōla* and *nēma*. The performers of a particular *būta* (deity) mostly recite the lines of the *pāḍdana* at the time of putting on make-up. Usually a woman of the performer's family joins in reciting the alternative lines of the *pāḍdana*. The recitation is accompanied by rhythmic beating of a drum *(tembarE)*. Considering this context of the recitation of the *pāḍdana* as preliminary to the *būta* performance, one should not be led to the simple conclusion that *pāḍdanas* can be defined as a genre in terms of the context. The question which should be posed here is whether this is the only natural context of *pāḍdana* recitation, and the answer may not be a simple one. In the context of the *būta* performance, only a few lines of the *pāḍdana* text are recited and many times the recitation/performance cannot be explained in relation to the *pāḍdana* text. There are some occasions when no *pāḍdana* recitation takes place and the participating folk do not think that the performance is incomplete. A small portion of the text, even when it does have a context, cannot be useful for identifying *pāḍdana* as a genre.

People also sing *pāḍdanas* (or *sandis*) in paddy fields while plucking 'paddy seedlings' *(nēji)*. The worksongs sung in the context of planting the paddy seedlings are called *kabitas*. These will be discussed later in this paper. The very fact that the *sandis* or *pāḍdanas* of *būtas* are sung as worksongs denotes that there is no bar from singing such *pāḍdanas* outside the *būta*-performance context. In the paddy fields, the *sandis* or *pāḍdanas* are normally sung by womenfolk. The women may be two or three in number, and the singing goes along with their work. Even here, many times the whole text of *pāḍdana* might not be recited, and the duration of the *pāḍdana* recitation will be dependent on the magnitude of work in the paddy field.

Pāḍdanas/sandis are sung sometimes at night in homes. Here the purpose and situation might not be much different from those of folk-tales.

If a researcher wants to have the 'complete text' of a *pāḍdana*, he/she cannot get that satisfactorily in any of the contexts mentioned above. He/she can go to a *pāḍdana* singer and collect the 'complete text' only after hearing it for hours together. But folklorists belonging to the contextual and performance school object to such recordings of bare texts without contexts; for if there is no audience, there is no performance. But the problem for the folklorist is, with such verbal forms, how to to do both: satisfy theoreticians and also get 'complete texts'.

Folk Genre and Meaning

As a partial resolution of the problem, *pāḍdanas* can be viewed as specific genres having different communicative efficacies. The concept of 'genre-specific meaning' can be profitably utilised to understand and explain culture-specific genres like *pāḍdanas*. Folkloristic studies of meaning are discussed by eminent folklorists like Lauri Honko, Roger D. Abrahams, Daniel R. Barnes, Lutz Röhrich, and Anna-Leena Siikala (Scandinavian Yearbook of Folklore 1984; cf. Jonsson 1986). Discussing genre-specific meaning, Honko says: 'Genres could be conceived of as units of communication which focus, direct, and limit meaning; favour some and avoid other topics; regulate expression and encourage typical ways of speech and action.' (Honko 1986a: 52). He also writes, 'The concept of genre-specific meanings serves by its very nature as a bridge from contextual consideration back to text semantics. Genre - typical meaning should be visible in folklore texts, and probably in many ways. A preference for certain themes and the avoidance of others is certainly one lead to follow in attempting to draw a profile of possible messages within a genre.' (Honko 1986a: 54). Lutz Röhrich in a paper entitled 'The quest of meaning in folk narrative research' raises such questions as what does 'meaning' mean, and what is the meaning of 'mean.' (Röhrich 1986 *passim)*. Though complicated, the 'theory of meaning formation of folklore' can be profitably used in explaining culture-specific genres like *pāḍdanas*.

Selected portions of the Kōṭi-Cennaya *pāḍdana* are recited in ritual performance *(nēma)*, in paddy fields as a work song, and also while tapping toddy from the palm trees.[2] In the first instance, the reciters are the traditional performers like *paravas;* in the second, it is working women irrespective of caste; and in the third, i.e. in the toddy-tapping situation, it is the Biruva community men, of the

[2] Dr. K. Chinnappa Gowda of Mangalore University has given me this last piece of information.

same social group to which the characters Kōṭi and Cennaya belong. In a ritualistic performance like *nēma,* the Kōṭi-Cennaya *pāḍdana* is utilised in order to create an atmosphere of the mythical realm. Here, the *pāḍdana* functions as a myth emphasizing heroic qualities such as valour, dignity and courage of ordinary people, in general. The recitation of the Kōṭi-Cennaya *pāḍdana* in this context serves the purpose of creating the concept of an intermediate realm where the folk and the mythical characters meet each other. In the paddy fields, the *pāḍdana* recitation functions mainly as a worksong, focusing primarily on the story. The message from the story of the Kōṭi-Cennaya is from the working class to the working class. Here the *pāḍdana* functions as a medium of traditional communication. In the toddy-tapping context, the recitation of Kōṭi-Cennaya *pāḍdana* is by the Biruva community men and the meaning we can extract is dependent on the caste bond. Since Kōṭi-Cennaya, the cultural heroes depicted in the *pāḍdana,* were of the Biruva community, the Biruva folk — here the traditional toddy tappers — identify themselves with the mythical characters, Kōṭi-Cennaya, and thereby get the message of involving themselves wholly in their traditional profession. Here the *pāḍdana* functions not as a part of a ritual like *būta-kōla,* but as an instrument with a totemic symbol.

We folklorists come across occasions for collecting *pāḍdanas* in full length with the reciters singing the whole text without any ritualistic or professional context. My recent experience is of collecting the Kōṭi-Cennaya *pāḍdana* in Belthangady Tālukā, where it was sung by two informants belonging to the Gauḍa community, who learnt and practice this *pāḍdana* in a more secular folk-theatrical, '*puruṣa* dance'. These two Gauḍa men participate as Kōṭi and Cennaya in the *puruṣa* dance performance which ridicules the traditional folk religion including *būta* performances. Though they don't recite the Kōṭi-Cennaya *pāḍdana* wholly in this satirical theatrical performance, the *pāḍdana* they recite jointly, with alternative lines in succession, is a product of such a theatrical performance. Here the point of the *pāḍdana* is relaxation and not ritual effectiveness.

The *katE*, or story of Kōṭi-Cennaya in prose form, is told as a folk tale; the purpose and meaning of such *katE* are different from that of the *pāḍdana*. The question is whether the *pāḍdana* in prose form should be termed a myth or a legend or just a tale. I think, in its structure, it is more like a legend than a myth. As I have mentioned in the beginning of this paper, *pāḍdana* scholars like Claus consider *pāḍdanas* to be myths or legends (Claus 1975, 1978). The reason may be because some episodes concerning the main characters like Kōṭi-Cennaya, Siri or a particular *būta* (Pañjurli, Jumādi etc.), can be seen as legends while others can be seen as myths. In a way, many of the *pāḍdanas* are a mix of legends and myths. But even this statement is a qualitative one and should be understood only in the light of the discussion undertaken in the preceding pages of this paper.

In order to highlight the nature of this problem, the Kōṭi-Cennaya *katE*, or story, can be compared with a popular legend in the Tuluva region *Agoli Mañjaṇṇa*. This is a *katE* which exists only in prose form and not in *pāḍdana* form at all. It is about a character, 'Mañjaṇṇa', belonging to the Baṇṭ community, known for his voracious appetite and Herculean might. But no *pāḍdanas*, no ritual performances, no shrines exist for him; there is only the story in the form of a legend. The non-existence of *pāḍdana* and ritual performance are complementary and, therefore, a non-mythical form of the story exists.

A systematic study of *pāḍdanas* began only about 20 years ago, and the collecting of *pāḍdanas* in their different contexts has not yet been done extensively in this region. So a comprehensive interpretation cannot be undertaken until further research is carried out. Interpretations by a larger number of investigators and folklorists are necessary to arrive at concrete conclusions.

Kabitas

Kabita[3] is an important genre of Tuḷu poetry, which functions as a worksong. *Kabitas* are normally sung by women as group songs in paddy fields while the paddy seedlings (*nēji*) are being planted. *Kabitas* are not sung while plucking the seedlings in the paddy field. *Kabita* as a generic term is not pan-Tuḷuva in nature, though people in some regions use it in that sense. In many places people either use the chorus line of each *kabita* independently, or sing *Obēlē* songs. *Obēlē* is a *kabita* which is very popular and is pan-Tuḷuva in distribution.

The singing of *kabita* by the womenfolk in a group is controlled by one woman who is well-versed in singing and who also has a rich repertoire of *kabitas.* She sings each line of the *kabita* and the rest join in the chorus. This process continues with different texts, depending upon the amount of work to be done in the paddy field.

The theme of the *kabitas* varies, but most of them are not complete narratives in nature. Compared to *pāḍdanas,* they are shorter in length and looser in structure. The structure of a *kabita* of this kind can be interpreted in relation to the context in which it is sung. The message it conveys can be understood by considering this context: working in the field is a relaxed, non-ritualistic context.

The popular *kabita 'Obēlē'* deals with the working situation in paddy fields. The very word *'bēlē'* in Tuḷu means 'work'. A landlord seeks the help of a traditional labourer to get women to work in the fields. He goes to fetch the women labourers and on his way back he mortgages two women in order to buy liquor and betel leaves. The landlord gets angry and the narrative suddenly tells us that his wife becomes pregnant. The concluding portion of the *kabita* has a

---

[3] The word *kabita* can be derived from *kavitā* (Skt.), meaning 'poetry'. Here *kabita* refers only to those songs which are sung during the planting of paddy seedlings in the field.

positive tone: the landlord gets a boy and a girl child, and in appreciation of the children's generosity, the *kabita* comes to an end.

Though there are many variants to this popular *kabita*, the central theme is very common. One variant reflects the wishes of the ordinary people whose work song says: 'Let new crops come up with the seedlings we have transplanted. Let the wife of our landlord become pregnant. Let there be prosperous crops in the field. Let there be prosperity in the house of the landlord.' This is the message that the *Obēlē kabita* conveys in a traditional set-up of land ownership, existing in villages. Ordinary people identify their happiness with that of the landlord in the feudalistic set-up. There is also a close connection between content, context and meaning in this *kabita*. The themes of having plentiful children and crops are two manifestations of the same ideology. The concept of wish-fulfilment is also pronounced in *kabitas* of this sort.

An interesting *kabita*, *'ye dā balla magā dūji kemmairā,'* describes a magnificent bull, the different parts of its body, its gestures and its various actions. At the end of this *kabita*, there is a reference to this *Dūji Kemmairā* (magnificent bull), its waiting for the cows in hiding, and also to the appearance of calves. Though not in the text, in the actual singing context the women, at this juncture, catch hold of each other in fun and enjoyment. On enquiry we were told that they were mimicking the action of the tiger catching the cattle. But throughout the text, there is no reference to the tiger at all. Though this section conspicously comes immediately after the mention of calves in relation to the admiration of the bull. Moreover, the whole situation is enacted in a relaxed, contented manner, and not in an atmosphere of fear. Thus considering the text and its context, the *kabita* can be interpreted as a symbolic representation of the desire for mating and motherhood on the part of women. In a way, the paddy fields also symbolize women. Hence, in such fields village women cut across all the boundaries of caste, family, social and mental restrictions.

There are many *kabitas* which just list the ornaments of women; except the words denoting the ornaments, the whole of such a text employs repetitive words, *e.g. yelyāle yelya bāle, ponnu Rāmasvāmi magalāl, ḍimbisāle ḍimbisāle* etc. Such *kabitas* are open-ended and they can be extended or contracted to any extent by adding or deleting the number of ornaments, depending upon the situation. Here the names of the ornaments do vary, but otherwise the text is fixed. The reference to various ornaments, in *kabitas* of this sort sung by women, is meaningful to them. Tuḷuva women normally love to have gold ornaments of different varieties, but cannot actualise their wishes because of their economic condition. Such *kabitas* fulfil their wish for gold ornaments.

There are other *kabitas* whose structure is very similar to those mentioned just now, place names substituting for ornaments. The desire to go to different temple festivals of different places is the theme of another type of *kabita*. Here also the desire of women to go to different temple festivals has been expressed in a repetitive style.

Kabitas are sung in the fields by women and they mainly reflect women's aspirations, dress and ornaments, their wish to go to temple festivals, as well as sexual desires. Some other *kabitas* reflect women's relationship with birds and plants. One can comfortably arrive at the conclusion that women were the actual creators of *kabitas*. Such *kabitas* have messages to be passed on from generation to generation of working women. The female consciousness inherent in the *kabitas* and the participation of women in singing are very important factors in the understanding of folk culture.

References

Abraham, Roger D. 1986. Story telling and achieving meaning: A West Indian case. In B.R. Jonsson (ed.), 57-66. Uppsala.

Barnes, R. Daniel 1986. Interpreting urban legends. In B.R. Jonsson (ed.), 67-78. Uppsala.

Brückner, Heidrun 1987. Bhūta worship in Coastal Karṇāṭaka: An oral Tuḷu myth and festival ritual of Jumādi. In *Studien zur Indologie und Iranistik* 13/14: 17-37.

Claus, Peter J. 1975. The Siri myth and ritual: A mass possession cult of Tulunadu. In *Ethnology* 14: 47-58.

Id. 1978. Oral traditions, royal cults and materials for a reconsideration of the caste system in South India. In *Journal of Indian Folkloristics* 1.1, 1-25.

Id. 1979. Spirit possession and spirit mediumship from the perspective of Tuḷu oral traditions. In *Culture, medicine and psychiatry* 3: 29-52.

Id. 1989. Behind the text: Performance and ideology in a Tuḷu oral tradition. In S.H. Blackburn *et al. Oral epics in India*. Berkeley: University of California Press.

Id. (this volume) Text variability and authenticity in the Siri cult.

Honko, Lauri 1986a. Folkloristic studies on meaning: An introduction. In B.R. Jonsson (ed.), 35-56. Uppsala.

Id. 1986b. Empty texts, full meanings, on transformal meaning of folklore. In B.R. Jonsson (ed.), 95-126. Uppsala.

Jonsson, B.R. 1986. *Scandinavian yearbook of folklore, 1984*. Uppsala.

Rai, Viveka B.A. 1982. *Tuḷuva adhyayana: Kelavu vicāragaḷu*. Mangalore.

Id. 1985. *Tuḷu Janapada Sāhitya*. Bangalore.

Id. 1986. Pāḍdanas as folk epics. In U.P. Upadhyaya (ed.) *Folk epics of Tulunad*. Udupi.

Rao, Damodara B. 1986. Folk poem as epic. In U.P. Upadhyaya (ed.) *Folk epics of Tulunad*. Udupi.

Röhrich, Lutz 1986. The quest of meaning in folk narrative research: What does meaning mean, what is the meaning of mean. In B.R. Jonsson (ed.), 127-138. Uppsala.

Siikala, Anna-Leena 1986. The praxis of folk narratives. In

B.R. Jonsson (ed.), 139-152. Uppsala.

Id. and Upadhyaya, S. 1986. Structures of pāḍdanas. In U.P. Upadhyaya (ed.) *Folk epics of Tulunad*. Udupi.

Upadhyaya, U.P (ed.) 1986. *Folk epics of Tulunad*. Udupi.

Scandinavian yearbook of folklore 1984. See B.R. Jonsson (ed.) 1986. Uppsala.

KANNALĀYE: THE PLACE OF A TUḶU PĀḌDANA AMONG INTERRELATED ORAL TRADITIONS*

Heidrun Brückner

I. Introductory

This article deals with the oral traditions of a folk religious cult of South India.[1] It consists of the worship of local deities found in the Dakṣiṇa Kannaḍa District of Karṇāṭaka State, i.e. roughly the coastal region between Mangalore and Udupi, covering a stretch of less than eighty miles in length and between ten and forty-five miles in width, depending on the distance of the mountain ranges of the Western Ghats from the Arabian Sea. The cults are indigenous to castes of Tuḷu-speaking agriculturalists who cultivate paddy, the toddy-tapper caste, closely linked to them, oilpressers, barbers, musicians and castes of impersonators of the local deities. The social set-up among these castes still appears as feudal as when rich landlords occupied the position of rulers over small principalities which they governed along with these deities. The deities themselves, viewed as kings or noblemen as well as warriors, controlled, confirmed and reflected the position of the local rulers. In spite of

---

* My thanks are due to the Deutsche Forschungsgemeinschaft whose travel grants enabled me to first record the text in 1984 and witness the connected rituals in 1986/87 as part of a research project on *bhūta* worship in Coastal Karṇāṭaka sponsored by the same organisation.

[1] My use of the term 'folk religion' is based on G.D. Sontheimer's understanding. See esp. Sontheimer 1989a, 1989b and 1989d.

social and political change, this older social structure is still expressed and in part maintained by the cults in question. They combine elements of fertility cults, and the worship of ancestors, local heroes and village goddesses.[2]

The focus of the present paper is on a particular oral text which tells the story of a deified buffalo driver, recited at the latter's small shrine during his annual festival rituals. The deified person is worshipped only at two neighbouring places in the same village. His story appears — at first sight — to be unique. But as soon as related textual and ritual traditions are taken into consideration, it becomes evident that the text and its ritual performance have to be viewed in close continuity with those traditions. My aim is then to show how a particular text can be understood in terms of the larger system of Tuḷuva culture, and how, at the same time, seemingly minor changes in the story and in its performance context achieve to establish the uniqueness of a local tradition.

The following section (II) outlines the general features of the genre to which the text belongs, gives a detailed account of it and sketches its ritual performance. In the subsequent section (III), the text as a whole as well as its different narrative episodes and a number of individual motifs will be utilised as points of departure to demonstrate the interrelation of various textual and performance traditions. Having placed the text in such a wider framework, its specificity will be re-examined in the final section (IV).

II. Text, localisation and ritual performance

There are in all only about one million Tulu speakers, but although the language area is small, linguistic and religious diversity

---

[2] A number of deities are androgynous.

is considerable. In both, there is regional as well as social variation. For example, the *būta*[3] cult in the south and southeast of the district exhibits more similarity with elements of *teyyam* worship in northern Kerala,[4] whereas in the north a certain impact of the popular Kannaḍa folk theatre of Yakṣagāna can be observed.[5]

I am going to deal here with materials from the middle region, corresponding roughly to the area of settlement of the Pambadas, one of several castes of impersonators of the local folk deities. The Pambadas mainly live and operate in the coastal region around Mangalore, up to about twenty miles inland. To the east and north of them is the region of the Paravas. A third group, the Naḷikes, are found all over. They can be distinguished from the Pambadas and Paravas by the type of deities they impersonate rather than by their place of settlement. The region most densely populated by families of Pambadas and by the deities they impersonate is the area between Nētrāvati river in the south and Gurpur river about fifteen miles further north.

The mythological texts of the cult recited by the impersonators of the deities form a blend of myths, legends and ballads. In Tuḷu, they are called *pāḍdana*.[6] Rai (1982: 1-2) and others connect the word

---

[3] On the following pages Skt. words, like *bhūta*, *dharma*, etc., are spelled according to the Tuḷu pronounciation, i.e. without aspiration. The word *tuḷu* is spelt throughout the article with a retroflex - *ḷ* -, following the practice of the dictionaries (Cf. Männer 1886a, Upadhyaya 1988). In the texts of the appendix, however, it is spelt with a dental - *l* -, in accordance with the pronounciation of the singer.

[4] For example the possession rituals. They have traits in common with the *teyyams* of Kerala (cf. Nambiar and Freeman, this volume). A connecting link between the two regions is — apart from similar ecological conditions — the matrilineal system of inheritance followed by most worshippers of *būtas* or *daivas* as well as of *teyyaṃs*.

[5] As in the costumes and make-up worn by the impersonators during the annual festival rituals.

[6] For a preliminary discussion of terminological problems, see Rai and Claus (both in this volume) as well as Brückner 1990. I am going to use these words in a non-technical way here, for want of a more adequate term. *Pāḍdana*, too, is a very general designation.

with a Dravidian root *pāḍu/pāṭu*, meaning "to sing". A text can only be called a *pāḍdana* if it is sung or recited. A mere prose account of the same myth would be called a *katE* (Skt. *kathā*), i.e. a narrative in the wider or unmarked sense of the term.[7] The term *pāḍdana* refers to a genre of Tuḷu folk literature which is performed in various contexts; e.g. the *būta pāḍdanas* are recited during rituals mainly by male specialists of the performing castes, the field-song *pāḍdanas* are recited by women at work in the paddy fields (cf. Rai and Claus, this volume) and the Siri *pāḍdanas* form part of a special variety of possession cult in which mainly females are involved (cf. Claus 1975, 1979a). My presentation focusses exclusively on the first group.

The hundreds of *pāḍdanas* of the *būta* cult current in the region generally describe the origin, wanderings and deeds of the local deities. These inhabit the same localities as their human worshippers, but can move between invisible and visible modes of existence (*māya* and *jōga*). In the absence of written records in Tuḷu, the *pāḍdanas* also constitute a kind of local history for the people.[8]

Even within the repertory of orally transmitted Tuḷu texts of the Pambada tradition used as ritual invocations in the annual cult rituals, several groups of texts and patterns or types of composition can be distinguished. By systematically investigating the original context of each recitation of a particular corpus of texts, insights can be gained into their composition and structure (Brückner 1987, 1990). Dozens of these deities and hundreds of their shrines exist in the region. Whereas some of them are worshipped only at one place,

---

[7] In the more restricted or technical sense of the term, *katE* is a specific genre within oral Tuḷu literature, corresponding to a "tale". Cf. e.g. Rai 1985, passim.

[8] A dating of the texts is, however, extremely difficult. Portions of them may date back to the 16th or 17th cent. In some of them, we find references to Vijayanagara as well as to the local dynasties of the Vijayanagara period, such as the Baṅga and Cauṭa chieftains (15th/16th cent.). But since, in this type of oral literature, one can — strictly speaking — never hear the "same" text twice, a performed text as a whole has to be dated on the moment of its recording.

others have dozens of shrines and a few of them might even have hundreds. Accordingly, a particular myth or ballad is recited either at only one or at many places.[9]

The text presented here belongs to the first group. Its singer, Aitappa Pambada, one of the senior professional impersonators in his caste, impersonates about ten to twelve different *būtas* at about fifty to sixty different localities where his family has the right and the duty to perform. Each *pāḍdana* ends at the very place at which it is recited.[10] The *pāḍdana* of the *būta* Kannalāye[11] has been chosen in order to demonstrate how, in spite of its uniqueness — suggested by the fact that the person whose deification is described is worshipped only at a single locality — the myth forms an integral part of a particularly Tuḷuva cultural context. This context is constituted on several levels.

Rituals and texts of other deities worshipped at the same locality provide the first frame of reference. Kannalāye's myth and cult are specially linked with a local form of the *daiva* Jumādi, who belongs to the group of very widespread Tuḷuva deities.[12] Jumādi, in his local *pāḍdana*, enters the scene already in a superhuman, divine state, whereas the account of the deification of the herdsman Kannalāye forms part of his *pāḍdana* and is effected by the local

---

[9] In any case, each ritual recitation of a *pāḍdana* of a particular deity at a particular place contains what I call a "local section," which relates to local history and local conditions.

[10] It appears as though different local portions are added to a basic set of singer's *pāḍdanas* to link them to the respective place of performance. This is, however, not a mechanical process. Such a mode of composition can mainly be traced in the texts of widespread *būtas* like Jumādi, whom e.g. Aitappa impersonates at about fifteen to twenty places. The local sections of the corpus collected by me generally focus on the last three places of a *būta's* wanderings, including the place of performance (cf. Brückner 1987, 1990).

[11] For a complete translation cf. appendix I.

[12] Forms of Jumādi are worshipped all over the district at hundreds of places and the different versions of his myth consequently name, in total, hundreds of localities.

Jumādi. A second level of reference concerns the position of the text and its ritual performance in the repertory of its singer. Thirdly, parallels in the texts of other singers will be taken into account.

The text

In September 1984, I made a tape recording of Aitappa Pambada reciting the *Kannalāye-pāḍdana* in a private session. In 1986, it was re-recorded in the original performance context, namely at two interrelated festival rituals in Kulavuru village, twenty miles north-east of Mangalore in the foothills of the Western Ghats. In the performance, the text, which consists of altogether 114 double lines or stanzas, is divided into two sections, the first one comprising stanzas 1-52 and the second 53-114. To make the organisation of the narrative content more transparent, I have subdivided these two sections into two parts each.

1) The first part (1-34) begins by introducing a family, father, mother and four sons, with their respective names. The following stanzas concern the children's education: the four boys are said to reach the age of seven to seven and a half years. They say they want to learn writing and reading. They start by writing on sand, next on a wooden board and, finally, on palm leaves.[13] Then the brothers state they have learnt enough and should start some business. They open four shops. On being successful, they want to try their luck in yet another venture. They journey to the top of the Ghāṭs to purchase buffaloes.

2) At the Ghāṭs, the second part of the narration starts (35-52): They meet a Kannaḍa-speaking buffalo dealer with a herd of 4000 buffaloes. The way this person is introduced lends him a tragic air. He tells them that there is no place for him, that he has lost direction and that he is going to a kingdom not seen by the eyes, to a land not heard of by the ears. They purchase his

[13] It is particularly interesting to find the preparation of the leaves described in detail in an oral text. Cf. also Blackburn 1988, xxi.

buffaloes and invite him to come along with them (34-44). Driving the buffaloes, they descend into the Tuḷu kingdom.[14] When the time for their evening meal comes, they halt at a certain field (45-52).[15]

3) Here, the change of tune of the recitation signals the beginning of the third part of the text, which is longer than the two previous ones (53—92). This point is also marked in the rituals, as will be discussed later. It opens by introducing a lady referred to as Svāmi Nandēdi. The four brothers come to her palace and ask for cooking facilities to prepare their meal. She answers that she will provide the food herself. The feast is then described elaborately in poetic language. At the end (67/68), the guests praise their hostess. The lady expresses her wish to see the 4000 buffaloes (69). She puts on her best dress and ornaments, takes her small silver dagger and her umbrella and sets out (81). When she arrives at the field and sees the beauty of the 4000 buffaloes, she wants to purchase the most beautiful pair.

4) Here, the fourth and last part starts (93-114). The four brothers quote the price and a quarrel arises, because the parties do not agree about the price (91-93). Infuriated, the lady returns to her estate and calls out to her deity Jumādi to help her (94-99). In the meantime, the buffalo driver takes the buffaloes to a near-by pond to drink (100-103). At that moment, Jumādi turns the 4000 buffaloes into stone (104/105). The driver, bereft of his buffaloes, addresses Jumādi and asks what is to become of him now. He is offered a position below a god *(dēveru)*, but above a *būta* and is transferred to an invisible realm *(māya)*. Jumādi has a seat of stone made for him and a bench with scissor-shaped legs. He entrusts three of his six estates to him and names the new deity Kannalāye.

Thus the text ends by providing the protagonist with a "tuḷuised" identity.[16] He, who has been without a specific place of his own

---

[14] The wording of this line resembles the opening lines of other *pāḍdanas* which begin with the descent of a deity from the Ghāṭs, e.g. Sārāla Jumādi (cf. Brückner 1987).

[15] From the name of this meal, *pōsa*, we can assume that they were Jainas.

[16] Tuḷu names of local deities are often formed by adding the pronoun of the third person singular masculine to a place name to indicate that the god is "he who belongs to or stems from such and such place". In the present case, Kannalāye is

during his life-time, is — through his premature death — given a position in the visible and the invisible world.

Localisation

After recording this *pāḍdana*, I visited the temple of Kannalāye along with the singer and asked the people of the locality where the deification of Kannalāye took place, where the buffaloes were turned into stone etc. Using the *pāḍdana* text in my notebook as a guide, I was shown all the localities of the last part of the *pāḍdana* in the actual topography of the place.[17]

Kannalāye has a small shrine of stone at upper Agari, the place mentioned in the *pāḍdana*. The shrine is situated halfway up a mountain densely overgrown with trees, bushes and shrubs. (See plates VII and VIII). The mountain is covered with blocks of granite stone. These are the transformed buffaloes of Kannalāye. At the foot of the hill is a pond, where Kannalāye took his herd to drink. Next to it is an open field, where Svāmi Nandēdi had come to see the beauty of the buffaloes. Some of them underwent the transformation into stone in that very place. A special position is occupied by the most beautiful pair: the two stones that represent them are situated just behind Kannalāye's shrine. A stone slab has been put across them to make a bench. During the annual festival rituals, these buffaloes receive food offerings on the bench along with several ancestors.

---

said to stand for *kannaḍa* + *āye*, "he of the Kannaḍa region or Kannaḍa-speaking community" (the change of -*ḍ*- to -*ḷ*- can occur; retroflex -*ḷ*- is pronounced as dental -*l*- in the speech of the informants).

[17] I do not advocate the historio-geographical method of earlier folklore studies here (cf. Brückner 1990 for a methodological discussion; cf. also Finnegan 1977, passim, for criticism of that approach). The localisation of a text by local people is no end in itself, but it can provide clues for the interpretation of the text and its contextual meaning.

The house referred to as Svāmi Ṇandēdi's palace in the *pāḍdana* is said to be the manorial house of Kulavuru situated nearby.[18] The present lady of the house, too, worships Jumādi as her family deity in a chamber by the side of the large front hall of her house. This farmhouse, Kulavuru guttu, heads a group of altogether six estates whose paddy fields and palmyra- as well as areca-palm trees stretch from the foothills of the Western Ghats to the banks of Phalguṇi river. Each one of these beautiful old farmhouses is situated in the middle of the land belonging to it. It is the deity Jumādi who is responsible for the overall protection of these lands, the people and the cattle.[19]

Ritual performance[20]

Annually, the former landlords and tenants, the agricultural labourers and other villagers hold a series of festival rituals after the second harvest of paddy: first two festivals of one night each for Jumādi and Kannalāye are held in a temporary shed near the river which forms the border of the territory of the six estates. This takes place at the beginning of March. Four weeks later, two festivals on two consecutive nights are held for Jumādi; the first, at his temple belonging to Kulavuru estate and patronized by it, the second one at the shrine of another estate at lower Agari. Subsequently, on the following night, festival rituals for Kannalāye take place at his small stone shrine described above. These will be dealt with below.

---

[18] During a later visit I heard the opinion that Svāmi Nandēdi belonged to another of the neighbouring manorial houses.

[19] Some other *būtas* found there have more specialised functions; e.g. the tiger-*būta* Pilicauṇḍi is in charge of protecting the crops against theft.

[20] This section of my paper is very preliminary. My study of the ritual complex is still in progress. For a fuller understanding, the entire annual cycle of rituals at the locality, the social background, the history of the village and especially of the families figuring more prominently in the cult would have to be discussed in detail.

Once a year, Kannalāye meets Jumādi during the festival rituals near the river. At this time, their paraphernalia are kept together on a bench in the same shed. At the end of the separate celebrations for the two deities, their paraphernalia are taken back, and their two priests become possessed again.[21] They jointly set off in procession and - at a certain field - take leave of each other for the rest of the year by ceremoniously crossing their swords. (See plate IX). The procession is then split into two groups, each consisting of the representatives of the respective three estates of the deities. As described in the *pāḍdana*, Jumādi is in charge of three estates, Kannalāye of the other three.

Kannalāye's paraphernalia are kept in the chamber of a nearby farmhouse belonging to a family of toddy-tappers and farmers in charge of Kannalāye's shrine. A younger male member of this family has served as Kannalāye's priest for the last few years. Another local person, said to be a descendent of the Kannaḍa buffalo driver, acts in the rituals as the buffalo driver, up to the moment of the latter's deification. The herdsman's stick that Kannalāye used for driving the buffaloes is part of the paraphernalia. When the man who impersonates him holds this stick, he becomes possessed. Jumādi, enacted in this scene by Kannalāye's Pambada impersonator, then approaches him and, in a fight, takes the stick away. The Pambada once again takes the part of Kannalāye after the latter's deification, alluded to in the ritual dramatization. The other person sinks down and is carried away to the side. His part as Kannalāye is over.

The common practice among Pambadas is to recite a *pāḍdana* as an invocation before the impersonation of the deity, but this *pāḍdana* is recited in between the first and the second stages of impersonation. During the first stage, the *daiva* makes his appearance in the light of torches and repeatedly exposes his body to the flames. He interacts with his worshippers through pantomimic ges-

---

[21] The possession of the priests and impersonators is of the controlled and induced type described by Freeman in the present volume.

tures. He does not speak at this stage.[22] After about one and a half hours the impersonator withdraws and reappears in more elaborate costume and decoration. It is at this point that Kannalāye's *pāḍdana* starts being recited after a short introductory dance. As indicated above, in the ritual recitation of the *pāḍdana* the point in the narration when the four brothers halt and just before Svāmi Nandēdi is introduced, is marked by a change of tune and, secondly, by a change in the way of performance. While reciting the first part of the text, the impersonator is sitting on a three-legged stool. For the second part, he gets up and continues his recitation while dancing. In this way, the turn in the course of events appears to be marked.

As the second stage begins, a decorated bamboo frame — on which a crudely cut out facial mask of areca-palm spathe is fixed — and a coconut leaf are tied to the impersonator's back, extending well above his head. This symbolises the fullest representation of the deity. The face is removed again after a short while. The deity blesses the representatives of the local families. He is given two burning straw torches, with which he dances and again blesses the audience. Followed by people, especially children, carrying similar torches, he sets out on a short trip down from his temple to a nearby field, where all the torches are burnt in one heap and a cock is cut for the *daiva*. Back at his temple, the scene showing the fight for the herdsman's stick is enacted (cf. above). After a dance with the stick, the two *pūjāris* of Jumādi and Kannalāye take it away from the *daiva* and put it back on the altar. Kannalāye sinks down for a moment and is then given his sword, bell and yak tail. He blesses the people with the sword. There is also an opportunity to consult the *daiva*.[23] Finally, he is offered a meal of chicken curry. After eating, he purifies and re-invigorates himself by sticking small

---

[22] For a more detailed account of annual festival rituals for *būtas*, see Gowda 1983, Claus 1989a and Brückner 1987, 1990.

[23] In the 1986 festival rituals a conflict about the distribution of property in the Agari family, who patronized the function, was passionately discussed.

red *kēpula* flowers (Ixora coccinea) onto his face. He gets his sword, bell and yak tail back and blesses the people one more time. When he returns them to the *pūjāri* and the latter sprinkles water on him, the impersonation is over. The deity leaves his medium.

As mentioned above, Kannalāye is not only impersonated at his *māḍa* at Agari but also - four weeks earlier - at a temporary shed erected in a field on the banks of the river which marks the village border. Whereas his rituals at Agari are sponsored mainly by a single family and, in 1986, included lengthy discussions of problems concerning this family, the rituals at Terejal are sponsored by the entire village and organised by a committee including representatives of the six estates.[24] They relate Kannalāye more closely both to Jumādi and to other village deities: these include the goddess Māri or Mammāyi and the *būtas* Kalkuda and Kallurti. Jumādi's and Kannalāye's priestly media are present for the rituals of Māri on the night previous to their own festivals. Māri has a Kannaḍa-speaking *dāsa* as her medium. She demands a pig, but gets only cocks as a sacrifice. The day after the impersonations of Jumādi and Kannalāye, the *būtas* Kalkuda and Kallurti are enacted by two men of the Naḷike caste of professional impersonators. These two *būtas* pay respect to Jumādi and Kannalāye. At Terejal, Kannalāye wears Jumādi's mask or "face" during a certain stage of the impersonation. He takes on functions which are performed elsewhere by Jumādi's assistant *būta*, Baṇṭe, such as the driving-out of the goddess Māri beyond the village border. During consultation, the problems of the Agari family referred to above were relegated to the rituals at Agari. The focus was on general village affairs. The fight for the herdsman's stick was, as far as I could observe, not enacted.[25]

---

[24] The use of the term "village" is problematic, but cannot be discussed here. Several systems of social and territorial organisation seem to overlap. See Brückner 1990, Tarabout 1986, and this volume.

[25] I thank all the participants and organisers of the festival rituals for accepting me as a guest and for tolerating my inexperienced behaviour and questions. Besides the

Even a superficial comparison of the two rituals makes it clear that a minimal shift of context implies a number of changes in ritual performance, in the functions of the deity, whose status is established in a relational way, and in the significance the rituals have for the participants. The analysis of performative, social and even topographical factors involved in this shift can help us to understand the processes by which a specific meaningful representation of an individual deity is created or constituted.

Firstly, the scene moves from the exact spot of Kannalāye's deification, on the border between village and hilly wilderness, to the other end of the territory of the six estates and to its other border on a riverside. It is removed from its original topographical setting. Secondly, the deified buffalo driver enters into a whole set of relations with other deities. All of them, namely Kannalāye himself, Jumādi, Māri, Kalkuda and Kallurti, are worshipped by the entire village, but at the same time, all have their special communities or families of worshippers.[26] The festival rituals at Terejal mark the integration of gods of various origins as well as of their worshippers into the realm of a single village. Kannalāye and Māri in particular are recognisable as figures from the Kannaḍa-speaking region east of the Ghats. The difference between them is that Māri has widespread, firmly established cult features, which (including the Kannaḍa language) have been maintained at Terejaḷ, and that the integration appears to consist mainly in a spatial and temporal contiguity vis-à-vis the Tuḷuva gods. Kannalāye, on the other hand, became part of Tuḷuva mythology from the moment of his death as

---

singer and impersonator Aitappa Pambada, whom I have known for several years, my special thanks are due to Shri Jivaraj Bhandary of Nonal estate for his hospitality, explanations and practical help. I also owe thanks to Dr. Chinnappa Gowda (and his wife) and Shri Shivaram Shetty of Mangalore University as well as to Shri Tonse Krishna Bhatt of Udupi, who all accompanied me to Kulavuru and Agari at different times. The responsibility for misunderstandings or misinterpretations is entirely mine.

[26] In the case of the former landlords, their sponsoring of the worship of all deities of the realm can be viewed in continuity with the classical duties of kings.

a human being. His ritually expressed integration at Terejal complements his mythological integration as expressed by the *pāḍdana*.

The observations based on the rituals at Kannalāye's own shrine at Agari illustrate the interrelatedness between myth and ritual, as well as between both these categories on the one hand and physical and social "reality" on the other. Myth and ritual seem to achieve an actual "restructuring of the social world within a narrative one" (Blackburn/Ramanujan 1986: 8); they not only mirror social life, but also have an impact on it.

The discussion, in the rituals, of problems of distribution of property, which also involved the deity himself, could serve as an example for such dynamics. The deity, on the one hand, functioned as an arbitrator between different factions of the family and specially looked after the welfare of the weakest member. On the other hand, Kannalāye strongly insisted on making the necessary economic provisions for the maintainance of his shrine and the observance of his festival rituals. Representatives of the village and the other estates were also interested in the continuation of Kannalāye's cult at Agari in order to guarantee the ritual and social balance of the locality and thereby its welfare and prosperity.

The rituals, in this perspective, not only appear as part of the social life but, reversely, social life also appears as part of the ritual transactions.[27] The affairs of the deity include those of men and vice versa. The structure also applies to the spatial organisation. The locality where the temple is situated is part of the village territory, and the latter also forms part of the realm of the local gods.

---

[27] Dichotomies such as the "sacred" and the "profane" do not seem to be easily applicable to the material. For a general discussion of the problems involved in the application of this opposition, see Das 1976. Sontheimer, while speaking about the nature/culture dichotomy in connection with the notions of *vana* and *kṣetra*, observes that these two categories are perceived as being partially co-extensive (cf. Sontheimer, 1987a, passim and 1989b: 197).

A similar relationship of — partially — mutual inclusion exists between the myth and the ritual proceedings. This involves, among other things, a linkage between a spatial and a temporal dimension. The narration of the myth refers to a reality viewed to have happened in the past. By the myth being recited during the rituals it also becomes part of the present and provides it with meaning. This impact of the *pāḍdana* recitation is strengthened by other, spoken, utterances of the impersonator and the possession priest which make the linkage between the mythological narration and the surrounding social and physical reality even more explicit, and thereby bring the past closer to the present: when, in the rituals, the possession priests speak of the past, they often say that everything happened only yesterday.[28] Moreover, the people involved in the rituals are addressed by ancient names, in use from the time of their ancestors, during whose lifetime the events of the narration are said to have happened.[29]

In this way, the past is narrated, enacted and continued at the same time. It becomes an intense experience of the present — a process amounting to a suspension of linear, chronological time. This suspension is re-enforced by the cyclical structure of the myths: at the end of a *pāḍdana* recitation, the impersonator often starts to recite the very first line of the text once again. The text is not recited to convey any new information to the audience, but rather to re-assert and re-create things as they are. This accords with Leach's notion of the self-referential message of rituals and recalls his remarks on ritual sequence.[30] Both, on the ritual and on the tex-

---

[28] The word can refer to the previous day as well as to the past in general. For the remote past, however, other expressions are used.

[29] At one place, for example, a descendant of the deified hero of a *pāḍdana* acts as his ancestor's priest and, during the rituals, is addressed by the latter's name.

[30] "The performers and the listeners are the same people. We engage in rituals in order to transmit collective messages to ourselves." and "Moreover the message as a whole, although it takes time to transmit, has a unity. The end is implicit in the beginning; the beginning presupposes the end." (Leach 1976: 45, 44).

tual level, an observation applies, which Burghart makes on the twofold purpose to which genealogical knowledge is put, namely to "fix identities" and to "transform identities" (Burghart, this volume).

The relation between myth and topographical reality is one aspect of the described dialectics which has a bearing on questions of localisation. As I have pointed out above, the topography of the scenario of the *pāḍdana* refers to the topography of the locality where the protagonist is actually worshipped. There is reason to assume that topographical features such as the granite blocks on the hill and the field, stirred the people's imagination and lead to that particular localisation of the legend. But, reversely, the legend, which is alive in the minds of the local people, also sanctifies the locality and makes its topographical features meaningful.[31]

A certain problem involved in analysing localisation lies in accounting for the fact that - with slight variation in the narrative - localisation of very similar, if not the same, stories can be observed at different localities - just as, e.g. a *svayambhū-liṅga* can come up and is said to have come up at various places (cf. also Claus, this volume). Although the deity Kannalāye and his myth appear peculiar to this locality and very closely linked to it, the text and some features of its performance have parallels at a number of other places. Whereas these parallels might be understood to express a larger cultural continuity, the variation relates to the specific contextual set-up of a locality — confirmed annually by the observance of the rituals.

[31] It certainly makes a difference whether the story of Jumādi and Kannalāye took place on a hillock one sees every day, or, for example, on remote Mount Kailāsa. That may also be why so many places claim to have been the original scene of mythological events. One could try to distinguish, in this connection, between "primary" and "secondary" localisation.

III. Textual and performative parallels

In this section, textual and performative parallels of the Kannalāye *pāḍdana* will be adduced in order to place it in a wider formal, topical and conceptual context.[32] These comprise of, (a) the *pāḍdana* of the local Jumādi, (b) similar styles of ritual recitation as well as narrative parallels in the repertory of the same and (c) of other singers, and, finally, (d) a comparison with a version of the story collected in the 19th century.

a) A text which the performance context brings into close relation with the present one is the *pāḍdana* of the local Jumādi *(Paṣṇa Jumādi)*, who, in Kannalāye's own *pāḍdana*, is said to have deified the latter. There is, however, no reference to this event or to Kannalāye in the Jumādi-*pāḍdana*. It constitutes rather a complement to than a parallel of the first text. The Kannalāye-*pāḍdana* exemplifies, in a way, a process of adaptation and integration of an outsider, which is not reflected in the *pāḍdana* texts but only in the rituals of the other gods involved.

Paṣṇa Jumādi's story takes us right to the core of the rural Tuḷuva life of the castes of agriculturalist *būta* worshippers. It also forms part of the repertory of Aitappa Pambada who impersonates Paṣṇa Jumādi as well. In the *pāḍdana*,[33] three episodes can be distinguished: The first one (1-30) narrates how the *daiva* came to a manorial house two villages east of Kulavuru by way of a marriage alliance. The second one (30-48) brings him to the village neighbouring Kulavuru, just across the river, where he helps a farmer to

---

[32] I am aware of the limitations in dealing exclusively with the *pāḍdana* narratives here. Other forms of speech in the rituals play an important role in establishing, reaffirming and modifying their impact and meaning. It is, however, beyond the scope of the present paper to take all those factors into account. For a more comprehensive treatment of similar material see Brückner 1990.

[33] For a complete translation of the *pāḍdana* see appendix II. The Tuḷu text is given in Brückner 1990.

water his *kambula* field.[34] In return he receives a shrine and worship from him.[35] The *pāḍdana*, whose performance is itself part of a ritual, abounds in references to other rituals — such as the *kambula* and the wedding — as well as to the one where it is recited.

Finally (48-57), the *daiva* travels on to Kulavuru, shows his presence, comes to be worshipped and establishes the present ritual setup. The two narrations of the first two episodes refer to events vitally connected with fertility - one concerning the auspicious act of marriage, the other the ritual fertilisation of the fields. *Būtas* are said to be closely associated with both, brides and buffaloes. Several *pāḍdanas* state that they follow a family line by following the brides and also that they follow the ropes of buffaloes. By describing the purpose for which buffaloes are mainly needed in the rice-growing area, the Paṣṇa Jumādi *pāḍdana* can be viewed in continuity with the episode of the buffalo deal in the Kannalāye text. As will be discussed below, its themes might also be taken to support a different understanding of the Svāmi Nandēdi scene.

b) Parallel modes of performance of other texts in the same singer's repertory allow us to place the Kannalāye-*pāḍdana* in yet another context. Thus, in the *pāḍdana* of Balavāṇḍi, the same change of tune as in Kannalāye's text occurs after about two thirds of the narration. The subsequent portion is recited while dancing. It is to the temple of the powerful *daiva* Balavāṇḍi at Perra that Aitappa Pambada has his major ritual affiliation. Besides Balavāṇḍi, he also impersonates the tiger-*būta* Pilicauṇḍi there. The performance of the latter's *pāḍdana* again resembles that of Kannalāye

---

[34] *Kambula/kambla/kambala* refers to a particular large paddy field as well as to a ploughing ceremony with buffalo racing conducted in it. In Kulavuru, it takes place in November. Cf. also fn. 86.

[35] This is the only text in my collection which refers to Muslims and does so in an inimical way. Jumādi uses tiles from a mosque for his own temple and kills the *mukri*. Nowadays, Jumādi's temple at that village is no longer in use; the neighbouring mosque is.

and Balavāṇḍi.[36] The manner of performance of these three *būtas'* texts distinguishes them from all others in Aitappa's repertory. With respect to Kannalāye, the style of recitation also forms a contrast to the recitation of Paṣṇa Jumādi's *pāḍdana*, which is sung as an invocation at the beginning of the rituals. This is in line with the common practice of Jumādi performances.[37] One could speculate whether the absence of an initial invocation for Kannalāye and Balavāṇḍi might have to do with the fact that they are deified humans, whose deification is described only in the course of the ritual recitation and forms part of the ritual enactment.[38]

Not only in features of performance, but also in the narrative content of the Kannaḷāye-*pāḍdana*, a number of parallels can be adduced from the Balavāṇḍi-*pāḍdana*. For example, as mentioned above, Balavāṇḍi, too, is initially a human, whose transformation into a deity forms part of the narration. He is transposed to the realm of *māya* by the god Bemmeru̥, who assigns to him a position one step below a god and one step above the *būtas*. Bemmeru̥ transforms his horse into stone, just like Jumādi made Kannalāye's buffaloes into stone. Kannalāye and Balavāṇḍi are the only two *būtas* in Aitappa's repertory who can be identified as former humans and who are confined to one locality.[39]

---

[36] But one more feature seems to be distinctive for Pilicauṇḍi: in full costume, the impersonator performs a number of somersaults. Moreover, during part of the recitation, the performer's assistant acts as a tiger who tries to catch children from the audience and pretends to devour them.

[37] In most of them it is followed by a second recitation at a later stage. This is not done for Paṣṇa Jumādi.

[38] Another way of looking at these differences would be to examine possible borrowings from the performance styles of the other two communities of impersonators. It must not only be observed that a deity moves, for e.g. from the Paravas' to the Pambadas' area of settlement and performance, but also that the patrons of a deity start inviting a member of another performing community (presumably of higher status) to impersonate their god. In this way, too, mixed styles of performance develop — the impersonator trying to keep up the traditions of the place, but also bringing in the conventions of his own group.

[39] Only recently, about twelve years ago, a second temple for Balavāṇḍi was con-

The purchase of buffaloes is described in a number of other texts in Aitappa's repertory.[40] In the *pāḍdana* of Jārandāye, one of the rather widespread *būtas*, a group of four Baṭṭas (i.e. Brahmaṇs) sets out to purchase buffaloes on the Ghāṭs for ploughing their fields. On the way back, their buffaloes are made to disappear by the *daiva* Jārandāye. When they promise him worship, the buffaloes reappear in their buffalo shed. In the Koḍamanatāye-*pāḍdana* two Baṇṭs go to a god's temple to make an offering. Subsequently, they purchase a cock and a buffalo. While halting underneath an Aśvattha tree, the *daiva* Ullāye possesses the buffalo and Darma Daiva possesses the cock. Back at the Baṇṭs' estate, the *daivas* make their presence known and demand worship. They get temples and establish themselves at the place. Thus, the Kannalāye-*pāḍdana* shares the motifs of the purchase of the buffaloes as well as their disappearance through the agency of a *daiva* with a large group of other texts. The differences are, firstly, that in the Kannalāye story the buffaloes are not made to reappear, and that, secondly, the disappearance or rather transformation of the animals is linked to that of their driver.

c) Parallels to the story of the *pāḍdana* are also found in texts of other singers. A close similarity exists between the first part of the Kannalāye text and a *pāḍdana* of the Deyyoṅgulu[41] *daivas* recorded from the Pambada *būta* impersonator Lokkayya at Bantval town[42] during the 1986 festival rituals for a group of three deities, Deyyoṅgulu, Jumādi and Mūḍadāye. The *pāḍdana* of Deyyoṅgulu provides an important link between the first one and a whole series

---

structed in another village. He is said to have followed a bride (cf. Paṣṇa Jumādi for this motif) from Perra to that second place. The last part of the Balavāṇḍi-*pāḍdana*, recited there by the same impersonator, describes the route by which the *būta* came there from Perra. This permits a glance at a text in the making.

[40] Cf. Brückner 1990.

[41] The Deyyoṅgulu, as the plural ending indicates, are normally considered as two deities, an older and a younger brother. The singer explained that in this text the name refers only to one *daiva* called Darma Arasu (cf. below).

[42] Bantval is situated in a plain on the banks of Nētrāvati river about 12 km south-east of Agari.

of other related texts. Its parallel portion is, however, shorter than in the Kannalāye version. The differences are such that, for example, the second text often fails to name people and places. It does not mention the names of all family members in the beginning. Later, it refers to the writing on sand, but not to writing on a board or on palm leaves. It mentions the wares of only three of the four shops and the lists of wares quoted differ slightly. The brothers go to a fair where they quickly purchase one thousand, not four thousand, buffaloes. They do not ask the dealer to come along. That the main protagonist of our first text is not mentioned here is the first major difference between the two texts. As in the first text, they approach the lady Svāmi Nandēdi and have a meal at her place. Next, they invite her to see the beauty of the buffaloes. She wishes to purchase the most beautiful pair.

From this point onwards, the narration takes an entirely different turn from the first text: they agree on the sale very quickly and, along with her two buffaloes, the lady returns to her estate. After one and a half years, the animals disappear. With the help of an astrologer she finds out that a deity, Darma Arasu ("King Dharma"), has seated himself on the buffaloes and wants to be worshipped by her. She does so. After another one and a half years he takes her leave to move towards the seashore. On his way he meets two other deities, who are looking for a king. He joins them and gets a *māḍa* next to their shrine at Bantval.[43] A tradition is established according to which, in the annual festival rituals, Darma Arasu has his rituals performed on the first night, the other two, Jumādi and Mūḍadāye, on the two subsequent nights.[44] Basically,

---

[43] Kannalāye's shrine at Agari also is called a *māḍa*. They differ from *sānas* in that they have a small sanctum in the upper storey.

[44] After the first recording of the text, I couldn't rule out the possibility that its relative brevity was due to the circumstances of the ritual recitation in 1986: the beginning of the rituals was delayed; the singer and impersonator might have tried to make up for this delay. This could have accounted for some of the minor differences, which occured, mainly at places where this second text omits a detail mentioned in the Kannalāye-*pāḍdana*. Another recording made in December 1988 outside the rit-

the Kannalāye- and the Deyyoṅgulu-*pāḍdanas* are very much alike up to the point when the lady wants to purchase the buffaloes. In view of the different continuation of the story, the fact that the brothers don't ask the buffalo driver to come along with them is consistent here, although it constitutes a difference from the Kannalāye text.

The continuation of the *Deyyoṅgulu*-pāḍdana, in the version from Bantval as recited by Lokkayya Pambada can, in its turn, be placed in the context of the latter's repertory. He impersonates a number of powerful *daivas* in a region extending from about ten to about twenty miles inland of Mangalore, along both banks of the Nētrāvati river, ending at Bantval town (where the Deyyoṅgulu text was recorded) and at the neighbouring temple and village of Nandāvara, the former capital of the local Baṅga chieftains. Some of the texts seem to reflect political changes which occured when the Baṅgas arrived from the east and tried to establish themselves in the region so far ruled, according to a local account, by the Bhairarasu kings. The *daivas* whom Lokkayya impersonates comprise several local variants of the Deyyoṅgulu or Ullākulu brothers, local forms of the female deity Ullāldi, the unique Nālkayitāye, as well as forms of Jumādi and Pañjurli.

The themes of their *pāḍdanas* overlap to some extent and the narratives relate to each other, but have only few parallels in the repertory of Aitappa Pambada. The motive of local deities inviting an outsider to be king occurs in several of them. Another conspicuous topic is hunting (battue of a boar). This seems to be related to the royal character of the deities. In ritual impersonations they appear as kings. Their comportment is very dignified. They carry a large silver bow and arrow and, at one point, shoot an arrow into each of the four quarters. The references to hunting in the texts

ual context for the tape-recorder shows, however, no significant differences from the 1986-recording — except for very minor variations which normally occur at each fresh recital of a text.

recall the old Tuḷuva practice of the royal hunt by which the balance between forest and settlement was re-established.[45]

Themes referring to buffaloes only occur in his repertory, as far as I have observed, in the above-mentioned Deyyoṅgulu text and in a *pāḍdana* of Pañjurli. Those two *daivas* very much connected with buffaloes in Aitappa's *pāḍdanas*, namely Jārandāye and Koḍamanatāye (cf. above), do not form part of Lokkayya's repertory.[46]

d) Before analysing his Deyyoṅgulu text in more detail and returning to the interpretation of the Kannalāye story, a third important parallel remains to be drawn:

I have not mentioned so far that a number of *pāḍdanas* were collected in the 19th cent. by Basel Missionaries (cf. Männer 1886) and by A.C. Burnell (Burnell 1893-97), who was a judge in Mangalore in 1871/72. One of these *pāḍdanas*, Burnell manuscript no. 18, is entitled "Kannalāye" - just as our first text - and was published in translation, along with other texts, in the Indian Antiquary in the 1890's. In view of what I said about the dating of the *pāḍdanas* and considering the limited fixity of this type of oral literature, these older collections are of immense value. We learn, however, very little about the informants, the original context, etc. It is extremely difficult to reconstruct that context.[47] This also renders it difficult to work with those texts. The fact to be noted is that a *būta* Kannalāye has been mentioned as far back as the middle of the 19th century.

---

[45] See Claus 1978, passim; Sontheimer, this volume, and Brückner 1990.

[46] As I have tried to show elsewhere, these differences also have to do with the specific political history of the various sub-regions of Tuḷuva. Certain families of singers were closely associated with certain families of local rulers and the deities in charge of the latters' territory. Cf. Brückner 1990.

[47] In Brückner/Poti 1992 we have attempted to "contextualise" some of the old texts.

Since I could not trace his cult at any other place than the one where the newly recorded text is performed, I assume that Burnell's text, too, may have belonged to that locality. It is worth considering because it follows the first text in yet another detail. The earlier parts of the new text, too, have parallels in texts in Burnell's collection. After tracing the handwritten Burnell Manuscripts in the India Office Library, I was able to compare the published translation of the *pāḍdana* with the original Tuḷu wording.[48] This allows a comparison of the terminology with that of the newly collected texts. Such a comparison also permits a glimpse at diachronic variation, thereby complementing the analysis of synchronic variability.

I list here some of the differences between Burnell's text and the one recorded by me:

The first difference is that, initially, this text mentions the mother first, then the father. It further adds the name of the uncle. It is tempting to take this as an indication that matriliny was more intact a hundred years ago — at least in the minds of the singers. In that system, the mother *(appe)* figured more prominently than the father *(ammE)*, and the maternal uncle *(sammale [= tammalE])* played a very important role as well. The Tuḷu text of the manuscript goes on to say: *they* had four children. The English translation seems to take the plural of the personal pronoun as a honorific referring only to the father and reads: *he* had four children. Grammatically, this is incorrect. The translator may have adapted the text to his own notions and/or to that of an English audience.

In both texts the brothers start by writing on sand, next on a wooden board and then on palm leaves, the preparation of which is described in both of them. The older text, however, adds one more stage: it says, "Then they took ink saying, 'we will hereafter write in

---

[48] I am grateful to the staff of the India Office Library, London, for making the manuscript available to me. Appendix III reproduces the English translation in the Indian Antiquary. Since the text is very short, I do not give a summary here.

English'. — They wrote superior writings on stamped papers and kept them safe in their house." This last point might be taken to illustrate the impact and prestige of the British administration of that period.[49] It is perhaps similarly signifieant that this hierarchy of writing materials does not seem to have survived the British rule: my contemporary recordings at least don't include ink and paper any more.[50] The succeeding parts of the narration agree largely with the other two texts. Another difference is that the brothers seem to buy only one buffalo and pay 300 *varāhas* for it.[51]

The two major differences concern the last part of Burnell's text: firstly, it is important to note that, after the purchase of the buffaloes, they come to Svāmi Nandēdi's palace alone, without the buffalo driver. This is, however, in agreement with the Deyyoṅgulu text. The most important difference lies in the way the text ends. Its last sentence is: "Then Kaṇṇalāye caused Saminandēdī to disappear and he went to his matam."[52] This amounts to an inversion of the scene of the first text, in which it is Svāmi Nandēdi's family deity who makes Kannalāye disappear.

It is indeed very strange that the protagonist, Kannalāye, after whom the whole text is named, is mentioned for the first time only

---

[49] South Kanara was part of the Madras Presidency from 1799 onward.

[50] Such references to contemporary matters appear to be more typical for the style of singers of the Parava caste than for the Pambadas. The mention of ink, paper and the English language might, therefore, also be an indication of the fragment belonging to a Parava tradition. To illustrate the ease of the Paravas — in contradistinction to the Pambadas — to include new details, I can narrate a recent fieldwork experience: while recording a lengthy *pāḍdana* with a Parava family (the mother was the lead-singer, the elder sons took turns in singing the refrain), they came to a point in the text where the several languages the hero knew were enumerated. While singing, the mother confirmed with one of her sons the name of my language, German, and jokingly included it in the list.

[51] At the beginning of the 19th cent. one *varāha* was equivalent to four Rupees (cf. Männer 1886a).

[52] The text reads *Kaṇṇalāye* and *Saminandēdī*.

at the end. The device adopted by the first Kannalāye text, to have the brothers take the buffalo driver along, is missing here. But they, too, bought their buffaloes from a Kannaḍa dealer of the Gauḍa community.[53] No reason is given for Kannalāye's action to cause Svāmi Nandēdi to disappear. The existence of the *būta* Kannalāye as well as of his shrine is presupposed in this text. It may be doubted whether its final scene is valid in the form in which it has come down to us, or whether it has been confused either by an informant or by a scribe. That the text breaks off is also confirmed by the fact that the next three pages are left blank in the manuscript. They were probably reserved for the latter part of this text. The last sentence of the manuscript appears like an attempt to indicate or sum up the further development of the plot. As it is, it is a document which starts in the style of a *pāḍdana*, but then turns more and more into a summary account of the story.

Apart from these very important differences, all three texts on being examined more closely show great similarity. This refers to the course of narration as well as to details such as the name Svāmi Nandēdi and the term *māḍa* used for the respective *būta's* shrine.[54]

A few more references have to be provided here to render the interpretation of the three texts more comprehensible:

---

[53] I take "Gauḍa" in the Tuḷu text to refer to a Kannaḍa community of that name. They today are one of the groups of Kannaḍa-speaking agriculturists settled in Tuḷuva, especially in the east and southeast of the district. The English translation of the text in the IA has "Ganda" instead of "Gauḍa". This may be a mere printing mistake or transliteration error but it may also point to the Kannaḍa notion of *gaṇḍa*, "a strong, heroic man," cognate with *gaṇḍu*, "husband". This is part of the expression "husband buffalo" *(gaṇḍa/gaṇḍu koṇa)*, denoting the sacrificial buffalo in some of the Kannaḍa cults of village goddesses. Whitehead quotes the term as *gauda kona*, either misspelt for *gauḍa kōṇa*, or, more probably, for *gaṇḍa kōṇa*, since he translates it as "husband buffalo" (Whitehead 1976: 73).

[54] *matam* in the English translation appears to be Burnell's spelling for *māḍa*.

A very important parallel, in particular for Lokkayya's Deyyoṅgulu-*pāḍḍana*, is "The Story of Toḍakināra" (Burnell 1894: pp. 96-99, Tuḷu text and English translation; Männer 1886: 31-33). Its first part, in turn, closely resembles the initial portion of an "Attavar Daiyongulu" text (Burnell 1894: 190-193; 1895: 113-114; Männer 1886: 24-27). The protagonist is referred to as "King Dharma" (cf. Lokkayya's Deyyoṅgulu; Aitappa's and Burnell's Koḍamanatāye). The text starts by mentioning his birth. When he is seven years old, he sends for a barber in order to be shaved. An elaborate description of the procedure is given.

In our context, the next part is significant: King Dharma wants to descend to the Tuḷu country and see the Tuḷu people. On his way, two gods oppose him. He meets a dealer in cattle with a herd of four thousand buffaloes and mounts one of his buffaloes, named Channamaṅgale Chaluwarāye, just as the two buffaloes in the Kannalāye text. Later on this very buffalo is sold to someone who, on his way back, ties it to a tree in order to go and perform *japa*. Upon his return, the buffalo is missing. The *būta* possesses the man's servant and informs him that he will give the buffalo back if he gets a temple at his place. He gets a temple and a festival. The *būta* is named Toḍakināra. Later on, he receives another temple and then wants to go and bathe in the western ocean. With Ullalti and a group of other *būtas* he goes to Ullal, bathes in the sea and establishes himself at the place.[55]

[55] A few more references will just be listed here: The process of learning how to write on sand, boards and palm leaves is described in the story of Bobbarya (Burnell 1896, 237 Tuḷu, 239 English). The same passage also refers to the way in which leaves of the palmyra palm are prepared for writing on them. In the Attāvara Deyyoṅguḷu- (Männer 1886, 1; Burnell 1894: 191) and Toḍakināra-*pāḍḍanas* (Männer 1886, 31-33; Burnell 1894: 96—99) a similar description is given in another context, i.e. a person wanting to write a letter. The third reference to be mentioned here is Aitappa Pambada's Balavāṇḍi-*pāḍḍana*. Aitappa's Jārandāye- and Koḍamanatāye-*pāḍḍanas* also have parallel versions in Burnell. The purchase of buffaloes at the Ghāṭs from a Gauḍa is found in the story of Pañjurli (Burnell 1896: 273; Männer 1886: 10). Buffaloes being possessed by a *būta*, or made to disappear by him, are mentioned in the stories of Jārandāye, Koḍamanatāye, Pañjurli and

To sum up: of the texts presented here, one group starts in the west and another is set in the east of the district. The first set of texts has a group of four persons start from the west and proceed to the top of the Ghāṭs to purchase buffaloes. In a second scene, this transaction is described. In Aitappa's text, the standard description is given at this point. In Lokkayya's text, the first deal is passed over quickly and the standard description is saved for the more central deal between the Seṭṭis and Svāmi Nandēdi. The transaction seems to mark the transition of a deity into a Tuḷuva context. The third part contains localised elaborations and blends with various other strands of tradition. In Aitappa's text, the Svāmi Nandēdi episode is the final scene, in Lokkayya's, it is just a link in a different narrative chain. By mentioning the name Darma Arasu and the latter's intention to go and see the western ocean, the text is also connected to another group of texts represented by Burnell's Toḍakināra, which I have summarised above.

The second group consists of texts which are set in the east of the Ghāṭs and describe the birth of one (Darma Arasu) or two (Attavar Daiyongulu) royal personages, who at some stage want to go to the Tuḷu country of their own accord. In Lokkayya's Deyyoṅgulu text the identity of Deyyoṅgulu and Darma Arasu oscillates, probably due to the similarity of the two narrations and personalities. For these deities the passes of the Western Ghats constitute an important point of transition, where they have to face opposition and overcome barriers. In those texts in which people from Tuḷuva go to the Ghats and bring them back the transition is facilitated and a confrontation like the one between the Attavar Daiyongulu and God Subrahmania avoided (cf. Burnell, loc.cit.).

Both groups of texts have in common the motif of the *daiva* taking possession of a buffalo.[56] Particularly the image of king

---

Toḍakināra (cf. above).

[56] In Burnell's Toḍakināra it is said that king Dharma "mounted an ox... this he did by magic." The Tuḷu text reads: "*yeruta mittu kuḷḷuderu, wolagāyeru, māyoḍu*

Dharma being seated on a buffalo recalls depictions of the God Yama, also called Dharma Rājā, riding his buffalo. Forms of Yama or Dharma are known all over India.[57] But once this king enters the Tuḷu country, he is integrated into a Tuḷuva setting by associating him with the local deities, giving him localised names, such as Toḍakukināra or Koḍamanatāye, which mostly are derived from place names, and having him figure in local Tuḷuva legends. Except for the image of a deity riding a buffalo, no traces of Yama mythology can be found in the *pāḍdanas*.

Concerning his acquisition of local names, the process is the opposite of a parallel one by which an existing local deity is absorbed into the mythology of a more widespread one, i.e. local deities being viewed as forms of Jumādi or Pañjurli. Practically, the result is the same, namely identification. The Tuḷu genre of *pāḍdana* provides specific patterns of description and narration to achieve both the integration of deities and their cults into Tuḷuva culture as well as the spread of extremely localised gods to a sub-regional level.[58]

IV Conclusions

1. The comparison of different *pāḍdana* texts and different versions of the same text allows us to see - among other things - how a new content is fitted into an existing framework of traditional poetic formula and narrative elements. Stock descriptions and stock narrative episodes seem to have served as a store from which they were

---

kuḷḷuderu." Literally: "He sat down on the buffalo, he ceremoniously seated himself, in an invisible form *(māya)* he sat down." In *pāḍdanas*, "*vōlega āyeru*" is normally used only for royal personages. In the other texts, the *būta* either makes the buffaloes disappear or makes them shake or tremble in possession.

[57] Cf. for example the material presented by R. P. Das (Das 1983 and 1987). On Yama in the religion of a South Indian tribe cf. Kapp 1982.

[58] I owe this terminology to Bhardwaj, who applies a fivefold geographical division to places of pilgrimage, namely pan-Hindu, supra-regional, regional, sub-regional and local (Bhardwaj 1983: 226 and passim).

taken to make up a large part of the text in question. In this way, the narration peculiar to this *pāḍdana* is whittled down to, at the most, about one fifth, i.e. the last portion of the text. But even here, parallels could be adduced from other texts for many of the phrases and expressions. At least 80% of the texts I have reviewed are composed of parts and elements not peculiar to them.

The first point I want to make here is that this lack of originality does not in the least diminish the impact and validity, or authenticity of the text. On the contrary, validity is achieved on a poetic and narrative level by the fact that not one single element is alien to it. In this way, it accords with the standards of the genre as a whole.

The agreement of a text with the standards of the genre to which it belongs, does not, however, suffice to establish its authenticity in the context of the cult. The authenticity of a text in this sense is constituted by its functioning at the level of the rituals in which it is performed and accepted. As has been shown in part II, text and ritual reflect the social and even topographical environment of the people concerned. Conversely, the myth and its performance help to constitute the very reality they reflect and, thereby, make it meaningful. In this way, they help to establish and maintain identity and authenticity in the lives of the followers of these cults.

2. My second point is somewhat contrary to the first. It is remarkable how stock elements can be combined in such a way as to make up a unique composition. The change of a single element can have an impact on the entire story and the meaning the latter achieves in a particular context. I have shown that in spite of the extremely localised character of the last part of Kannalāye's *pāḍdana*, i.e. Jumādi's turning the buffaloes to stone and transferring the buffalo driver to an invisible realm *(māya)*, it has many elements in common with other *pāḍdana* texts.[59] What is unique, is the

---

[59] Namely, the entire first part, containing the narration about the four brothers, their studies and their business. Even one of the most central motives, the turning of

device to have the Kannaḍa buffalo driver accompany the four brothers and, from the outset, to characterise him as a tragic figure. For example, he does not seem to have a family or a home, he is all alone. In this way, the earlier part has not just been prefixed to, but has been integrated into the local core narration, which thus, in its turn, is also joined to the mainstream of current oral traditions.

Another unique feature concerns the appearance of the lady Svāmi Nandēdi in Aitappa's, Lokkayya's and Burnell's texts alone and in no other *pāḍdana* known to me. Some elements of the scenes involving her have parallels in other texts, some do not.[60] Both, Aitappa and Lokkayya describe her wish to purchase buffaloes. With Lokkayya she succeeds, with Aitappa she fails to do so. Each of these two different solutions are common in *pāḍdana* narrations. Only one detail is unique to both texts: that it is a woman who wants to purchase buffaloes. In the dozens of other texts describing such deals no woman is ever involved in them. The continuation of the scene in Aitappa's version, namely the enraged Svāmi Nandēdi approaching her family *daiva* for help, again has parallels in other texts which also describe how a person, in anger or despair, approaches her or his family deity for help.[61] Only the name Svāmi Nandēdi connects the above episode with the final scene of Burnell's text, in which Kannalāye makes Svāmi Nandēdi disappear from the visible realm.

---

buffaloes to stone, is not peculiar to this text (cf. Balavāṇḍi, above). Deals comparable to that between Jumādi and Kannalāye, the sharing of Jumādi's property, are made in other *pāḍdanas* as well (cf. Burnell, Jārandāya, loc.cit.). In the Mañjeṭṭi goṇE-*pāḍdana*, a text of the women's field-song tradition, too, Jumādi once turns a buffalo driver and his two buffaloes to stone (cf. Brückner 1990).

[60] There is, of course, a chance of coming across yet another version of the text which will make all these speculations futile.

[61] Jumādi, in particular, is famous for taking such emotional requests too literally, thus causing more harm than help. Often, those people who cannot control their anger and thereby lose what is dearest to them, in the texts, belong to the Baṇṭ community. See Claus 1989b and Brückner 1990.

All three scenes can be described as aspects of a constellation in which this woman, the four brothers, a pair of buffaloes and a *būta* are involved. In all three the act of transference to the realm of *māya* plays an important role, but in each of them the agent and the object differ: in Aitappa's text, Svāmi Nandēdi's deity Jumādi transfers the buffalo driver and transforms the buffaloes; in Burnell's text, Kannalāye — being already in an established, deified state — transfers Svāmi Nandēdi; and in Lokkayya's version, the *daiva* Darma Arasu temporarily transfers a pair of buffaloes belonging to Svāmi Nandēdi in order to exercise pressure on her.

All three patterns are familiar, but have very different implications: in the last-mentioned one, a god from outside urges the lady, a rich landowner, to establish his cult. In the old text, a *daiva*, on behalf of a group of males, seems to punish the lady for her pride or stubbornness — a recurrent motif specially in the field-song *pāḍdanas*. In the first text, the lady is closely associated with her deity Jumādi, who makes himself the instrument of her anger.

3. Finally, I want to point out how — on a conceptual level — the last-mentioned scene can be placed in the wider context of South Indian religion. To this end I shall juxtapose certain traits of Jumādi, known from other sources, with elements of the present narrative. Firstly, as I have already mentioned, Jumādi is an androgynous deity, although — in the *pāḍdana* texts — he is referred to by a masc. pronoun. The Sanskritic and Kannaḍa forms of his name, Dhūmāvatī / Dhūmāvati, have a feminine ending. The paraphernalia often include a coat of mail with breasts (cf. Brückner 1987). Secondly, some texts of Sārāla Jumādi associate him with smallpox, a trait which connects him with Māri and other smallpox goddesses of the Deccan. Concerning Svāmi Nandēdi, the following two details are significant: firstly, the attraction the buffaloes exercise upon her; and, secondly, the fact that she makes herself up "like a bride" in order to visit the herd of buffaloes.

These traits recall the notion of the "husband buffalo" (cf. Whitehead 1976: 73 and passim; cf. fn. 53). In festival rituals for Māriyamma studied by Beck (1981), Māri weds a water buffalo, who at the same time is her sacrificial victim. The cult of Māri is part of the immediate ritual context at Terejal (cf. section II).[62] It is tempting to assume that the Tuḷu narrative constitutes a variant of a pattern familiar from the cults of the village goddesses of the Deccan. To account for the absence of the sacrificial element in the Tuḷu material, we can point to a feature which might have replaced that element, namely the "transference to the realm of *māya*". The notion of a wedding is present in the water-buffalo races which form part of the annual ritual cycle at Kulavuru: the procession of the beautiful, decorated racing buffaloes to the *kambula* field, headed by the local ruler's pair and accompanied by an orchestra, has the appearance of a wedding procession. The consummation of the wedding in the field is perceived as dangerous. Those who enter the field run the risk of being transformed to the realm of *māya* — as is testified by several *pāḍdana* narratives and local legends.[63]

In the Kannalāye-*pāḍdana* the bridal aspect of the goddess is represented by Svāmi Nandēdi. The notion of the two buffaloes as grooms[64] is suggested by their beauty and attraction for the "bride" and by the roles the racing buffaloes of estate owners play in the *kambula* rituals. The aggressive aspect of the goddess, who demands a buffalo sacrifice, is — in a mildened Tuḷuva way[65] — represented

---

[62] Beyond the river there rules the goddess Ullāldi or Rājarājeśvarī perceived as a killer of demons and also referred to in the Paṣṇa Jumādi- *pāḍdana* (cf. appendix II).

[63] In the context of the *kambula* the wedding is between the king, represented by his racing buffaloes, and the earth — a notion well known from ancient Indian literature. The relation between the soil and the king's deity cannot be discussed here nor can other features of the races, such as ritual competition.

[64] A pair is perceived as a unit. Cf. the Deyyoṅgulu- *daivas* variously spoken of as one or as two deities.

[65] Incidentally, *tuḷuve* also means "soft". According to some scholars, this meaning characterises the Tuḷu people and corresponds with their self-perception.

by Jumādi, who transfers the buffalo driver to the realm of *māya*. But making him disappear from the visible world is not only an act of aggression, it also leads to a union in Jumādi's own realm, *māya*.[66]

Thus, peculiarities of an individual local text can be identified as culture-specific expressions and — at the same time — as variations of concepts of Hindu folk religion current on a regional and supra-regional level.[67]

---

[66] The buffaloes in the text are transformed to stone. "The most beautiful pair", however, which Svāmi Nandēdi wanted to purchase, are given a place next to Kannalāye's shrine, where they receive food offerings (see section II above).

[67] In other cases the continuity is more immediate. See, for example, the motif of the god with two wives studied by Sontheimer (Sontheimer 1989c).

APPENDIX

I. Kannalāye-pāḍdana (translation)[68]

1) (Line establishing the tune of the piece)
2) Being called "father," there is a man by name Guru Sarapōli Nāyeru̥

3) Being called "mother," there is a woman by name SonnE Solilamma Deyyāru̥
4) To them four Seṭṭis were born:[69]

5) Uttu Seṭṭi, Uttama Seṭṭi, Nācu Seṭṭi [and] Nācamma Seṭṭi.
6) When they reach the age of seven to seven and a half years, the four Seṭṭis say:

7) "We have to learn reading and writing," they say. They learned reading and writing.
8) "Hereafter we have to learn writing on sand," the four Seṭṭis say.

9) They went (probably: had someone go) along the seashore and they had [someone] fetch very fine sand.
10) In the middle of the front hall [of their mansion] they had a line of sand laid out, they, the four Seṭṭis.

11) They learned the writing on sand. "We should learn yet another [way of] writing," they say.
12) "We should learn writing on a wooden board," they say. They had a big *pālE* tree cut.

13) They did the work of the board (i.e. they prepared it or had it prepared). They learned writing on the board.
14) "We should learn yet another [writing], the writing on a palm leaf," the four Seṭṭis say.

---

[68] My thanks are due to Dr. Vivek Rai of Mangalore University, who introduced me to *pāḍdana*-Tuḷu and also helped me to understand the present text.

[69] The sons who were born to them are referred to by their family name. The name occurs among Baṇṭ cultivators as well as among Jaina merchants — the family seems to belong to the second group, cf. below.

15) They went to a long dry field in the eastern direction; they had tender leaves of a young palm tree brought.
16) They had the bundle of palm leaves spread out in the burning sun-heat of the east (i.e. in the morning); in the cool (i.e. evening) sun of the west the leaves [were ready].[70]

17) And they had a bundle tied. They took out selected leaves from the bundle. They have cut the bottom of the leaf, they have trimmed the top of the leaf.
18) They have applied oil and turmeric to the leaf. They learned the writing on the leaf.

19) "We have become well versed in reading and writing; we have to do business;
20) we have to go to the seashore," they say. Out of dried palm leaves they had a shop constructed.

21) For one shop the four Seṭṭis made four compartments, four doors.
22) In one door (i.e. compartment) they set up a textile business.

23) In another compartment they set up the *mukasiri* business.[71]
24) In another compartment they put up the business of Bengal gram and wheat.

25) In another compartment they put up the business of iron.
26) The Seṭṭis became well versed in business. "We should [take up] another business;

27) we should go to the top of the Ghats," they say. "We should buy a herd of buffaloes," they say.
28) They had a big clean bag stitched. They counted their pagoda-coins [and] tied them up [in the cloth bag].

---

[70] Line 16b can also be connected with the initial words of 17a. The sentence would then read: and in the cool sun of the west they had the leaves tied up in a bundle [again].

[71] The meaning of this word is not clear; *muka* means face, *siri* refers to auspiciousness and is sometimes prefixed in expressions such as *sirimonE* "good face" to confer the meaning of beauty, respect and auspiciousness.

29) The Seṭṭis come to their palace, which is called "Koṅganāḍu Naṇḍedēsa
30) CeṇḍE Cīmulla Palace." On an auspicious Tuesday early in the morning they got up.

31) They put oil on their head, they rubbed oil on their body. Having applied oil [and washed it off with hot water], they felt good.
32) Having taken off their dirty clothes, they put on clean ones. [For breakfast] they ate a meal of rice left over from the previous day.

33) In a lunch carrier they put [some food along with] hot milk. They left (lit.: descended from) their palace.
34) The Seṭṭis come to the top of the Ghats. They wander in the dry fields of the Ghats.

35) At that time there comes, driving four thousand buffaloes,
36) the "buffalo-Kannaḍa". When he comes driving and grazing the four thousand buffaloes,

37) the four Seṭṭis see the "buffalo-Kannaḍa." "Oh buffalo-Kannaḍa, do you hear,
38) from where do you come [and] where do you go?" say the Seṭṭis.

39) "Oh children, do you hear, I have lost direction, my position [in life] has come to be ruined;
40) I am going to a kingdom not [previously] seen with [my] eyes, to a country not [previously] heard of by [my] ears—"

41) thus speaks the "buffalo-Kannaḍa" to the Seṭṭis. The Seṭṭis ask:
42) "You should give your four thousand buffaloes to us," they say.

43) The Seṭṭis gave the bundle (lit.: knot) of pagoda-coins to the "buffalo-Kannaḍa."[72]
44) "You should give your buffaloes to us [and] you should come along with us," the four Seṭṭis say.

45) They come driving [and] grazing the four thousand buffaloes.

---

[72] Variant: The Kannaḍa gave the rope of the buffaloes to the Seṭṭis.

46) "Where shall we descend along the Ghats into the Tulu kingdom?" they ask.

47) "If we descend via Kolyūru, the God Kolyūru Kokke Subrāya will not leave us [in peace] (or: will not let us pass)," they say.
48) "Whatever may happen, we should descend at the Naḍuvala Nalpa Muḍi field along with the buffaloes," they say.

49) There the four Seṭṭis descend with the buffaloes at Naḍuvala Nalpa Muḍi [-field].
50) They tied the herd of four thousand buffaloes at the Naḍuvala Nalpa Muḍi field,

51) the four Seṭṭis. At that time,
52) the [right] time for the *pōsa* [-meal] has come for them, the four Seṭṭis.[73]

53) The four Seṭṭis come to the house of the woman Svāmi Nandēdi.
54) "Who is there in the house, who is there in the house?" the Seṭṭis ask.

55) "A pot for cooking and a house to dwell in has to be given to us," they ask.
56) At that time, the woman Svāmi Nandēdi says to the four Seṭṭis:

57) "Oh children, oh children, in olden days
58) I did not give a house to dwell, I did not give a pot to cook," she says.

59) "In the middle [room of the house] there is cooked food, oh children, there is a meal with *pañcāmruta* (a sweet dish); go ahead!
60) In the stone tub they have put a hand mug, wash your hands, feet, teeth and face."

61) On the well-smoothed platform [on the front wall of the entrance hall] they have spread a coloured mat. The four Seṭṭis sat down.

---

[73] The first part of the text ends here. The beginning of the second part (53sqq.) was marked in the recitation by a change of tune.

62) At that time, in the middle of the front hall they have laid out [the leaves] in a row.

63) Having taken the cooked food to the middle [of the hall], the woman Svāmi Nandēdi serves it to the four Seṭṭis there.
64) Then there they have eaten [food cooked in] buttermilk, they washed their hands in milk.[74]

65) They have eaten [food cooked in] milk, in buttermilk the four Seṭṭis washed their hands there.
66) "Oh woman Svāmi Nandēdi, such a meal we have not eaten before

67) [and] we shall not eat it hereafter," say the four Seṭṭis there.
68) At that time [to] the woman Svāmi Nandēdi they say:

69) "Our four thousand buffaloes [are there] at the Naḍuvala Nalpa Muḍi field,
70) at the Naḍuvala Nalpa Muḍi field the herd of buffaloes has halted;

71) you should come to see the beauty of the buffaloes," they say.
72) "Oh children, you go first (or: ahead), I shall come afterwards (or: behind);

73) if I come along with you, the *ālikāras* will make fun [of me],
74) the *pōlikāras* will say nasty things"— thus speaks the woman.

75) The woman Svāmi Nandēdi enters the southern room [of her house]; the best *sīrE* (Sāri) of the bundle to be worn,
76) the best *sīrE* of the bundle[75] she wore; the best gold [-ornaments] of the jewelbox she put on.

77) She made herself up like a bride. She arranged for an escort in front and a servant [to go] behind [her].
78) In her right hand she held a silver knife, in her left hand a *ponnE* umbrella,

---

[74] These are expressions of abundance.

[75] Possibly a pun: the word could also mean "for the herd" [of buffaloes].

79) holding the umbrella, there, at the Naḍuvala Nalpa Muḍi field,
80) she comes, the woman Svāmi Nandēdi, [to see] the beauty of the four thousand buffaloes.

81) For the woman Svāmi Nandēdi they have had made a stool to sit, a cot to lie down;
82) the four Seṭṭis have had it made. At that time, Svāmi Nandēdi,

83) the woman Svāmi Nandēdi there, saw the beauty of the buffaloes.
84) Among the four thousand buffaloes there are two [exceptional] buffaloes:

85) there are [two] buffaloes called Cenna-Maṅgala [and] Celuva-Rāya;
86) they are buffaloes [who have] a white mark on the forehead, a white tuft on the tail [and] on the four legs *sonambu/sonambulla.*[76]

87) At that time the woman Svāmi Nandēdi asks the four Seṭṭis:
88) "Among the four thousand buffaloes there are two [exceptional] buffaloes;

89) you should tell me the price for those buffaloes," she says.
90) "For the front step a thousand pagodas, for the back step a thousand and one pagodas

91) you should give," the four Seṭṭis say. At that time,
92) [the price] for the buffaloes is not agreed upon; the woman Svāmi Nandēdi in anger,

93) in anger [and] rage leaves [and] comes to [her] estate of Kulavūru.
94) She comes to the estate of Kulavūru; there she stood in Jumādi's *cāvaḍi* hall.[77]

95) "Oh Jumādi, do you hear, there are two buffaloes suitable for our buffalo shed,

---

[76] The meaning of this word could not be traced. It might refer to white marks or to golden anklets.

[77] The *daivas* have places of worship in the front halls of houses.

96) there are two buffaloes there; [the price] for the buffaloes is not agreed upon;

97) you should make it agree;" in this manner, there, the woman Svāmi Nandēdi at Kulāra guttu estate,
98) standing in the middle of the *cāvaḍi* hall, makes a request to Jumādi.

99) At that time, the "buffalo-Kannaḍa" comes driving the four thousand buffaloes
100) to Sārada Guṇḍi Māru̥ to drink water.

101) He passed Malla AṭṭE Padavu, he descended Yelya AṭṭE Padavu.
102) At the time when he makes the buffaloes drink water at Sārada Guṇḍi,

103) exactly at that time, Jumādi transforms the four thousand buffaloes
104) into stone. There, at that time, he says,

105) the "buffalo-Kannaḍa" says: "Oh Jumādi, do you hear,
106) my buffaloes you transformed into stones; what is to become of me?" (lit.: "what for me?") he asks.

107) "To you I [shall give a position] one step smaller than a god [and] one step bigger than the *būtas*,"
108) thus he speaks there. And he transposed the "buffalo-Kannaḍa"

109) into [the realm of] *māya* (i.e. an invisible realm). "At the shrine of Agari I shall have a stone seat carved for you,
110) and I shall have a cross-legged cot put up; a left stone and a right stone I shall have put up;

111) among [my] six estates three estates are for you, three estates are for me," thus he speaks.
112) At that time at the shrine of Agari he had the stone seat carved, the cross-legged cot,

113) the cot he had put up there, he, Jumādi.

II. Pasna Jumādi-pāḍdana (translation)[78]

1) At the manorial house of Rāyi [there lives] Magrādēre Ballāl, Magrādēre, [the nephew of] the Ballāl (nobleman) Kōca Ālverụ.
2) Magrade Ballāl [reaches] the age of seven to seven and a half years; when he becomes ten [and then] sixteen years of age, [he thinks:]

3) "For [other] youths like me the right moment for the wedding has [already] come;[79] [to where do] the marriage alliances established by our ancestors [direct me]?
4) Where is the meal [prepared by the bride to be] eaten [by the bridegroom]?" thus he asks there. They say, "It is in the manorial house of Ambaḍādi;"

5) thus they speak there; in the manorial house of Rāyi [there assembled] the four [men] of the Nāḍu, the four [men] of the manor,
6) eight or sixteen Bāragas[80] assembled in the manorial house of Rāyi; they made themselves up in grand style.

7) They left the manorial house of Rāyi [and] passed the Peral tree with the stone platform [around it]; they passed the temple of [the goddess] Ullāldi;
8) they [crossed] the "Red Hillock," crossed Baḍajeda Bailụ there; they crossed the rivulet of Kalasandaḍka Yerụ.

9) When they come to the dam bordering the *kambula* field at the manorial house of Ambaḍādi, the dear niece of Kōcālverụ [is looking] from a distance;
10) from a distance she is looking there [and says:] "Oh uncle, do you listen, what guests [are approaching] our house,

[78] The text has been first recorded with Aitappa Pambada in September 1984 outside the ritual context. It was compared with the ritual recitation at Kulavuru on 24th April 1986. My thanks are due to Shri Amrith Someshvar, of Kotekar and to Dr. Vivek Rai of Mangalore University for going through the text with me and making valuable comments.

[79] I.e. passed, they have already gotten married.

[80] Bāragas are agriculturalists of the Banṭ caste (cf. Männer 1886a).

11) [what] guests are coming [there]?" she says. Thereupon Kōcālvarụ says: "Oh niece, do you listen," he says,
12) "guests who [want to] come will come, guests who don't [want to] come, won't come;[81] you go [and] enter the southern room,

13) make yourself up [like] a bride," thus he speaks there; wear the best *sīrE* (Sāri) of the bundle [of cloth and] from the jewelbox,
14) from the jewelbox put on the best gold [-ornaments]," he says; come with your right [foot first and] tie [your hair] in a knot [like] a bride;

15) make yourself up [like] a bride," he says. To the guests who had come they gave water for [washing] the feet.
16) They washed the dust off their feet and the dust off their hands. On the well-smoothed platform[82] they spread an ornamented mat. The guests sat down wherever there was space.

17) Kōcālverụ says, "To the guests who have come in the heat of the sun, we must serve a meal suited to the heat."
18) "Before the meal, before the feast, we must first attend to the task [and] duty for which we have come."

19) "Name the task [that has to be] named, oh children, don't name the task [that does not have to be] named" - thus speaks Kōcālverụ.
20) "If there is a maiden [to be] given [as a bride], if there is a buffalo [to be] sold [will you give them to us]?" they ask.

21) "The maiden [to be] given [as a bride] has [already] been given away; the buffalo [to be] sold has [already] been sold off," says [Kōcālverụ]. "Whatever is there may be given," they say (or: he says).[83]

---

[81] I.e.: "why do you bother?"

[82] I.e. on the low front wall of the entrance hall.

[83] Their are two ways of translating the passage. Kōcālverụ either wants to say that their request is already fulfilled the moment they pronounced it or - as I have translated following Amrith Someshvar's suggestion - the sentence expresses extreme modesty. It would then imply that a superior girl and a superior buffalo apt to be offered to such a high-born suitor have already been given away and that he pretends to offer only the girl and the buffalo left with him.

22) They sent for the Baṭṭa of the Nāḍu, they called the soothsayer of the manorial house. In the middle of the *cāvaḍi* hall,

23) in the middle of the *cāvaḍi* hall they heaped up [the nuts for soothsaying]. "Between a girl of seven to seven and a half years
24) and a boy of ten to sixteen years there results a correspondence from the calculations," they say there.

25) At that time the engagement for the marriage was made: "On the eighth day of the following week
26) the marriage procession should come from the manorial house of Rāyi to the manorial house of Ambaḍādi," they say.

27) On the eighth day of the following week they lead the marriage procession from the manorial house of Rāyi to the manorial house of Ambaḍādi.
28) The auspicious moment of the wedding has passed. When the lady (i.e. the bride), who has gone [back home] once [and] has come back a second time, comes back for the third time, after having gone for the second time,

29) the *daiva* comes following the lady from the manorial house of Ambaḍādi to the manorial house of Rāyi.
30) He (the *daiva*) comes to the manorial house of Rāyi. In the manorial house of Rāyi he receives [worship]. From the manorial house of Rāyi he comes,

31) following [another] lady (i.e. bride), to Irandilla Janana.[84] At Irandilla Janana there is, at the time,
32) Pinanulla Candirābu Seṭṭibālu. He has lain down because of worry about the water for the *kambula*.[85]

33) At that time the *daiva* asks: "Oh Pinanulla Candirābu Seṭṭibālu, why are you worried?
34) Have you lain down out of worry over the water for the *baṇḍimāra-kambula* [-field] or have you lain down in order to sleep?" he asks.

---

[84] Following brides is one of the devices by which *daivas* move from estate to estate. Verse 30 also marks the transition from the first to the second narrative episode.

[85] See fn. 33.

35) "Oh *daiva*, do you listen, I have lain down because of worry over [procuring] water for the *baṇḍimāra-kambula*," he says.
36) "Don't worry about the water for the *baṇḍimāra-kambula;* before the morning star has risen and the day has dawned,

37) I shall procure water for the *kambula*, I shall have the *kambula* prepared [for the race], I shall have the *pūkarE* [-pole] erected" - thus he speaks.[86]
38) He assembled a thousand *būtas* [and] gave them pots and buckets. From the Sārada Guṇḍimāra [-well]

39) he had the water filled [into the buckets]; he procured water for the *baṇḍimāra-kambula;* he had the *kambula* prepared; he had the *pūkarE* [-pole] erected.
40) At that time the *daiva* comes to Irandilla Janana. "Oh Pinanulla Candirābu Seṭṭibālu, do you listen,

41) for the *kambula* I have procured water, I have had the *kambula* prepared, I have had the *pūkarE* erected; what [will you give] me [in return]?" he says.
42) "At Koṭyadaḍka I shall have one place constructed for you [and] one place for [the goddess] Ullāldi," he says.

43) "I shall give you a hoisted flag[87] [and] five days of *ceṇḍu*,"[88] he says.
44) At Koṭyadaḍka he had the shrubs removed [and] the ditches made level; he had the foundation for the temple laid.

45) At that time, the *daiva* Jumādi, he, removed the tiles of the temple

---

[86] After flooding it, the field is prepared by ploughing it repeatedly and then smoothing the mud with wooden planks pulled by pairs of water-buffaloes. The embankments of the field are smoothed as well and decorated with ornamental designs. Finally, a pole decorated with flowers and called *pūkarE* is erected in the middle of the field.

[87] A hoisted flag stands for a grand festival ritual for a deity.

[88] *Ceṇḍu* is a ritual football match between two villages. The most famous *ceṇḍu* games are those held for the goddess Rājarājeśvarī (Tuḷu: Ullāldi) of Purāḷu (Kann.: Polāli) at her temple two or three miles beyond the river from Terejal. The reference in the text seems to be to a smaller temple of Ullāldi.

46) [and] had them put on the [roof of] the mosque; he removed the tiles of the mosque and put them on the temple. The *mukri* who called for prayer in the morning,

47) the *mukri* who called for prayer in the morning he killed in the evening; the *mukri* who called for prayer in the evening he killed in the morning.[89]
48) In [the form of] *māya* he made the regulation [that he was to be called] "Ainūra Jumādi" (the Jumādi of five hundred households). He crossed [the river at] Minaṅgila Kariya. To the estate of Kulavūru,

49) to the estate of Kulavūru he comes. He started [to show his presence] in a crying child [and] and a lowing calf. "What strange happening is this,
50) what a *kalijiga*?"[90] they say. When consulting the palm leaf almanac [they find out:]

51) "A *daiva* has come, suitable for the hundred households of the place," they say here. "What [has to be given] to the *daiva* who has come," they say.
52) "He wants a swinging cot beset with pearls in the middle of the *cāvaḍi* hall," they say. "He wants arrangements [to be made] for [building] a temple," they say.

53) On the Kaḍurāḍu Ula hillock they had a temple constructed for the *daiva*. In the temple which had been constructed they installed the *daiva*.
54) In his *māya* [-form] the *daiva*, he himself, made a regulation: "[My domain extends] from Dharmasthala in the east

55) up to the Kaḍurāḍu Ula hillock in the west;" this regulation he made in his *māya* [-form]. Below [at the foot of the hillock] he had a platform constructed [around a tree];
56) on top [he had the temple of] Kaḍurāḍu Ula hillock. This regulation the *daiva* Jumādi made, he himself.

---

[89] 45-47. This way of interlinking two statements (in 45/46 and in 47) is a typical feature of the *pāḍḍana* style. In both cases, only one action is referred to, i.e. he takes the tiles away from the mosque and he kills the *mukri*.

[90] *Kalijiga*, Skt. *kaliyuga*, is used here in the sense of a strange occurence, just like the previous expression, *sōjiga*, which I have translated as "strange happening."

57) At sunrise [he occupied] the estate of Kulavūru, at sunset [the temple of] Kaduṛāḍu Ula hillock; having created *nāga bermeṛu* at the left side, he had [the place] called Kaduṛāḍu UlaguḍḍE.

III. Kannalāye (Burnell ms. 18, Indian Antiquary 25, 1896: 65)

There was a mother named *Soyiramma Taiyar*, a father named *Guru Sarapoli Naika*, and an uncle named *Bābe Sēṇava*. *Guru Ṣarapoli* had four children. One of them was called Aru Adana Śēṭṭi; another named Unnappa Śēṭṭi; another Darama Śēṭṭi; another Sundaram Śēṭṭi. For these four children he built a building on the seashore. He brought some sand for them to write on. He put up a sloping table for them. Then the children began by writing on the sand, and when they could write on boards, their father brought some leaves of a palm tree, put them in the morning sun and heaped them together in the evening sun. He cut off both ends of the leaves, and trimmed the edges. He put turmeric on the leaves. The children wrote on a bundle of such leaves and tied them to a tree in the street.

Then they took ink saying, "*We will hereafter write in English.*" — They wrote superior writings on stamped papers and kept them safe in their house.

"We have become clever, and so now let us build four shops on the seashore," said they. They put curry stuffs into one shop, wheat and Bengal gram into another; into another a kind of rice called *samē*: into another, clothes. In this way, they had separate things in four shops.

Then they left off this trade and began to deal in bullocks. At *Karmin Salē* on the Ghats there was one *Yellappu Ganda*. They went to him and said: —
"Yellappu Ganda, we want a pair of bullocks. Tell us the price and give us the bullocks quickly and the straw for them! Give us a superior kind of bullocks."

He brought bullocks differing in the colours of their four legs. Brown was the colour of their tails; white the colour of their heads and white were their tongues! He sold them with the straw for them. They paid hundred rupees, and then they brought them to the *chāvaḍi* of a woman named *Saminandēdī*. They called her and asked her a foot's length of ground on which to cook.

"We give food to those who take it, and fruit to those who will not take food; but our ancestors never gave a place for cooking, and we will not give it now," said she.

Then she asked their caste and supplied them with water.

Then *Kaṇṇalāye* caused Saminandēdī to disappear and he went to his *matam*.

References

Beck, Brenda. 1981. The goddess and the demon. A local South Indian festival and its wider context. In *Puruṣārtha* 5, 83-136.

Bhardwaj, Surinder M. 1983 *Hindu places of pilgrimage in India. A study in cultural geography*. Berkeley etc.

Blackburn, Stuart 1988. *Singing of birth and death. Texts in performance*. Philadelphia: University of Pennsylvania Press.

Id. and Ramanujan, A.K. (eds.). 1987. *Another harmony. New essays on the folklore of India*. Berkeley: University of California Press.

Brückner, Heidrun. 1987. Jumādi: an oral Tuḷu myth and ritual of bhūta-worship in Coastal Karṇāṭaka. In *Studien zur Indologie und Iranistik*, 13/14 1987, 17-37. Reinbek. (= Festschrift für Wilhelm Rau).

Id. 1990. *Königliche Kulte: Mythologie und Rituale von Volkskulten an der Westküste Südindiens*. (587pp., manuscript).

Id. and Poti, Narasimha 1992. Dhūmāvati-bhūta: A oral Tuḷu-text collected in the 19th cent. Edition, translation, analysis. In *Studien zur Indologie und Iranistik* 16, 13-64.

Burnell, A. C. 1894-1897. Devil worship of the Tuḷuvas from

the papers of the late A.C. Burnell, ed. by Maj. R.C. Temple. In *Indian Antiquary, Vols. 23-26.*

Claus, Peter J. 1975. The Siri myth and ritual: A mass possession cult of Tulunad. In *Ethnology* 14: 47-58.

Id. 1978. Oral traditions, royal cults and materials for the reconsideration of the caste system in South India. In *Journal of Indian Folkloristics* 1: 1-25.

Id. 1979. Spirit possession and spirit mediumship from the perspective of Tuḷu oral traditions. In *Culture, Medicine and Psychiatry* 3: 29-52.

Id. 1989a. Behind the text: performance and ideology in a Tuḷu oral tradition. In *Oral epics in India* Blackburn et. al. (eds.), Berkeley: University of California Press.

Id. 1989b. Kinsongs (manuscript).

Das, Rahul P. 1983. Some remarks on the Bengali deity Dharma: Its cult and study. In *Anthropos* 78: 661-700.

Id. 1987. More remarks on the Bengali deity Dharma, its cult and study. In *Anthropos* 82, 244-251.

Das, Veena 1976. The uses of liminality. In *Contribu-*

tions to Indian Sociology 10, 245-263.

Finnegan, R. 1977. *Oral poetry. Its nature, significance and social content*. Cambridge.

Gowda, Chinnappa 1983. *Bhūtārādhane: Kelavu adhyayanagaḷu*. Mangalore.

Kapp, Dieter B. 1982. The concept of Yama in the religion of a South Indian tribe. In *Journal of the American Oriental Society* 102, 517-521.

Leach, Edmund. 1976. *Culture and communication. The logic by which symbols are connected.* Cambridge: Cambridge University Press.

Männer, August 1886. *Pāḍdanoḷu*. Mangalore: Basel Mission Press.

Id. 1886a. *A Tuḷu-English dictionary*. Mangalore (reprint: Delhi 1983).

Rai, Viveka 1982. *Tuḷuva adhyayana: Kelavu vicāragaḷu*. Mangalore.

Id. 1985. *Tuḷu janapada sāhitya*. Bangalore (Ph.D.thesis).

Sontheimer, G.-D. 1987. The vana and the kṣetra: The tribal origins of some famous cults. In *Eschmann memorial lectures*, Vol. I (1978-86), G.C. Tripathi and Hermann Kulke (eds.), Eschmann Memorial Fund, Bhubaneswar, 117-164.

Id. 1989a. Between ghost and god: A folk deity of the Deccan. In *Criminal gods and demon devotees: Essays on the guardians of popular hinduism*. Hiltebeitel, Alf (ed.), Albany, N.Y.: State University of New York Press.

Id. 1989b Hinduism: The five components and their interaction. In *Hinduism reconsidered*, Sontheimer, G.-D. and Kulke, H., (eds.). Delhi.

Id. 1989c. The myth of the god and his two wives: Two pastoral versions from Maharashtra. In *Living texts from India*, Thiel-Horstmann, M. and Barz, R. (eds.), Wiesbaden.

Id. 1989d. *Pastoral deities in Western India*, (tr. by Anne Feldhaus) New York: Oxford Univ. Press.

Upadhyaya, U.P. 1988. *Tuḷu nighaṇṭu (Tuḷu lexicon)*, Vol. I. Udupi.

Whitehead, H. 1976. *The village gods of South India*. Delhi: Sumit. (Reprint of 1921 edition).

TEXT VARIABILITY AND AUTHENTICITY IN THE SIRI CULT

Peter J. Claus

Like many other local religious cults in Tuḷunāḍu and elsewhere around southern India, text and context have an intimate relationship in the Siri cult.[1] But in the way the text and ritual context are linked, the Siri cult differs from other Tuluva cults. While many of the local religious cults of Tuḷunāḍu — *bhūta* cults — are confined to a specific village, or at most a few neighboring villages, and linked, as Brückner (1987 and this vol.) has shown, by the tenuous threads of *pāḍdanas* known only by low caste ritual specialists (Pambada males), the Siri cult is region-wide, and the story of Siri, unique in the vast repertoire of Indian story traditions as far as I can tell, is

---

[1] For a more extensive discussion of the relationships between the Siri text and ritual see Claus 1975a, 1979a, 1986, 1987. In Claus 1975a, 1986 and 1987 there is a brief summary of the Siri story.
Many other ritual traditions utilize narrative text as an integral part of the performance. See for example Blackburn's study of Tamil *vil pāṭṭu* (1981, 1988); Beck's description of the ritual performance of the *aṇṇanmār katai* (Beck 1982) and Ashley's analysis (1979) of Kerala Teyyams. In Tuḷunāḍu there are many examples: see Brückner 1987 and Claus 1979b, 1989. Since the text is performed (sung, chanted) in one form or another as part of the ritual, the relationship is far greater than that between *sthala purāṇas* (Shulman 1980) and temple rituals. *Sthala purāṇas* are generally related only to the origins and iconography of a temple (but see Welbon 1982 for an intermediate case where dramatic possession ritual takes place at a Hindu temple).

known throughout Tuḷunāḍu.[2] The purveyors of the Siri cult are non-professionals: the numerous women who sing the *pāḍdana* in the fields; and men, called Kumārs in the context of ritual spirit possession, who are responsible for organizing local cult groups. Once a year the women and men who participate in the cult gather at certain locations, called *āluḍe* (most likely from *al-*, 'to rule' + *-aḍe*, 'place'), or *mūlasthāna* (*mūla*, 'root, origin' + *sthāna*, 'place'), dispersed around the district. They come from different villages, different castes, different backgrounds, and frequently have little or no contact with one another at other times of the year. Nevertheless, their association during the cult ritual is exceedingly intense and effective at all levels, psychologically, socially and religiously (Claus 1979a).

In this paper I primarily want to up-date my research on the Siri myth (or story, legend[3]), correct some possible misunderstandings in my earlier papers on Siri and report some of my more recent find-

---

[2] There are several other *pāḍdanas* which have this sort of culture-wide circulation, but all of them are epic-like stories of male caste heroes: Koti-Cannayya (of the Billava caste) and Kordabbu (of the Mundala caste). Unlike these, the main characters of the Siri *pāḍdana* are female and the tone is tragic. The Siris are not regarded as *bhūtas* as in the case of these other examples.

[3] The texts I have collected could be characterized by a number of English terms. In as much as none of these English terms have very widely agreed upon technical definitions and none of them corresponds with native genre categories, I myself will not use them in a technical sense. The Tulu word *pāḍdana* covers a wide variety of sung narrative forms which could be described as epic, ballad, chant and even dirge. The Tulu word *kathe*, too, is applied broadly to cover formal folk-tale narration, the spoken narration of the "story line" of other genres, description of events in conversational narrative and as a rough equivalent to the English word "story".
In this paper, I shall use Tulu and Kannaḍa terms to refer to specific genres, i.e. the specific texts in the forms *(pāḍdana, kathe, hogalikke)* in which they are manifest. I shall use the English word "story" to refer to the major theme (story line) of a *pāḍdana*. In some instances this corresponds to one Tulu usage of the term, *"kathe"*. In this sense, the story of Siri could be loosely described as either a legend or a myth; its formal recitation as a *pāḍdana* could be called a song, a ballad, or an epic, depending in part on the context in which it is sung and in part on what characteristics one focuses on in defining terms for genres.

ings. The recent findings have not been the result of systematic research devoted to the study of the Siri cult, but rather mostly fortuitous discoveries gained in the process of carrying out systematic research on the variation and dynamics of the *pāḍdanas* women sing in the fields while transplanting paddy seedlings.[4] For this reason, my presentation is perhaps less complete than might be desired. What I wish to argue, however, is that the Siri *pāḍdana* (myth, story, legend) and cult (place and activity) may not have been as fixedly linked throughout their history as their present-day association would lead one to suspect when simply gathering information from a given informant. My more recent findings increasingly point to the probability that the images, motifs, episodes, names, places and story connectives in the contemporary Siri *pāḍdana* are derived from a number of different sources and stitched together. There is, at any given time, a great deal of variation in the Siri story as it is found in its various contexts, variation which speaks to a dynamic compositional process which is still very active.[5] This claim, while it will not surprise the anthropologist or folklorist, flies in the face of

---

[4] See Claus 1988 for a preliminary discussion of this research. The main goal was to understand the variation and dynamics of the women's field-song *pāḍdana* tradition. Another object of the research was to understand the relationship of women's field-songs to the *pāḍdanas* sung by men during religious rituals. A portion of the long Siri *pāḍdana*, the Abbaga-Daraga (or Sonne-Ginde) *pāḍdana* has been part of this research, as has been (more tangentially, though) the collection of Kannaḍa *hogalikkes* in the region immediately to the north of the Tulu-speaking area.

[5] There is similar evidence that the ritual acts at the Siri cult rituals in various locations are similarly dynamic and hence variable from place to place. Presentation of my recently gathered material on the variability of text and ritual activity in the ritual context will be saved for another occasion. I do, however, allude to some of the ritually recited textual material in this paper. That textual tradition, I should point out, seems to be transmitted independently of the actual *pāḍdana*. Many of the women (perhaps the majority) do not sing the *pāḍdana* in the fields — indeed, they may not even work in the field — and *cannot* sing the *pāḍdana*. Yet during the *jātrE* many recite long "texts". The texts are apparently learned in the ritual context only. The ritual texts, sung during possession, and associated with specific acts and impromptu situations, introduced by new participants and supplicants, require special analytic considerations which I cannot fully discuss in this paper.

both believers and local scholars, who would combat it with powers of authority they possess.[6] But it is not in learned (urban, literate, Sanskritizing) assemblies and arenas in which the Siri *pāḍdana* is most effectively integrated and linked to particular places, ritual activities and historical events. Rather, it is in varying ritual and secular contexts, amongst the dispersed participants, and in the context of women singing in the fields and even in the particular lives (families, personalities) of the participants that the integration takes place. Yet if this is so, how can such unrelated, disparate sources yield such uniformity? My data shows that there is not, in fact, the uniformity that believers so adamantly supposed. Furthermore, it is clear from my data that there is not normally a *direct* interaction between the text and rituals. The myth, not actually sung during the ritual, is *referred* to. The full story is sung only in the fields (if at

---

[6] Local scholars have a powerful, if indirect, influence over local tradition. Indian culture continues to hold the literate, urban class in high regard and the rural masses defer to their opinion even in matters of rural folk tradition. Some of the processes local writers often take upon themselves are the compilation, rationalization and Sanskritization of folk tradition, thereby not merely adding to it, but altering its very course of development. Local groups not only accept these changes, but often commission them (see also Shulman 1980). Recently, mass media, radio, television, cinema, popular magazines, etc. have contributed to the development and standardization of folk tradition. Frequently, it is the same group of local scholars who are asked to write articles for magazines, who write scripts for cinemas and act as consultants for other types of productions.

My own research and scholarship has even begun to influence, albeit in a yet more indirect way, public opinion about these traditions, with the publication in Kannaḍa of Tuluva Darshana (Claus 1987b), and through a series of workshops on folkloristics in which several folklorists of the area participated. It is too early to assess the effects of these involvements, but I expect it will have only a very limited influence over the people, for whom I will always be a foreigner, a non-believer.

For believers, one of the most powerful influences is direct communication with the supernatural. The Kumār, for example, is sometimes asked to use his divine inspiration to answer theological questions. I have known local researchers to put their research questions to the Kumārs and to use their answers as fact in their written work. The Kumārs, themselves, sometimes read the works of local scholars and their responses, inspired or not, cannot be said to be impartial. In any case, most divine responses are vague enough to allow local writers ample room to provide their own interpretation and claim it is "God's Truth".

all), and there, too, its referential association with the actions of the ritual, while strong, lacks important elements of the cult context. Singing portions of the Siri *pāḍdana* in the fields is apt to bring about possession for those women who participate in the cult, but the possession is essentially meaningless and is not utilized by those present for any of the purposes to which it is put during the cult possession. Thus myth and ritual have independent existences and, I would hypothesize, independent histories. Their integration is constantly being worked out in numerous, disparate events. What I would like to present in this paper, then, are some of the possible sources of the textual tradition. The texts I present are entirely haphazardly encountered. It must be kept in mind that an incalculably large number of past associations, of which we shall never have a definite knowledge, must certainly have had powerful effects on the development of the text and that tomorrow, too, there may be important events which could change the entire course of the cult tradition, the myth, the ritual and their relationship.

The "Authentic" Siri Myth

The Siri *pāḍdana* ranks as one of the longer *pāḍdanas* of Tuḷunāḍu. It takes 6-8 hours or more to sing in its entirety. Although it is usually regarded as the sort of *pāḍdana* women sing in the fields, it is one of the few of that type I have found that some men of various castes also know and can sing.[7] However, it is not one in which the men of the bardic castes (Pambada, Parava and

---

[7] It might be noted here that the Siri *pāḍdana* has a very distinctive style of singing. It has long, open-ended lines of varying length, sung in a very rapid, un-melodic manner. It's refrain "Naaraaaayana, Naarayanaaaa, Naaraaayanaaa ..." instead of the usual *pāḍdana* refrain of "Dennaana, dennana, dennaaana ..." is also distinctive. The distinctiveness of its singing style may differentiate it from the women's field-song tradition and thus make men more comfortable about singing it. The sing-song manner of recitation is carried over even to conversational modes of speech while being possessed by the spirits in the cult rituals.

Nalke), who sing the *bhūta pāḍdanas*, are especially knowledgeable.[8] It is clear, then, that at present, at least, the Siri *pāḍdana* is, like the Siri rituals to which it is linked, not a specialist tradition, but, on the contrary, one of the most widespread Tulu oral traditions and one in which both men and women of all non-Brahmin castes may participate. In fact, as a prose narrative, not fixed in *pāḍdana* song and verse form, it has an even far greater distribution. Except in the Kāsaragōḍ area, now a part of Kerala, I have seldom met a Tuluva of any caste who did not at least know the major events of the story.

Despite this widespread popularity, and despite the absence of a specialist class to control its authenticity, there is a strong feeling that a legitimate standard exists: there is, it is felt, a true version, a correct account. However, precisely locating where this correct account might exist is problematical. Women who sing the *pāḍdana* in the fields with confidence are apt to demure at having full knowledge of the song and refer to another, older, more experienced woman, who is a participant in the Siri cult at the closest *āluḍe*. When that woman is then tracked down and asked to sing, she feigns surprise that she is regarded as an authority. When pressed, she agrees to sing, but usually, if she is a participant at the annual rituals, she insists that only during the Siri *jātrE* will the full and correct *pāḍdana* be sung. This, however, is patently not the case, if by full, correct version she means the narrative of Siri's life, for during the *jātrE* the *pāḍdana* is not, in fact, sung at all.[9] Only small

---

[8] In my experience, when these specialist caste men are asked to sing a Siri *pāḍdana*, they either deny knowledge of it, or sing a *pāḍdana* which contains the story, but which is sung by them in the context of one of the *bhūtas* associated with the cult (see below). Women of these specialist castes do not generally participate in the Siri cult and usually deny knowledge of the *pāḍdana*.

[9] I have available to me numerous recording taken at Siri festivals. Typically, the Siris, accompanied by the Kumārs, remain for 4-6 hours in a possessed state and all of their discourse is sung during this period. Their song contains a welter of different kinds of references to the Siri *pāḍdana*, but only once, very recently (March 1989), did I hear a nearly complete version of one portion (the Abbaga Daraga section) of

sections, fragments, are recited and then usually chanted repeatedly. When confronted (gently, of course) with this observation, our authority readily admits that nowadays there is no time to sing the entire *pāḍdana* during the festival because of the great crowds which come for worship and to give offerings *(parake)*. In the past, she says, the full *pāḍdana* was sung. Her observations are, however, contradicted by my own documentation, based on tape recordings, over a twenty-year period. My tape recordings show no substantial change in the style or content of the ritually performed text. What I am forced to conclude is that it is only here, with a particular woman who is identified locally as an authority, as I record the *pāḍdana* at her house, that the "full", "authentic" version is perpetuated in the women's tradition.

At the *āluḍe* I am sometimes referred to the authority of the *mūla kumār*, a *pātri*, male priest, of the Siri cult, who is the chief among the priests of that place. His residence will be at another village, where he is engaged in his normal occupation, as school teacher, farmer, retired postal clerk, etc. The priests comes from a variety of castes and educational backgrounds. When approached, he will provide a great deal of information and he may narrate the story, answer theological questions, interpret the text, explain the rituals, identify the deities, point out historical landmarks and even quote scholarly books, but, in my experience, he does not usually sing the *pāḍdana*.[10] Instead, I am asked to attend the *jātrE*, where, he, too,

---

the *pāḍdana* sung.
Much of the formulaic discourse implies an intimate knowledge and understanding of the themes of the *pāḍdana* without actually singing it. One example of this is the elaborate, formal question-and-answer discourse carried on by the Kumār and two Siris while enacting the game of *cenne*, sitting on the specially designated *mantapa* during the Siri *jātrE* at Urmbitota. This mode of presentation is found only at a few places where the Siri *jātrE* takes place, and all of these cases are located in the Belthangadi region, and all are of relatively recent date. This mode of presentation is probably an innovation based on the more widespread, less elaborate and less formal types of discourses one commonly hears during the possession.

[10] There are Kumārs who do sing the *pāḍdana* and these have been recorded by

insists the true version is sung. When the difficulties of doing this are explained to him, he refers me to a knowledgeable, experienced woman in the village or amongst his cult group, saying she knows the "real" version. Thus, I am referred back to the women's tradition described above.

The temple management, no differently than the general public, refers questions of authenticity to these Kumārs and to knowledgeable women. Frequently, however, literate informants refer to one of the several books on Siri written by local scholars (see note 6). The temple Brahmins *(tantris)* will generally comment only on their rather restricted ritualistic duties toward the deity, Bermeru, and to the main deity of the place, Mahāliṅgēśvara, which duties they say has no direct relationship to the Siri cult.

To the extent that the *pāḍdana* is connected to the rituals and is authenticated by the rituals, the authority, we must conclude, lies distributed with hundreds of women and men around the countryside. The search for an authoritative, legitimate, true, complete, original or accurate text lies in finding a version to which all would agree is correct. In collecting dozens of versions, however, I find only variation. I have not, it is true, systematically canvassed Tuḷunāḍu in search of the "true" version and I have not questioned every one of the "authorities" about the differences between their versions and the others. This would be a most arduous task, and one fraught with uncomfortable confrontations, given the sensitivity of believers toward the feeling that there *is* some authentic text, and it is *theirs*. After innumerable interviews, I have to conclude that only the most general outline of the story is relatively constant, but that a large amount of specific detail lies outside this area of agree-

---

several collectors. Based solely on the texts, I see no reason, however, to regard their recitation as any more authentic than any other texts. The social position (males) and ritual authority (*Kumāra, pātri)* alone make their recitations more highly regarded.

ment. Even so, the agreement often lies in acknowledging the authority of the singer, not necessarily of the text. When it comes to the *pāḍdana*, with its specific phraseology, inclusion of specific events, episodes, incidents, places, names, etc., it is always the current informant's version which is correct and the others' incorrect. This, I have come to learn with regard to other *pāḍdanas* which women sing in the fields, is a common assessment. At best, one hears the comment, "In different places they sing it differently. They don't know — " usually followed by a comment about their own region preserving "pure Tulu" traditions. There is here, as elsewhere in the world (see eg. Kvideland 1983), the conviction amongst the folk that the most authentic version must also be the most ancient version, created in a time when Tulu was pure, unsullied by the influences of neighboring languages and foreign domination.

What this leaves us with is, that the "standard" Siri *pāḍdana* is not a *pāḍdana* at all, but a text, call it perhaps a story, or even a reference text of the "Collective Mind", that exists outside the realm of a specific traditional, formal, ritual recitation text and context. What is meant by "standard" is a broad area of agreement in the general events of a story linking women of a matrilineal family, the names of these women, and the places of significance. The story is put to song (a distinctive *pāḍdana* form) in the fields by women planting paddy. In this context, the story exists in the form of elaborate mental notes about the births and the lives of the Siri spirits and a number of formulaic phrases of varying length used in oral composition. In the ritual context, the Siri *jātrE*, the spiritual relationship between the possessed women and men is determined by the story, and the text they recite implies an intimate knowledge of the story, but the story itself is not recited. The mental text takes on more the function of a script for a play (or like the text of a novel on which a cinema is based) than a story recited. The spontaneous, impromptu text they actually recite takes many different forms, but often consists of only formulaic phrases shared with the *pāḍdana*. These they combine with discourse pertinent to specific ritual acts, reference to specific shrines and the particular problems of their supplicants. Yet its presence is obviously strongly felt for there is unanimous agreement that it is there we find the true *pāḍdana*. The implied story, to which the words that they *do* sing make constant reference, legimates their presence and their relationships and their problems. The legitimating effect of the ritual performance, in turn, establishes those who participate in it as authorities on the *pāḍdana* itself. They need not, however, be able to put the story to song, as women are so skilled in doing, but the distinctiveness of the style in which the Siri *pāḍdana* is sung — a style of singing in which all conversation by the possessed men and women at the ritual is presented — allows both men and women to recite it if they wish. The "full" Siri *pāḍdana,* that which is able to integrate the greatest number of formulaic phrases, episodes and incidents, is thus regarded as the most authentic.[11] However, this is a matter of negotiation, for there is no complete unanimity as to what events are regarded as pertinent. The issue of the source of the welter of pertinent images and events is what I shall take up next.

---

[11] For example, I have very recently encountered versions of the Abbaga-Daraga *pāḍdana* in the Mangalore and Puttur areas which considerably extend the *pāḍdana* and the twin motif in a fascinating manner. After Abbaga and Daraga are cremated, they reincarnate in *jōga*-form *(jōga rūpa)* and request to be married. Twin boys (called Rāma-Lakṣmaṇa, as twin boys often are) are found in the village (Nandolige) and a marriage ceremony is performed. Once married, the twin sisters then return to their heavenly realm in their *māya*-form *(māya rūpa)*. Whether this version, with its additional story content would be regarded as legitimate in other areas, I don't know. In the far northern area the story of Siri does not include those of Sonne-Ginde and Abbaga-Daraga. I do know that some informants regard the inclusion of these stories as illegitimate versions (see below, page 7-8??). There are thus regionally standard stories.

This version suggests links with the ghost marriage sometimes encountered in Tuḷunāḍu and elsewhere in southern India. In Hiriyadka, for example, I encountered a case where a woman dreamed frequently of her daughter, who had died at a young age, before marriage. In her dream, the girl appeared as a bride. In this case, a family was found which was bereaved of an unmarried son and the two ghosts were married with a special ceremony. It is believed that, if a person dies before basic desires are fulfilled (marriage in this case), he or she will return to trouble their living relatives.

Representation of Siris in Texts and Temple Contexts

Not only is it probable that the current "standard" legend is a construct generated outside of the reference frame provided by the Siri shrines and the ritual context, but my suspicion is that it is of relatively recent construction, or, more likely, a product of continuous, gradual construction, joining two or more *pāḍdanas* together, and linking them with connectives associated with places around Nandolige.[12]

Even the most general features of the story (as I have left it in the previous section) are difficult to match with the places, rituals and stated beliefs of the participants. One of the difficulties is that such cross-references are made mostly in terms of specific versions of the *pāḍdana*, which, as I have already indicated, are quite variable and often at odds with one another precisely on these sorts of issues.[13] The appearance is always such that there is a close rela-

---

[12] This would imply that at one time Nandolige, the village in the story where the three-generational linkage is set, had a wider prominence than it does today. Unfortunately, it is rather difficult to discover whether this is true or not, or what the nature of that prominence might have been. Other than through the evidence of the Siri myth itself, no independent history of the place has been developed on the part of competent historians.

Currently, at several of the recently (20th C.) established shrines in the southern region of Tuḷunāḍu, local authorities point to landmarks in the surrounding territory and claim these to be particular features mentioned in the Siri myth. Without a large body of independent evidence to confirm their claims, we must regard this as a typical "localization" of mythological events. One encounters similar localization, folk exegesis and etymology surrounding other *pāḍdanas*. A visitor to the "homes" of Koti-Cannayya, Kordabbu, Karniga, etc. will be similarly taken to specific fields, paths, river crossings, trees and the like which are identified with those in the story. These short, semi-formal commentaries linking specific locations with legends, resembling *sthala purāṇas*, are worked out in conversational discourse, and no doubt get added to local versions of the recitation texts (both ritually sung texts and extra-ritual *pāḍdanas*), causing the formal text and its identification with local places to merge into a single body of ever-growing, self-confirming tradition. It is not unlikely that such a process has occurred earlier at Nandolige, too.

[13] There are two sorts of variations having to do with names of characters and

tionship between myth and ritual, with each legitimizing the other (see note 12). But in comparing more diverse materials with one another, even at the most general level, one quickly encounters inconsistencies.

One of the most curious situations is that Siri, herself, is not represented at the major temples where the Siri *jātrE* is held. Instead, we find either inside the temple or in a separate shrine, along with a deity identified with a pan-India figure (Mahāliṅgēśvara), two female figurines identified as Abbaga and Daraga, Siri's "granddaughters", the victims of sororicide and suicide. In the *pāḍdanas* it is at the end, after the death of Abbaga and Daraga, that their spirits travel to the places where they are now worshipped. No such travels are attributed to Siri. It is not clear why Siri herself is missing, and one gets a variety of answers to inquiries.

One reason she may not be represented is because, according to the "standard story", she had two husbands. As a woman who had sexual relations with more than one man, she is hardly the ideal of

---

places. One is in the main body of the text and one is at the end of the text after the spirits have become *māya*. The former sort of variation can be found to some extent in the texts recited at the *jātrE*, but takes on little significance in the general melee of associative phrases which are pronounced. Outside of the *jātrE* context these sorts of variations may spark debate. The "post-māya" recitation is rarely sung outside the *jātrE* context; or, if it is, it is sung while the singer is possessed and she is not regarded as being individually responsible. My tape recordings show that during the *jātrE* the place and character (spirit) names and their kin relationship are of central concern and prominence and often fill a great deal of the spiritual dialogue. The reasons for the concern are several: on the part of novices (both male and female) they must assert their right to stand in the *dalyas* (a line of sacred cloth on which the participants stand) and their claim to this shrine as their *āluḍe*. The adepts must assert their legitimacy *(wora)* and the legitimacy of the place as one which the Siris visit. Neither set of assertions are taken for granted. These references vary from one place to another and from time to time, and serve to legitimate the place and the individuals involved, and so take on the character of dogma. However, since these concerns do not extend beyond the ritual place, they rarely become an issue debated outside of the immediate context, except when questioned by research investigators and irate kinsmen.

Indian womanhood, and although she is regarded as *satya* ("true, pure, innocent"), this taint on her image appears to disqualify her from being housed in the temple.[14] However, since they are orally presented, the myths and commentary may be seen to be only current interpretations of an existing situation. They may be regarded as formidable arguments against introducing her image, bringing about any change in either fact or interpretation of fact, but they need not have great historical depth.

A second curious situation presents itself: with the exception of Nandolige, the major locations of the Siri cult are not mentioned in the main body of the standard story and some of the most important locations mentioned in the story are not to be found on the map today. Here, however, we must be quite precise as to what we mean by a "standard" text, since local variants differ from one another precisely on these points, and only ritual versions (the highly abbreviated phrases and portions of the story chanted under possession at the *jātrE*) deal extensively with where the Siris originated and to where they have traveled. The question of localization in the ritual text is, obviously, a highly critical one (see note 12), but it is not one we can rely on for establishing historical relationships. One might say it is precisely *because* it is so critical, that it is not reliable. Indeed, because it is on this matter that we find variability (when we find mention at all) in the larger story context sung in relatively more secular contexts, and because we find concentrated discussion on this point only in localized ritual contexts, where ritual legitimation is itself the major concern (for reasons dis-

[14] According to one general interpretation of her character, Siri is regarded as overly head-strong, willful and haughty. There is a phrase in Kannaḍa, known throughout Karnataka, which identifies any overly proud woman as a 'Siri'. It seems doubtful that this reference could stem directly from the Tulu story, but even in Tuḷunāḍu, Siri, herself, may be charged with this accusation, as she, in fact, is in the *pāḍdana*. In other *pāḍdanas* where women are victims of male misconduct they die or commit suicide (Claus in press). Such women are glorified for their self-sacrifice and suffering. When Siri is held up against such an ideal, she fails the test.

cussed more thoroughly in Claus 1975, 1979, 1987), out of the context of the larger narrative, that interpretation of the historical relationship of text and context is most questionable.

Finally, the three-generational matrilineal structure which links the major portions of the full Siri story is evidenced even now, outside of the ritual context, normally only in terms of extra-textual commentary. The Siri *pāḍdanas* are normally sung as separate episodes, not one continuous narrative. A number of informants tell me that the three *pāḍdanas* (Siri, Sonne-Ginde and Abbaga-Daraga) are separate *pāḍdanas,* linked in terms of the Siri story in a way which they will then describe to me in prose commentary. This is also the case in several other long *pāḍdanas* of the women's field-song tradition. In fact, some *pāḍdanas* seem never to be sung naturally as a single long performance. They exist as epics, in a way not well-understood, only in the minds of the people and are available to the researcher only in the form of extra-textual commentary. The recitation of the entire story in *pāḍdana* form may well be, in this sense, an artificial result of the collection activity, where the researcher asks for, and provides an opportunity for, the combination of elements joined by links only latent in the minds of the tellers. As I have already mentioned, the text which is directly related to the ritual context is not the larger standard *pāḍdana.*[15] That only has a general referential function. The text presented within the ritual context often makes reference to Siri only within the kinship (spiritual kinship) relation of the participants. It is thus a structural relationship, not one of great textual elaboration. Indeed, it is often collapsed into a two-generational framework, with Siri called *apparē* (mother), or even *akkarē* (elder sister) by Abbaga and Daraga, "officially" her granddaughters.

---

[15] This statement is based on many hours of taped recordings taken in context at six different locations.

In any case, in the mind of one of my most knowledgeable informants, Kargi, the *pāḍdanas* of the Siris are quite independent. I have already published two of these in another article (1987). In her recitation, the Abbaga-Daraga *pāḍdana* has no direct connection to the Siri *pāḍdana*. Their mother is not Sonne, the daughter of Siri. In fact she sings a separate *pāḍdana* of Sonne-Ginde, also twins who commit sororicide and suicide while playing *cenne*, but, who, like Siri herself are born of *prasāda* received by Berma Ballaveru̥ at his *mūlasāna*. She also sings a *pāḍdana* of Mayage and Maipage, who similarly die as a result of playing *cenne*. Their parents are Gala Badrakumār and Cenneda Paravati. While it may be said that her *pāḍdanas* merely fragment the longer three-generation pattern of the "standard" Siri story, separating the portion about Siri from that of Sonne and her twin daughters, and triplicating the story of the twins' ill-fated game of *cenne*, she presents some rather convincing arguments to the researcher in defense of her tradition. Siri, according to her, could not have remarried, could not have given birth to a second child, Sonne, after Kumār. Not only would that deny, according to Kargi, from Siri the status of *satya*, but it would make Kumār's status questionable, as the son of a woman whose conduct is less than faithful to her vows of marriage, and would make Sonne an illegitimate child altogether.[16] In her set of Siri *pāḍdanas* no such conflict arises. While one can't weight a single informants interpretations over that of many other informant's, nor regard her *pāḍdanas* as more authentic, on several very general points, unimportant for the theological debate, but interesting in an historical light, her *pāḍdanas* support the hypothesis that the "standard" ver-

---

[16] In one version of the "standard" *pāḍdana* Kumār says, "I was born to one father. Don't make me take another. People will call me a son of a prostitute. Make me māya here." Siri asks why he is saying this. Kumāra tells her the future events, how she will marry Kodisar Alva and says he does not want to be a mere servant at that house.
At one Siri *jātrE* I attended recently, Kumār accusingly reminds his mother, Siri, "For you there is the continuity of a family. For me, who is without a position in life, you must give a place also. My head is burning (with worry and concern)."

sion is a compilation of separate *pāḍdanas*. As I have already indicated, many other informants also assert that the three *pāḍdanas* are separate, and although they assert that Abbaga and Daraga are Siri's granddaughters by Sonne, this connection is made only by means of oral commentary. (See plate X).

The Twin Motif in the Siri Pāḍdanas

There are other lines of inquiry, however, which would seem to support the hypothesis that the phrases, images, motifs, episodes, names, places and story connectives of the contemporary Siri story are derived from independent sources.

One of these pertains to the widespread twin motif. The names of the Siris are always mentioned in pairs: Abbaga and Daraga, Sonne and Ginde, Mayage and Maipage. The triplication of the twins' stories, each independent of the other in the northern (Kargi's) versions, also suggests a possibility that the cult is historically a cult of twins. In the northern versions Sonne and Ginde are twins, like Abbaga and Daraga. To these pairs, the northern versions add another, Mayage and Maipage, to make a total, along with Siri herself, of "seven Siris". This phrase is the common means to refer to the Siri spirits all over the district, but it is only in the northern versions that it has much significance.[17] In the southern versions, Gin-

[17] In some places I have encountered only rather *ad hoc* lists of who the "seven Siris" are supposed to be: Siri, Sonne and Ginde, Abbaga and Daraga, Daru and Kumār. Daru is an incidental figure in the "standard" story and Kumār, a male, cannot be called a "siri". Some informants include Sama (or Swami) Alvedi, the first wife of Siri's second husband, who would thus be *paldi* (elder sister, *akka*, in address terminology) to Siri. In the region around Mangalore I am told, there is a separate *pāḍdana* of Sama Alvedi.
The names Abbaga and Daraga, at the core of the Siri tradition, are interesting. If I may be allowed a bit of historical and etymological speculation, I would suggest that these terms might not have originally been applied to twins. The term *abba*, or *abbakka*, sometimes refers to an ancestress, or a Lady of an aristocratic matrilineal

de's story is quite independent of the rest and she is only loosely associated with Sonne, as a half-sister.

This would also explain why Siri is not to be found in the temples amongst the images and why only twins are. To be sure, the twins' images are often identified as Abbaga and Daraga, but they are often called merely *sirikulu*, "Siris". It does not seem unlikely that this simple iconography of pairs of females is what Kargi's northern tradition has collected its *pāḍdanas* of twins around.

The Maisandāya Pāḍdana

Quite incidental to my research on Siri, I happened to collect a Tulu *pāḍdana* from a Kannaḍa-speaking Panar from the region just north of Tuḷunāḍu. The Kannaḍa-speaking Panars maintain marriage ties with the Tulu-speaking Nalkes, from amongst whom they claim to have originated before their migration northward. The *pāḍdana* was that of Akkaraisiri Poṇṇjewu and Gala Badra Kumār. The story is that of twins who play *cenne* and subsequently commit sororicide and suicide, clearly the same set of motifs found in the Siri *pāḍdana*. I later found out that the same story exists in the Nalke repertoire and is sung in connection with the Maisandāya *kola* wherever they perform it.[18] I was even able to collect the

---

family. The term *dāru* refers to a subordinate female, currently interpreted as a maid servant, but possibly at one time a younger female in the matriline, or descendant. Thus, the terms may have, at one time, indicated a female relationship of super- and subalternation, ancestor and descendant, elder and younger. This kind of relationship is commonly found in certain *bhūta* cults (eg. Jumadi and Banta) and characterizes many of the most ancient social dimensions of Tuluva cults (see Claus 1978). Here, in its present manifestation as twins, the older-younger, super-subalternation is still stressed, but the role of ancestress has been shifted to Siri, herself. As twins, within a single generation, what becomes magnified is jealousy, desire and rebellion and the disastrous effects of these emotions.

[18] More recently, I have collected a version of the Maisandāya *pāḍdana* from a Parava in the Vitla area which has essentially the same story. The Pambadas,

pāḍdana from Nandolige, the center of Siri worship. It is significant to know, then, that the story of the twins, so critical to the Siri cult, exists also outside of this cult, in association with a closely related religious tradition.

The details of the Nalkes' versions are of interest, too. Although they consistently link Hiriyadka and Nandolige, two famous locations of the Siri *jātrE,* they do not do so in terms of Siris wanderings.[19] In fact, they do not mention either Siri or Kumār at all. The phraseology differs in so many regards, it is hard to imagine it is derived from the "standard" Siri *pāḍdana* and every aspect of both the text and context argues for its independent existence and independent historical development. Nevertheless, since the story is essentially the same as one portion of it, it must share an historical origin with the Siri myth, at a time earlier than the elaboration of today's "standard".

Cikku Cults

The Kannaḍa-speaking Panars of Kundapur Taluk are performers in a religious cult devoted to a class of spirits called Cikku, in which myth and ritual are linked in yet another of the ever-varying ways found all over Southern India. Amongst their songs — called

---

according to information collected by Heidrun Brückner (personal communication), sing a very different *pāḍdana* in connection to the Maisandāya *kola,* with a story having no apparent relationship to the one under discussion.
It is of interest to note that the Siri *jātrE* often takes place within the larger frame of a series of *bhūta* kolas, usually including the Maisandāya *kola.* However, the connection the Nalkes make is that the Nandi-gone often found at the *āluḍe* along with the Siris is the same as Maisandāya. The place name Nandolige is also almost certainly related to the name of this deity.

[19] It is interesting to note that the family of Kanyabettu, so prominent in the story of Abbaga and Daraga, has Hiriyadka as its *mūlasthāna.* This may be of little historical value since we do not know for certain how far back the current family has lived in the house.

hogalikke, 'to praise, spread the fame of' — are two, whose place of action is Nandolige, called in the song, Ullala, after the Devi there, who is locally called Ullalti. One of these, the *hogalikke* of Dodkal Cikku, is the story of the twins, Abbaga and Daraga, who play *cenne* and commit sororicide and suicide.[20] There can be little doubt that the Panars' song is related to the Siri story, but exactly how is not possible to guess at this point. Yet again, since 1) it differs in many details from the "standard" Siri story, and, 2) its phraseology indicates that it is part of a tradition separate from the Siri story — it is certainly *not* a translation of the Abbaga Daraga *pāḍdana* — and, 3) it is firmly embedded in its own ritual context, yet 4) it preserves the essential story, we are led to the conclusion that it shares an historical origin with the Siri story, dating from a time earlier than that when the "standard" story had taken its present form.

While it cannot be proven, on the basis of these variants of the story of the twins, that the "standard" Siri story is a compilation of relatively recent date, it is true that one portion — that of the twins — has a far wider and independent distribution. Given also that this portion is firmly embedded in traditional contexts of its own, it seems that it is unlikely to have been the result of fragmentation and subsequent dissemination of the larger story. On the other hand, it seems that at least some of the twins' stories share a common origin with the place Nandolige itself. What this would suggest, although somewhat more tentatively, is that the separation of the traditions occurred before the development of the larger story took place. It is, however, not possible to date this with any accuracy, given the rather poor condition of much of Tuluva social-historical scholarship.

---

[20] It is worth mentioning that the other *hogalikke* is that of Haleyamma, whose 100 daughters are Cikkus. The story is somewhat reminiscent of the story of Siri, but concerns mostly Haleyamma's brothers, Deva Shetru and Cikka Shetru.

Other References to Siris in the Tulu Pāḍdanas

At this point I would like to take up the idea that *pāḍdanas* can be a compilation of independent stories. The dynamics of *pāḍdana* composition has not been well investigated yet, so my presentation will have to be very tentative. I will use only *pāḍdanas* which have some relationship to the Siris and thus try to serve several purposes at once. Up to now, I have discussed only the possibility that they are either quasi-historical, legendary individuals (Siri and her descendants of the "standard" Siri story), or, as my evidence would indicate, mythological figures, twins, whose story motifs are symbolically connected with a cult which centers around an *āluḍe*. The Siri motif, however, is even wider than this: so wide, in fact, that it will not be possible to cover all references in this paper. I will limit myself, therefore, to instances where twins are specifically linked to Siris and to several occurrences of the name Siri in other *pāḍdanas* and Tulu story traditions. It must be pointed out, though, that these are not regarded by my informants as "the same" Siris, in the sense that the others which I have already discussed above would be. All that this may mean, however, is that the Siris in the discussion above are found in the stories which have become closely connected to the ritual, while the ones I discuss below are not.

***

The Parnderu Pāḍdana

Women who sing *pāḍdanas* in the field are often unaware that a particular *pāḍdana* is a part of religious ritual elsewhere. Kargi, for example, does not know that the Parnderu *pāḍdana* she sings is sung by Paravas in connection with their Jumadi *kola* fifty miles away, in Belthangadi Taluk.[21] In the Parava tradition, the *pāḍdana* becomes considerably shortened, because, as they themselves admit, they are used to singing only portions of it in the midst of the many other ritual activities which have to be attended to. But not only does the *pāḍdana* vary from one context to another, it varies considerably in each context from one end of the district to another. There are essentially two parts to this particular *pāḍdana:* 1) the story of the death of Parnderu's sister Parndedi; and 2) the story of Kapura and Karniga, Parndedi's twin daughters, Parnderu's nieces. While each major portion *could* stand alone as an independent story, I have found this to be true only of the second part, the story of Kapura and Karniga. This, of course, is the more dramatic, more tragic portion, and the only portion that is directly related to Jumadi and cult worship. Since it is the more widespread of the two, we may suppose (at least as a working hypothesis) that it is the more basic portion and that the first portion has been added to it.[22] The second portion of the story itself has several versions (in brackets, below) which combine or omit certain episodes. This portion of the story may be briefly summarized:

Second Portion of the *Parnderu Pāḍdana,* the story of Karniga:

1. The girls are raised at Parnderu's house, their matrilineal home.

---

[21] I have unconfirmed reports that it is sung by Nalkes in connection with the Jumadi *kola* held at Kordabbu shrines in the area around Katil. A Parava family in Bantwal tells me they sing this in connection with the *kolas* of Angai Jumadi.

[22] See Blackburn 1989 for instances of this sort of "back-building" of Indian oral epic story traditions.

2. Parnderu is called to a meeting of the local chieftains. Karniga prepares a meal for him.

[3A. She picks vegetables from a garden protected, at Parnderu's request, by the household deity, Jumadi. Jumadi causes stones and other objects to appear in the food served to Parnderu.]

[3B. Duwu (Parnderu's wife) puts stones and other objects in the food served to Parnderu.]

4. When Parnderu goes to eat, he discovers the objects in his food and becomes angry with Karniga.

[5A. He beats her (in some versions he attempts to rape her), she escapes by climbing a tree. He follows her. She jumps into a well.]

[5B. He curses her in the name of Jumadi. When the girls go to the tank to bath, Jumadi pushes the girls into the tank and they drown. Parnderu returns from the meeting and regrets the consequences of Jumadi's powers.]

[6A. Karniga's corpse is cremated. Jumadi comes in the form of a hawk and takes a piece of the partly cremated flesh and places it in a curry so that Parnderu eats it.]

[6B. Karniga (and her twin sister in some versions) are reincarnated by Siris from a heavenly realm.]

The original form of this, more basic, second portion is rather difficult to reconstruct, not only because of the great variation in its versions, but because along with that variation the inclusion or exclusion of its variable episodes entails (it seems) additional elements (connectives) to make the actions comprehensible in relation to the contexts in which it is recited. It even appears that certain broad theological assumptions and associations influence the development of versions and variation in the tradition.[23]

---

[23] None of the versions I have are entirely consistent from a theological perspective. The suppositions of the story predominate.

The versions [B] collected in the northern part of Tuḷunāḍu contain reference to Siris and twins. Parndedi gives birth to twin girls, *ullayi* (inside) Karniga and *pidayi* (outside) Kapura.[24] Only the one, however, *ullayi* Karniga, plays a significant role in the story. It is she who is asked to prepare a meal for her uncle before he sets out for a council meeting. His wife, Duwu, in this version sabotages the preparation by adding the unpleasant objects to the rice. Karniga is blamed for this and as a consequence of a curse uttered in his anger the household deity, Jumadi, pushes Karniga and her twin sister into the well (see 5B., above). When he learns of the ruinous effects of his curse, Parnderu asks his brother-in-law, the father of the twins, for help. Their father then (mystically, not made very clear in the *pāḍdana*) communicates with the lord of *mittu̦ mēdima lōka,* (a place not well described, but found in many other *pāḍdanas* as well) and asks him to bring the girls back to life. The Lord of this heaven chooses two Siris and commands them to go to earth *(tirtu̦ Siri lōka)*, fashion bodies out of the girls' ashes and then enter the bodies and give life to them. The mode of communication, the description of the father's actions and the reference to the role of the Siris all bear such striking resemblance to the Siri cult activities that I am convinced that this and the Siri myth are historically related to the same cult. Kargi, who sings this version, is not aware of any connection and declines to confirm my historical reconstruction.[25]

---

[24] In some versions the inside-outside distinction is assigned to husband's sister's daughter and mother's brother's wife (i.e. Karniga and Parnderu's wife) respectively. Both configurations are consistent with women's hierarchical relations within a matrilineal structure, but the first refers to the order of sisters, while the second, the relationship between consanguineals and affines.

[25] There are some fascinating similarities to Southeast Asian material mentioned by J. Gonda (1954: 221), such as a goddess by the name of Sri, who is "described as a divine princess, closely related to the *widadaris* (< Skt. *vidyādhārī*), a sort of kindly fairies who in part of the Archipelago are considered to preside over love, and in Java are held to be able to revive the deceased: they maintain relations with the waters and exercise a salutary influence on agriculture and on the wealth and prosperous condition of the house in which they take up their residence."

It is true that many other versions of the *pāḍdana* do not contain this segment, and instead, on the basis of a motif shared with a very popular and widespread folk-tale (Bilimale and Claus 1988), build the *pāḍdana* in a different direction, linking it to a different set of ritual actions and theological assumptions. This in itself is instructive and helps us to understand the dynamics of variation in the *pāḍdana* recitation tradition and their continual adjustments and readjustments to ritual cults. In other words, even if there are not direct historical connections between the Siri *pāḍdana* and the Parnderu (Karniga) *pāḍdana*, there are many parallels in the dynamics, compositional development and relationship to ritual.

Other Siri pāḍdanas

There is a relatively rare *pāḍdana* called the Seven Siri (Elverụ Sirikulu) *pāḍdana*. Its manner of singing is uniquely chant-like and highly repetitive. Aside from the Siri *pāḍdana(s)*, which are also sung in a unique style, I know of no other *pāḍdana* more likely to be associated with one of Tuḷunāḍu's many trance cults; however, it is not so linked, at least at the present time.[26] Its story, taking 45 minutes to complete, is as simple as it is inscrutable:

---

[26] However, on a tape in the archives of the Regional Resource Centre for Folk Performing Arts in Udupi, I found a version of a Kumār's spirit-possessed recitation recorded during the Siri *jātrE* at Nidegal (1988) in which a portion of the repeated phrase *("pañcanaṇgaḍi, janma būmiḍụ, ...")* of this *pāḍdana* was included. I have myself heard the repeated phrases of this *pāḍdana* uttered by participants during Siri possession, but I have not had the opportunity to follow up on this potentially important lead.
I have also recorded Parava a version of the Maisandāya *pāḍdana* in Bantwal Taluk which contains this phrase. The story contained in the *pāḍdana* is different from that of any of the standard Siri *pāḍdanas*, but does make reference to Abbaga and Daraga and is set in Nandolige. Its story, however, bears close relationship to portions of the Bama Kumār (Ganapati?) *pāḍdana* collected and published by Amrith Someshwara, and discussed below. This relationship, too, needs to be further investigated.

> Seven Siris are created along with a palace and a tank. They get up (as if from sleep), perform household duties (cleaning and sweeping) and go to the tank to bathe. They then prepare a meal. Finally, they return to the tank, immerse themselves and become lotuses.

This simple story is told with considerable detail, step by step, in the specific activities, especially the selection of rice and the preparation of the meal. Their three-fold connection with the tank (creation with/from, bathing/purification, and final return/emersion) seems to be its contextual theme.[27] What makes it such a long *pāḍdana* is the repetition of a particularly enigmatic phrase after every line of

sāna, sāna, sānada arāmane
pañcanaṅgaḍi janma būmiḍụ
nandigoṇe cāwaḍi
elverụ sirikulu

'Shrine, shrine, shrine palace; Five shops (town?), creation on Earth; The throne of Nandi, The Seven Siris.' I have no clue as to the references made in this phrase, however. One possible line of historical inquiry is that it may have had some connection with local Jain rituals at one time. A version of the Abbaga-Daraga *pāḍdana* collected at Nandolige describes how after their death the spirits of Abbaga and Daraga go to *mittụ mēdima lōka,* where they are instructed by the lord of that realm to return to earth *(tirtụ siri lōka)* and rid themselves of the pollution of having been born of a human woman (Sonne). Abbaga and Daraga go to a tank where the Jain women of

[27] This is, of course, a consistent theme of the Abbaga-Daraga *pāḍdana* as well. It also occurs in some versions of the Parnderu *pāḍdana*. It is, however, uncommon in other *pāḍdanas* In some versions of the Abbaga-Daraga *pāḍdana* the theme is linked to Jain families and the association of Siris with lotuses strongly suggests a Jain influence. It may also be significant that all of the locations where I have encountered the Seven Siri *pāḍdana* are places where there were Jain chieftains in the past.

the town of Belma (a place near Nandolige) are ritually purifying themselves in the water. They possess these women and obtain the necessary purity to return and stay in *mittu mēdima lōka.*

A *pāḍdana,* called the *Bama Kumār Pāḍdana,* collected and published in Tulu and Kannaḍa by Amrith Someshwara (1962), contains many features of interest to my present argument. The story is rather long and complex and so I will only summarize it here:

> Śiva created Paravati, a palace and various requirements of a household, including a flower garden and a boy to collect flowers and do *pūjā.* But when the boy went to collect them, the flowers ran away to the land of the Siris (identified in various parts of the *pāḍdana* as *sirināḍu, miri lōka* and *siri lōka*). The boy chases after them.
> Meanwhile, in Siri land, the youngest of seven Siris insists that they should go to their tank and bathe. Her older sisters consent, and while they are bathing, they "smell a human", something they had not known before. The elder sisters send their youngest sister to see what it is. When the boy sees her, he swoons, but she revives him. She gives him flowers and sends him back to earth with the warning not to say what he saw or where he got the flowers.
> Needless to say, he tells Śiva, who then transforms himself into a beetle and goes to the land of the Siris and becomes a lotus in their tank. The six older Siris see the lotus but are unable to pick it, because whenever they approach it, it moves into deeper water. When the youngest Siri attempts to remove it, it dances across the water to her. She puts it in her hair. Later, when she retires to her room at night, Śiva transforms to his normal self and seduces her.
> The youngest Siri becomes pregnant and returns with Śiva to his palace, where Paravati accepts her and treats her as a younger sister. Śiva is called to war and while he is gone, Siri gives birth to a son, Kumār.
> Kumâr rapidly grows up to become a strong youth who beats everyone in sports, even the Rakṣasas. The Rakṣasas insult him, saying Śiva had dishonored his mother. Furious, he does battle with them and defeats them. As they retreat, he chases after them. They race to Śiva and beg him to protect them. When Kumār arrives, he confronts

> even Śiva, not knowing that he is his father. Śiva, not knowing that Kumār is his son, cuts off his head. Śiva then proceeds home, where he gives an account of the battle to Paravati. Paravati is disconsolate until Śiva promises to replace the boy's head and revive him. However, they are unable to find a proper human head and have to settle for the head of a royal elephant, the only being sleeping with its head to the north. Śiva presents the re-built boy to Paravati, asking whether this is her son. She replies, "Below the waist (sic) he is my son, above the waist he is not." The boy is then renamed as Ganapati and given the work of protecting the people and receiving the offerings on Ganapati Caturti.

I would not say that this *pāḍdana* has any great claim to authenticity, in the sense that it might be the standard version of a widespread story.[28] It is, however, representative of the dynamic potentials of the way women sing *pāḍdanas* in the field. It, like the Siri *pāḍdana* itself, combines many formulae, motifs, episodes and whole stories, shared with other *pāḍdanas* and even more diverse sources, into a reasonably coherent narrative whole. Although the central persona in this *pāḍdana* is Śiva, for example, he is described with many of the same trait formulae which are used to characterize Krishna in other *pāḍdanas* I have collected. The seduction motif, similar in effect to that in other *pāḍdanas* under the name of Krishna, receives almost endless metamorphosis.[29] The creation episode at the beginning can be found, with different names and places, associated with *nāgas* (cobras) in yet other *pāḍdanas*. The remarkable addition of the Ganapati story, widely known all over southern India, is probably the reason the earlier portion is cast in the name of Śiva. The motif of Śiva taking the form of a lotus and dancing across the water to the youngest Siri is shared with a version of the Maisandāya *pāḍdana* sung by a Parava from the same

---

[28] This is the only version of it published, and I have not collected other versions in the field myself, so little can be said about its authenticity.

[29] For a comparison, see "Lord Krishna's Wives", Beck, et.al. (1987: 155-60).

region in which explicit reference is made to the Siris as being Abbaga and Daraga and the location as being Nandolige. And so it is with virtually every image through which this story is presented.[30] The "standard" Siri story, I would maintain, has undergone the same process, although at the present time it has become more consolidated and stable.

My interest for the moment, though, is with the Siris portrayed in this *pāḍdana*. Clearly these Siris are based on the same mythological tradition as those in the other *pāḍdanas* we have been considering. Their names are very similar: Janāga, Janapaga, Mayaga, Maisaga, Daraga, Ganapaga and Ummaga. Listed like this in the *pāḍdana,* it can be seen they are conceived in pairs, although the action of the story focuses only on one (Maisaga), who is called in the later part of the story merely Siri. There are few overt parallels in this story to the standard Siri story other than that, like Siri, Maisaga is brought to the home of a man who is already married and must first be accepted as a co-wife before she can enter the house. Both Maisaga and Siri have a son called Kumār, who is sensitive to the accusation that his mother has had illicit sexual relations.

There is a possible historical source for the image of the Siris in this and the other *pāḍdana* traditions, in a very widespread folk-tale motif (D361.1 or tale type A-T 400*) "the Swan Maidens" (Aarne/ Thompson 1981). The motif is found in several well-known Tulu

---

[30] Another image worth discussing is that of Kumār. The passage here, where he plays games and does battle with the Rakṣasas is almost identical to that in a *pāḍdana* about the origin of Parāmale Ballal, a part of the long Koti-Cannayya epic cycle (see Burnell, 1895, (May) 116-8). In the Tulu Lexicon Project collection at the Regional Resource Centre for Folk Performing Arts, in Udupi, there is a tape-recorded version of this which is sung in the same distinctive manner as the Siri *pāḍdanas,* with the initial line-phrase of "Naraayana, Naraayana ..." This, and other, internal features, make it almost certain that this portion of the Koti-Cannayya *pāḍdana,* the Nalkes' Maisandāya *pāḍdana* and some of the versions of the Siri stories all draw from a common source.

tales where the maidens are even called Siris.[31] The inclusion of folktale motifs in *pāḍdanas* is not uncommon and even the inclusion of tales, although probably relatively rare, is not unknown (see the discussion of the Parnderu *pāḍdana*, above). What this suggests is, again, that the Siris of the *pāḍdana* are probably conceptually related to a more widespread set of beliefs at some point in their history. That is, the Siris of the *pāḍdanas* may have been regarded as a specific instance of the more general class of deities. Concentrating only on the Siri *pāḍdana*, admitting only the Siris of the *pāḍdanas* of this cult as representatives of a unique class of deities, we are left with only legendary accounts of them and accounts solely explicable by reference to the *pāḍdanas* themselves. This would lead us by tautology to the conclusion, contrary to our working hypothesis, that there was a close historical relationship between the Siri myth and ritual. However, if the Siris can be shown to be historically linked to widespread tale traditions, then the historical linkage between a specific class of deities, the legends about them and the specific cult practices associated with these is brought into question and each set of phenomena (class of deity, text and ritual) may be seen to have at least partially separate sources and historically independent dynamics.

To these examples of Siri traditions I must add a very recently collected *kabita* of Siri twins.[32] The *kabita* (a term used in some parts of the district to distinguish *pāḍdanas* sung while planting paddy seedlings; see Rai 1982, Claus in press) was called by the singers "Trulele bāle", but the title refers only to the chorus; the stories identified by this term are entirely different from one another (see Rai 1982 for a different story under this same title). In brief, the story in the version I collected is:

---

[31] The motif occurs in all of the South Indian language tale repertoires. In other languages, however, they are usually termed *dēvakanyās*. Whether the Siris, as a class of spirits, can therefore be historically linked with that class of spirits, is open to question.

[32] The *kabita* was collected in April 1989 from Unyakka Shedti of Kumbelāje village, Kāsaragōḍ, *Kerala*.

> Two Siris, elder sister and younger sister, are created by the god, Suri Devere. They are given a palace, fine clothes, a swing to sit on, a tank to bathe in and maids to serve them. Thus they live their lives in comfort. One day, however, the younger sister says to the other, "The Lord gave every being children *(santana siripala,* literally "generational continuity"). We were born mysteriously *(maraṇe)* and we will die mysteriously *(nanku maraṇe puṭṭoḍu, maraṇe saipuna")*. Let us go to the Lord and ask for children. So, they bathe and bring an offering to give to their Lord. They arrive at an inauspicious time *(galige)* and are asked to return on a good day, at an auspicious moment.
>
> When that time comes, the younger sister urges the elder to go. The elder, however, persuades the younger to sit for a while and put her head on her lap while she, the elder, picks the lice from her hair. The younger falls asleep and the elder leaves her and goes to their Lord alone. The god receives her, but is angry that she came without her sister. He refuses her request for children and instead grants them to the younger sister. Thus the younger sister became pregnant. On the 7th month a *bāyake (* pregnancy ceremony *pōrita madme)* is duly performed by their Lord. In the 9th month she begins her labor. The elder sister (helpful to the younger throughout) brings a midwife, called Ajje. The younger sister bears twin girls. The midwife warns them that there is a danger that spirits *(kale)* might harm the newborn babies. Indeed, when the afterbirth is disposed, it is eaten by the spirits, which then come and kill the two babies. The two Siris are left to weep and cry.

The story, while said not to be connected to the Siri *jātrE,* was described by the singer as concerning the origin of the Siris. In it are contained the motif of the twins, the concern for children, the jealousies between sisters and their disastrous effects on succeeding generations, all themes which we find at the core of the Siri tradition, associated with Abbaga and Daraga. The story was collected entirely fortuitously, suggested by the singer, who knew of my interest in the Siri cult, having participated in the singing of her version of the Abbaga Daraga *pāḍdana*. How many other such story traditions exist in parts of Tuḷunāḍu cannot be foretold at this point in Tuluva research.

Other Sources of the Tradition

There are, of course, many other lines of comparative and historical inquiry which we might take to identify Siri, or the Siris, outside the Tuluva ritual context with which they are presently associated. One obvious one would be a connection with Śrī, or Lakṣmi. But not only does the present day Tuluva ethnography fail to support this, neither the ritual setting nor the story reveal any connection to this deity. The Siri shrines, to the extent they are associated with any pan-Indian gods, are found at Śiva temples, not Viṣṇu ones. Theologically, it would seem inconceivable that Viṣṇu would send his wife to earth for the reasons the Siris come to the aid of their cult practioners. There is only, as far as I can discern, the ancient (though also one of the most persistent) characteristics of Lakṣmi shared with the Siris, that they are both associated with the power, wealth and beauty of royalty and with procreation, progeneration, propinquity and fertility. But the characters of Śrī/Sri and Siri, as they develop in the *purāṇas* (Sri) and *pāḍdanas* (Siri), take these characteristics in very different directions.

If there is any close parallel to the Siri *pāḍdanas* in other Dravidian languages (other than the Kannaḍa *hogalikkes* discussed above), I have been unable to find them, despite repeated inquires through folklorists and Indologists working in other regions.[33] This is not to say, of course, that there does not exist material from around south-

[33] Attempts to connect Siri to the vast array of Kannagi stories, both literary and folk (including the Malayali Bhagavati myths), yields little except some very widespread and general common themes, all of which, like the role of the prostitute, are the most secular portions of the story with little direct relevance to the relationship of the myth to the ritual.

ern India which would be of great help in discerning the history of the Siri myth and rituals. Regional folklorists have collected vast amounts of material which Indologists, with their preference for literary texts and a small range of favorite themes, have almost totally ignored. However, very little of the folk material has been translated into an international language and thus remains hidden from the comparativists' eyes. Indologists, even when they deal with local traditions, tend to favor the literary renditions.[34] As I hope I have already demonstrated, it is not only the "legitimate", "standard", "authoritative" texts, nor even the "text in ritual context" which is important, but also the ordinary folk text. Indeed, these, I have argued for the case of the Siri cult, are the *most* important.

Even within Tuluva culture there are many sources of influence on the development of the myth and ritual and the characterization of the Siris themselves. I have already discussed at length what I believe to be the two most important contexts in which the story is recited, women singing in the fields and the *jātrE* ritual context. Other important lines of inquiry would include the *yakṣagaṇa* presentation of "Tuḷunāḍu Siri" (a story in a traditional drama form immensely popular during the late '60s and early '70s), cinema, parallel styles of *bhūta* worship and an investigation of now extinct forms of Jain popular worship.

Conclusion

It is true that at a given time and place, or for a given participant, the texts and rituals of the Siri cult exist as a relatively unified, self-affirming dogma. Yet it is also true that at a given time (to which students of oral literature are bound) from place to place there is considerable textual variability and inconsistency between texts and ritual activity. The texts and rituals are both in very

---

[34] Eg., Zvelebil, 1987.

dynamic states and each has a contextual existence partially independent of the other in which their continual development takes place. The texts themselves are temporal manifestations of stories put into song, which even within the tradition vary from context to context, and are maintained by a disparate, loosely organized group of people, many of whom never have contact with one another. The main textual tradition, upon which other textual derivatives depend, is that of the women's field-song. The text in this tradition, while distinctive in some ways, shares with the hundreds of other songs in the women's field-song tradition many motifs, a formulaic mode of composition, and certain characteristics of textual development. The women's field-song tradition is related to other religious traditions as well, and shares with them (often unawares) many story traditions. This is also true with the Siri texts, forms of which occur in Tuluva *bhūta* cults and Kannaḍa Cikku cults.

Unfortunately, despite its obvious importance for the textual traditions of Tuḷunāḍu, very little work has been done on the women's field-song tradition. Until recently, few of the vast number of texts had even been collected and there had been no studies of the nature of these texts, or the manner in which they are composed. In my own field research over the past few years I have had the opportunity to survey this oral literature and I have been exposed to its dynamics to some extent. It has become increasingly clear to me that the tradition contains a large number of stories, motifs and episodic formulae which, because of common modes of composition which distinguish the genre, are easily and frequently transported from one story frame to another. Whole stories become fused and then become reworked in their new arrangement. In this paper I have presented evidence that this is what has happened in the case of the Siri *pāḍdanas* as they are currently found in many, but not all, parts of the region. While it is unrealistic to expect that we could ever document this process with any precision, all of the motifs, themes, formulaic fragments, types of relationships and moods found in the "standard" Siri *pāḍdana* can be evidenced in other *pāḍdanas*, each with their independent textual and ritual contexts. It is not implausible to suppose, then, that they all draw from a common source, the tradition itself.

Some texts in the broadly defined *pāḍdana* genre (including *kabitas)* remain in a state of such fluidity of story content that only the title and names of the characters remain constant. Scholars of folk-tales are familiar with this situation, having traced stories and motifs all around the world. Generally, however, they have not concerned themselves with contextual constraints of variability nor how this process of motif combination takes place. In the *pāḍdana* tradition, the manner in which some texts become relatively more fixed than others seems (from my limited data) to depend on their association with religious cults.

The challenge that faces the researcher studying *pāḍdanas* associated with religious cults, is to understand how the specific contexts effect the development of the texts. While both ritual and secular contexts are found to be capable of introducing variability, outside the ritual context, women are freer to introduce material from other *pāḍdanas* and even more diverse sources. It is this topic on which I have concentrated in the present paper. In the ritual context, much of the recitation is derived from the field-song *pāḍdana*, but is highly formulaic and selective. The recitation takes place in an altered mental state and the selection of texts depends on the complex social and psychological background of the participants (see Claus 1975a, 1979a and 1986). What allows the continual re-integration of the ritual and field-song contexts is the presence of extra-textual commentary, which occurs both in the ritual context and in secular situations. The commentary, in ordinary conversational speech forms, is part of ordinary life, day-to-day activity, influenced by surrounding societal concerns and the religious and artistic developments of the society at large at any given time. It is part of the cultural and religious history of the region. The commentary gradually and continually interprets the texts and in turn influences the texts by influencing the minds of the composers, the women and men who sing the *pāḍdana*. While the texts remain in an artistic form of abstraction, with their peculiar structure and manner of presentation, they must be continually brought to bear on the problems of particular women and their families. It is in this regard that the story, the mental text, which is also used to construct and reconstruct the *pāḍdana,* plays an important role for the many participants and their relatives, who may not even participate in the *pāḍdana* singing in the fields. They are familiar with the standard story, albeit often in a much abbreviated form. But a tremendous amount of material would have to be gathered and interpreted to understand this process well (see Claus 1984). In the cult context, the textual commentary is more focused and more stylized. The direction is more from the story to the lives of the participants via the formulaic texts which make reference to the story. The lives of particular women do not, of course, change the story, but rather their lives and the story share a common structural source in the ideology of the matrilineal family, which lies at the root of both.

I would speculate that an earlier form of the Siri cult consisted of the worship of twins, variously identified as Abbaga and Daraga, Sonne and Ginde, Mayage and Maipage. The concerns revolved around fertility and the perpetuity of matrilineal lines and the jealousy (and guilt) that arises between collateral lines as their fortunes evolve separately. This itself involves a host of associated religious themes and emotional anxieties which is still at the core of the tradition. To this is added an inter-generational dimension, with another set of concerns and emotions. Kumār, representing the multiple roles of a single male kinsman who serves to mediate between his female relatives, adds another dimension (for the significance of male kinsmen in the integration of matrilineal families see Claus 1975b). Eventually, each of the structural roles of a matrilineal family are represented. A *pāḍdana* integrating these roles, explaining their relationship and legitimating their presence, is formed. It is drawn, as explained above, from existing *pāḍdana* traditions and fused together into a single story. The process, however, is not complete. The story in no region of the district is entirely fused in the *pāḍdana* form. In some regions it consists of entirely independent stories. In other regions there are additions to the story which have not been incorporated into the "standard story". Throughout Tuḷunāḍu, there is a great deal of variation in specific recitations. The story, however, being far less specific and detailed, is far more standard and widespread, extending nearly the length and breadth of Tuḷunāḍu, and known by virtually everyone. Mass media, modern transportation, the appearance of cinemas and traditional dramas and texts written by local scholars have all facilitated this process of standardization and continue to alter its course of development.

References

Aarne, Antti and Stith Thompson 1981. *The types of the folktale.* (FF Communications No. 184). Helsinki: Suomalainen Tiedeakatemia.

Ashley, Wayne 1979. Teyyam Kettu of Northern Kerala. In *The Drama Review* 23.2: 99-112.

Beck, Brenda E.F. 1982. *The three twins: The telling of a South Indian folk epic.* Bloomington: Indiana University Press.

Bilimale, P. and Peter J. Claus 1988. Research note *Karnataka Folklore Newsletter,* vol. 1, n. 1, p. 8.

Blackburn, Stuart H. 1981. Oral performance: Narrative and ritual in a Tamil tradition. In *Journal of American Folklore* 94: 207-27.

Id. 1982. The distribution, development and position of oral epic traditions in India (revised version). Presented at the Conference on Indian Oral Epics, Madison, Wisconsin, June, 1982.

Id. 1988. *Birth stories, death stories: Oral performances in a Tamil folk tradition.* Philadelphia: University of Pennsylvania Press.

Brückner, Heidrun 1987. Bhūta worship in coastal Karṇāṭaka: An oral Tuḷu myth and festival ritual of Jumādi. In *Studien zur Indologie und Iranistik,* Heft 13/14, 17-37.

Claus, Peter J. 1975a. The Siri myth and ritual: A mass possession ritual of South Indian. In *Ethnology* 14, 1:47-58.

Id. 1975b. Determinants of household organization among tenants and landowners of the Bant-Nadava caste complex. In *Contributions to Indian Sociology* (NS) 9.1: 91-110.

Id. 1978. Oral traditions, royal cults and materials for a reconsideration of the caste system in South India. In *Journal of Indian Folkloristics* 1: 1, 1-25.

Id. 1979a. Spirit possession and spirit mediumship from the perspective of Tulu oral traditions. In *Culture, Medicine and Psychiatry* 3: 29-52.

Id. 1979b. Mayndala: a myth and possession cult of Tulunad. In *Asian Folklore Studies* 38.2: 94-129.

Id. 1984. Medical anthropology and the ethnography of spirit possession. In Judy Pugh and Valentine Daniel (eds.) *Contributions to Asian Studies.*

Id. 1986. Playing *cenne:* The meanings of a folk game. In S.H. Blackburn and A.K. Ramanujan (eds.) *Another harmony: New essays on the folklore of India.* Berkeley: University of California Press, pp. 265-293.

Id. 1987a. Mancala (cenne) in Tulu myth and cult. In Peter J. Claus, D. P. Pattanayak and J. Handoo (eds.) *Indian folklore, vol. II*. Mysore: Central Institute of Indian Languages Press.

Id. 1987b. *Tuluva darshana*. Kundapur, India: Pradesika Vyasanga. [In Kannada, a collection of eight research articles translated by A.V. Nadava and Subhashcandra.]

Id. 1988. *Future research in Tulu culture*. Academy Silver Jubilee Lecture 4. Manipal (India): Academy of General Education, Manipal.

Id. 1989. Behind the text: Performance and ideology in a Tulu oral tradition. In Stuart Blackburn, Peter J. Claus, Joyce Flueckiger and Susan Wadley (eds.) *Oral epics in India*. Berkeley: University of California Press, 55-74.

Gonda, J. 1954. *Aspects of early Viṣṇuism*. Utrecht: N.V.A. Osthoek's Uitgevers Mij.

Rai, Viveka. 1985. *Tulu Janapada Sāhitya*. Bangalore: Kannada Sahitya Parishath.

Shulman, David D. 1980. *Tamil temple myths: Marriage and sacrifice in a South Indian Śaiva tradition*. Princeton: Princeton University Press.

Someshwar, Amrith 1962. *Pāḍdanagaḷu*.

Welbon, Guy R. 1982. The caṇḍāla's song. In Guy R. Welbon and Glenn E. Yocum (eds.) *Religious festivals in South India and Sri Lanka.* New Delhi: Manohar, 77-79.

Zvelebil, Kamil. 1987. *Two Tamil folktales: The story of king Matanakama and the story of peacock Ravana.* Delhi: Motilal Banarsidass.

AVATĀRA, AVENGER, AND KING: NARRATIVE THEMES IN THE RĀJASTHĀNĪ ORAL EPIC OF DEVNĀRĀYAṆ

Aditya Malik

Introduction

In the last decade or so there has been an increasing interest in oral epics in India and their place within folk cults.[1] The deification of mortal heroes, spirit possession during the performance of some of the epics, their structure and world-view vis-à-vis epics of the "established" Sanskrit tradition like the Mahābhārata and Rāmāyaṇa are some of the issues that have been examined. Alongside this, it has been a general concern among scholars of South Asian culture to postulate the existence of social paradigms that generate the structure of Indian society. One of these social models, *viz.*, that of the king, in which status is determined by reciprocal sets of obligations and duties of individual members towards the king and *vice versa,* appears to play an important role in the construction of folk deities, who quite often bear the characteristics of royalty. Analogous to the realm of the king, a distinguishing feature in the case of such deities is, perhaps, the reciprocality of devotion expressed by a member of the cult towards the god and *vice versa.* Thus, at least two interconnected issues seem to be pertinent with regard to the study of folk epics: (a) an examination of the epics in

---

[1] See, for example, Beck (1982), Roghair (1982), Blackburn (1985) and Blackburn *et al.* (1989).

the context of folk cults (deification of heroes, spirit possession, etc.) and (b) the unraveling of social and religious ideals that sustain and generate both the epic narratives and the folk-religious phenomena accompanying them.

The following paper is a preliminary attempt in the above terms at examining a narrative about Devnārāyaṇ, a folk deity of Rajasthan. The discussion centers around Devnārāyaṇ's *'byāvlo,'* a short narrative dealing with circumstances and events leading upto the deity's marriages.[2] The *'byāvlo'* forms part of the epic tradition of Devnārāyaṇ, major portions of which are constituted by narratives of the Bagaṛāvats and Devnārāyaṇ.[3] The paper is divided into three parts. Part I deals briefly with (a) the origins and history of the Gujars, who are the main bearers of the tradition and (b) a short synopsis of the epic prior to the point of the deity's birth/incarnation. Part II contains a summarized prose translation of the *'byāvlo.'* Part III looks at the *byāvlo'* in terms of its place within the larger context of folk/classical traditions, and what it tells us about perceptions of society and divinity in an essentially pastoral, folk cult.[4]

---

[2] The *'byāvlo'* is in fact a heavily condensed version of a section (called *Devnārāyaṇjī ro janampatrī)* of a considerably lengthy narrative named *Devnārāyaṇ kathā*. The author plans a full length study including an edition and translation of this text of which he was able to record a "complete" version in summer 1991. The narrative, together with a prior section dealing with the lives of 24 Gujar heroes, is over 50 hours long. Not even this, however, constitutes the entire length of the corpus of narratives associated with Devnārāyaṇ and the 24 Gujar heroes. (Joseph Miller, University of Pennsylvania, has collected 109 hours of audio tape dealing with Devnārāyaṇ and the Bagaṛāvats; personal communication).

[3] See below for an explanation of who the Bagaṛāvats were. Locally printed versions of the narrative of the Bagaṛāvats are sometimes called Bagaṛāvat "Bhārat," signifying the epic character of the narrative. Similar to the Mahābhārata, the Bagaṛāvat Bhārata also culminates in a great and bloody war.

[4] The material collected on Devnārāyaṇ resulted from a field-trip to Pushkar between autumn 1984 and spring 1985. The story presented here was recorded in a village approx. 30 km west of Pushkar. Although the main focus of the study was on understanding the development of Pushkar as a center for the worship of Brahmā, it

I.

The Gujars

Devnārāyaṇ is the principal deity of the Gujars or Gurjaras as they are called in Sanskrit texts. The Gujars are now a pastoral community living in Rajasthan, Saurashtra, Uttar Pradesh, Gujarat as well as parts of Kashmir and Himachal Pradesh. The literature on this community has taken pains to discuss the question of their "origins," an issue that has, nevertheless, remained fairly undecided. Following the orientalists' penchant for identifying migrations in the early history of the Indian subcontinent, Bingley writing in 1899 considered the Gurjaras to be an offshoot of the Scythians called the Yuchi, who migrated to the North Western parts of India probably from the region of the Oxus river (and other Central Asian regions). According to him these early Scythians eventually settled down and intermarried with the "original" inhabitants of the region around Saurashtra, claimed to be the Ahirs. The descendants of both these groups are supposed to have ultimately established the

---

soon became clear that in order to do this it would be necessary to understand the influence of the folk/pastoral background in which the pilgrimage center is physically and culturally situated. This concern was supported by two other reasons, *viz.*, a) There are three important temples in Pushkar dedicated respectively to Devnārāyaṇ, Bhuṇojī (Devnārāyaṇ's cousin; one of the main characters in the narrative), and Savāī Bhoj (Devnārāyaṇ's father; perhaps the most important figure in the first part of the epic), and b) in a number of villages I was informed that Devnārāyaṇ's "*thān*" (Rajasthani: "place") was considered to be older than the village itself or conversely that the *thān* was the spot around which the village grew. To add to this I later discovered in Sir Jadunath Sarkar's "History of the Dasnami Naga Sanyasis" that: "The holy city of Pushkar had been taken possession of by the wandering robber tribe of Gujars. But in the Diwali night of 30 Kartik Badi, Vikram Samvat 1214 (1157 A.D.) Naga Sannyasi troops defeated and expelled the Gujars and restored the city to the Brahmans. They planted the Bharatis in the Varaha temple, the Jnan-Naths in the Vaidyanath temple, and the Puris in the temple of Brahma and Savitri, - where they are still in possession." (s.d., 274). Although the date for this event could be questioned, the role played by the Gujars in the history of the pilgrimage center becomes fairly evident.

country of Gujarat.[5] Unlike Bingley, however, B.N. Puri concludes that the Gujars were a "native tribe living in obscurity near about the Mount Ābu in Rajputana." (1957: 18). After migrating to the north-west region of Swat and to Kathiawar in the south-west, the Gujars established the powerful dynasty of the Gurjara-Pratiharas, which played a crucial role in the history of early medieval North India.[6] This more recent view about the origins of the Gujars is supported by B.S. Suryavanshi (1962), who associates the Gujars with the Abhiras or Ahirs as they are called today. Following Puri, Suryavanshi sees the Abhiras as constituent of the original group out of which various subgroups emerged. These subgroups or castes as Suryavanshi calls them include the Nandbans in Uttar Pradesh, the Ghosin, Nandgop and Goyaria in Bengal, the Ghosis in Madhya Pradesh, the Rawat and Gahra in Orissa, the Gohel, Nandania and Sisoṭia in Kutch and Saurashtra, the Gollas and their endogamous groups in Karnataka as well as the Gujars in the areas mentioned above. Besides their geographical distribution and the debate concerning their "origins," it is important here to mention certain cultural characteristics that are shared by these groups. One of these cultural markers is perhaps the consistent reference in their mythology, legends and festivals to Kṛṣṇa[7] and to the Goddess. Ch. Vaudeville writes in this context: "It was probably the Abhīras and related castes who spread the legend of their hero, Kṛṣṇa-Gopāla, throughout India... Like all the non-Aryan castes from the North to the South of India the pastoral tribes recognized as the supreme deity the great goddess Devī, in her warlike form of Durgā or her fertile and maternal form of Umā, the wife of Rudra-Śiva." (1975: 104f.).[8]

---

[5] An important aspect concerning the religion of the Scythians, or Takṣakas as they were called, was that they were serpent worshippers and were also refered to as Nāgas (Cp. Basak Nāg/Vasuki).

[6] On the early medieval period (c. 650-1200 A.D.), see, for example, R.C. Majumdar (1955), D.R. Sharma (1966), A.K. Majumdar (1956), J. Tod (1829/1971).

[7] See Suryavanshi (1962: 53-80, 90ff.).

[8] Parallels between Kṛṣṇa and Devnārāyaṇ, and the decisive role played by the goddess are distinguishing features of the epic.

The epic background

Devnārāyaṇ's cult extends over a region approximately 320-540 km in diameter, covering most of Rajasthan and the north-western tip of Madhya Pradesh. The epic has been classified as "regional," by Blackburn (1989: 18), who has attempted to map known epic traditions in India in relation to their geographical spread, terming them "local," "sub-regional," "regional" and "supra-regional." The epic tradition of Devnārāyaṇ,[9] according to Blackburn, moreover, belongs to the category of "martial" epics, such as those of Pābūjī, Palnāḍu, Ālhā etc. Both the category of "martial" and "sacrificial" epics like those of Kanyaka and Ellamma, emphasize "group solidarity." "Romantic" epics such as those of Lorik-Candā, Gūgā and Ḍholā, on the other hand, "often celebrate individual actions that threaten that solidarity." *(ibid.,* 5). Furthermore, martial epics like those of Devnārāyaṇ, "are concerned with power, social obligation, and social unity; they turn on the themes of revenge, regaining lost land, or restoring lost rights... Martial epics celebrate external - often military or political - conflict and a warrior ethic." *(ibid.,* 5).

The story that will be presented here is entitled *"Śrī Devnārāyaṇjī ro byāvlo"*[10] *(byāvlo:* A tale associated with marriage; Rājasthānī: *b/vyāh,* or Sanskrit: *vivāha).* On account of its being sung the chronicle (as I have chosen to call it) can, as a genre, be classified as "epic." Individual episodes and the sequence of events in the story correspond, on a number of counts, to stories about heroes in other Indo-European settings. One such detail is Devnārāyaṇ's "immaculate" conception and descendancy from a god, i.e., from Viṣṇu. As already mentioned, the text forms part of the second half of an essentially two part epic sequence and appears to be a narrative unit within itself, i.e, it may be recited independant of the main corpus.[11]

---

[9] For a brief outline of the epic, see also Blackburn *et al.* 1989: 216-217.

[10] *"The marriage (chronicle) of Śrī Devnārāyaṇjī."*

[11] Although by and large in performances of the epic the section on Devnārāyaṇ is

The first part of the epic deals with episodes centering around the 24 Bagaṛāvats (Gujar heroes),[12] culminating in their annihilation at the hands of the Goddess.[13] The second part begins with the birth of Viṣṇu in the form of Devnārāyaṇ,[14] who later avenges the death and defeat of the Bagaṛāvats. The first part thus constitutes the background and reasons for Viṣṇu's incarnation as Devnārāyaṇ. This part of the epic relates the story of the 24 Gujar heroes and their battle against a Rajput chieftain (Rajasthani: *rāṇā)*. The outcome of the battle is that the Bagaṛāvats are all killed and their wives, with the exception of Sāḍū, Devnārāyaṇ's mother, commit *satī*.

The epic begins with an episode in which Bāgh Siṃh (or Rāv) the father of the Bagaṛāvats is conceived.[15] Hari Siṃh, the nephew of

---

always preceded by the section on the Bagaṛāvats. According to a senior singer this is done in order to please the deity's ancestors (i.e., the Bagaṛāvats) first.

[12] See Singh, this volume.

[13] J.D. Smith (1989: 177, fn. 2) notes: "the heroes of the Rajasthani epics are said to have been "duped" *(chaḷiyā)* by the Goddess." This notion has parallels in the classical Sanskrit tradition, in which, for example, the goddess causes Rāma and Rāvaṇa to engage in battle against each other (Kālika Purāṇa 62.26-28ff.):

> (She) went to the city of Laṅkā, where Raghu's son formerly stayed (26).
> When she came there, the great Goddess caused Rāma and Rāvaṇa to be engaged in a battle, but Ambikā herself remained hidden. (26-27).
> After she had eaten the flesh and the blood of the Rākṣasas and the monkeys, she caused Rāma and Rāvaṇa to be engaged in fight during seven days. (27-28).
> (Trans. K.R. van Kooij 1972: 109, Ch. 62.26-28).

[14] For a discussion of the evolution of the appellation 'Nārāyaṇa' within Vaiṣṇava mythology, see R.N. Dandekar (1979: 229ff., 257ff.).

[15] In reality the roots of this event extend much further, pushing back the epic's "intergenerational" character (see Blackburn *et al.* 1989: 31f.) into a previous Yuga in which the 24 Gujar heroes are Ṛṣis who are "unintentionally" devoured by Śaṅkar who has taken the form of an Aghori. After consuming 23 of the 24 Ṛṣis he returns to his more normal, benign consciousness and repents his cannibalistic deed. The surviving sage insists on also being consumed so as to remain together with the other 23. Before complying with his wish Śaṅkar promises that all 24 will be born as the

Bīsaḷdev Chauhan, the legendary ruler (10th-12th A.D.?) of Ajmer[16] kills a lion and heads for Pushkar to wash his blood smeared sword.[17] At the lake he encounters Līlā Sevṛī, a young woman who has vowed never to see the face of a man, and who has just finished performing ablutions in the holy lake in the light of the moon. She sees Hari Siṃh, who is carrying the lion's head slung over his shoulder, reflected in the lake in the form of a man-lion. Now that her vow has been broken, Līlā Sevṛī insists that Hari Siṃh marry her, something not possible without the king's permission because they belong to different castes: he is a Rajput[18] and she a Brahman or a Mahājan (a trader caste), depending upon the version of the story one chooses.[19] Their son, as it turns out, has the head of a lion and the body of a man and is therefore called Bāgh Siṃh or Bāgh Rāv[20] (Bāgh = "lion"). Because of his unusual features no one wants to give their daughter in marriage to him. He does, however, manage to trick 12 girls into marrying him. These girls are of different castes and each of them gives birth to two sons, who are collectively called the Bagaṛāvats.[21] Later on, because of a boon they receive from

---

sons of Bāgh Siṃh in the Kali Yuga. In a variant of this episode, which links the narrative to the Rāmāyaṇa, Rāvaṇa forcibly extracts tax from the 24 Ṛṣis, who pay in kind in the form of their own blood. Later they are reborn as the sons of Bāgh Siṃh, and Rāvaṇa as the Rajput Rāṇā whom Devnārāyaṇ ultimately destroys, thereby avenging the Ṛṣis'/Bagaṛāvats' humiliation and defeat. (See Malik 1990: 205, note 13).

[16] Neither the date nor the identity of Bīsaḷdev Chauhan is certain.

[17] Cp. Singh, this volume.

[18] Some informants claim that Hari Siṃh was a Gujar called Hari Rām, who was given the title of "Siṃh" only after his courageous act of killing the lion.

[19] Cp. Singh this volume: Līlā Sevṛī conceives immediately upon seeing Hari Siṃh.

[20] From which the name Bagaṛāvat is supposedly derived.

[21] In a way the figure of Bāgh Siṃh encapsulates the paradigm of the king: his marriages cut across caste distinctions and establish bonds within different groups in society. An amusing part of this episode is the experience undergone by a Brahman who has been Bāgh Siṃh's cook and caretaker. - As Bāgh Siṃh embraces 13 women (12 of whom he finally marries), the Brahman, also being unmarried, demands one woman for himself. Bāgh Siṃh allows him to choose one, on the condition that he should not inquire about the woman's caste *(jāt)*. The Brahman

Śiva, the Bagaṛāvats become rich and influential and "exchange turbans" (i.e. become brothers) with the Rāṇā of Rāṇ City. In an extended drinking session streams of alcohol flow over the earth and down into the underworld, aggravating Basak Nāg,[22] lord of the underworld, who complains about this to Viṣṇu. In order to test the Bagaṛāvats, Viṣṇu appears to them in the form of a leper, but the Bagaṛāvats are not deceived by his disguise, and wash Viṣṇu's wounds, treating the used water like nectar by drinking it. Unsuccessful with the Bagaṛāvats, Viṣṇu disguises himself as a holy man *(sādhu)* and visits Savāī Bhoj's (the eldest of the 24 brothers) wife, the future mother of Devnārāyaṇ, asking for alms. Sāḍū, who is bathing, responds immediately to his demand and approaches him naked, covered only by her long tresses. Although finding this revolting at first, Viṣṇu is then convinced that this is a sign of true devotion and grants her a boon. Sāḍū spreads her *jolī*,[23] and asks Viṣṇu to be born in it as her son. The god promises to do this and also to avenge the prophesized defeat of the Bagaṛāvats. Later on in the story Viṣṇu, acting on the wishes of Basak Nāg, sends Durgā on a mission to destroy the Bagaṛāvats. Durgā, who takes birth as the daughter of the Rājā of Idarkoṭ, grows up at an amazing speed till

---

chooses a beautiful woman, who, as he later to his disappointment finds out, belongs to the Bhābīs - a caste at the lower end of the social hierarchy.

[22] Sanskrit: *Vāsuki*. Basak Nāg and Rājā Vasak signify the same serpent deity. With regard to the deification of dead heroes amongst the Minas of Chitorgarh Dist. of Rajasthan, J. Jain (1973: 61) observes that the hero is believed to be reborn as a serpent or rather serpent deity and is called *Vasak*. The term, though found in classical Hindu mythology, does not have this association for the Minas and is used as a general term for serpent deity. Among the Minas, thus, memorial stones usually depict the engraving of a coiled serpent. On the other hand memorial stones of the Bhils in Central India usually show a horse-ridden man. Since we are dealing here with cults of deified heroes, these facts are interesting with regard to Devnārāyaṇ, because we find both figures in his icons: the serpent (Rājā Vasak) and the deity riding a horse. Unlike in the case of the Minas, however, the symbol of the serpent and Devnārāyaṇ himself are actively associated with Vaiṣṇava mythology.

[23] *jolī* here refers to *oṛnī*(sash used by women). It also can mean either a pouch or a cloth bag in which children are put to sleep or a bag in which an ascetic collects alms.

it is soon time for her to be married. Although she promises to marry the Rāṇā of Rāṇ City, she secretly weds the Savāī Bhoj's (Sāḍū's husband and Devnārāyaṇ's father) sword. Ultimately the Bagaṛāvats engage in a tremendous Mahābhārata-like war on account of Rāṇī Jaimatī (the Rājā of Idarkoṭ's daughter, i.e., Durgā), in which the nearly invincible Bagaṛāvats are killed off one after another through the supernatural powers of the goddess. The wives of the Bagaṛāvats commit *satī*. Only Sāḍū, who has received Viṣṇu's promise, does not commit *satī*, and survives. She retires to the "Mālāsari Hill"[24] and begins to practice asceticism *(tapas)*. Soon after Devnārāyaṇ is "born" in a lotus flower. And this is the point where the *byāvlo* begins.

What is immediately noticeable in this first section of the story is the ambivalent role played by Viṣṇu. On the one hand he initiates the destruction of the Bagaṛāvats, promising at the same time to take birth as Devnārāyaṇ to avenge their defeat. If we remember that the Bagaṛāvats owe their wealth and influence to a boon given by Śiva, besides being a party to rituals that have a tantric tinge to them,[25] we could, at least in part, interpret the story as a conflict between Śaivism and Vaiṣṇavism. Once the "Śaivite," almost *asura*-like Bagaṛāvats are vanquished through Durgā's acting out of Viṣṇu's wishes, Viṣṇu is prepared to incarnate himself as the leader of the Gujars, and even to avenge the defeat of the Bagaṛāvats. Although this kind of interpretation may sometimes help to understand developments on a "sectarian"[26] or classical level, it will not be sufficient to understand a cult on a folk level. On this level there

---

[24] This is a small hill situated near the town of Āsind, and the temple of Savāī Bhoj in Bhilwara Dist. in South Eastern Rajasthan.

[25] See Singh, this volume.

[26] Although this may also be doubtful, since the term "sect" is a misnomer in the context of Hinduism. For an alternative to the "sectarian" interpretation of a Puranic myth, see, for example, E.C. Visuvalingam on the myth of Bhairava's brahmanicide (1989: 164ff.).

appears to be a mixture of both Śaivite and Vaiṣṇavite characteristics to the story/cult without the "self-conscious" distinctions found in the classical tradition. On the other hand, patterns found in the classical tradition may be reflected in the folk tradition and *vice versa*. Thus, for example, the Bagaṛāvats play out the role that demons usually do in Puranic myths. The parallels are striking: both, demons and the Bagaṛāvats, accumulate enough influence to upset the balance of power in the world and both are vanquished by the goddess. But there are other intricacies too, as for example, Rāṇī Jaimatī's secret marriage to Savāī Bhoj. Again, like in the myth of Durgā and Mahiṣa, there is an undercurrent of "*Liebestod*" here: Savāī Bhoj's infatuation for Rāṇi Jaimatī sparks off the war in which he is killed at the hands of the queen, alias Durgā. Unlike Mahiṣa, however, Savāī Bhoj is not subsequently elevated to being the devotee *par excellence* of Durgā. A reconciliation, if at all, does not appear to occur here: there is apparently no "conversion" of the "transgressors" in the epic. All the Bagaṛāvats are simply annihilated.[27] And this is the important point here - there is a marked divergence from "conventional bhakti theology" (Smith 1989: 176).[28] M. Biardeau and others have tried to show that the transformation of demonic figures (here, partially substituted by the Bagaṛāvats) into "devotees" occurs through the workings of bhakti. Thus, for example, a violent, lustful Bhairõ (Bhairava) becomes the principal guardian and "bhakta" of the gentle, "vegetarian" Vaiṣṇo Devī (a goddess of Jammu Dist.), *after* his decapitation by the goddess; Maṇi, the demon enemy of Khaṇḍobā, becomes a symbol of fervent devotion, after he is defeated at the hands of the god.[29] On the

---

[27] If one wants to find a pattern in this tradition which is evident in other folk cults, then perhaps one could maintain that Viṣṇu's birth as Devnārāyaṇ represents a second generation transformation of the "*asuric*" Bagaṛāvats, but this would require closer examination.

[28] See also Singh's discussion in this volume on the ethics of the epic, which provide a contrast to the stereotyped view of Indian society as "spiritual" and "transcendental."

[29] See Biardeau, Erndl, Sontheimer and Stanley in Hiltebeitel (ed.) 1989.

other hand, Indian epics, according to Smith, deal mainly with themes of the transfer of evil onto men from the gods and not with its transformation: "Celestial beings propose to provoke and participate in human conflicts, causing enormous human carnage; and their reasons for doing so are purely to avoid trouble in heaven." (Smith 1989: 183). Although Smith's provocative analysis of the ideology of Indian epics, summarized in his description of their human heroes as "scapegoats of the gods," would appear to suit the first part of the Bagaṛāvat-Devnārāyaṇ epic, it does not appear to hold good for the second part which is discussed in the third section of this essay. In the latter part the hero is divine to begin with. The story is not marked by the gloomy fate of mortals, on the contrary it is miraculous, being characterized by the beneficial acts of the deity, whose behaviour is, in many ways, like that of an earthly king.

II.

The Text

The epic texts are usually sung or rather performed by Bhopās[30] who belong to Gujar, Kumahar or other castes. (See plate XIII).[31]

---

[30] The term Bhopā is probably derived from (a) *Bho/Bhūpāl*, meaning 'protecter of the earth' or king; (b) *Bhūp* (king) + the dimunitive suffix *'ā,'* meaning "small" king.

[31] Though the epic or parts of it may also be sung by other members of the community, it is only the Bhopās who are professional singers. The institution of the Bhopā is widespread among other cults in Rajasthan, e.g., Pābūjī, Tejājī, Gugājī, Bhairū, as well as among groups like the Minas. J. Jain, who refrains from translating Bhopā into the term "shaman," describes the Bhopā in the following manner: "Als *bhopa* wird der religiöse Zeremonienmeister bezeichnet. Im Verlaufe einer bestimmten Zeremonie wird ein toter Held oder eine Göttin gerufen, in den Körper eben dieses *bhopa* zu kommen... Der *bhopa* ist also ein Mann, der als geeignet angesehen wird, zeitweilig Sitz einer Gottheit zu sein." (1973: 19). No possession (Rājasthānī: *bhāv āvṇo*) takes place through Devnārāyaṇ, and as a consequence there is no possession, through the deity, of Bhopās or members of the audience during performances of the epic. Possession does, however, take place through Bhairū, who accompanies Devnārāyaṇ, but this is usually of an oracular kind and is some-

O.P. Joshi (1976: 30f.) distinguishes three groups of Bhopās: (a) the temple Bhopā, (b) the Jamāt Bhopā and (c) the Paṛ Bhopā. Of these only the last specialize in reciting the epic.[32]

Although the "*byāvlo*" is in verse I have chosen to summarize the chronicle in prose for the purposes of this paper and have divided the story into three main sections. These sections can be further divided into subsections. The choice of these divisions is based on the movement of the story through different episodes and phases.

Śrī Devnārāyaṇjī ro byāvlo

I. Devnārāyaṇ's birth
Sāḍū's flight to Malwa.

While his mother, Sāḍū, performs *tapas* on top of the Mālāsari hill in the year *vi. sam.* 968 (= 911 A.D.), Devnārāyaṇ appears in a lotus flower. At his birth the Rāṇā's throne begins to quake, the legs fall off his bed and four of his teeth crack. He summons four paṇḍits and orders them to kill the boy.[33] They journey to the place where Sāḍū lives, demanding on their arrival *dakṣiṇā,* and later water to cook with, from her. While Sāḍū is away fetching water, the paṇḍits try to kill the child by feeding it with poison. But the child resists these attempts by confusing the paṇḍits. He appears varyingly to each of them: once as an old man, once as a youth, once as a snake and once as a child. In their confusion they drop the poison and begin quarrelling amongst themselves. They return to the Rāṇā and inform him that the child is an "*avatāri lāl,*"[34] The

what restricted to places that are specially dedicated to Bhairū.

[32] See Joshi (1976) and appendix for details of the different functions of the Bhopās.

[33] Since the Bagaṛāvats and the Rāṇā have "exchanged turbans" (see above), i.e., have become brothers, the Rāṇā's kin status is that of Devnārāyaṇ's uncle. Cp. the myth of the birth of Kṛṣṇa, in which Kṛṣṇa's maternal uncle (actually his cousin) Kaṃsa tries to kill him (Harivaṃśa 47.1-57; 48.1-37a).

[34] Divine child or incarnation of god.

Rāṇā then sends a *dūtī*[35] to kill the child. The woman disguises herself, and claiming to be the child's paternal aunt, she reprimands Sāḍū for not informing her earlier of his birth. Then, after smearing her breasts with poison she suckles the child. The child, however, is not harmed by the poison and instead begins to suck the woman's life-energy away.[36] She, too, realizes that he is an "*avatāri lāl,*" and begs forgiveness, promising to serve him thereafter. She returns to the Rāṇā and, like the paṇḍits before her, tells him of the child's divine nature. Upon hearing this the Rāṇa grows even more apprehensive and summons another Brahman.

Meanwhile, Sāḍū who anticipates the Rāṇā's evil intentions, sends a message to her brothers Āmbā and Nimbā Vīr. She informs them of the Rāṇā's attempts to kill the child. Āmbā and Nimbā Vīr set off and arrive quickly with their army. Then, together with buffaloes, cows and the two Bhils, Kānyo and Kiṣṇo, they place the child in a *pālṇo* (crib) and depart in the direction of Malwa, which is Sāḍū's paternal home. Sāḍū leads the group of buffaloes and cows while Kānyo carries the *pālṇo* on his head. On the way a Brahman suddenly appears and warns Āmbā, Nimbā and the Bhils that the child will cause them great misfortune. He advises them to abandon it. Āmbā and Nimbā along with Kānyo follow this advice and throw the *pālṇo* into a gorge. Here, however, the child is sheltered by Bhavānī, who suckles him in the form of a lioness. Shortly after the child has been abandoned, Sāḍū notices that the *pālṇo* is missing and demands that Āmbā and Nimbā take her to it. They rush back to the gorge and find the lioness feeding the child. Thereafter, Sāḍū carries the *pālṇo* on her head and they proceed to Malwa.

II. Devnārāyaṇ realizes his purpose.

Devnārāyaṇ grows up in Malwa and the text now describes his taking the cattle to graze, exhibiting miraculous powers.

---

[35] *dūtī* can either mean a female messenger or a woman who instigates quarrels.

[36] Cp. the story of Pūtanā, the ogress, who tried to kill the child Kṛṣṇa by smearing her breasts with poison and suckling him (Bhāgavata Purāṇa 10.6.1-20, 30-44).

[37] Chochū Bhāṭ is often identified with Nārada. The role he plays is also somewhat similar to the one played by Nārada in puranic myths: his presence creates a rupture

In the meantime Chochū Bhāṭ,[37] the family chronicler-geneaologist[38] of the Bagaṛāvats, makes plans for going to Malwa in order to inform Devnārāyaṇ of his family's history and of his true purpose, i.e, to avenge the Bagaṛāvats' death. The Bhāṭ arrives in Mālwa and tells Devnārāyaṇ about the Bagaṛāvats and about his three other brothers,[39] *viz.*, Mādurāv, Bhuṇo and Bhageśvar. Devjī,[40] who hears this for the first time, promises to find his brothers and to avenge his father's death.

Devjī brings Chochū home for a meal. Sāḍū is pleased to see Chochū, but entreats him not to inform Devjī about the Bagaṛāvats. She instructs Chochū to collect some leaves of the Banyan *(baṛ)* tree for the meal. Chochū goes and finds a Banyan tree. Before collecting the leaves he washes himself in a rivulet and prays to Śiva. Sāḍū who does not want the Bhāṭ to tell Devjī about the Bagaṛāvats, conceives a way of eliminating him. She mixes poison into the food. Meanwhile Chochū climbs up the tree in search of leaves, which he drops to the ground. But as he does this the 52 Bhairavas and 64 Joginīs who inhabit (?) the tree (literally) "show their teeth" and devour him.

Since Chochū does not return within a reasonable space of time, Devjī goes searching for him. He discovers Chochū's *dhoti* hanging from the tree and his turban and shoes on the ground. He goes to the rivulet and asks Śaṅkar, who sits there, to tell him what has happened to Chochū. Śaṅkar laconically denies any knowledge of the matter. But because Śaṅkar does not help him, Devjī decides to commit suicide. Thereupon, Śaṅkar quickly changes his mind and informs him that the Bhāṭ has been devoured by the Bhairavas and Joginīs. After tracking down the Bhairavas and Joginīs, Śaṅkar makes them disgorge all the meat and bones and then sprinkles *amṛt* over the heap. Chochū is revived and Bholanāth (Śiva)

---

in an otherwise harmonious scene, ultimately leading to new and perhaps necessary configurations.

[38] For a discussion of the social function and historical role of family bards and genealogists in Rajasthan and Gujarat, such as the Bhaṭṭas, Bhāṭs and Cāraṇs, see, for example, C. von Fürer-Haimendorf (1961). See also Burghart, this volume.

[39] The longer version mentions four brothers.

[40] Devjī = Devnārāyaṇ

departs. Kālājī and Gorāji[41] scare off the Jogiṇīs.

The Jogiṇīs go to Nagvanti, the daughter of Nāgdev and ask for shelter. Nagvanti relates the incident to her father and asks him to marry her to Devjī. He agrees and calls the paṇḍit to place *ṭīkas* on the couples' forehead. In this manner Devjī reaches Singh(dh)vāṛā and marries Nagvanti. After this, Devjī, Nagvanti and Chochū Bhāṭ return to Sāḍū.

Finally, they all sit down for the meal and Devnārāyaṇ knowingly eats the poisoned food that was meant for the Bhāṭ. He vomits on account of this, and then eats the leaves from a Neem tree as a cure. The next lines are in praise of the Neem tree, informing listeners that the world shall worship the tree and that it shall relieve whosoever suffers in the same manner.

III. Devnārāyaṇ's decision to avenge his father's death: the "return journey."

Encounter with Śaṅkar

The next thing that Chochū suggests is that Devjī should obtain his (maternal) uncle's blessings and, along with his three brothers, return to Goṭhā[42] to avenge the Bagaṛāvats' defeat. Sāḍū is against his departure and his intention to fight the Rāṇā, since he is only a boy of thirteen. Devjī says he has no fear and asks his uncle for his blessings. Even his uncle advises him to wait for a while, but Devjī insists on leaving immediately. After having received his *māmā's* (maternal uncle) and mother's blessings, Devjī departs and proceeds towards Goṭhā along with Chochū, Nāpā the Gvāl (cowherd) and 900,000 cows. After some time they reach river Saprā.[43]

---

[41] These are forms of Bhairava that accompany Devnārāyaṇ. Cf. fn. 55 below..

[42] *goṭhā* literally means "small village." There is some ambiguity in the usage of the term. In this text it is used as a proper noun denoting a particular place, *viz., Goṭhā nagar*. In other texts, such as the longer one recorded by the author, it is written in the plural: *goṭhā̃* (= "small villages"), thereby refering to unspecified hamlets. Cp. Skt. *goṣṭha-* 'cow-pen,' 'meeting place,' etc.

[43] Śiprā river?

There is an interlude here in which Pīpal, Devjī's future queen, is introduced. Her father is Jaisal Rāj Puvār. Pīpal is a devotee of Ambā, whom she worships in her garden. Ambā, impressed by her devotion, grants her the strange boon of having horns on her head, until the time when she sees her husband. "Once you meet your husband," promises Ambā "the horns will fall off." In the meanwhile Devjī has gone to sleep for a month on the river bank[44] and Nāpa takes the cows out grazing. While the cattle graze he plays a game with a ball[45] *(daḷi)*. Once he throws the ball so high and far that it lands on Śivjī who is sitting in *samādhi*. The *gvāl* demands the ball back from Śiva, who refuses and instead rubs some dirt off his body and creates a *bhūt* (ghost/demon) that scares the *gvāl* away. The *bhūt* drinks up all the river's water as a result of which the cows have nothing to drink. The *gvāl*, not knowing what to do, blows his conch loudly enough to wake up Devjī. Devjī remedies the calamity by sitting on his horse, thrusting his spear into the ground and causing water to gush out of the earth.

Devnārāyaṇ's second and third marriages

They continue their journey and arrive at the town of Dhār, where they rest under a Banyan tree. After resting, Devjī goes together with Chochū to the bazar where the king's daughter Pīpal is sitting on her verandah. As soon as Pīpal sees Devjī, the horns on her head fall off. Overjoyed, Pīpal runs to her mother and informs her that the prophecy has come true and that she should be married to Devjī. The mother runs to the king and the king calls Devjī who is sitting in Dhanna Seṭh's shop. The king asks Devjī whose son he is and which village he comes from. Devjī answers "My mother is the Gujarī called Sāḍū. I come from the town Goṭhā and was born in a lotus flower." However, before he can marry Pīpal, the king, sets him the task of retrieving a "gate" *(phāṭak)*[46] that has been stolen by a Daitya (demon) and taken into the underworld *(pātāl)*.

Devjī enters the underworld on his horse and demands that the Daitya return the gate. The Daitya simply laughs and refuses to

---

[44] Cp. Viṣṇu's sleep during the four months of the rainy season *(Caumāsa)*.

[45] Cp. Zoller, this volume.

[46] Possibly this refers to one of the gates or doorways of the city or of . the king's palace.

give the gate back unless Devjī is willing to fight for it. The Daitya calls out his entire army but Devjī, armed only with his spear and double-edged sword, defeats the army, whereupon the Daitya falls at his feet, asks for forgiveness and promises to give his daughter Damyanti in marriage to Devjī. After marrying Damyanti, Devjī returns together with her and the gate to Dhār town. He relates all that has happened to Pīpal's father.

Pīpal and Devjī are married. Bālū, the barber, comes running out with a torch. Mohan, the Khāti, comes with the *toraṇ* and Devjī sitting upon an elephant strikes down the *toraṇ*. Wealth is then distributed amongst all. The three wives Nagvanti, Damyanti and Pīpal, pay their respects to Sāḍū. As they are about to leave Dhār town, they see a Seṭhāni weeping aloud because she is about to commit *satī*. Devjī revives her husband with *amṛt*. But then she still laments about the fact that she has no children. Devjī promises her that she will have a daughter. But then she continues to lament about the fact that she has no brother and so Devjī makes her his "*dharm*"-sister.

Devnārāyaṇ encounters his brothers

In the meantime, the Rāṇā from his palace sights a great cloud of dust flying up (from the herd of cattle). He summons Bhuṇo and tells him to ride down and collect a tax on the cows. So Bhuṇo rides down with his double-edged sword and demands a tax, which Devjī refuses to pay. As they draw their swords and are about to fight with each other Sāḍū stops them, informing them that they are brothers (i.e. cousins).

Then Bhuṇo sends Devjī off to Bhīlvāṛā, advising him to be wary of the Bhils on the way. He gives him his shoulder sash *(rūmāl)*. promising that it will protect him and bring victory. On the way to Bhīlvāṛā Devjī arrives at the Khāri river. Rūpnāth, the Bagaṛāvats' guru, sends Bhageśvar, who is in his care, to collect tax from the owner of the cattle. Devjī refuses to pay the tax and Bhageśvar draws his weapons, whereupon Sāḍū once again intervenes and informs them that they are brothers (i.e. cousins). Devjī pays his respects to Rūpnāth.

With the promise that every man and woman who hears the "kathā" of Devnārāyaṇ will be freed of his/her bonds (or suffering) by Śaṅkar, the tale ends.

III.

Analysis of the "byāvlo"

The tale may be examined at various levels, each resulting in different sets of meaning. One way of examining it would be to look for the structure of the tale by analysing the text in terms of the sequential development of its elements.[47] Thus, a tale beginning with the hero's birth and ending with his marriage could be described in terms of what the individual episodes denote, e.g., 1) The initial situation 2) Interdiction intensified through promises 3) Violation of the interdiction 4) Departure from home on a quest, etc. The advantage of this method lies in the fact that it results in an abstraction through which a pattern applicable to more than one tale may be arrived at. It has, however, been criticized on the grounds that it completely neglects the context of a tale, concentrating solely on its formal organization.

In the following section of the paper I shall attempt to circumvent this shortcoming not by *not* discussing the narrative structure, but by trying to "fill-out" the structure by refering to the cultural matrix in which the *byāvlo* is embedded. The latter will be done by examining sets of configurations that appear in the text, such as a) Devnārāyaṇ's multiple marriages, b) the relationship between Devnārāyaṇ and Śiva, and c) other elements like the journey to Malwa and Devnārāyaṇ's association with the *"avatāra"* sequence, within the larger context of classical and folk-religious patterns found in Hinduism. This approach is, in itself, one step removed from, say, a Proppian analysis which would deal solely with the formal elements of the story. I have divided the story into three main sections each of which have subsections. This division is based on the following considerations: geography, chronology, and "purpose":

---

[47] See, for example, V. Propp 1968.

I. Devnārāyaṇ's birth; In Goṭhā.

1. Devnārāyan's birth.
2. The Rāṇā's attempts to kill him.
3. Sāḍū's decision to retreat/travel to Malwa, her father's home.
4. Arrival of Āmbā and Nimbā.
5. Āmbā and Nimbā abandon the child.
6. Devnārāyaṇ is suckled by a lioness.

II. Devnārāyaṇ realizes his purpose; In Malwa.

1. Devnārāyaṇ is older now (10-12 years).
2. He exhibits divine/magical abilities.
3. Chochū Bhāṭ appears, informs him of his destiny.
4. Sāḍū plans the destruction of Chochū.
5. Chochū is devoured by the Joginīs.
6. Devnārāyaṇ moves Śankar into saving the Bhāṭ.
7. Devnārāyaṇ's first marriage with Nagvanti the daughter of Nāgdev.
8. Interlude in praise of the Neem tree.

III. Decision to avenge his father's death: the "return journey."

A. Encounter with Śankar.

1. Devnārāyaṇ pronounces his decision to avenge his father's death.
2. Both mother and uncle try holding him back.
3. Departure with 900,000 heads of cattle, Chochū and Nāpā the cowherd.
4. Arrival at the river Sapra.
5. Interlude introducing Pīpal.
6. Pīpal is a devotee of Ambā, with horns on her head.
7. Nāpa plays ball.
8. Encounter with Śankar.
9. Śankar refuses to return the ball, creates a *bhūt*.
10. The *bhūt* drinks up all the water in the river.
11. Devnārāyaṇ is woken up.
12. He creates a fresh source of water and resolves the problem.

B. Devnārāyaṇ's second and third marriages.

1. Arrival in Dhār town.
2. Pīpal sees him in the bazar and her horns fall off.
3. Her father, the king, sets up a task for him.
4. Devnārāyaṇ enters the underworld and defeats the Daitya.
5. Marriage with the Daitya's daughter Damyanti; return with her and the "gate."
6. Devnārāyaṇ's third marriage (with Pīpal).
7. All the three wives pay their respects to Sāḍū.
9. Devnārāyaṇ stops a Seṭhāṇi from immolating herself.

C. Devnārāyaṇ encounters his brothers.

1. Devnārāyaṇ meets Bhuṇo, his brother. Both are ignorant of their relationship.
2. Sāḍū resolves their enmity.
3. Devnārāyaṇ travels to Bhīlvāṛa.
4. Here he meets his brother Bhageśvar. Both are ignorant of their relationship.
5. Sāḍū resolves their enmity.
6. Devnārāyaṇ meets the clan-guru Rūpnāth.
7. The tale ends with Devjī paying his respects to Rūpnāth.
8. The promise of "being taken across" by Śankar.[48]

The narrative has a dual movement begining and ending at the same locus after moving out both spatially and temporally. Whereas the first section is characterized by danger and flight, the second and third sections are marked by well-being, refuge, and, ultimately, vengeance. The first section is geographically located essentially in and around Devnārāyaṇ's birth place. Chronologically, it is also limited to the deity's birth and events immediately following. The second section is situated mainly in Malwa, Sāḍū's paternal home. There is a chronological jump here: in Malwa Devnārāyaṇ is

[48] In the *Devnārāyaṇ kathā* the narrative continues upto the point where Devnārāyaṇ and his brothers avenge the Bagaṛāvats' deaths by defeating the Rāṇā.

already about ten or twelve years old. There are no details about the period between his birth and the events in this section. This section is, among other things, distinguished by an emerging sense of purpose on the part of Devnārāyaṇ. The Bagaṛāvat's genealogist Chochū Bhāṭ interrupts the childhood idyll in Malwa informing Devnārāyaṇ of his clan's history. By providing him with details of the past Chochū sparks off the creation of Devnārāyaṇ's future identity as avenger, god and king. Succeeding events are now motivated by a specific purpose, namely avenging the defeat and death of Devnārāyaṇ's father Savāī Bhoj, and the other twenty-three Bagaṛāvats. The third section covers a large locale spreading from Malwa in Madhya Pradesh to Bhīlvārā in South Eastern Rajasthan. Here the chronology of adulthood continues: Devnārāyaṇ's "return journey" is marked by his three marriages, and the reunion with his brothers.

Another level of meaning that emerges from the development of the story could lie in perceiving the hero's growth in terms of a movement from the realm of the mother to that of the father. Thus, the hero's mother rescues him after his life has been threatened by his father's enemy (also the father's "brother."). The journey that follows ends at the mother's paternal home, a symbol of the maternal realm. Here he is cared for by his maternal uncle and his mother. During the journey he is briefly abandoned and suckled by a surrogate mother, a lioness. After an idyllic childhood under the protection of his mother, the hero is confronted by the family genealogist, who informs him of his destiny, which is essentially linked to matters belonging to the paternal domain. The implicit conflict between maternal and paternal realms surfaces here when we find that the hero's mother tries having the genealogist, a symbol of the paternal realm, killed. Her attempts are unsuccessful and the hero decides to return to his paternal home in order to avenge his father's death and restore the clan's lost dignity. The return journey in which the hero is, incidentally, accompanied by his mother, is marked by various tests of endurance and by the hero's marriages. Even though his wives finally pay their respects to the hero's mother, at least briefly establishing her superiority again, she ultimately merges with the male quest that is now gathering momentum. She reconciles the hero with his brothers. The last encounter is with Rūpnāth, the clan's guru, representing in some ways the hero's final disassociation from the maternal realm. Thus, in a sense, the final section of the story is a mirror image of the opening section: the dominance of the mother is replaced by the dominance of the father's allies and male interests.

Apart from this, there are a number of points in the above list that correspond to the lives of Indian epic heroes. Thus, the heroes usually have miraculous births and are divine to begin with. Often there is a threat to the hero either at birth or soon after. A period of exile or growth, in which the hero is ignorant of his origins, follows. Once the hero is informed of his destiny there is a return to his original home, preparing the ground for a final conflict which usually takes place between "related clans."[49] In Devnārāyaṇ's case his birth takes place in a lotus flower. Soon after this unsuccessful attempts are made to kill him. His mother, Sāḍū, who plays a key role in the narrative, flees with the help of her brothers to distant Malwa, her paternal home. No details of Devnārāyaṇ's childhood are given, and when Chochū Bhāṭ, the family genealogist, arrives on the scene to inform him of his destiny, Devnārāyaṇ is already about twelve or thirteen years old. Besides describing his various marriages, the narrative also moves through a series of "encounters" between Devnārāyaṇ and his brothers, one of whom, interestingly enough, has been adopted by their joint enemy, the Rāṇā. Though the *byāvlo* does not develop further, these encounters and Devnārāyaṇ's return journey point to the imminent conflict between him and the Rāṇā, on whose account the Bagaṛāvats have lost their lives. The struggle, one between uncle[50] and nephew, echoes one of

---

[49] See Smith 1989.

[50] See above, the Rāṇā and Savāī Bhoj have exchanged turbans, i.e., are "turban" brothers *(pagaḍ bhāī)*.

the central conflicts of other legends and myths, the foremost, perhaps, being that between Kṛṣṇa and his uncle (actually cousin) Kaṃsa.

The spatial as well as to a degree temporal framework of the narrative is provided by the journey from Goṭha to Malwa and back. The journey which is located in an existing geographical area, possibly reflects transhumance routes the Gujars once took. Thus, unlike certain other genres, the *byāvlo*, in accordance with its epic character, *specifies* the territory covered by Sāḍū, Āmbā-Nimbā, Kānyo-Kiṣṇo, the buffaloes, cows and Devnārāyaṇ. Along the way attempts are made to tax the cowherds, something not uncommon within the feudally structured society during the early medieval period of Northern and Western India.[51]

In Malwa, Devnārāyaṇ marries thrice, and in two cases the towns in which his wives live are mentioned. Nagvanti, the daughter of Nāgdev, lives in Singh(dh)vāṛā. Pīpal's father is the king of Dhār. Whereas the figure of Nagvanti probably represents a clan belonging to the Ahirs or Gujars, Pīpal, on the other hand, is the daughter of a Rajput ruler (Jaisal Rāj Puvār). Pīpal, the devotee of Ambā, is in all likelihood divine herself. Thus, we find that certain towns in the vicinity of Dhār are called Pīpalod, and that the Minas of South Rajasthan, for example, worship a clan goddess called Pīpalod Mātā.[52] Although it is too early to definitely state the significance of Devnārāyaṇ's multiple wives,[53] perhaps it could tentatively be stated that these symbolize the fusion of different communities within the context of the cult.

---

[51] Cp. Smith (1989: 184): "The world into which the epic heroes make their spectacular entrances is essentially a feudal one."; for a discussion of feudalism in early medieval India, see R.S. Sharma (1965).

[52] See J. Jain (1973: 111).

[53] This is a motif found in different regions of India in varying contexts. See, for example, Murty and Sontheimer (1980); Sontheimer (1989c); Malik (1990: 198ff.).

The relationship between Śiva and Devnārāyaṇ is ambivalent. Here Devnārāyaṇ hardly appears like a resolute god. He is a mortal, - albeit with an extraordinary destiny. For the present, he is somewhat at the receiving end of tests from a taciturn Śiva, who is associated with some of the obstacles that he confronts. The first incident in which he appears is soon after Chochū Bhāṭ has been devoured by the fifty-two Bhairavas and sixty-four Joginīs. Initially denying any knowledge in the matter, he complies only after Devnārāyaṇ threatens to take his own life. Later, on the banks of the river Sapra, he creates the *bhūt* that sucks up all the water in the river. Though Śiva is connected with these obstacles we encounter no overt rivalry between him and Devnārāyaṇ. On the contrary, Devnārāyaṇ seeks the latter's assistance in finding and reviving Chochū Bhāṭ and is not angered at the fact that Śiva has indirectly caused the river to dry up. Instead he resolves these setbacks.

Furthermore, the juxtaposition of Śiva and Devnārāyaṇ, who, in this context, symbolize ascetic and king, suggests an ordering of society in which ascetic and king are connected in large measure by an egalitarian partnership, although the ascetic retains his independant and somewhat aloof status.[54] The fact that Devnārāyaṇ is accompanied by Kālājī and Gorājī Bhairū, points[55] additionally to the "martial" or "royal" paradigm of the cult. It is seldom in the classical tradition that Bhairava, on account of his ritually impure

---

[54] On the relationship between ascetic and king, see also Burghart (1978), and this volume.

[55] Sanskrit: *Bhairava* - the terrifying aspect of Śiva. Observing the universal presence of Bhairū in Rajasthan, J. Jain cites Carstairs with reference to a village in Udaipur dist.: "Even where the chief deity was a goddess, a snake god or a locally worshipped minor incarnation of Viṣṇu... there was always a Bheruji in attendance as well." (Carstairs 1961: 93. Cited in Jain 1973: 74). Bhairū also occupies a central place amongst the Minas of South Rajasthan. Similar to the case of Devnārāyaṇ, Bhairū is sometimes represented in two complementary forms: "Manchmal wird *Bheru* durch zwei Bildnisse dargestellt, ein zinnoberrotes und ein schwarzes. In dieser Form wird er als *Karaji-Goraji* (schwarz und hell) bezeichnet." (J. Jain 1973: 73).

status, is placed in such an immediate ideological as well as spatial vicinity of the deity.[56] Although this feature would appear to rest, in part, on the less "self-conscious" nature of a folk cult itself, it may be a result of the fact that the idea of "purity" or "pollution" is not central to the model of a society in which the king ranks highest. Thus, the domain of the king or "lord of the land is a terrestrial world which comprises all human beings, regardless of their caste, tribe, or sect, who dwell within the territorial boundaries of the kingdom and who are differentiated from one another by their respective rights and duties vis-à-vis the king and his land."[57] In this order, however, the brahman is subordinate to the king. In both the brief incidents in which brahmans appear in the story they are sent on missions commanded by the Rāṇā. They arrive to destroy the child, and by implication are characterized as "cunning" and "evil." The second incident in which Āmbā and Nimbā abandon the child shows the traditional faith in the brahman's command over the religious and ritual realms (omens etc.). Nevertheless, in both instances there is clearly antipathy expressed towards the child by the paṇḍits. On the other hand, this antipathy is also an extension of the Rāṇā's intentions. And in this sense the paṇḍits function as mere instruments in the Rāṇā's hands. On the whole, this is in contrast to the values inherent in the "sacrificial" model of society where the status, function and relationship of the four *varṇas* is determined by their relative purity/impurity and where the brahman occupy the highest position. In this model Bhairava, for example, represents what has been termed the "trangressive pole" of Hinduism, providing an extreme contrast to Viṣṇu (and Brahmā), who represents the "interdictory pole."[58] On the other hand, Devnārāyaṇ, who is an *avatāra* of Bhagavān or Viṣṇu, is always accompanied by Kālā and Gorā Bhairū. It could thus be maintained on the basis of this preliminary

---

[56] Bhairava usually occupies the position of a guardian on the periphery of a temple or sacred space.

[57] Burghart 1978: 523.

[58] See E.C. Visuvalingam (1989).

study of the *byāvlo*, that the epic tradition and cult of Devnārāyaṇ "... does not permit us to emphasize *a priori* the importance of the *varṇa* hierarchy,..."[59]

In conclusion we may summarize the answers to two interlinked questions underlying the observations made in this paper: (1) How are society and divinity perceived in the text? and (2) What is the text's place within the continuum of folk and classical traditions? Clearly, society is not perceived in terms of the caste hierarchy generated by brahmanical notions of the world. That is not to say that caste, as a system which provides social identity, is non-existent or is dissolved, rather, that relationships within that system are "reordered" in terms of the direction and definition that they receive via the figure of the king/deity. Perceptions about society and divinity are, therefore, in this sense co-terminous. On the other hand, Devnārāyaṇ's appellation and his inclusion into the "avatāra" sequence as well as the generally harmonized relationships between himself and his brothers would suggest a tendency towards the classical or puranic level of Hinduism.[60] But this feature may well be of marginal importance to members of the cult, adding only to its status and, as Blackburn claims, perhaps facilitating a broader identification among different groups in a large geographical region.[61] Its central features, *viz.*, the pastoral-feudal setting of the tale, the deification of mortal heroes (in the first part of the epic), and the perception of Devnārāyaṇ as a "divine" and almost "secular" king, who is "alive, attentive, ... and responsive" (Sontheimer 1989a: 205f.) to his devotees needs, emphasize the place of text and cult within the domain of folk religion.[62]

---

[59] Sontheimer (1989b: 301).

[60] Compared to the other names in the story, such as Sāḍū, Mādu, Chochū, Āmbā-Nimbā, Kānyo-Kiṣṇo, and Pīpal, Devnārāyaṇ's name stands out in its classical tone.

[61] See Blackburn *et al.* (1989: 8).

[62] For a discussion of the term folk religion in the Indian context, see Sontheimer

Note

The author is grateful to Professor Heidrun Brückner, University of Tübingen, and to Professor Veena Das, School of Sociology, Delhi University, for reading through and discussing earlier drafts of the paper with him.

Appendix

Three categories of Bhopās

1) The temple Bhopā resembles a "priest-custodian." He need not necessarily belong to the Gujar community. His duties include the performance of the daily *pūjā* and the organization of other religious festivals and rites. He must also perform life cycle rites for individual members of the community and function as care-taker of the *paṛ*, which is used by the Paṛ Bhopā. He may have disciples who assist him in the performance of rites.

2) Among the followers of Devnārāyaṇ there are ascetic groups, which form the Jamāt (Arabic/Persian: *jamā' at* - 'society,' 'corporation,' 'union,' 'federation,' etc.). Only members of the Gujar community may join the Jamāt. Among the three existing Jamāts, the Jamāt of Savāī Bhoj is the most strongly represented. Often the first born sons are given over to the order. The Jamāt, whose members observe a vow of celibacy, usually wander from village to village without having to perform any specific rites for the villagers.

3) Paṛ Bhopās recite the epic of Devnārāyaṇ with the help of a *paṛ* (a painted scroll which depicts scenes and characters from the epic). Usually there are two Bhopās who recite the epic, one is the main Bhopā, the Paṭāvi, and the other is his assistant, the Diyāla. (See

---

1989a: 204-206. In printed versions of the text there is an increasing emphasis on its classical associations. Thus, the story is entitled: "*Devnārāyaṇ avatāra kathā.*"

plate XIII). Paṛ Bhopās may belong to different communities - Rajput, Gujar or Kumahar. The profession is not necessarily hereditary, being based on an aptitude to sing and perform the epic.

References

Aarne, A. 1964. *Types of the folktale*. Helsinki.

Carman, J.B. and F.A. Marglin 1985. *Purity and auspiciousness in Indian society*. Leiden.

Asopa, J.N. 1976. *The origin of the Rajputs*. Jaipur: Rajasthan University.

Babb, L.A. 1986. *Redemptive encounters*. Berkeley: University of California Press.

Banerji, A.C. 1944. *Rajput Studies*. Calcutta.

Beck, B.E.F. 1982. *The three twins*. Bloomington: Indiana University Press.

Bingley, A.H. 1899/1978. *History, caste and culture of Jāts and Gūjars*. New Delhi.

Blackburn, S.H. 1985. Death and deification: Folk cults in Hinduism. In *History of Religions*, 24: 255-274.

Blackburn, S.H. and A.K. Ramanujan (eds.) 1986. *Another harmony: New essays in the folklore of India*. Berkeley: University of California Press.

Blackburn, S.H., P.J. Claus, J.B. Flueckiger, S.S. Wadley (eds.) 1989. *Oral epics in India*. Berkeley: University of California Press.

Burghart, R. 1978. Hierarchical models of the Hindu social system. In *Man*, 13: 519-536.

Burghart, R. and A. Cantlie (eds.) 1985. *Indian religion*. London.

Callewaert, W.M. (ed.) 1980. *Early Hindī devotional literature in current research*. Leuven.

Carstairs, M. 1961. *The Twice-Born*. Bloomington.

Census of India 1961. Vol. XIV, Part VII-B, Fairs and festivals of Rajasthan.

Cort, J. 1989. Review of T.N. Madan *Non Renunciation*. In *History of Religions* 29,1: 68-71.

Dandekar, R.N. 1963. *Insights into Hinduism*. Delhi.

Das, V. 1976. The uses of liminality: Society and cosmos in Hinduism. In *Contributions to Indian Sociology* (N.S.), 10: 245-263.

Id. 1977. *Structure and cognition*. Delhi.

De Vries, J. 1963. *Heroic song and heroic legend*. (Trans. B.J. Timmer). London and Oxford: Oxford University Press.

Dumont, L. 1972. *Homo Hierarchicus*. London: Paladin.

Dundes, A. (ed.) 1965. *The study of folklore*. Prentice Hall.

Id. 1980. The life of Jesus and the hero-pattern. In A. Dundes *Interpreting folklore.* Indiana University Press.

Id. 1984 (ed.) *Sacred narrative.* University of California, Berkeley.

Finnegan, R. 1977. *Oral Poetry.* Cambridge University Press.

Fürer-Haimendorf, C. von 1961. The historical value of Indian bardic literature. In C.H. Philips (ed.) *Historians of India, Pakistan and Ceylon.* London: Oxford University Press.

Gold, A. 1989. *Fruitful journeys. The ways of Rajasthani pilgrims.* Delhi: Oxford University Press.

Gonda, J. 1954. *Aspects of early Viṣṇuism.* Utrecht.

Hahn, G.J. von 1876. *Sagwissenschaftliche Studien.* Jena: F. Mauke.

Hiltebeitel, A. (ed.) 1989. *Criminal gods and demon devotees.* Albany: SUNY.

Jain, J. 1973. *Bavaji und Devi.* Wien: Europa Verlag.

Joshi, O.P. 1976. *Painted folklore and folklore painters of India.* Delhi.

Kavoori, P.S. 1991 Transhumance in Western

Rajasthan: Trends and transformations. In *Studies in History*, (New Series) Vol. VII,2: 255-278.

Leshnik, L.S. and G.D. Sontheimer (eds.) 1975. *Pastoralists and nomads in South Asia*. Wiesbaden.

Lewis, I.M. 1971. *Ecstatic religion: An anthropological study of spirit possession and shamanism*. Harmondsworth.

Lincoln, B. 1976. The Indo-European cattle raiding myth. In *History of Religions*, 16: 42-65.

Lingat, R. 1973. *The classical law of India*. (Trans. J.D.M. Derrett). Berkeley.

Majumdar, A.K. 1956. *The Chaulukyas of Gujarat. A survey of the history and culture of Gujarat from the middle of the 10th to the end of the 13th century*. Bombay.

Majumdar, R.C. (ed.) 1955. *The age of imperial Kanauj (750 - 1000 A.D.). (The history and culture of the Indian people, Vol. 4)*. Bombay.

Malik, A. 1990. The Puṣkara-Māhātmya: A short report. In H.T. Bakker (ed.) *The history of sacred places in India as reflected in traditional literature*. [Panels of the VIIth World Sanskrit Conference, Leiden 1987]. Leiden: E.J. Brill.

Marcus, G.E. and Cushman, D. 1982. Ethnographies as texts. In *American Review of Anthropology,* 11: 25-69.

Marglin, F.A. 1985. *Wives of the god-king*. Delhi.

Miller, J.C. 1980. Current investigations in the genre of Rajasthani *Paṛ* painting recitations. In W.M. Callewaert (ed.) *Early Hindī devotional literature in current research.* Leuven.

Murty, M.L.K. and G.D. Sontheimer 1980. Prehistoric background to pastoralism in the southern Deccan in the light of oral traditions and cults of some pastoral communities. In *Anthropos,* 75: 163-184.

Pandey, S.M. 1982. *The Hindi oral epic Canainī*. Allahabad.

Id. 1987. *The Hindi oral epic Lorikāyan.* Allahabad.

Propp, V. 1928/1968. *Morphology of the folktale.* Austin: University of Texas Press.

Puri, B.N. 1957. *The history of Gurjara-Pratihāras.* Bombay.

Ray, H.C. 1931-1936. *The dynastic history of Northern India, early and medieval period.* 2 Vols. Calcutta.

Raglan, Lord 1934. The hero of tradition. In *Folklore* 45: 212-231.

Rank, O. 1959. *The myth of the birth of the hero.* New York: Vintage.

Roghair, G.H. 1982. *The epic of Palnāḍu.* New York: Oxford University Press.

Sarkar, J. (s.d.) *A history of Dasnami Naga Sanyasis.* Allahabad.

Sharma, R.S. 1965. *Indian feudalism.* Calcutta.

Sharma, D.R. 1966. *Rajasthan through the ages.* Vol. I: From earliest times to 1316 A.D. Bikaner.

Singh, B. 1980. The Bagaṛāvat - a popular heroic narrative of Rājasthan. In W.M. Callewaert (ed.) *Early Hindī devotional literature in current research.* Leuven.

Smith, J.D. 1989. Scapegoats of the gods: The ideology of the Indian epics. In Blackburn *et al. Oral epics in India.* Berkeley: University of California Press.

Sontheimer, G.D. 1989a. Hinduism: The five components and their interaction. In G. D. Sontheimer and H. Kulke (eds.) *Hinduism reconsidered.* New Delhi: Manohar.

Id. 1989b. Between ghost and god: A folk deity of the Deccan. In A. Hiltebeitel (ed.) 1989.

Id. 1989c. The myth of the god and his two

wives: Two pastoral versions from Maharashtra. In R.K. Barz and M. Thiel-Horstmann (eds.) *Living texts from India*. Wiesbaden: Otto Harrasowitz.

Srivastava, S.L. 1974. *Folk culture and oral tradition (a comparative study of regions in Rajasthan and eastern U.P.)*. New Delhi: Abhinav Publications.

Suryavanshi, B.S. 1962. *The Abhiras*. Baroda.

Thompson, S. 1946. *The folktale*. New York.

Id. 1955-58. *Motif-Index of folk-literature*. 6 Vols., Indiana University Press.

Thompson, S. and W.E. Roberts 1960. *Types of Indic oral tales*. Helsinki.

Tod, J. 1829/1971. *Annals and antiquities of Rajasthan*. Delhi.

Vaidya, C.V. 1924. *History of medieval Hindu India*, Vol. II: Rajputs (A.D. 750-1000). Poona.

Vaudeville, C. 1975. The cowherd god in ancient India. In Leshnik and Sontheimer (eds.) *Pastoralists and nomads in South Asia*. Wiesbaden: Franz Steiner.

Van Kooij, K.R. 1972. *Worship of the goddess according to the Kālikāpurāṇa*. Leiden: E.J. Brill.

THE EPISODE OF THE GOLDEN ŚIVA IMAGE IN THE BAGAṚĀVAT

Bahadur Singh

On the 8th of March, 1979, at about 10 in the morning, the Bhopas Dhannā Rām and Jaya Rām began a recital of the Bagaṛāvat-Devnārāyaṇ Epic at the Rūpāyan Sansthān, Borundā, in the Jodhpur District of Rajasthan:

> *dhuṃdāḷāṃ dukh bhāṃjaṇā... vināyak siṃvarjau,* "...invoke Vināyak, ...the pot-bellied one who overcomes adversity."

Dhannā Rām and Jaya Rām continue invoking various other deities: Vidyā (Sarasvatī); Agni; Hanumān; Bhavānī; Brahmā-Viṣṇu-Maheśa; the Bhairavas, dark and fair; Mother Earth; Narasiṃha, the protector of Prahlāda; Dhruva; Rām and Lakṣmaṇ (but Sītā is conspicuously absent); and finally, Haṃsa.

It may be noted that the logic behind the selection of those deities and their sequence - Gaṇeśa apart, of course - is not clear, and it remains as much of a problem in the version of Pannā Rām and Durgā Rām (PD); note also that the latter two, "concentrate with devotion" on the main characters of the epic they go on to recite, whereas, Dhannā Rām and Jaya Rām (DJ) don't. That is to say, the very beginning of the recital poses a number of problems which still require a solution, only the present paper has a different aim.

Now to approach this aim, the story always begins with prose narration - and, I am afraid, this too poses a problem, for what may be the reason for an extensive *prose* introduction to an epic in *verse*? This does not, of course, detract from the interest and significance of the prose, and Dhannā Rām, the sole narrator of the prose, begins thus:

> *rājā ho bīsaḷ, jako choṭā bhāī hā māṃḍaḷdevjī...*
> "there was a king, Bīsaḷ, the younger brother was Māṃḍaḷdevjī. He said to him, 'O brother Māṃḍaḷ, go to Kathiawar and procure horses.' Then Māṃḍaḷdevjī set forth. He went to Kathiawar, *horses* he did not buy, but where there were good chances of water collecting, there he set about getting a tank constructed. He got it dammed well and fair, and after getting it dammed well and fair, he returned to Ajmer. The king asked, 'O brother Māṃḍaḷ, where are the horses?', whereupon he said, 'O Royal Court (= king), *horses* I haven't procured yet; in Mewāṛ, around the wells the fenugreek is waving in the breeze, when the Four Months (= the rainy season) arrives, then I shall bring the horses."[1]

Briefly, very briefly: Dhannā Rām continues with the tale of Māṃḍaḷ taking Bīsaḷ to Kaṭhiāwāṛ; upon being shown the tank, Bīsaḷ suspects that it was his own money that had been misspent to have it constructed, and in order to find out the truth, he challenges Māṃḍaḷ to cross the tank riding his horse, saying that Māṃḍaḷ would drown if he had lied. Māṃḍaḷ does cross the tank, but he suddenly reflects that Bīsaḷ, his very brother, has wished his death; thereupon, he turns his horse to recross the tank, and only half way through he deliberately drowns because the very idea of seeing his brother again is hateful to him.

---

[1] That is to say, Māṃḍaḷ hides behind the excuse of the imminent fenugreek crop, which is harvested before the rains. — For the text see Appendix.

Shortly after, Māṃḍaḷ's wife gives birth to a son, Harisiṃh, and Harisiṃh, once he is young man, slays a tiger which has become a menace in Ajmer and its surroundings. Carrying the tiger's head and the still blood-smeared sword, Harisiṃh goes to the Pushkar lake to wash the sword. It is then midnight, and Līlā Sevṛī, a pious young woman, who has come to the lake for a holy bath, becomes pregnant upon seeing the reflection of the tiger's head appear upon Harisiṃh's body. She then gives birth to a boy, appositely given the name Bāghsiṃh (Bāgh = tiger). Now Bāghsiṃh, precisely because of his tiger's head, finds nobody willing to marry him, and yet by a trick (which is most entertaining and funny, but too long to be recounted here) he does manage it, and even gets 12 brides. These brides give birth to 24 sons in all, known in our epic as the Bagaṛāvat brothers, who become cattle breeders.

We have now reached the point of the story that directly leads to the argument of the present paper. The observations which now follow are based upon the two versions of the story already noted, both recorded at the Rūpāyan Sansthān. One is of 15 hours duration, the other 25.

For the purposes of the present paper, I shall limit myself largely to two questions, that is, to the problems of composition and to the ethics which the episode of the golden Śiva image reflects.

In descriptive terms, it is best to begin with our episode as it is narrated in the PD version:

One of the cows of the Bagaṛāvat brothers returns home without any milk. Savāī Bhoj, one of the brothers, follows her and discovers that an ascetic living in the Nāg mountain consumes her milk. The ascetic understands that Savāī Bhoj desires compensation and gives him 10 seers of food grain. On the way home, Savāī Bhoj feels that for a large family like his, 10 seers are of no real help and, instead, he feeds pigeons with the grain. The next morning, he sees that the few grains that had remained attached to his blanket have turned into diamonds. He now realises that the ascetic is endowed with supernatural powers, and he returns to him to become his disciple.

Since it is the Holi festival, the ascetic tells Savāī Bhoj to heat oil in a cauldron. He also tells him that he has to go on his alms-round, gives him four keys, warning him at the same time not to open the four chambers the keys are for. Savāī Bhoj opens them, of course. In the first, there are three heads which laugh at him and tell him that the ascetic would slay him too, as he has slain them. In the second chamber, he finds the goddess Durgā, who tells him that she will become his wife for 12 months if he survives. In the third chamber, there is a mare, and she tells Bhoj that if he survives, she would carry him on her back for 12 years. In the fourth chamber, he finds Nārad, the bard, who tells him that if he survives, he will spread his glory throughout the world.

On his return, the ascetic asks Bhoj if he has opened the chambers. Bhoj says, no, he has not. The ascetic proposes that they circumambulate the cauldron. Once Bhoj is in the front, the ascetic tries to push him into it, but he does not succeed. Bhoj realises the peril he is in, and manages to push the ascetic into the cauldron instead. The ascetic turns into a golden image weighing three-and-a-half maunds (about 140 kg). Now Mahādev appears and grants Bhoj the image, saying that the Bagaṛāvat brothers will survive for 12 years and that during this period the immense wealth in the form of the golden image will endure for them, without ever getting exhausted.

In terms of narrative composition, the point to note here is that the motif of the four chambers and the golden image are, in essence, a prefiguration of things to come in the entire Bagaṛāvat-Devnārāyaṇ story: Durgā is Rāṇī Jaimatī in the Bagaṛāvat and causes the destruction of the brothers; the mare, *baṃvḷīghoṛī*, is central to both the Bagaṛāvat and Devnārāyaṇ sections; the bard is Chochu Bhāṭ, and a key figure in the Devnārāyaṇ story; and, of course, the story can only proceed at all because the heads of the first chamber put Bhoj on guard against the ascetic; finally the immense wealth in the form of the golden image leads to the excesses which bring about the destruction of the Bagaṛāvats.

But what is the compositional or narrative purpose of the ascetic giving Bhoj the keys and telling him not to open the chambers? The immediate answer is clear: the ascetic wants to tempt Bhoj to open the chambers and thus be warned of the peril he stands in. But again, why did the ascetic at all wish to warn Bhoj?

The DJ version gives us additional information in this regard. For in this version we not only find the pivotal elements of PD, but also the following:

The ascetic, confronted with Bhoj wishing to become his disciple, re-evokes the memory of an earlier birth in which he was an Aghorī and had, in order to perform his rites, fried and consumed 23 of the 24 brothers — the later Bagaṛāvats — who had then been his disciples. The 24th brother — the later Bhoj — survived because the rites were complete even without him; the Aghorī promises that in the Kaliyuga he, in his turn, will be fried and "consumed," as it were, by all the 24 Bagaṛāvats.

In other words, the conduct of the ascetic in the PD version becomes fully intelligible if we turn to the DJ version and argue that the ascetic wants to be slain in order to fulfil a promise he had given in an earlier birth. Note too that it is an ending which is largely equivalent, for the ascetic too is fried, though not consumed literally — the Bagaṛāvats are not Aghorīs! — but possessed in the form of the gold into which the ascetic changes.

At this point, it is necessary to avoid coming to all too simple conclusions. In theory, the DJ version could be the original and the PD version its abbreviation; in theory again, the DJ version could be an explication of the all too brief PD version; and, of course, all of us can easily imagine other possibilities. But the point is, I think, that we have no objective means to prove that any one possibility is historically the true one. We must be content with the fact that there are versions which are mutually elucidatory.

I conclude this part of the discussion with two more examples of the sort of many problems of interpretation any student of the Bagaṛāvat is faced with. What is the significance of the number 12? Why will Durgā be Bhoj's wife only for 12 months? Again, to put an earlier question from another point of view: why does versification commence only when the story of the golden image begins? I am afraid, at the moment at least, I have no answer to these and other similar questions.

Let us turn now to the most interesting notions of ethics our episode contains. It is common that everywhere in India all life is described as impermanent, passing, transient. And our episode, too, subscribing to this idea, illustrates the passing nature of everything and everybody by saying, for example, that kings and warriors and saints and ascetics both Muslim and Hindu have all perished; even Karṇa of the Mahābhārata, even Rāvaṇa of the Rāmāyaṇa. But the conclusion drawn from this is to enjoy life, to exploit the immense wealth in the form of the golden image. That is, in the Bagaṛāvat we find a strand of Indian thought which is hardly ever mentioned but is central to it, for while non-attachment is certainly important in India so is desire for worldly success. And in the Bagaṛāvat it is the very impermanence, the short duration of everything, which is the main argument for enjoying life. Let us take the following example illustrating impermanence:

kesariyā rājkaṃwār, kaṃwrāṃ cejārā (cālyā re giyā)
giyā cuṇāwaṇhār (dādā cejārā cālyā o giyā)
giyā cuṇāwaṇhār mardāṃ lākhaṃ par lekho (karai(ṛ)tā)
kāṃī legā lār (dādā lākhāṃ par lekhau re karai)
kāṃī legā lār wai to lankāpat ko (rāṃvaṇ whiyau)
giyau lank nai choḍ (mardāṃ lankāpat rāvaṇ ai whiyau)
giyau lank nai choḍ jamaṛā āyā o rājā (rām kā)
legā chin meṃ ṭol ḍāngiyā (āyā o rājā rām kā)
legā chin meṃ ṭol jyāṃkai sūrjī rasoṛai re (tāptau)

cāṃd cirāgai loy (jyāṃkai sūraj jī rasoṛai re tāptau)
cāṃd cirāgai loy jyāṃkai indrājā (pāṇī o bharai)
pawan buārau kāṛh (jyāṃkai bemātā poṛhyā re daḷai)
pawan buārau kāṛh (rāṃvaṇ kā hāthī o raigā hīṃḍtā)
ghoṛā pāyagāṃ māṃy (rāṃvaṇ kā hāthi o raigā hīṃḍtā)
ghoṛā pāyagāṃ māṃy (maṃdodar raigī o bādaḷmail meṃ)[2]
kop gayau ho bhagwān rānī nai rākhī bādaḷmail meṃ...

Translated broadly this means:

> ".... the masons are dead, the owners are dead, what have the millionaires carried with them while departing this life? There was Rāvaṇa, king of Laṅkā. When the messengers of the God of Death appeared he had to abandon Laṅkā at once. And this was the Rāvaṇa for whom the Sun provided fire in the kitchen and the moon provided light, for whom Indra was the water-carrier, Wind dusted his house, Bemātā, the fate-goddess, ground grains for him! (And he died) leaving behind his swinging elephants and horses all ready for service, and Mandodarī entirely alone in her sky-scraping palace. When God showed anger, the queen was left alone in her sky-scraping palace."

Let me adduce one more example which has the merit, besides, of helping us draw a literary parallel. In the proclamation about impermanence, we also read:

ūgyā sau nar aṃthwai, phūlyā sau kumḷāy
cuṇiyauṛā mandar ḍhah paṛai, dhartī meṃ
jaḷmai so nar mar jāy.

The translation is again roughly as follows:

> "Whatever rises, whatever blossoms, withers; palaces constructed collapse; man born on earth, dies."

---

[2] The bracketed text is recited by the supporting Bhopo, Mr. Jaya Rām.

Now this very passage is found in Kabīr also, where we read:

jo ūgyā so āṃthve, phūlyā so kumilāi
jo ciṇiyāṃ so ḍhahi paṛai, jo āyā so jāi[3]

How to explain this close correspondence, not only here but also in a few other instances? Here again we are faced with the problem of proof; and, perhaps, we should assume that both Kabīr and the Bagaṛāvat are simply using popular maxims. But if this is true, where is the exact dividing line between 'literary' literature, which is what Kabīr is taught to be, and folk/oral literature?

But to return to our starting point which was the ethics of the Bagaṛāvat. Kabīr teaches impermanence in order to exhort men to abandon wordly ties; the Bagaṛāvat, on the other hand, is true to the strand which values the enjoyment of life; and because of this too, the Bagaṛāvat is of great interest, for it saves us from a very one-sided view of Indian ethics as teaching only non-attachment to the world.

To avoid misunderstandings, I should add that the Bagaṛāvat demands that wealth be used not only for one's personal pleasure but also for the well-being of others, for money should be distributed and wells and tanks should be constructed. Certainly this, too, aims at personal glory, but the point is that the Bagaṛāvat does not stop at merely exhorting personal pleasure.

There is one more point in this connection which I should not omit. Our present knowledge of the Aghorīs is mostly horrid, and let me sum up this knowledge with a quotation from Jonathan Parry's essay "Sacrificial death and the necrophagous ascetic": "The 'true' Aghori is entirely indifferent to what he consumes, drinks not only liquor but urine, and eats not only meat but excrement, vomit and the putrid flesh of corpses"... "Or again, Tod (1839: 84) reports

[3] Shukla *et al*. 1969: 295.

that, 'one of the Deora chiefs told me that... when conveying the body of his brother to be burnt, one of these monsters crossed the path of the funeral procession, and begged to have the corpse, saying that it would make excellent "chatni", or condiment'".[4]

But the Aghorī in our episode is different even though he did indeed eat up the 23 brothers; for he wishes to compensate for his act, and obviously he looks upon this act as a misdeed. His is an example of the ethics of reciprocation, and this shows there is still much to be discovered about the Aghorīs and their view of life.

Let me conclude this part of my paper on a general note. The episode of the golden image is an excellent example of a certain technique of communication, for, in order to elucidate impermanence, the singer of the narrative draws upon various literatures and religions of India, citing the Rāmāyaṇa, the Mahābhārata, Śaivism, Vaiṣṇavism, and Muslim asceticism. It would be interesting to know if other oral literatures of India too use this technique and to what extent.

Now some remarks on the *paṛ*. It is rather difficult to explain all the principles of its composition; therefore I shall confine myself to a few points: The top strip from the left is clearly the area where the narrative begins, for here we find Gaṇeśa, incarnations of Viṣṇu and other deities. Immediately below this strip, we find the golden image of our episode, and, this too, is logical, for as we have seen, the episode is the key to the story, both as it is narrated and as it is depicted on the *paṛ*. (See plate XI). It is interesting to note that most of these scenes regarding the deities and other heavenly bodies are painted on the top part of the *paṛ*, which could be compared to heaven in the Hindu cosmology. But there are, of course, exceptions.

---

[4] Parry 1982: 89.

The centre is always reserved for the key figures of the narrative, Devnārāyaṇ and his four brothers in our *paṛ*. (See plate XII). At the area around the face of Devnārāyaṇ we always find the details regarding the production of the *paṛ*: the painter's name, the ruler of the area, the date, at times the name of the patron, the price paid, etc.

It is of course clear that no *paṛ* can depict each and every element of the narrative; a *paṛ* has to be selective and has to include only the major elements. Some of the scenes on the *paṛ* are even used by the singers to illustrate more than one narrative event during the recitation. The *paṛ* does not depict events in their narrative sequence and the Bhopo moves along the *paṛ* and connects scenes with each other although they stand farther apart on the *paṛ* itself.

The colour distribution seems to follow two principles, the natural colour and the iconographic colour. Thus water is blue, the tiger is yellow, the buffalo is black, trees and plants are green. On the other hand, Kṛṣṇa is blue. But then the boar of the Varāha incarnation is also blue and Devnārāyaṇ's steed is always green. In this regard, I am afraid, our knowledge is still limited.[5]

Appendix

rājā ho Bīsaḷ. jako choṭā bhāī ha Māṃḍaḷdejī. jakānai kahyo re bhāī Māṃḍaḷ! kāṭhiyāwāṛ meṃ jāo jo ghoṛā lāo kharīd ar. janāṃ Māṃḍaḷdejī baṭhūṃ vhir whiyā. jako kāṭhiyāwāṛ giyā. ghoṛā to konī kharīdiyā. jaṭhai pāṃṇī ro āccho moko dekhiyo jako talāb baṃdhāwṇau surū kar diyo. baṃdhā baṃdhāya khūb. khūb baṃdhā baṃdhūr pāchā Ajmer āyā. rājā būjhyau re bhāī Māṃḍaḷ! ghoṛā kaṭhai hai? to kayo darbār ghoṛā to abār lāyo konī Mewāṛ meṃ berā māthai methī rijkā khāwai. chaumāso ā hī janāṃ lāwāṃ.

---

[5] I am most grateful to Peter J. Claus and S.A. Srinivasan with both of whom I could variously discuss the argument of the present paper.

References

Parry, J. 1982. Sacrificial death and the necrophagous ascetic. In Bloch, M. and J. Parry (eds.) *Death and the regeneration of life*. London: Cambridge University Press.

Shukla, S. and R.P. Chaturvedi 1968. *Kabirgranthavali.* Prakashan Kendra: Aminabad, Lucknow.

Tod, J. 1839. *Travels in Western India*. London: W.H. Allen.

ITINERANT VAIṢṆAVITE GENEALOGISTS OF THE GANGES BASIN

Richard Burghart

The quality of a person's ancestry serves to establish his credibility in Hindu society: the credibility of his word, of his fitness to act, of the fitness of his daughters for marriage and so on. It is no surprise that certain castes, or lineages within a caste, are authorized to record and state the authenticity of one's pedigree. There are, however, few ethnographic studies on the organization and role of such genealogists in Hindu society. The accounts at hand include the Ghaṭakas of middle period Bengal (Inden 1976: 137-42), the Pañjikars who serve the Brahmans of Mithila (Jha 1980), the Vahivanca Barots of Gujarat (Shah and Shroff 1959) and the Kāyastha Munshijis retained by Gayāwāl Paṇḍas (Vidyarthi 1961: 71-82). Interestingly, such services are provided not only for Hindu householders but also for ascetics who have, in some sense, renounced the temporal world. The aim of this paper is to describe the itinerant Brahman genealogists who travel throughout the Ganges basin recounting the history of the Vaiṣṇavite redemptive traditions and telling tales of Vaiṣṇavite saints. In the first section, I present some details on the history and social organization of this caste; and, in the second section, I describe their work as genealogists. There is considerable ambiguity in the purposes to which genealogical knowledge is put. On the one hand, genealogists keep records in order to fix identities, thereby enabling others to control membership and entitlements within Vaiṣṇavism; on the other hand, they use their knowledge to magnify persons, make saintly reputations and in this way transform identities. In the third section, I describe both these aspects of a Vaiṣṇavite genealogist's work; and, in conclusion, analyse them in the light of the comparative material on the Ghaṭakas, Pañjikars, Vahivanca Barots and Gayāwāl Munshijis.

I

Throughout the Ganges basin an itinerant Brahman caste, known as Bhurā Bhaṭṭ, travel from monastery to monastery praising the forms and incarnations of Viṣṇu, reciting Vaiṣṇavite religious mysteries, telling tales of Vaiṣṇavite saints and keeping the records of pupillary succession for Vaiṣṇavite abbots. Their patrons and audiences are exclusively ascetics of the *catuḥ sampradāya* — that is, the four Vaiṣṇavite redemptive traditions founded in the name of Rāmānand (in some accounts, Rāmānuja), Nimbārk, Viṣṇusvāmī and Mādhavācārya. The caste of Vaiṣṇavite genealogists is not numerous and their future is uncertain; but they can still be heard within the courtyards of monasteries, particularly on the occasion of major festivals.

How the Bhurā Bhaṭṭ came upon their role as Vaiṣṇavite genealogists is explained by the Bhaṭṭ themselves as follows:

> Many years ago there was a ruler of Hastinapur, called King Piṇḍ, who gave in alms 56 crore rupees to a Brahman from Bhim. The Brahman disposed of the gift with alarming rapidity, throwing money onto friends and relatives and buying all sorts of things. Within a short while only eight crore remained. The Brahman's prolifigacy came to the attention of King Piṇḍ, who happened by one day. Upset to see how the Brahman squandered his gift in such an unmeritorious way, he demanded its immediate reimbursement. The Brahman was shocked to hear that the king sought to reclaim his original gift, and anyways how could he come up with the missing 48 crore rupees in a matter of days? He went

around to the people to whom he had previously given money, asking for its return, but they refused to come to his aid or they had already spent it. In despair the Brahman slipped away to Kāsi, where he awaited his death on Maṇikarṇa Ghāṭ.

At that time King Vikramajīt of Ujjain was a very old man who had come to Kāsi to spend his final days. One evening, while walking along Maṇikarṇa Ghāṭ, he heard someone muttering from the shadows:

> Hunger pain, mental pain, bodily pain, the pain of a bad man's words;
> I live in pain, the pain adds to my pain, as I await my painful end.

Hearing these words, King Vikramajīt stopped and asked the man what could possibly have happened to him to cause such despair. The Brahman told him his story. King Vikramajīt was amazed that the Brahman had been so fortunate as to receive 56 crore rupees and then to suffer the misfortune of having the donor demand its return. Wishing to right the situation, the aged ruler immediately gave the Brahman nine times 56 crore rupees and then led him away to the nearby Pañcbaṭṭi Kuṭī where lived Svāmī Rāmānand.

Svāmī Rāmānand enjoined the Brahman never again to accept monetary gifts from householders. In future he was to accept only firewood and water from pure householders. For money and grain he was to rely solely on gifts from ascetics of the four Vaiṣṇavite traditions: the Rāmānandīs, Nimbārkis, Visnusvāmīs and Mādhavācāryas. In order to derive his livelihood he, and his descendants, would have the authority to visit each Vaiṣṇavite monastery once a year in order to recite the mysterious origin of Vaiṣṇavism and to recount the pedigree of the abbot. In the fulfillment of this duty he may receive a token of the abbot's pleasure *(kuśī)* and expect a parting gift *(bidāī)*. He can visit the same monastery more than once a year but is entitled to only one parting gift *per annum*. From Kāsi the Brahman returned to his ancestral home in Bhim where he met his relatives, repaid King Piṇḍ's gift and began to serve as the Vaiṣṇavite genealogist. His descendents thrived,

> spreading across the Aryan heartland from the Himalayas to the Vindhya mountains.

I shall return to this story in the third section below. For the moment, let me state that the several genealogists whom I met in Janakpur (Dhanusa District, Nepal) came from Gaya district, Bihar, and they claimed that all Bhurā Bhaṭṭ, including themselves, originate from twenty-seven households of Gaur Brahmans in Bhim (Ramgarh *thānā*, near Jaipur) and that these households are all related to the Brahman who had been brought back from the edge of despair by King Vikramajīt and subsequently authorized by Svāmī Rāmānand to serve as genealogist for the *catuḥ sampradāya*.

Bhurā Bhaṭṭ learn their trade as young men from their father, grandfather or uncles. At the time of their initiation into the Sacred Thread, in the course of which they become ritually Brahman, they are also intitiated into the mysteries of Vaiṣṇavism. The same person (usually a paternal grandfather) undertakes the role of the guru in both rituals. The Vaiṣṇavite initiation is that which is appropriate for a householder, not a celibate ascetic. That is, the Bhurā Bhaṭṭ adept receives the *tulsī* necklace, the forehead *tilak* (not the 'twelve *tilak*') and the Rām mantra (without the preliminary *oṁ* used by celibate ascetics). This guru-disciple link doubles as the line through which the Bhaṭṭ may expect to inherit his family's records of Vaiṣṇavite pupillary succession, which become later the source of his livelihood.

After his initiation a young Bhaṭṭ accompanies his father or grandfather on his travels and in this way perpetuates his family's contacts with ascetics. Married Bhaṭṭs often travel with their wives and children, hiring bullock carts where necessary to make good deficiencies in local transport. In a joint family of three generations at least one generation, however, remains behind in the village, looking after the house and property.

Although the abbots of Vaiṣṇavite monasteries are *jajmān* for Brahman priests and patrons of numerous servant and artisan castes, their relationships with Bhurā Bhaṭṭ are not of the so-called *jajmānī* type. Genealogists regularly visit the same monastaries, where they are remembered, but they have at present no exclusive, hereditary contractual arrangement with particular abbots. This, of course, does not deny the possibility that Bhurā Bhaṭṭ have certain arrangements among themselves. Unfortunately I overlooked to ask whether Bhaṭṭs have divided upper India and Nepal into regions, each being under the authority of a particular lineage. Nevertheless the genealogists seem to have a regional competence. The Bhurā Bhaṭṭ, who visit Janakpur, have records for Bihar, southeastern Nepal and eastern Uttar Pradesh, including Ayodhya; but not for Rajasthan, the Indian Himalayas and central India, including Citrakut, where important Rāmānandī monasteries are also situated. In short, either by caste arrangement or practical difficulties the Bhaṭṭ seem to be regional in their coverage of monasteries.

According to their tale of entitlement Bhurā Bhaṭṭ may visit Vaiṣṇavite monasteries throughout the year, but they are entitled to receive from the abbot only once a year a token of his pleasure *(kuśī)* and a parting gift *(bidāī)*. In point of fact Bhurā Bhaṭṭ visit the monasteries of Vaiṣṇavite pilgrimage centres at the time of major festivals: the Janakpur monasteries for the Marriage of Rām and Sītā, the Ayodhya monasteries for the Birth of Rām Candra, the Vrindaban monasteries for the Swing Festival, and so on. At the conclusion of a major festival the genealogist, together with his family, makes his way in the direction of the next big religious fair, stopping off at the various Vaiṣṇavite monasteries that lie on his route. At each place he recounts the lives of saints and recites Vaiṣṇavite mysteries and, at the same time, keeps himself informed of local events and updates his books. Genealogists are fed out of the same monastery charity kitchen as are visiting ascetics; and the two gifts they expect from their host — the token of pleasure and the departure gift — usually amount to no more than a few rupees. The Bhaṭṭ, whom I met in Janakpur, recalled past times when their caste members received munificent gifts from abbots. None of them were satisfied with their present condition.

In explaining their caste duties to me, Bhurā Bhaṭṭ stressed their double identity as Gaur Brahmans and Vaiṣṇavite devotees. The significance of this double identity, formed in adolescence at the time of the Sacred Thread ceremony, can be seen in their fourfold classification of genealogists. I was informed of the existence of four different castes of Bhaṭṭ, depending upon the ritual status of the Bhaṭṭ's patron: Brahma Bhaṭṭ, Khuda Bhaṭṭ, Betāl Bhaṭṭ and Bhurā Bhaṭṭ. Brahma Bhaṭṭ and Khuda Bhaṭṭ record the genealogies of householders, the former for Hindu householders and the latter for Muslims. Betāl Bhaṭṭ and Bhurā Bhaṭṭ keep the records of pupillary succession for ascetics: the former for Daśanāmi Saṃnyāsī Śaivites and the latter for the Vaiṣṇavites of the *catuḥ sampradāya*.

Setting aside the genealogists for Muslims — who are themselves Muslim —, the other three castes of Bhaṭṭ all claim to be Gaur Brahmans. The Śaivite and Vaiṣṇavite Bhaṭṭs, however, claim by virtue of their initiation into the mysteries of the Śaivite and Vaiṣṇavite religious traditions, to be Ādi-Gaur Brahmans — that is, Primal Gaur Brahmans — and thus to be separate from the Brahma Bhaṭṭ. As for the Ādi-Gaur, they see themselves as comprising two lineages: the Betāl Bhaṭṭ who keep the genealogies of the Daśanāmi Saṃnyāsīs and the Burā Bhaṭṭ who do the same for the four main Vaiṣṇavite traditions. In the same way that Bhurā Bhaṭṭ claim to have received their caste entitlement from Rāmānand, so the Betāl Bhaṭṭ claim to have received theirs from Śaṃkarācārya. Both these lineages see themselves as being superior to Brahma Bhaṭṭ, who keep records for mere householders and who lack the dual initiation of those who serve ascetic patrons.

The intra-caste superiority of the Ādi-Gaur Brahmans is signified and enforced by restrictions on connubial and commensal exchange. Ādi-Gaur Brahmans do not intermarry with Brahma Bhaṭṭ. Bhurā and Betāl Bhaṭṭ may, however, marry one another (although such arrangements were said to be rare, for the two lineages work from different books, have different ascetic patrons and go on different itineraries). In order not to present themselves as 'greedy' mendicants, I was further informed, that at the time of marriage, Ādi-Gaur Brahmans accept from the bride's father no dowry and only 1.25 rupees in *tilak*. In a similar vein Bhurā and Betāl Bhaṭṭ do not accept *kaccā* food or cash gifts from Brahma Bhaṭṭ, for such observances would go against Svāmī Rāmānand's injunction that they accept no religious gifts *(dān)*, other than firewood and water, from pure householders. Predictably Bhurā Bhaṭṭ accept *kaccā* food from Betāl Bhaṭṭ (and vice versa). It is interesting to note, however, that Rāmānandī ascetics do not accept *kaccā* food from Daśanāmi ascetics (but not vice versa).

It may be fitting to conclude this section by mentioning how scrupulous the genealogists were in their relationship with me and unscrupulous they were to one another. For several weeks I worked separately with two Bhurā Bhaṭṭ and one Betāl Bhaṭṭ, listening to their tales and recording the guru-disciple succession of some six hundred Rāmānandī and Daśanāmi monasteries in Uttar Pradesh, Bihar, West Bengal and southern Nepal. Being an untouchable European householder, it was rather outside the genealogists' remit to impart their knowledge to me or to accept any form of payment. Each was willing to reveal some of his knowledge, but not to let on that he was doing so. We could not be seen together in public. Into a rented hotel room I invited a local Rāmānandī ascetic whom I respected as my guru and who was willing to collude with me in my purpose to reconstruct the sacred history of Janakpur. The Bhaṭṭ sat facing the Rāmānandī and recited his tales and genealogies while I sat out of view behind the Bhaṭṭ, taking notes from what I 'overheard'. At the end of the day I, as a householder, offered money as a religious gift *(dān)* to the ascetic who promptly used the money to offer a token of his pleasure *(kuśī)* and a departure gift *(bidāī)* to the Bhaṭṭ. I had to swear myself to confidentiality, never to mention the name of any Bhaṭṭ nor to publish the genealogical material in a usable form. Each genealogist feared that I was acting in cahoots with his rivals, using me to fill in the gaps of their knowledge. Each genealogist was extremely jealous of his notebooks and dismissive of the knowledge of all other genealogists, claiming the others to be totally incompetent and unreliable. The fact that I relied separately upon three different genealogists, seeking in this way to corroborate each other's testimony for my historical research, drove them to desperation. My working methods excited their jealousy and exacerbated their rivalry. Meanwhile, they tried to drive me to desperation by inventing all kinds of stories of ongoing court cases involving abbots where their expert testimony was urgently awaited. At the end of every day in the little hotel room a drama unfolded in which their professional duty was pitted against my desire for knowledge. Desire eventually triumphed, but only by revealing itself with greater and greater tokens of pleasure.

II

The primary duty of the Bhurā Bhaṭṭ is to record the guru-disciple succession at Vaiṣṇavite monasteries of the *catuḥ sampradāya.* There are two types of pupillary relationships that are of consequence. The first is that which binds an ascetic to his preceptor guru *(dikṣa guru)* who bestows the redemptive mantra. The mantra is essential for the ascetic's ultimate release from transience, but it does not, in itself, have any methodological import. More important is the optional, secondary initiation, from one's doctrinal guru *(sādhak guru)* in the course of which one is entitled and instructed in a particular spiritual discipline. So-called Rasik ascetics, who follow a devotional path, undergo a secondary initiation in the course of which they receive a *sambandh patra* from their doctrinal guru. The *sambandh patra* grants them access to personal service at their redemptive deity's celestial palace. So-called Renouncer ascetics receive the sacred ashes, together with the mantra by which the ashes are consecrated, from their doctrinal guru. Out of all these types of guru-disciple relationships, the disciple who has been designated to succeed his guru to the abbotship is of central importance for Bhurā Bhaṭṭ. In the case of sedentary Vaiṣṇavites the abbot designates his successor from among those disciples for whom he was the preceptor guru. For itinerant Rāmānandīs, nearly all of whom are so-called Renouncers, the abbots of other itinerant monasteries elect a deceased abbot's successor from among those candidates for whom the deceased abbot was the doctrinal guru. Thus the Bhurā Bhaṭṭ aim to keep records of pupillary succession for sedentary preceptor gurus and itinerant doctrinal gurus.

In the past Bhurā Bhaṭṭ served as expert witnesses in disputes concerning rightful accession to the abbotship. They regularly attended the Kumbh *melā,* held triennially at Hardwar, Prayag, Ujjain and Nasik, where internal disputes among Vaiṣṇavite ascetics were resolved, and they also gave testimony in disputes settled at royal courts. I was informed by the two Bhurā Bhaṭṭ who visited Janakpur that their caste members still serve as expert witnesses in succession disputes. These would be civil disputes brought by one disciple against another. For this purpose Bhaṭṭs make some effort to keep their records up-to-date, their annual tour of monasteries serving not only for the recitation of tales and genealogies and the receipt of gifts but also for recording new information on monastic succession.

Bhurā Bhaṭṭ jealously keep their records. I was allowed only a fleeting glance in which I discerned that relations of succession were listed vertically and relations of generation horizontally, but nothing more. Bhaṭṭ do, however, prepare written genealogies for the benefit of the abbot who is their host. Such genealogies, called *praṇālī* (literally, a 'stream' of spiritual descendancy) are represented diagrammatically as follows:

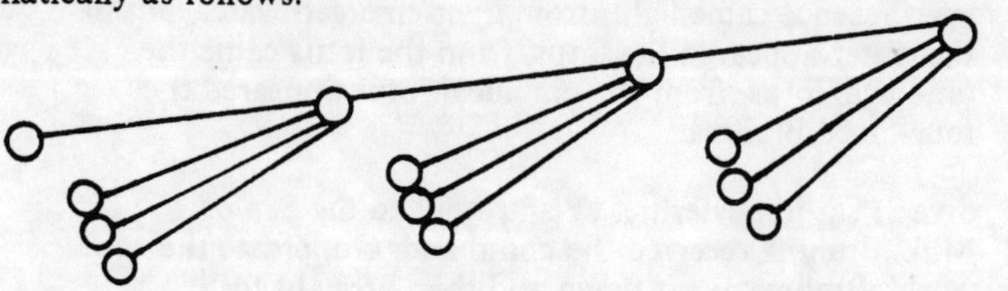

More common than a written genealogy is a formal recitation of the abbot's spiritual ancestry *(utpatti)* in front of the abbot and assembled ascetics in the monastery compound. The recitations I witnessed took place in Rāmānandī monasteries at mid-morning while the cook prepared the *rājbhog* for Rām and Sītā and groups of ascetics sat in the courtyard — chatting among themselves, smoking *gāñjā*, engaging in individual acts of devotion, or possibly receiving a visit from a devotee. In their midst a visiting Bhaṭṭ would stand up and declaim in a loud voice the origin of the Rāmānandī religious tradition. As the impact of the voice and message spread, everyone would fall silent. The end of the recitation would be greeted by exclamations of "Jay Rām Jī", and the gift of a rupee or two from the abbot as token of his pleasure.

These narratives may be conveniently divided into three sections. The Bhaṭṭ recounts, in the first section, the emergence of the universe; in the second, the genealogical history of the redemptive tradition from its origin to the time of the Kali Age preceptors; and in the third the transmission of the mantra is recounted from these preceptors down to the present day. Material could be substituted from within, but not between, the first and second sections of the narrative.

An example of the cosmogonic section is translated below:

> Out of emptiness appeared great emptiness, from great emptiness appeared ultimate emptiness, from ultimate emptiness came inner emptiness, from inner emptiness appeared everpresence. From everpresence came light, from light emerged water, out of the water appeared the lotus, from the lotus came the umbilical lotus, from the umbilical lotus appeared the four-faced Brahma.
>
> Siva Jī sat in austerities. Visnu went to the Sea of Milk. Brahmā received the command. Go, create the world. Brahmā Jī sat down and then brought forth the earth below and the heaven above. Then he created the

moon and sun and in the four directions upon the earth
he created the 8,400,000 beings.

Then follows the second section in which the Bhurā Bhaṭṭ recounts the origin of a Vaiṣṇavite religious tradition and its early stages of pupillary succession. Here again some variation is possible, but as a redemptive tradition its origin must lie in eternity. Taking Brahmā to be the endpoint of the first section, one possible starting point of the second section are Brahmā's four 'mind-born' sons: Sanak, Sanandan, Sanātan and Sanatkumar. These sons were 'mind-born' (that is, not born of Gāyatrī and Sāvitrī). Rather than have offspring, they have remained sexually continent, thereby retaining their youth. They are almost as old as the universe but are envisaged as young boys, seemingly five years of age, dressed in a *kaupīna* style of loincloth and sacred thread, and carrying a staff and water pot. The four Sankādik are the original Bairāgī, each of whom started one of the redemptive traditions which became known in the Kali Age through the teachings of Rāmānand, Nimbārk, Mādhavācārya and Viṣṇusvāmī. A variant middle section is the account of the transmission of the Rām mantra down through the ages. This begins, invariably, with the heavenly Rām revealing his personal mantra to his spouse Sītā who reveals it to her devotee Hanuman who then tells Brahmā who passes it down to Vasiṣṭha who gives it to Parāśara who gives it to Vyāsdeva and so on down through the generations to Svāmī Rāmānand in the Kali Age.

The third section traces the lines of pupillary succession from the founder of the religious tradition in the Kali Age, down to the guru of the abbot before whom the Bhaṭṭ makes his recitation. There is, in theory, no scope for substitution in this section. Many abbots know the details of their pupillary succession, and any Bhaṭṭ who wavered from the recognized line would lose credibility. The Bhaṭṭ's recitation of the third section supports the view that the abbot listens to the genealogy not in order to come to know his ancestry, but rather to hear it as a performance. The significance of the recitation, therefore, lies, not in making known the unknown, but in uttering aloud what is already commonly known. I shall return to this point in conclusion below.

Bhurā Bhaṭṭ also recount informally, but in public, the life histories of Rāmānandī ascetics. These tales may be of great saints who are remembered throughout the Ganges basin, or the tales may be of more local significance, such as the circumstances surrounding the founding of his host monastery and the life history of the early abbots. Two possible themes structure such tales: either that the founder received the deity's grace in establishing the monastery at that place (e.g. the deity appeared in a dream to the ascetic at that place or a form of the deity emerged out of the ground at that place); or the founder himself was a liberated ascetic such that his everpresent form still consecrates the place as a *siddha sthān*.

An example of the latter theme is the story of the founding of the Samuvapur monastery in Champaran District, Bihar.

> One day, many years ago, Rām Dās arrived in the region of Samuvapur which at that time was almost entirely covered with jungle. Rām Dās, being a Renouncer, began to chop trees from the forest in order to make his smouldering fire *(dhūnī)*. Since he liked to warm himself both at night and day beside a huge fire, in no time at all he had cleared several acres of trees from the jungle. In that clearing he lived in the company of his bull, called Bholva, who travelled with him wherever he went.
>
> One day the police happened to come upon the clearing and saw Rām Dās felling trees without a permit. When they asked the holy man who had permitted him to fell trees, Rām Dās remained silent and continued chopping.
>
> The policemen returned to the palace and informed the Queen who came the following morning with a large company of policemen intent on banishing Rām Dās from the kingdom. But when the Queen arrived at the campsite, neither Rām Dās nor Bholva was there. In

> vexation she asked aloud, "Now where has that ascetic gone?" To which Rām Dās' waterpot, lying beside the fire, replied: "He's gone to bathe in the river and will be back shortly." The Queen was astonished to hear a waterpot speak, and realized that Rām Dās was no ordinary ascetic.
>
> When Rām Dās returned to the campsite, the Queen — instead of wanting him driven from the kingdom — begged him to stay, offering him whatever he desired. Rām Dās replied that he was a Renouncer and, therefore, he did not desire anything. The Queen persisted in her offer and Rām Dās eventually said: "There is nothing wanting in my life, but maybe the bull wants something." The Queen asked the bull whether he desired anything and the bull nodded his head. So the Queen offered Bholva as much land as he wanted to graze upon. The bull then set off walking in a large circle, the circumference of which he marked by urinating as he walked. The Queen then gave Bholva all the land within that circle (about 4000 acres) and upon that land Rām Dās built the Samuvapur monastery.

Although this tale is unique in its details, the claims made about Rām Dās are conventional: that he was an accomplished yogi, that his spiritual powers superseded the terrestrial authority of the monarch, and so on. It is perhaps only necessary to note that as an accommplished ascetic Rām Dās is still alive today. Most Rāmānandī abbots, who have 'renounced their soul', are buried in the monastery courtyard in an attitude of 'living meditation' *(jīvit samādhi)*. One of the popular themes of temple tales is how such abbots come out of their earthen pits at night, while everyone else is asleep, to protect the monastery from thieves and tax collectors. Should a Bhurā Bhaṭṭ tell such a tale at the Samuvapur monastery, it can be assumed that his audience includes not only the 'living' abbot but all of his predecessors, including Rām Dās himself, who are buried on the monastery grounds. Everyone understands that the past has lapsed and that genealogists perpetuate the past in memories, but there is also a sense in which liberated persons remain everpresent and this everpresence inhabits both past and present. The Vaiṣṇavite tradition lives in this double sense and the tales of the genealogists remember and evoke both.

III

Bhurā Bhaṭṭ work as genealogists; but from what I heard and 'overheard' in Janakpur, it is clear that they are more than record-keepers who fix a person's identity by reference to his descent and generation. They also enhance a person's identity and magnify the circle in which he is known, thereby giving him a reputation in which his identity may be transformed.

These observations imply a distinction between identity and reputation. Identity has to do with personhood: it is the way by which a person becomes knowable through his actions and thoughts. One may speak of national identity, caste identity, lineage identity, personal identity, and so on. A complex of such identities has an individualizing function, such that a unique person may be located and have rights and duties ascribed to him. Although nations, castes, lineages and persons may be variously esteemed, the individualizing function of identity is both neutral and universal in its import. By contrast, reputation has to do with the attribution of value to one's identity and the extent to which one is known. Like identity, reputation has an individualizing function but it is neither neutral nor universal in import. Not everyone has thoughts and performs actions of positive or negative value; hence not everyone has reputation.

Both the concepts of identity and of reputation are implied in the Indo-Aryan term *nām*. Personal names have invariably to do with identity. Brahmanical naming practices have an individualizing function in that all personal names within the seven generation *sapiṇḍa* group should be unique. In this way members of a common *sapiṇḍa* group are not confused with one another. Yet the word *nām* also contains within it the sense of reputation, as in the Indian-English expression "What is your 'good name' *(śubhnām)?*" and in the Indo-Aryan rendering of the English 'name' as a rhyming compound *náim áiṇḍ pháim.* There is furthermore a sense in which a 'nobody' is somebody without a 'name'. Persons of value have 'names'. One can also lose (lit. spoil) one's name, meaning reputation; or have a bad name *(badnām).*

These linguistic usages merely map the subject-object ambiguity of a personal name. On the one hand, one's personal name is unique to one's *sapiṇḍa* group, and its first syllable, the so-called *rāśi phal,* is intrinsic to one's personal identity. It is fixed according to the time of one's birth and is unchangeable (even a Vaiṣṇavite ascetic of Brahman birth, who receives a new name upon initiation, should retain the initial syllable of his previous name). On the other hand, a name is that by which one is known, and the extent to which one is knowable is testimony to the greatness of one's name. Only persons of repute are known and remembered. Great persons die, but their name lives on in the world they leave behind.

The work of the Bhurā Bhaṭṭ, described above, entails both an identifying and a magnifying function. Bhaṭṭ both record identities and they make reputations. The identifying function is apparent in the historical circumstances surrounding their caste entitlement. Despite my informant's reference to King Vikramajīt and Svāmī Rāmānand, it is more likely that Raja Sevai Sinha of Jaipur authorized the Gaur Brahman from Bhim to record the genealogies of the four main Vaiṣṇavite religious traditions. Sevai Sinha played a leading role in the defence and purification of eighteenth century Vaiṣṇavism. He is credited with having recognized the militant Vaiṣṇavite orders which engaged with Naga Saṃnyāsīs and Muslim Faqirs for access to the pilgrimage centres of upper India. He is also said to have ordered the 'clean up' of north Indian Vaiṣṇaivism by having genealogists trace the pupillary succession of all Vaiṣṇavite ascetics back to the four founders of the *catuḥ sampradāya.* Those who could not trace their ancestry back to Rāmānand (alternatively Rāmānuja), Nimbārk, Mādhavācārya or Viṣṇusvāmī were excluded from royal favour (Burghart 1978).

It is perhaps not unfortuitous that Bhim, the ancestral village of the Bhurā Bhaṭṭ, is said to be situated seven *koś* east of Jaipur, putting it in the vicinity of Galata, the Vaiṣṇavite monastery whose abbot was the Rājguru of Jaipur. At the turn of the eighteenth century a dispute occurred within the monastery as to whether celibacy was a prerequisite for renunciation. All parties to this dispute traced their pupillary succession from Narayan through Rāmānuja to Rāmānand, but in the course of the dispute the Rāmavat tradition split into two groups, the celibate branch calling themselves Rāmānandīs and the married Vaiṣṇavite ascetics of Brahman birth Rāmānujīs. The Rāmānandīs lost control of the abbotship, but in their departure from Galata they spread throughout the Ganges basin, eventually coming to eclipse the Rāmānujīs. The elimination of the Rāmānujīs from upper India did not entail their physical elimination; rather they had the record of the historical transmission of the mantra — that is, their record of guru-disciple succession — rewritten in such a way as to avoid all mention of Rāmānuja. Although the defense of Vaiṣṇavism against Śaivism and Islam required ascetic-warriors, the eclipse of the Rāmānujīs in upper India required genealogists. I presume the Bhurā Bhaṭṭ were instrumental here.

These surmises about the role of a caste of genealogists in the purification' of a corporate group at the behest of a king are supported by the other ethnographies. The Pañjikars of Mithila received their entitlement from King Harisiṃha Deva in 1386 AD, after concern that irregular marriages among Brahmans would lead to social disorder. A somewhat similar situation prevailed in the middle-period Bengal, only in the Bengal case it was Muslim rule that led Brahman and Kāyastha caste councils to assume the royal function of maintaining order within the caste society, by engaging genealogists to keep track of one's ancestry, and to ensure that marriages would be contracted within proper bounds.

Although the identifying function, by which Vaiṣṇavite ascetics were located and controlled through their pupillary descent, was critical to the historical role of the Bhurā Bhaṭṭ, the magnifying function, of genealogical recitations, endures as the major public role of the Bhurā Bhaṭṭ. In their recitations of temple tales and the traditional origin of Vaiṣṇavism, the Bhaṭṭ praise — and thereby magnify — the spiritual ancestry of their host. Such praise should not be interpreted as an accolade, but rather as a rhetorical gesture that enhances the greatness of the object of praise. The term is *guṇa lagānā,* that is 'to draw out the qualities' of the person being praised. Although greatness naturally attracts praise, the drawing out of positive qualities is also said to magnify the soul, thereby making the other a greater person, expanding his field of action. Hence greatness merits praise and praise makes for greatness. In this sense then the Bhurā Bhaṭṭ enhance the spiritual power of the Vaiṣṇavite saints, enabling them to work their grace upon their living disciples and devotees.

The magnifying function of genealogical recitations was particularly evident in the way in which Bhurā Bhaṭṭ added anecdotes to the life histories of saints who founded monasteries. The foundation themes were often unique in certain details, as is the case with the founding of the Samuvapur monastery, but to this story were added anecdotes, such as the following about Rām Dās:

> Rām Dās' elder co-disciple decided one day to pay Rām Dās a visit. It was morning and Rām Dās was seated atop the boundary wall of the monastery, cleaning his teeth with a toothstick, when he sensed that some miles away his elder co-disciple was coming to visit, riding a tiger. He turned the brick wall around and, still astride it, made the wall move several miles forward so that he could meet his co-disciple half way. Before he could leap down from the wall and salute his elder co-disciple, his co-disciple had dismounted and saluted him, saying, "I thought I was a great ascetic to be able to mount a tiger, but you are even greater to make a brick wall move."

I heard this anecdote on numerous occasions, each time with reference to a different saint. I assume that it is expected of a Bhurā

Bhaṭṭ that he have enough personal integrity to record and state the truth in his written genealogies, but in the magnification of persons through the public recitation of genealogies and temple tales, there is considerable license to alter the material. Here the aim is not to record another's identity but to work effects upon it.

IV

The distinction between the identifying and magnifying functions of a genealogist's work — like the distinction between fact and value — is not absolute. Each function mutually entails the other; sometimes each seems to shade into the other; and both are implicit in the meanings of the word 'name'. Nonetheless, both functions can be distinguished in their different aims, modes and social aspects.

With regard to aim, one may note the presence of the identifying function when the genealogist compiles records about a corporate group at the behest of a third party. Caste purification was the aim of the genealogies compiled by the Bengali Ghaṭakas and Maithil Pañjikars. The exclusion from North Indian Vaiṣṇavism of ascetics, who had obtained the initiatory mantra by irregular means, was the initial aim of the Bhurā Bhaṭṭ's genealogical knowledge; and restriction on improper competition over *jajmān* between Paṇḍas that of the Gayāwāl Munshijis. In all cases the aim was one of social control by means of fixing identities, and in all cases a third party — be he king or Paṇḍa — authorized or employed the genealogist to record this personal knowledge. In short, there is a triadic structure to the aim, and the identifying function has to do with reference.

By contrast, there is no third party to consider with regard to the genealogist's magnifying function. It takes place in a dyadic structure and has to do with address. Bhurā and Betāl Bhaṭṭ enhance 'living' saints, and the Ghaṭakas recited genealogies in public, to the families whose offspring are to be united in marriage. The Vahivanca Barots of Gujarat double as bards, and praise their Rajput hosts. The only case of a genealogist caste not addressing the persons about whom they have the knowledge are the Kāyastha Munshijis of Hindu Gaya; and, interestingly, they do not work in situations in which identities are transformed. All the other castes carry out both identifying and magnifying functions, structured both in relations of reference and address. In the middle period Bengal the Ghaṭakas not only confirmed entitlement of Brahmans and Kāyasthas to marry, but also enhanced their value as persons in their hypergamous *kulina* marriages. So did, in this respect, the Pañjikars of Mithila. Meanwhile in Gujarat the Vahivanca Barots played a critical role in magnifying Koli identities so that they could contract hypergamous alliances with Rajputs.

These different aims, of identifying persons in reference, and transforming persons in address, are signaled by their different modes. The identifying function is written. It entails acts of inscription, such as the record books, called *khātā,* kept by Munshijis. By contrast, the magnifying function entails acts of speech. Praise may be written, but it must be uttered to work its effects. The Bhurā and Betāl Bhaṭṭ, Ghaṭakas, Pañjikars, Vahivanca Barots and Kāyastha Munshijis all keep written records. All but the last-mentioned, however, make oral performances in public. And, again, all but the last-mentioned, enhance the persons about whom they have knowledge.

One might assume that there is no society in which praise comes legitimately from the self, for self-praise is a symptom of arrogance. Culturally variable is the other who expresses praise. In Hindu society persons of superior status should not praise their inferiors: for example, parents do not praise their children. Praise should come from someone completely outside the social group: say, a woman who praises her neighbour's child. Or it should be directed within the social group from persons of inferior status toward their superior — a dependant to his patron or a disciple to his guru. In their dependency, such persons are thought to be part of the same social body as the benefactor who sustains them. It is perhaps not too far-fetched to detect a tendency for genealogical magnifiers to be subjectified by the persons whom they magnify. The Bhurā Bhaṭṭ are

Vaiṣṇavites who not only receive initiation, but also adopt, in some measure, the itinerant, mendicant way of life of the persons whom they praise. The Pañjikars who work for Maithili Brahmans are themselves Maithil Brahman. Rajputs, or Kolis claiming to be Rajput let themselves be praised by Vahivanca Barots, who themselves claim to be Rajputs. Yet, in their identifying function, genealogists objectify the persons about whom they have knowledge and see them as being members of a different corporate group. Despite their initiation, the Bhurā Bhaṭṭ are householders; and Rāmānandī ascetics do not accept *kaccā* food from them. The Pañjikars are a separate lineage of Maithil Brahmans. And so on.

What becomes clear from this analysis is that when the same caste performs both identifying and magnifying functions, its structural relationship with the persons about whom it has knowledge is ambiguous. Bhurā Bhaṭṭ are like Vaiṣṇavite ascetics, but not really. The Ghaṭakas of Bengal Brahmans are often Brahman, but not necessarily. The Vahivanca Barots of Gujarat are said to be Rajput, but somewhat uncertainly. The only caste of genealogists in a structurally unambigous position are the Kāyastha Munshijis of Gaya, but they merely identify *jajmān*, they do not magnify them. All the others, on whom we have information, both identify and magnify their patrons, and accordingly find themselves both within and without the corporate group they know.

References

Burghart, Richard 1978. The founding of the Rāmānandī sect. In *Ethnohistory* 25: 121-39.

Inden, Ronald 1976. *Marriage and rank in Bengali culture.* Los Angeles and Berkeley: University of California Press.

Jha, Ugranath 1980. *The genealogies and genealogists of Mithila: A study of the Panji and Panjikars.* Varanasi: Kishor Vidya Niketan.

Shah, A.M and R.G. Shroff 1959. The Vahivanca Barots of Gujarat: A caste of genealogists. In Milton Singer (ed.) *Traditional India: structure and change.* Philadelphia: American Folklore Society.

Vidyarthi, L.P. 1961. *The sacred complex in Hindu Gaya.* Bombay: Asia Publishing House.

NASĪRUDDĪN AND ĀDINĀTH, NIZĀMUDDĪN AND KĀNIPHNĀTH: HINDU-MUSLIM RELIGIOUS SYNCRETISM IN THE FOLK LITERATURE OF THE DECCAN*

Hugh van Skyhawk

Unlike the orthodox forms of Islām, Ṣūfīsm adapted itself quickly to the Indian way of life. From the 12th century onwards Ṣūfīs became increasingly involved both in the religious life and in the personal problems of Indians from all walks of life. Worldly people sought help from Ṣūfīs for their wordly problems; spiritually inclined people sought the guidance of Ṣūfīs for their spiritual problems. The attachment that many Indians felt for a famous *shaikh* during his lifetime was transferred to the *dargāh* of the *shaikh* after his death. Visiting his *dargāh (ziyārat)* was often seen as having even more spiritual benefit than performing the *hajj.*[1] The attraction

---

* In the present paper the following conventions of transliteration have been used: 1) Marāṭhī words have been transliterated according to their pronunciation; 2) bibliographical references to publications in Indian languages have been given in full transliteration, that is, with the inherent "a" between syllables and at the end of a word; 3) words of Urdū, Persian, Arabic, or Hindustānī origin used in the Marāṭhī text have been transliterated according to their orthography in the Devanāgarī script; 4) other words of Urdū, Persian, Arabic, or Hindustānī origin have been given according to the transliterations found in Muḥammad Mujeeb's *The Indian Muslims.*

[1] With regard to the great importance of *ziyārat* for Indian Ṣūfīs Muḥammad Mujeeb observes: "Even a *ṣūfī* so careful of his words and acts as Shaikh Niẓāmuddīn declared that the *murīd* who just said his prayers five times a day and

of the spiritual power of a great *shaikh* or of his *dargāh* was by no means limited to Muslim devotees, but was felt by Hindus and other Indians as well.

In this connection we need to distinguish between the attitudes of "orthodox Ṣūfīs,"[2] who remained aloof from and often mistrusted non-Muslims, and the open-minded liberalism of Ṣūfīs like *Shaikh* Farīduddīn Shakarganj, *Shaikh* Niẓāmuddīn Awliyā, and *Shaikh* Nasīruddīn Cirāg Delhī, whose missionary efforts were characterised by the "...appraisal, assimilation, or rejection of the spiritual and moral values of Hinduism. Visits of yōgīs are mentioned in accounts of Shaikh Farīduddīn and Shaikh Niẓāmuddīn. The latter, in particular, had a very open mind. He believed, apparently, that the acceptance of Islām by the Hindus should be a by-product of the spiritual endeavour and self-discipline of the Muslims, and on one occasion he definitely refused to say anything to induce the brother of a convert to accept Islām. We do not know whether Shaikh Niẓāmuddīn studied the principles or the practice of yōgā or Hindū metaphysics. Shaikh Nasīruddīn may have studied them. He refers to Sidhs, the gurus of the yōgīs, who take a fixed number of breaths; he says that the *ṣūfī* must keep an eye on his breathing, and must be able to hold his breath in order to concentrate..."[3]

---

repeated some *waẓīfah* (litany) for a while, but had absolute faith in his *pīr* and was intensely devoted to him, was better than the *murīd* who spent his time in prayer, fasting, and the repetition of litanies and who performed the *hajj*, but was wanting in faith and devotion to his *pīr* (Mujeeb quotes here from the *Fawā'id al-Fuwād* of Amīr Ḥasan Sijzī). 'He (Shaikh Niẓāmuddīn) said, "After the death of Shaikh al-Islām Farīduddīn, I had a strong desire to go for the Great *Hajj*. I said to myself, Let me go to Ajodhān for a pilgrimage to the *shaikh*. When I had accomplished the pilgrimage (to the tomb of) Shaikh al-Islām, my desire was fulfilled, with something added on. Again I had the same desire, and again I went on pilgrimage to (the tomb of) the *shaikh*, and my need was fulfilled".'"(See Mujeeb, 1967:126).

[2] See Ahmad, 1964:131. With regard to the Ṣūfīs of medieval Bījāpūr, Richard Maxwell Eaton draws a distinction between "rustic Literati" and "urban Reformer" Ṣūfīs, the former having contacts with the non-Muslim population, and the latter disdaining such contacts. See Eaton, 1978:132f.

[3] See Mujeeb, 1967:165.

For their liberal-mindedness and for their efforts to bring Hindus and Muslims closer, Shaikh Niẓāmuddīn and Shaikh Nasīruddīn are also remembered in the folk literature of the Deccan. According to a popular tradition of the *Nāgeś-saṃpradāya,* Shaikh Nasīruddīn even travelled from Delhi to the Deccan for the sake of a Hindu devotee. This popular tradition forms the basis of a Marāṭhī pamphlet with the title *Alakhaniraṅjana*", which was published in Puṇe in 1981 by Shaikh Abdul Rajhākśāh Isma'īl Biyābānī, a retired police officer and *shaikh* of the Biyābānī-Rifā'ī-Qādirī- *silsila.* Biyābānī's chief aim, in compiling the several sources of the folk tale of Nasīruddīn and Hegras-svāmī and publishing them in a Marāṭhī pamphlet, is to bring Hindus and Muslims closer by making them aware of the roots they share in the religious and cultural history of the Deccan. Although Biyābānī's attempt to trace the origins of several bhakti movements in the Deccan back to Nasīruddīn Cirāg Delhī may be historically incorrect, the examples he presents of Hindu-Muslim popular traditions about Nasīruddīn Cirāg Delhī and his Hindu devotee Hegras-svāmī provide valuable insights into Hindu-Muslim religious syncretism — especially with regard to the attraction felt by non-Muslims for great *shaikhs*.

The story in its present printed form consists of a fragment from an anonymous Urdū manuscript (which has since been lost), scattered excerpts from several medieval Marāṭhī and Persian sources, an excerpt from an old copy of a Marāṭhī pamphlet of the *Nāgeś-saṃpradāya* known as *"Saṅkaṭ-haraṇ"* ('the remover of calamities') and of Shaikh Biyābānī's own account of witnessing a divine confirmation of the truth of the story. On the whole, Shaikh Biyābānī's narrative combines elements of oral tradition with the familiar hagiographical accounts of the lives of the Bhakti-saints of Mahārāṣṭra:

"Śrī Najhīrśāh was originally from Wāī, in District Sātārā. As a resident of Puṇe he lived for many years in the old *Modīkhānā*. And in 1948 he went to Pākistān. In his possession there was an Urdū manuscript, which he took with him to Pākistān. (Here is) some information contained in that manuscript: 'Khvājā Nasiruddin (sic)[4] Cirāg Delhī ('the Lamp of Delhī'), who was of the family of Hajrat Umar — May Allāh be merciful unto him! — , who was the *kaliphā* of the most revered Muḥammad Paigaṃbar — May peace be upon him! — , after obtaining the condition of spiritual perfection *(pūrṇa-avasthā)* from Khvājā Nijāmuddīn Avaliyā on 17 Rabīūl Ākhir in the Hijra year 725 (1347 A.D.), received an order to have his *gādī* (literally: 'throne') moved immediately and travel to the South, and in the name of the *Caitanya-saṃpradāya (cistiyā)* spread monotheism *(ekeśvarī vād)* and spiritual knowledge *(adhyātma)* of the *dharma* of Islām among the Hindus, and bring Hindus and Muslims near (to one another).

The *sadguru-paramparā* of this *Caitanya-saṃpradāya* has been given below. It has been taken from the books *Haśyeba-hasyata, Nāgeśa-līlāmṛta,* and *Tajakeratula-avaliyā*.[5] Detailed information will be obtained from these books; in addition one might even examine an old *Gazetteer* of the Solāpūr District:

1) Khvājā Nasīruddīn Cirāg Dehlī alias Ādināth alias Nāgnāth; 2) Macchindranāth; 3) Gorakhnāth; 4. Gahinīnāth; 5) Nivṛttināth; 6) Jñāneśvar; 7) Sopan; 8) Muktabāī; 9) Visobā Khecar; 10) Yogirāj Cāṅgdev; 11) Nāmdev Śiṃpī.

II. The Garland of the Disciples of the *Vārkarī-saṃpradāya:*

From Khvājā Nasīruddīn Cirāg Delhī alias Nāgnāth Śivyogī there evolve three branches of succession: branch A: 1) Rāghav Caitanya, i.e. Allāhuddīn Māśāyakh, Āḷand; 2) Bhakta Mujumdār, Junnar; 3) Siddhaliṅg, Āḷand; branch B: 1) Keśav Caitanya, i.e. Khvājā Bande-

---

[4] As a rule Biyābānī writes the name *"Nasiruddin"* in his Marāṭhī publications instead of the more widely accepted "Nasīruddīn". For the remainder of the present paper we have used "Nasīruddīn" and "Nijāmuddīn" for the sake of uniformity. Otherwise, the transliteration of proper names and titles follows the Marāṭhī text, e.g. "Husenī" instead of the more widely accepted "Hussainī".

[5] *Haśyeba-hasyata* and *Tajakeratula-avaliyā* were not accessible to me.

navāz, Gulbargā; 2) Navkoṭ Nārāyaṇ, Kalburge (?);[6] branch C: 1) Bābājī Caitanya, i.e. Śahābuddīn Bābā, Mānyahāḷ; 2) Sant Tukārām, Dehu.

III. The Garland of Disciples of the *Liṅgāyat-panth:*

From Hajrat Kamāluddīn Ālama Prabhū there evolve five branches of succession: branch A: 1) Hiṃmant Svāmī, Muḷgund; branch B: 2) Siddheśvar Siddharāmeśvar, Solāpūr; 3) Bhakta Basaveśvar Kalyāṇ Moglāī; 4) Canna Basaveśvar; 5) Tresaṣṭh Purāṇ; branch D: 1) Aminuddīn, Vijāpūr (Bījāpūr); 2) Phakīrsvāmī Sirhaṭṭī, Dhārvāḍ; 3) Maḷī Prabhū Muḷgund, Dhārvāḍ; branch E: 1) Rāmaliṅg Āḷte, Kolhāpūr;

IV. The Garland of Bhaktas of Khvājā Śekh Nasīruddīn alias Nāgnāth:

1) Datta Caitanya Siddha, Vaḍvaḷ; 2) Rāmbhaṭ, Mahgāv; 3) Raghunāth Khillārī, Moglāī; 4) Timaṇṇā Dhangar, Indūr; 5) Kṛṣṇabāī, Hirve; 6) Ekaliṅg Telī, Manūr (i.e. Mānūr, Dt. Bīḍ or Dt. Solāpūr?); 7) Hegrasvāmī Yogīrāj, Mohoḷ, whose disciples were: (1) Ajñānsiddha, Narade (i.e. Narenda), (Dt.) Kolhāpūr; (2) Narendra Siddha Phulārī, Vaḍvaḷ; and (3) Siddhaliṅg, the son of Bhakta Majumdār, the *pujārī* of Mohoḷ; 8) Varadammā alias Varad Basavaṇṇa, Mānūr; 9) Badakavvā, Mārḍī; 10) Narasiṃha alias Balarām, Āpegāv; 11) Bahiram Bhaṭ, Paiṭhaṇ.[7]

---

[6] "*Kalburge*" is probably a misprint for Gulbarga.

[7] The story of Bahiram Bhaṭ alias Bahirā Pisā ('Mad Bahirā'), his conversion to Islām, his reinstatement as a brahmin, his confusion concerning his true nature, and his ultimate liberation from doubt through the encounter with the *sadguru* Nāgnāth is told in at least three *caritre* in Old Marāṭhī: 1) in the *Hegras-caritra* of Ajñānasiddha (14th or 16th century; for a brief discussion of the dating of Ajñānasiddha see Tulpule:1979:371); 2) in the the *Bahirambhaṭ-caritra* of Uddhavacidghana (17th century); 3) in the more lengthy narration of Mahīpati (18th century) in the *Bhakta-vijaya*, 44.8-44.85. For a brief discussion of the three versions of the story see my article "Vaiṣṇava Perceptions of Muslims in 18th Century Maharashtra" in: Anna Libera Dallapiccola and Richard Maxwell Eaton (eds.), *Proceedings of the Conference on Regional Variations of Islām in Pre-Modern India* (Heidelberg, 1989), forthcoming.

A manuscript copy of the book *Nāgeś-līlāmṛt* is in the possession of Śrī (Bhāskarpant) Deśpaṇḍe's family in Moho!. A copy of it must be with Dr. Śrī Yu. Em. Paṭhāṇ, Head of the Marāṭhī Section, Auraṅgābād University (i.e. Marāṭhvāḍā University, Aurangabad). He has published a book in Marāṭhī with the title *Nāgeś-saṃpradāya* through the Auraṅgābād University.[8]

Śrī Va. Sī. Bendre has written the Marāṭhī book *Tukārām-Mahārājāṃcī-guruparamparā*.[9] In this book the following information has been given on page 49: 'Information on the *sants* and *sādhus* in the *Nāgnāth-saṃpradāya*is available in the *Nāgeś-līlāmṛt*. The parts therein that are relevant to the subject under discussion are these: "*Nāgeś-avatār*" and "*Caitanya-traya*" ('the *Caitanya*-trio').' In the eighth chapter of the third book the legend of the *Nāgeś-avatār* begins. Information about where and when this *avatār* originated is not given. However, while narrating the wonders of the *avatār* the author writes:

> 'Like that our *svadharma* (the specific duties proper to one's birth group) will be different.
> But the highest serenity *(uttama virama)* is only in one place.
> Thus the nature of the Self *(svarūpa)* has been shown.
> Know ye that the very one whom the Hindus call "Nāgeś" is Nasīruddīn for the *yavanas* (i.e. the Muslims).
> Verily, they say this name is hidden (i.e. Nasīruddīn).
> The cobras *(bhujaṅg*, i.e. his disciples in the *Nāgeś-saṃpradāya)* use the other one (i.e. "Nāgeś", 'Lord of the Snakes').'
>
> (8.80)[10]

Nāgnāth alias Ādināth — that was Nasīruddīn Cirāg Delhī. Hegras-svāmī, a resident of Moho! in district Solāpūr, was his disciple. Hegras-svāmī has a big temple. The booklet "*Saṃkaṭ-haraṇ*"

---

[8] See Paṭhāṇa, Yusufakhāna Mahaṃmadakhāna, *Nāgeśa-saṃpradāya*, Auraṅgābāda, 1963.

[9] See Bendre, Vāsudeva Sītārāmā, *Tukārāmācī-guruparamparā*, Muṃbāi, 1960.

[10] These *ovī*-s can be found in the eighth *adhyāya*, verses 76f., of the *Nāgeśa-līlāmṛta* edited by Śivājīrāva Sadāśivarāva Śeṭe Kolhāpūrkar in Kolhāpūr in *śake* 1900 (A.D. 1978).

was written by him.[11] I obtained an old copy of it in 1952. Therein, in the final *ślok* (here: generic term for a verse), it is clearly mentioned that Nasir Cirāg Dillī — May Allāh be merciful unto him! — came from Dillī for the sake of Hegras-svāmī. And he himself is Nāgnāth alias Ādināth. Someone took this booklet from me to read, but did not return it.

A certain goddess was pleased with Hegras-svāmī. For many days he stubbornly persisted (in praying) to her: 'Let me meet a *sadguru!*' One day the goddess told Hegras-svāmī to close his eyes and open them again. When he closed his eyes and opened them, he had a vision that he was standing on the bank of a certain river, while Khvājā Nasīruddīn Cirāg Delhī (was standing on the other) bank of the river and calling to him. He ordered Hegras-svāmī to return (to the Deccan) and said: 'I shall come to the South for your sake!'[12] According to this vision, Khvājā Nasīruddīn Cirāg Delhī came to the South on the order of his *sadguru* Nijāmuddīn Avaliyā Dehlī, together with Khvājā Bandenavāz Gesūdarāz (who is known to the Hindus as Keśav Caitanya) and many other *avaliyā* (literally: 'friends of God', i.e. saints). Many *pīrs* took up residence in Daulatābād. Among them was a certain *pīr sāheb* Khvājā Śekh Salāuddīn Cistī, who together with his disciples came to the *kasbā peṭh* in Puṇe and settled there.

While doing his "*Nāgeś-līlā*" (his divine sport as "Nāgeś", 'the Lord of the Snakes'), Nasīr Cirāg Dehlī came to Vaḍvaḷ.[13] (The palanquin in which he had travelled has been placed inside the

---

[11] Here *Shaikh* Biyābānī apparently confuses Hegras-svāmī with Ajñānasiddha, Hegras's grandson through his daughter Ahalya, who is considered to be the author of the *Saṃkaṭ-haraṇī*.

[12] In this connection it is striking that even today Delhī is mentioned by the devotees of the *Nāgnāth-saṃpradāya* as one of their seven *devasthān*, the remaining six being Mānūr (Dt. Bīḍ or Dt. Solāpūr?), Narenda (Dt. Kolhāpūr), Degāv (Dt. Solāpūr)), Mārḍī (Dt. Solāpūr), Vaḍvaḷ (Dt. Solāpūr), and Mohoḷ (Dt. Solāpūr). Whereas at the six other *devasthān* a specific Nāgnāth temple is the focal point of the cult, in Delhī no certain temple or holy place is mentioned. I was told that this is because in the six centuries since the time of Hegras-svāmī, devotees seldom visited this *devasthān*, it being situated a great distance from the Deccan. Thus, in the course of time, the exact location of Nāgnāth's manifestation in Delhī was forgotten.

[13] The place name "*Vaḍvaḷ*" is sometimes given as "*Vaḍvāḷ*". For the sake of uniformity, I have used the form *Vaḍvaḷ* throughout this paper.

precincts of the *dargāh* of Bandenavāz Gesūdarāz).[14] Moho![ ] is four miles from there. He saved Hegras-svāmī (from his entanglement in wordly life) *(tyāṃnī Hegras svāmīs uddhārile)*. Once Hegras-svāmī decided to offer food to his (Brahmin) ancestors. Accordingly, all the plans were made and everyone was invited to dine (together). But all the Hindus in Moho! decided that they should not go to this (inter-communal) dining; the reason was that Hegras-svāmī was keeping company with *Musalmān-phakīrs*, etc.[15] Hegras-svāmī went to Vaḍvaḷ and gave this news to Nasīr Cirāg Dehlī. Then Nasīr Cirāg Dehlī alias Nāgnāth himself came to Mohoḷ. And on a nearby hillock[16] he directed that the leaf-plates *(patrāvaḷī)* of all the

[14] I am grateful to Sayyid Shah Khusro Hussaini of Gulbarga, a descendant of Hazrat Banda Nawāz Gīsūdirāz, for informing me that, according to family records, the palanquin of Nasīr ud-Dīn Cirāg Dehlī was given to Gīsūdirāz by Shaikh Nasīr ud-Dīn as *tabarūk* (a gift of divine grace). The palanquin was then brought to Gulbarga by Gīsūdirāz when, at the age of eighty, he came to the Deccan for the second time in 1402 (his first visit to the Deccan was in 1326 when he and his father together with hundreds of other important Delhī *Ṣūfī*-s were exiled to Daulatābād at the orders of Sultan Muhammad bin Tughlug). According to the records of the Hussaini family, *Shaikh* Nasīruddīn Cirāg Dehlī, Hazrat Bandenawāz's *pīr*, never visited the Deccan. Dr. Carl Ernst of Pomona College (Claremont, California) has suggested that the story of Nasīruddīn Cirāg Dehlī coming to Mohoḷ might be a popular version of the story of the *Ṣūfī*-s being expelled from Dehli and sent to Daulatābād in 1326 at the order of Sultan Muhammad bin Tughlug (personal communication of 2 March 1990).

[15] At this point the various versions of the story diverge: Śekh Biyābānī's narration then follows the *sākhī* of Ajñānasiddha, while S. N. and V. S. Moholkar's pamphlet simply states that Nāgnāth then came to Mohoḷ and rescued Hegras-svāmī.

[16] The hillock in question is known today as *"vimān-ṭekaḍī"*. A small temple to Śiva as *"Uttareśvar"* ('the Lord of the North'(!)) stands on the summit of the hill. The *liṅga* in the *garbha-gṛha* forms the focal point of worship. Outside the temple, there is a beautiful hero-stone inlaid in the northern temple wall. It is striking that the villagers freely speak of this hillock as the place to which Nasīruddīn Cirāg Dehlī came to help Hegras. We were shown a Muslim grave covered with a green cloth that was said to be the grave of *"Śekh Nasīruddīn Bādśāh kī Hastinapur"* (the ancient name of Dehli). We were also told that *Shaikh* Nasīruddīn Cirāg Dehlī and Nāgnāth were one and the same person. This view is also shared by the devotees of Nāgnāth at the *samādhi* of Ajñānasiddha, Hegras-svāmi's grandson, in the village of Narenda in District Kolhāpūr. At Narenda it is especially striking that the devotees wash themselves at a water tank in the Muslim fashion before entering the *samādhi*. In the *samādhi* itself both the *kalimā* (profession of faith in Islām) and the *fātehā* (the opening *sūra* of the *Qur'ān)* are recited before devotees proceed to the underground

(villagers') ancestors be laid out by name. The villagers watched these proceedings from a distance. Just when the leaf-plates had been laid out, all those ancestors in whose names the leaf-plates had been laid out themselves came and began tasting the food. Seeing this wonder, the villagers were confounded *(stimit)*.[17]

Khvājā Nasīruddīn Cirāg Dehlī was himself a great *sadguru* in the tradition of the *Cistī-pīrs*. He is the very one whom they call Nāgnāth alias Ādināth. The very spot on which the *mūrtī* stands in the temple at Vaḍvaḷ is the place (he used) for sitting (in meditation) *(cilla)*. This very *Cistī-saṃpradāya* is the *Caitanya-saṃpradāya*. Through this *saṃpradāya* he brought pious Hindus to their basic doctrine of monotheism *(ekeśvarī vād)*, and from that the *Vārkarī-saṃpradāya* came into being. 'Allāh is one' — this was the message he gave. 'Allāh is pure *(pāk)* and flawless *(be aib hai)* — just this was his teaching. 'Allāh is one' *(Allāh ek āhe)* — the corrupted form *(apabhraṃśa)* of this became "*alakh*". And "*pāk aur be aib hai*" — as the sense of this was "*nirañjan*", the adherents of the *Nāth-panth* began giving the spiritual instruction "*alakhnirañjan*".

In 1947-1948 I myself went to the temple of Nāgnāth alias Ādināth in Vaḍvaḷ. In this temple there is a brass *mūrtī* of Ādināth. Standing in front of the *mūrtī*, I said in my heart of hearts *(manātlyā manāt mhaṇālā)*: 'If you give some sign that Khvājā Nasīruddīn Cirāg Delhī really was at this place, then I shall recite the *phātehā (al-fātiḥa*, the opening *sūra* of the *Qur'ān)*.' Instantly a

---

samādhi where they receive "*darśan*" of the "*svarūp*" of Ajñānasiddha. The *samādhi* consists of a small chamber, built upon a heap of stones approximately two meters in height, in which the *pādukā* of Ajñānasiddha are kept, and of the underground chamber mentioned above, which bears a striking resemblance to a Muslim grave. The shrine itself also faces the west, the direction of Mecca in relation to the Deccan, which is unusual for Śaivite shrines.

17 A similar story is told by Śrī Sant Ekanāth's hagiographer, Mahīpati. By feeding three hungry fakirs in his house, Ekanāth enraged the orthodox Brahmins of Pratiṣṭhān to the point that they threatened to excommunicate him unless his heavenly ancestors came down from heaven and ate from the leaf-plates laid out for them. Thereupon, Ekanāth called his heavenly ancestors to come down from heaven, and they appeared shining with divine lustre. The intense lustre of Ekanāth's heavenly ancestors blinded the Brahmins and forced them to hide their heads between their knees in shame. See Abbott, 1927:86-91.

wonder occurred. I saw a beard on the brass *mūrtī*. The hair on my whole body stood on end and I trembled. Immediately, I recited the *phāte hā*, offered my *namaskār*, and turned back.

Every year in Vaḍvaḷ a big *yātrā* is held for (Nāg)nāth.[18] I have heard that if, when lifting Nāth's palanquin at this time, (the people) don't give a shout "Yaroddīn is the friend of Nasir Cirāg!" *(Nasir Cirāgkī dostī Yaroddīn)*, the palanquin cannot be lifted.[19] I have not yet had the opportunity of going there and seeing for myself..."

Thus far, I have not succeeded in obtaining a copy of the edition of the *Saṃkaṭ-haraṇī* mentioned above by *Shaikh* Biyābānī, which was published in Solāpūr around 1950. However, in a recent edition of the *Saṃkaṭ-haraṇī* the story of Hegras-svāmī meeting his *sadguru* is told differently.

After propitiating the goddess Reṇukā by 16 forms of constant worship *(ṣoḍaṣopacāre nitya pujā)*, Hegras-svāmī receives *darśan* of Nāgnāth (Śiva). Nāgnāth then grants Hegras the following wish: the god will go with Hegras to Mohoḷ if, on the way, Hegras does not look back to see if Nāgnāth is following him. Hegras agrees, and both set out from Māhur to Mohoḷ. But Hegras cannot resist the temptation of looking back to see if Nāgnāth is still behind him. Thus, at Mānūr, in District Solāpūr (or Dt. Bīḍ?), Hegras looks back, and Nāgnāth becomes a stone *mūrtī* at that very spot. Even-

---

[18] Though the *yātrā* of Nāgnāth takes place at Mohoḷ, the village of Vaḍvaḷ, some six kilometers distant, figures importantly in the festivities. The festival is mentioned in part VII.B of volume 10 of the *Census of India* (1961), which is entitled *Fairs and Festivals of Maharashtra*. A detailed description of the *yātrā* of Nāgnāth at Mohoḷ is given in the *Gazetteer* of District Sholapur (published in Bombay, 1977, pp. 872-878).

[19] There is a slight difference of opinion regarding the exact wording of the shout. At Mohoḷ, I was told that the devotees shout: "*Śekh Nasīruddīn bādśāh kī do cirā hor din Hara Hara!*". At Vaḍvaḷ, however, devotees claim that the following shout is raised: "*Śekh Nasiruddīn bādśāh kī do cirā hor din Śiv bolā Hara Hara Mahādev!*". In both villages I was told that possession by Nāgnāth often occurs immediately after the shouting.

tually, Nāgnāth manifests himself to Hegras again at Mohoḷ and at Vaḍvaḷ in order to help his devotee out of a difficult situation (as in *Shaikh* Biyābānī's narration).

In the 1987 edition of *Saṃkaṭ-haraṇī* there is no mention of *Shaikh* Nasīruddīn Cirāg Delhī. Though mention is made of the difficulties Hegras had because of his association with fakirs in general, no fakir is mentioned by name in the narrative.[20] According to V. S. Mohoḷkar, a descendant of Hegras-svāmī, a fakir by the name of "Nasīruddīn" may have been associated with Hegras-svāmī, but as his *guru-bandhu*, (fellow disciple) and not as his *guru*.[21] However, in another collection of the *sākhī*-s of Ajñānasiddha and of another descendant of Hegras-svāmī, Siddhaliṅga-svāmī, that was published in Solāpūr around 1950 on behalf of the *Nāgnāth-mandīr* in Mohoḷ, Nasīruddīn Cirāg Delhī figures importantly, his name being mentioned no less than seven times. Moreover, in the story of the harassment of Hegras by the orthodox brahmins of Mohoḷ because of his association with fakirs, Nāgnath is referred to as "*...baḍe karāmata vallī, siddha Nāganātha cirāka Dehalī*" ('the great wonder-[working] holy man, Siddha Nāgnāth Cirāk Delhī'), thus identifying Nāgnāth with Nasīruddīn Cirāg Dehlī.[22]

According to S. G. Tulpule, Ajñānasiddha lived, not in the 14th, but in the 16th century, which would make it impossible that his grandfather, Hegras-svāmī, actually met *Shaikh* Nasīruddīn Cirāg Delhī, who died in 1356. Though Tulpule mentions the "liberality" of the *Nāgeś-saṃpradāya*, and substaniates this by referring to Alamkhān, a Muslim bhakta of "Siddha-Nāgnāth", he makes no mention of a tradition of the *Nāgeś-saṃpradāya* according to which Nāgnāth is identified with *Shaikh* Nasīruddīn Cirāg Dehlī, nor that

---

[20] See Ajñānasiddha, *Saṃkaṭaharaṇī*, edited by Śaṅkar Nānābuvā Mohoḷkar and V. S. Mohoḷkar, Solāpūr, 1987, pp. 7ff., 13, and 78f.

[21] Interview in Solāpūr, 7 June 1990.

[22] See *sākhī* number 15 of Ajñānasiddha in: Siddhaliṅga Viśvanātha Svāmī and Nāganātha Guṇḍubuvā Kuruḍe (eds.), *Ānaṃda-laharī-va-sākyā*, Solāpūr, no date given, circa 1950, p. 19.

Shaikh Nasīruddīn helped Hegras-svāmī in his difficulties with the orthodox brahmins of Mohoḷ.[23] Whatever the historical truth of the legend of Nāgnāth/Nasīruddīn/Hegras-svāmī may be, there can be no doubt that in the popular traditions surrounding these religious figures there arose a strong attraction to the great *shaikh*, Sayyid Nasīruddīn Cirāg-i-Dillī. Centuries later, in post-partition India, this devotion to the famous *Chistī-shaikh* of Delhi became the source of a controversy within the *Nāgeś-sampradāy* concerning the authenticity of sacred tradition, a controversy that has continued up to the present time.

***

[23] See Tulpule:1979: 370f. and note 322.

Setu Mādhavrāv Pagaḍī is a Marāṭhī-speaking brahmin from Bidar. After completing his higher education at Allāhābād and Banāras, he served as a gazetted official *(sandī nokar)* in the government of His Highness, the Nizām of Haiderābād. After 1948, he became an official in the Indian Administrative Service (IAS). For many years he lived at Auraṅgābād, in Marāṭhvāḍa, a region in which Hindu-Muslim religious syncretism was, and to some extent still is, especially strong. Pagaḍī himself is a good example of the cultural synthesis of the Deccan: he is fluent in Urdū, Persian, Hindī, Sanskrit, Kannaḍa, Telugu, Marāṭhī, and English. The style in which Pagaḍī writes Marāṭhī is well suited for describing Hindu-Muslim religious syncretism. Drawing freely on the rich stock of words of Arabic, Persian, or Hindustānī origin in Marāṭhī, he seldom requires a parenthetical explanation of the Urdū or Persian oral text. Moreover, through his intimate knowledge and obvious love of Deccanī culture Pagaḍī endows his Marāṭhī translations of Urdū *dantakathā* (oral traditions) with great sensitivity towards the cultural nuances of the unique world and world-views of the characters involved. The basis of the following English translation of the Urdu oral tradition "Nijāmuddīn of Paiṭhaṇ and Kāniphnāth" is Pagaḍī's *Sūfī-saṃpradāya (Muṃbāi, 1953)*, in which the author combines a short history of Ṣūfīsm in India with Marāṭhī translations of the Urdu oral traditions of the Deccan. The book is intended as an introduction to the spiritual teachings of the Ṣūfīs and their missionary work in medieval India, especially in the Deccan. It is primarily intended for the non-Muslim Marāṭhī reading-public.

Where Marāṭhī words of Arabic, Persian, or Hindustānī origin have been transliterated they have been placed in italics and marked with a *. As in the preceding translation, Marāṭhī words have been transliterated according to their pronunciation:

Paiṭhaṇcā Nijāmuddīn
('Paiṭhaṇ's Nijāmuddīn')

"Sayyad Ussādāt Sayyad Nijāmuddīn[24] was originally from the Sistān region (central Irāṇ).[25] He was born at the end of the 14th century. His father's name was Sayyad Mophamuddīn Idris. When he presented himself for admission to school he utterly astounded the schoolmaster by reciting and explaining the entire *Kurāṇ (Qur'ān)*. The schoolmaster made a report of this to his father and said: 'It seems that this boy read the *Kurāṇ* even while in his mother's womb.' Nijāmuddīn began concentrating on his devotion to God from childhood on. He would always be reading the *Kurāṇ*. He would always say: 'In the *Hadīs (ḥadīth)* — among the *sādhana* {means} of devotion to the Lord — reading the *Kurāṇ* has been recognized as the best of all.' He himself would read the *Kurāṇ* continuously while standing.

After some time, Nijāmuddīn began to become famous among the people. His (fame) grew to such an extent that it began to be an obstacle in his daily life. Finally, he decided to leave his native land. Nijāmuddīn was an adept in the art of wrestling *(mallavidyāpravīṇ)*. In order that people should not recognize his true nature, he made the exhibition of wrestling skills his outward occupation. He would walk about with an arrow in one hand and a stone weight *(vajanācā* dagaḍ)* in the other hand. He would say, 'I shall apprentice myself (spiritually) to the man who recognizes my inner nature.'

After leaving his native land, Nijāmuddīn wandered and wandered and (finally) came to Daulatābād. Sayyad Allāhuddīn Jiyā, a very famous Ṣūfī, was residing at Daulatābād at that time.

---

[24] Sayyad Ussādāt Sayyad Nijāmuddīn is more widely known today in Paiṭhaṇ as "Maulanna Sāheb". His *dargāh* is listed as one of the tourist attractions of Paiṭhaṇ on a sign displayed at the petrol pump on the Auraṅgābād road on the outskirts of Paiṭhaṇ. Numerous devotees of Kāniphnāth of Maḍhi visit the *dargāh* in order to pay homage to Kāniphnāth's *guru* before proceeding to the temple of Kāniphnāth at Maḍhi.

[25] Unless otherwise indicated all parentheses and brackets in the following English translation of Pagaḍī's Marāṭhī text are mine.

Nijāmuddīn went to his *khānkā* (hospice) and got down (from his horse). Then he gave a demonstration of his skill in wrestling. Allāhuddīn Jiyā discerned Nijāmuddīn's inner nature and said to him: 'But Nijāmuddīn, you are a *mumukṣu* (one desiring liberation). What's the sense of wandering about aimlessly? You need to increase your spiritual power (in contrast to the physical power of a wrestler).' Upon hearing this, Nijāmuddīn took refuge with Allāhuddīn Jiyā, and he received *gurūpadeś* (spiritual instruction) from Allāhuddīn..."[26] "...(One day, many years later, when Allāhuddīn's time of death was at hand) he summoned all his disciples and spoke: 'My disciples are many, but the best of all is Sayyadussādāt (i.e. 'the best Sayyad') Nijāmuddīn Idris al-Husenī. I ordain him as my *kaliphā* and put him in charge of *(havālīṃ*)* promoting religion in the Paiṭhaṇ region. He should proceed there and promote religion *(dharma-pracār)*...'[27]

"...The most famous of all of Nijāmuddīn's (Sayyid as-Sādāt Niẓāmuddīn) disciples was Kāniphnāth alias Śahā Ramjān. As it is generally known in Mahārāṣṭra that he was of the *Nāth-saṃpradāya,* the following information, which comes from an oral tradition of the Muslims, will be illuminating:

'In the succession of events (in the life) of Nijāmuddīn, Kāniphnāth has a place of importance. They say that he was the son of a king.

From childhood on, he had a passion for practising yoga and obtaining *siddhis.* After achieving success in this, he began performing miracles even at his young age. Becoming invisible, flying through the sky — he began performing such miracles. So, after some days had passed (in this way), he began longing to reach God *(īśvaraprāpti);* and he began wandering about in search of a guru. He made ready a palanquin and began to circle about in the sky. 'I shall become the disciple of that man who strikes down my yogic power' — such was the 'memory-knot' *(khūṇgāṇṭha)* that Kāniphnāth tied for himself. While wandering in this way by means of his palanquin, he once flew over Nijāmuddīn's *maṭh.* At that time Nijāmuddīn was washing his hands for prayer, and his disciple Śahā Tavvakul was pouring water into his hands. He saw the flying

---

26 Pagaḍī 1953: 87f.

27 Pagaḍī, p. 89.

palanquin. That his guru should be on the ground and some fellow should parade about in the sky — Śahā Tavvakul did not like that. 'Such a man's pride should be taken away' — thus he made his humble petition to Nijāmuddīn. 'We are *phakīrs**. What have we got to do with some other man?' — thus Nijāmuddīn pacified his disciple. But Śahā Tavvakul did not give up his obstinacy *(haṭṭa)*; and he persisted in pressing his guru: 'That man's palanquin should be made to descend!'. Finally, Nijāmuddīn threw his wooden shoes *(khaḍāvā)* into the air. And in the interval of time, in which Nijāmuddīn's shoes fell down, Kāniphnāth's palanquin crashed down with a loud thud *(dhāḍdiśī)*. While lying on the ground, Kāniphnāth assumed the form of a tiger and moved toward Nijāmuddīn. At that time Nijāmuddīn's son, Sayyid Badruddīn, was sitting next to him. Being irritated by him, the tiger tore open its jaws. Pacifying his son, he said: 'That isn't a tiger. It's a man. It isn't proper to harass him.' And from that day on Badruddīn got the name 'Whiskered Tiger' *(kalleśer**). At this point Nijāmuddīn cast some pebbles at the tiger. The instant that the pebbles fell upon the (tiger's) body, Kāniphnāth cast off the form of a tiger, appeared in a human body, and took refuge with Nijāmuddīn *(śaraṇ ālā)*. In accordance with his wish, Nijāmuddīn gave him the *dikṣā* of Islām and named him "Śahā Ramjān" (i.e. Ramaḍān). After some days, Śahā Ramjān made evident his wish of obtaining the guru's teachings. 'That will take a little time' — said Nijāmuddīn. As it was Nijāmuddīn's wish that Śahā Ramjān's *ahaṃkāra* concerning his *siddhis* and wonder-working *(camatkār)* should first be destroyed, he assigned him the work of serving the guru *(guruseva)*. The first labour that he told Śahā Ramjān (to perform) was filling the large stone water-jar in the *maṭh* (i.e. Nijāmuddīn's khānqāh or hospice) everyday. This water jar *(rāñjaṇ)* has come to be preserved to this very day in the hospice of Nijāmuddīn in Paiṭhaṇ. Nijāmuddīn gave him a rough earthen pitcher *(ghaḍā)* and assigned him the labour of fetching water and filling the *rāñjaṇ*. Śahā Ramjān thought: 'What's so difficult about filling the *rāñjaṇ?*' He picked up the earthen pitcher, put it on his head, and set out on the way to the river. They say that (at first) by power of his *yogbal* (pschyo-kinetic yogic powers) he would carry the earthen pitcher (suspended) in the air one and a quarter hands above his head. But the more his *yogbal* began to diminish, the more the *ghaḍā* descended, until, in the end, it lay on the ground.

Even after many days, Śahā Ramjān's labour of filling the *rāñjaṇ* was not completed. The reason was that the guru was making trial of his disciple. In the morning Śahā Ramjān would bring water from the river, and in the afternoon he would fetch wood from the jungle *(jaṅgal)*. He was very adept at playing the flute *(baṃsrī*)*. The snakes in the wilderness would become stupefied *(mugdha)* by the sweet sound of his (music). Thus it often occurred that Śahā Ramjān would catch the snakes that had become stupefied by the sound (of his flute), bind up his bundles of wood (with them) and take them to the *maṭh* of Nijāmuddīn. They say that even to this day snakes will not bite anyone in the *maṭh* of Nijāmuddīn.

Seeing that Śahā Ramjān had got the grace of the guru, Nijāmuddīn's other disciples began to fume and chafe *(jaḷphaluṃ lāgle)*. Śahā Ramjān had a cow by the name of 'Bholā' ('guileless'). The eyes of the (other) disciples fell upon this (cow). One day they petitioned Nijāmuddīn: 'The cow 'Bholā' should be slaughtered and a meal be made of her' — that is our unanimous wish!' At first Nijāmuddīn did not give his consent in this matter. Finally, because of their excessive pressing, Nijāmuddīn consented *(kabūl* keleṃ)* saying: 'You can kill the cow. But there is one condition: you must bring the cow's head, feet, and hide into the *maṭh*.'[28] The disciples did accordingly. In the evening, when Śahā Ramjān had fetched a bundle of wood and was about to set foot in the *maṭh*, the other disciples ridiculed him viciously and said: 'Today, on the guru's orders, we killed your cow and ate it!' Hearing this Śahā Ramjān felt very bad. Hanging his head, he went to Nijāmuddīn and sat down. Nijāmuddīn made out the reason for his disciple's dejection and said: 'Go, Śahā Ramjān, go outside and call your cow loudly.' Śahā Ramjān went outside the *maṭh*, stood in the town square (this square is known in Paiṭhaṇ up to this day as

---

[28] Nizām ud-Dīn's stipulation that "the cow's head, hide, and hoofs" be brought into the *math* bears a striking resemblance to the legend of Shaikh Aḥmed of Roh (Afghanistan), whose habit it was to slaughter daily 400 sheep for hungry wayfarers, then collect the animals' bones, heads, and hides. When the shepherd from whose herd Shaikh Aḥmed had taken the sheep for slaughter counted his sheep on the following morning, he invariably found his herd to be complete. Apparently, Shaikh Aḥmed had revived the slaughtered sheep at night by manipulating their bones, heads, and hides in a supernatural way. The belief is wide-spread among the Dards and Afghans that the bones, heads, hides, hoofs, and skeleton of an animal (especially an animal slaughtered by a hunter) possess a supernatural power that can be activated to revive a slaughtered animal and thus insure the abundance of game and domestic animals (see Müller-Stellrecht 1973:195-200, especially p. 196).

'phakīr-cauk') and shouted. 'Śahā Ramjān is calling the dead cow. He's really gone crazy!' — in that manner the other disciples began talking among themselves. Then, what a wonder! In front of (everyone) the cow together with its calf came running! In this way Nijāmuddīn completely confounded *(khajīl*)* all his disciples.

In this manner Śahā Ramjān served his guru for twelve years. One day Śahā Ramjān was massaging his guru's feet *(pāy dābat* hotā)*. At that time the insects (living) on Śahā Ramjān's head fell down (onto the ground). He picked them up and put them back onto his head. When the guru asked the reason (for this), Śahā Ramjān gave the following answer: 'But these insects are creatures of God *(īśvara)* and their food is on my head. If you turn from this pillow onto that pillow, the insects under you will be crushed. So, I picked them up and put them (back) onto my head.' The guru rejoiced at Śahā Ramjān's answer. He said: 'Go. Now my full grace *(pūrṇa kṛpā)* is upon you. Go. Bathe yourself, and return.' After Śahā Ramjān had bathed and returned, the guru brought him near and placed his hand of benificence *(varada hasta)* on his head. Because of this, the insects on Śahā Ramjān's head were completely removed, and in addition, he received the complete teachings of the guru.

They say that one day Śahā Ramjān was late in coming to the *maṭh*. When asked the reason, he explained: 'Today is *dasara* day, and Hindus by the thousands have taken up flagstaffs and banners and are walking about *(phirat* hote)*. I was standing and watching that. Hearing this, Nijāmuddīn said: 'If you like flagstaffs and banners, then in the future thousands will bring such flagstaffs to your place.' Even to this day when performing the *yātrā*, flagstaffs *(jheṇḍe*)* and banners are brought to Śahā Ramjān's, that is, Kāniphnāth's *samādhi*in Maḍhī (District Aḥmednagar). And it is believed that this is the fruit of Nijāmuddīn's blessing.

One day (some time after he had imparted his teachings to Śahā Ramjān), Nijāmuddīn said: 'Ramjān, the light of a lamp *(divī)* cannot be seen in front of a torch *(maśāl*)*. Now you should no longer stay at Paiṭhaṇ, but should be sent to another place *(pāṭhavāve*)* in order to promote religion — that is my wish' *(dharma-pracārā-karitāṃ)*.' Having said this, the guru gave Śahā Ramjān a staff *(chaḍī*)* and a large piece of cloth *(rumāl*)*. And he said: 'At the place, whither this cloth flies and then falls, that region shall be yours for promoting religion.' Śahā Ramjān said: 'May I spend my whole life toiling at your feet! — that is my wish! But you are driving me away from you!' Nijāmuddīn eased his mind and said: 'The whole world is the *jahāgīr** (proprietary estate) of a *phakīr*. A *phakīr* must be like water, which means that if his wish is (to flow) in this direction, then he should flow (away) in the other direction. If it is *Parameśvara's* wish, then you should spread (religion) in another direction.' Having most reverently understood the order of the guru, Śahā Ramjān let go of the cloth in the air and set out following it. The cloth flew and flew, and, in the end, fell in the vicinity of Maḍhī. At this place there was a *maṭh* of a certain *gosāvī*. Having brought (the *maṭh)* under his control, he drove away the *gosāvī* and settled at this place.

After that, Śahā Ramjān would visit Nijāmuddīn. One day, when he arrived for his visit with the guru, the banks of the Godāvarī were overflowing. Śahā Ramjān was distressed about how to reach the farther bank. Then a big fish came forth from the river. He cast his eyes upon the fish *(najar* paḍūn)* and commanded it. And riding upon its back, he reached the farther bank of the river. From that day on he got the name *Māhīsavār** ('he who has a fish'), that is, *Matsyarohī* ('he who is mounted upon a fish').'[29]

Śahā Ramjān lived to a ripe old age. He lived at Maḍhī for about fifty years and received death *(mṛtyu pāvlā)*[30] toward the end of the 15th century. How this *sādhu*, who adopted *Islām-dharma* at the hands of Nijāmuddīn and got the name "Śahā Ramjān," became known in the *Nāth-saṃpradāya* as a great adept by the name of "Kāniphnāth" is one of several secrets in the cultural history of Mahārāṣṭra. He must have proselytised for *Islām-dharma* in the Maḍhī region. In this capacity, what work did he perform *(bajāvilī*)* in the *Nāth-saṃpradāya?* It is necessary that this be explained..."[31]

---

[29] In numerous folk tales of the Ṣūfīs, power over water and all marine and aquatic creatures is attributed to Khwājā Khiḍr *(khiḍr* = 'sea-green'), whose vehicle is a big fish. In the above regional tradition, Śahā Ramjān (or Kāniphnāth) has apparently been associated with the traditional role of Khwājā Khiḍr, and has also been given a big fish as his vehicle. About Khwājā Khiḍr and his fish, see Titus, 1930:139f.

[30] Note Pagaḍī's use of the honorific euphemism in Marāṭhī for the death of a holy man: he 'received death'.

[31] Pagaḍī, pp. 94-98. In the Gazetteer of the Bombay Presidency Vol. XVII

The above story in its present form was intended primarily for the Hindu reading public in Mahārāṣṭra. For this reason, Pagaḍī translated it from spoken Urdū into literary Marāṭhī. But, while the original language of the story had to be translated in order to reach a wider, non-Muslim audience, the context of the story needed no translation or parenthetical explanations of unfamiliar ideas. For in each of the vignettes contained in the story of Nijāmuddīn and Śahā Ramjān a spiritual lesson is taught that is well known in the bhakti tradition of Mahārāṣṭra: Does not the humbling of Kāniphnāth's pride in his yogic powers remind us of Jñāneśvar, who broke the pride of Cāṅgdev Vāṭeśvar, the 1400 year old *yogīrāj* who rode upon a tiger and used a cobra as his whip?[32] Does not Nijāmuddīn's use of *guru-seva* in order to destroy the *ahaṃkāra* of his disciple remind us of Ekanāth's *guru-seva* for Janārdana-svāmī? Does not Nijāmuddīn's restoring the dead cow to life affirm the great importance of the ethical principle of *ahiṃsā?* Indeed, it is only after applying this lesson of respect for all forms of life even to the insects living on his scalp that Śahā Ramjān loses the last trace of his *ahaṃkāra* and receives the full grace and complete teachings of his guru. And who in Mahārāṣṭra would not see a similarity in Śaha Ramjān's reluctance to leave the service of his guru and Ekanāth's reluctance to leave the service of Janārdana-svāmī? Clearly, the world-view (Weltanschauung) that underlies the tradi-

---

(Ahmednagar), for the year 1884 (726f.) there is no mention of a Khāniphnāth in connection with the *dargāh* of the Muslim-Hindu saint Shah Rāmzān Mahi Savār who also was known and is still known as Kānhobā (a popular epithet of Śrī Kṛṣṇa).

[32] The story of the holy man who, by riding on a stone wall, breaks the pride of his pretentious rivals is well known in Ṣūfī traditions. In the *Fawā'id al-Fuwād* (14th century compilation of the sayings of Niẓāmuddīn Avaliyā) of Amīr Ḥasan Sijzī, the following story is told of Shaikh Luqmān of Sarakhs: "They say that on one occasion he (Shaikh Luqmān) had missed his Friday prayer or omitted to follow one or the other of the divine injunctions...The religious leaders of the town came out to interrogate him. People said to him, 'The leaders of the town are coming in order to argue with you'. 'Are they coming on foot or riding?' he asked. People replied, 'They come riding'. The Shaikh was at the time sitting on a wall. He said to it, 'Move, by the command of God'. The wall immediately began to move." See Mujeeb, 1967:121.

tion of Nijāmuddīn and Kāniphnāth differs very little from the world-view found in the popular traditions of the bhakti saints of Mahārāṣṭra. Here, in the story of Paiṭhaṇ's Nijāmuddīn and his disciple Kāniphnāth, we find ourselves in the colourful religious world of a medieval *Deccanī pīr*, a a world in which *yogīs* and Ṣūfīs confronted one another, fought one another, learned from one another, and, not infrequently, formed bonds of great affection for one another. Two important legacies of this fusion of ideas and spirits are the numerous cults of Hindu-Muslim saints in the Deccan and the folk tales of those holy men who brought Hindus and Muslims closer.

Acknowledgement

To Professor Dr. Ian R. Duncan, Department of Social Anthropology, Massey University, Palmerston, New Zealand, I owe a special debt of gratitude for introducing me to Śekh Biyābānī in Puṇe in the summer of 1982 and for accompanying me in my field work in Dt. Solāpūr in 1990.

References

Abbott, J. Edward 1927. *Eknath* (sic), Poona.

Ahmad, Aziz 1964. *Studies in Islamic culture in its Indian environment*. Oxford.

Ajñānasiddha 1987. *Saṃkaṭaharaṇī*, edited by Śaṅkara Nānābuvā Moholakara and Vi. Śī. Moholakara. Solāpūra, *śake* 1909, *isvī sān* 1987.

Ajñānasiddha and Siddhaliṅga-svāmī s.d. *Ānaṃda-laharī va sākhyā*, edited by Siddhaliṅga Viśvanātha Svāmī and Nāganātha Guṇḍubuvā Kuruḍe, Solapur, circa 1950? (place and date of publication not given).

Bendre, Vāsudeva Sītārāmā 1960. *Tukārāmācī-guruparamparā*. Muṃbaī.

Biyābānī, Śekha Abdula Rajhākaśāha 1981. *Alakhaniraṃjana*, Puṇe.

Eaton, Richard M. 1978. *The Sufis of Bijapur, 1300-1700: Social roles of Sufis in medieval India*. Princeton.

Government of the Bombay Presidency 1884. *Gazetteer of the Bombay Presidency, Ahmadnagar*.

Government of Maharashtra 1976. *Maharashtra State Gazetteers, Ahmadnagar District*, Bombay.

Id. 1969. *Bhir District*, Bombay.

Id. 1960. *Kolhapur District*, Bombay.

Id. 1977. *Sholapur District*, Bombay.

Müller-Stellrecht, Irmtraud 1973. *Feste in Dardistan. Darstellung und kulturgeschichtliche Analyse*, published in the series: *Arbeiten aus dem Seminar für Völkerkunde der Johann Wolfgang von Goethe-Universität Frankfurt am Main*, Volume 5, Wiesbaden [Franz Steiner Verlag].

Mujeeb, Muḥammad 1967. *The Indian Muslims*, London.

Pagaḍī, Setu Mādhavrāva 1953. *Sūfī-saṃpradāya*. Muṃbaī.

Paṭhāṇa, Yusufakhāna Mahaṃmadakhāna 1963. *Nāgeśa-saṃpradāya*, Auraṅgābāda, 1963.

Id. 1983. Contribution of the Muslim saints of Maharashtra to early devotional literature in Marathi. In M. Thiel-Horstmann (ed.) *Bhakti in current research, 1979-1982*. Berlin: Dietrich Reimer.

Titus, Murray T. 1979. *Indian Islam: A religious history of Islam in India*. Oxford, 1930; reprinted in Delhi.

Tulpule, S.G. 1979. *Classical Marāṭhī literature: From the beginnings to A.D. .1818*. Wiesbaden.

THE KING AND THE TRIBAL BARD
- PATTERNS OF PROTEST BY TWO MINORITIES -

Alokeranjan Dasgupta

The term 'minority', judging by the Indian context, offers an incredibly wide spectrum of connotations, often apparently colliding with each other. It points to a varied range of behavioral and aesthetic attitudes, such as resilience and radicalism, and yet moulds them into a multivalent totality. The basic characteristic of a minority consists, of course, as anywhere else in the world, in its vulnerability. And yet this quality perhaps acquires an element of dignity in Indian society where the sense of alienation or isolation is not so strong as in its western counterparts. The present paper attempts to understand the rather complex nature of the artistic expressions of two minorities, both aboriginal tribes: an Oriya-speaking group in Mayurbhanj, and the Santals in West-Bengal.

In this connexion we may recall the description, if not definition, of the word 'minority' in a Delhi symposium on the 'Minority Rights Group India' by Soli Sorabji, that 'it takes in all groups and sections of people who, on account of their non-dominant positions in society and because of their special and peculiar traits or characteristics, were subjected to disabilities and were victims of discrimination ... and exploitation'.[1]

---

[1] T .atesman, August 18, 1984.

Within the limits of the Mayurbhanj district of Orissa, however, these 'victims of discrimination and exploitation' happen to be in majority, so far as their numerical strength is concerned. Already the 1961 census for that district shows the ratio of the aborigines at 60,6%, a percentage which has certainly grown since then, although no strict record has been kept. One section of this majority has been turned into a victimised group through the vested interests exercised by, for instance, money-lenders, or landowners dependent on agriculture. Most of them are landless cultivators, forced to be content with income from their meagre seasonal employment. The rest of the time they love performing Jātrā, based on purānic legends, and composing parabolic stories where they couch their protest in an extraordinarily subtle way. These stories have a kind of *campū* character, interpersed as they are with popular rhyming. Here is a story narrated by a tribal bard during one interlude of a Kṛṣṇa-Jātrā, performed 17 August 1985 in a small village called Baripada.

At the royal court of Nayagarh appeared Jadumaṇi, the bard of the people. The king urged him immediately to compose a quatrain. Jadumaṇi took one day's time. The next day he brought to the king a leaf-packet prepared with Śāl-leaves, with four edges, covered under a piece of cloth in a big basket. The king asked, 'Where is the quatrain I asked for?' Jadumaṇi unwrapped the basket and retorted, 'This is your quatrain'. The people of the court greatly appreciated the trick and burst into laughter. The king, dumbfounded, had no other way out than to grant Jadumaṇi a strip of land.

It was soon found to be unproductive land, however. Next year Jadumaṇi sent a messenger to the king with the following verse:

> What the king so joyfully granted
> took a whole year to reach me
> it is so select a waste land
> that in monsoon rain
> coconuts smash
> if one flings thereupon -
> not even weeds can take root there.

The king, once again trapped, did not show his wrath. He tried a new play this time. He urged Jadumaṇi to accompany him on a hunt. The king rode on an elephant, while Jadumaṇi went on foot. The king complacently asked the poet: 'Now tell me who is the superior amongst us?' Jadumaṇi retorted immediately:

> The goldsmith's scale reveals to us
> that the heavier gold remains below.

The king felt put out, but did not display his anger. He waited for a future ocassion when he might overcome the folk bard. He arranged a special ceremony at his palace where all the invited subjects were to bring him offerings, placing a garland around his neck, and laying money at his feet. 'Now tell me', he asked the king, 'Who is the superior amongst us?' Jadumani answered in a spirit of holy sobriety:

> 'The king is revered in his own courtyard;
> beyond that is admired the people's bard'.

The king, demasked, had no other option left than to adopt Jadumaṇi as his court poet. But before he was in a position to admit to his own conceit, and find words to formulate his choice, the assembled people saw Jadumani walk out and disappear.[2]

***

[2] Girish Chandra Dhal, my local informant, mentioned, incidentally, about the possibility of a folk source of Radhanth Ray's popular short story 'Jadumani,' in this connexion, which was exploited, barring the resurgent conclusion almost *in toto*. Mr. Dhal vouched for a similar local legend where the bard did not ingratiate himself with the king and staged a dramatic retreat from the royal palace located nearby.

Here ends the story. Most of the other parables about the king and the tribal bard I have heard in this area of Orissa, have a similar strain of self-validation about them. The king symbolizes the empty-headed land-owner whose only intention is to cheat the landless labourer out of his claims. Jadumaṇi, the tribal bard, is the spokesman of these labourers. His mellow witticism clearly expresses the people's integrity of prevailing common sense: the true asset of which they can be really proud. One can legitimately raise the query why they accept their lot with forbearance and humour, and do not insurrect. There is no easy answer to be found; one can only surmise that, apart from their capacity to bear the given situation, their awareness of the fact that numerically and spiritually they are affiliated with all the rest of the Mayurbhanj aborigine minority whom the bard Jadumaṇi called 'the people'. The poet's alternate word-play with the 'tribesmen' *(jñati)* and 'people' *(jāti)* shows the real source of his sense of strength: the basic confidence that, at least potentially, a revolution is possible.

Returning to West Bengal one is tempted to look for more revolutionary spirit amongst the Ādivāsīs or aboriginals there. The Santals offer, quite naturally, the scope for an interesting case study in this context. W.G. Archer correctly observes that this Indo-Melanese group of people are 'the largest, most resilient tribe in Eastern India.'[3] This quality of their inborn temperament is still to be discerned in the Santal Pargana district of Bihar, despite the extent of their conversion to Christianity for reasons other than purely religious. The Santals in West Bengal have, on the other hand, been exposed to urbanization: this has proved far from an unmixed blessing.

The 1971 census shows the strength of the Ādivāsīs at about 2.6 million out of an approximate total population of 50 millions for West Bengal.

---

[3] Archer, W.G. 1974: 11.

The Santal share of the population is 845,395 in West Bengal: a very modest number. It can be said with a certain historical understanding that the peace-loving demeanour of the Santals towards the Bengali stems more from a strategy of suspicion than from their inborn nature. After the permanent settlement in 1793, their original lands were seized by landlords and as they could not bear the burden of the enhanced tax, many Santals started shifting from the end of the nineteenth century on to the districts of Bhagalpur, Birbhum and Murshidabad, where they found much unused earth to be tilled, without caring about the legality of these actions. They called their new settlement 'Damre Koh', cleared the jungles and brought the lands under cultivation. They thought the misfortunes caused by their exodus had come to an end. But at this juncture the non-Santal landlords began asserting their rights. From the very beginning, these zamindars took a profiteering line, demanding heavy taxes from these tillers of the soil. Business people too, mostly Bengali, started cheating them in money-lending practices and other forms of commercial transaction. The Santal rebellion of 1855 was a result of such exploitations. This uprising exerted an impact on the Bengal Indigo revolt (1860), and the insurgence of farmers in Bogura and Pabna (1872), now in Bangladesh; a parallel far away was the insurgent of the Marathi farmers of the Deccan (1875-76).[4] All these insurgent drives were shattered in no time. What is important in our context is that the Santals in West Bengal have never ceased to be sceptical about Bengalis in their oppressive roles of middlemen, police or co-operators with the usurpers. If one dwells on Santali tales, one can not but notice an ambivalent undertone which explains the nature of their complicated, strained relationship with the dominant Bengalis. These tales are generally called 'Kudum', meaning puzzle or riddle, and the first line is always, 'Kudum Kurit Kurit', which, literally translated, stands for 'a hawk giving chase to intelligence.' Santals claim that a riddle provokes or awakes sensibility, like a hawk pounding on its prey. One such Kudum is a won-

[4] See De, A. 1975.

derful example of the humorous way of describing the state of being persecuted:

> Hawk, hawk a riddle
> falls from above
> oh my father, oh my mother,
> where else on earth could this happen?
> The thing easily enmeshed everybody
> Tell us, oh father of a babu,
> is it a constable or just a policeman?

The answer of the puzzle is a 'fishing net'. But while unwrapping the riddle completely, we can just be sure that the chasing claws of the hawk clearly hints at the Bengali, 'the father of a babu,' known to the ordinary Santal as an unscrupulous opportunist. The metaphor still remains valid, despite the allegory of protest. And therein lies its charm. This mode of protest has nothing to do with self-pity or an inferiority complex. It just defines the trap that a persecuted group of people are in, using a mild irony, and thus defies their own defeatist leanings.

It requires the attention of a socio-politically conscious ethnologist to analyze the roles of the persecutors and the persecuted in these Kudums. For us it is important here to know how a Kudum operates. The structure and character of these riddles is that of *stichomythia* in Greek drama (though often exceeding the one-line-limit here) in its closely-woven mannerism of sophisticated repartee. It is not irrelevant to point out here that the Santals, irrespective of their environment whether rustic or urban are intrisically *urbane* in their way of looking at life. In this dramatic dialogue of riddles too, there resides an oblique will of the persecuted to confront the opponent. The quizmaster does not lam into the opposite side, and vice versa. If the opposite side fails to reply to the riddle, he will never give in or say 'I have failed.' He just says instead:

> The noises of the next habitation
> approach us;
> in which forest would you enter now?

This next habitation is nothing but the neighbouring, curious society. Hence both the groups, the quizmaster and the answerer, must enter a 'forest' of negotiation - actually a bamboo-grove - where the quizmaster condescends and says:

> I turn my cups and pots upside down
> come, let us go home,
> tomorrow I'll offer a couple of goats to
> the deity[5]

Subsequently it becomes evident that the quiz-master is made to submit to the opposite party and is even indirectly entrusted with the task of buying goats for consecration. My Santal friend Jaggu Marandi told me in no uncertain terms that a Kudum on the outskirts of Calcutta indicated the wishful thinking of the Santals that they were boastful of their victory over their quiz-master in real life, the Bengalis.[6]

A few other forms of Santali riddles can exemplify tendencies which are rather submissive. For example, the 'Pate sereng' (or the leaf festival) songs. The leaf festival occurs in *chaitra,* the last month of the Hindu calendar. These songs are sung to appease the Hindu Bengali audience and are studded with Bengali loan-words. The Christian missionaries don't deem these songs as typically 'Santali' as they apparently reflect a Hindu bias. But on a closer investigation we find that the so-called Hindu-Bengali listeners are not offered any unalloyed entertainment. On the contrary, they are exposed, as the following song exemplifies:

> The girls of the hill come down,
> they need work, sheer work,
> at times one rupee extra,
> at times four annas, the babus
> rob the girls of their honour
> worth gold and silver.

---

[5] Baske 1982: 58,71; see Introduction.

[6] Jaggu Marandi to the present author in Calcutta, September 6, 1985.

It would clearly be wrong to characterize this as a song of revolution. One can even read into it an attitude of compromising womanhood for evil ends. But an insider is sure to perceive a quiet demand pressed for the protection of women's honour. And this very sobriety of tenor makes such articulation a significant contribution in defence of woman folk who are dominated and humiliated. It is known that pleasure-seeking Bengali tourists thrust their ways into ethnic minority areas and handle the women, mostly day-labourers, as a commodity. At times the Santal women are inclined to tart themselves up in this mercantile process. A critic shows in his revealing article 'Ādivāsīs mirrored in the Bengali Fiction' how the Bengali story-tellers reflect this tendency in their novels. It is their beauty commercialized that fascinates them. A typical exemple can be found in Abdul-Jabbar's bestseller 'Mātāler Hāṭe'. (In the drunken village market): 'Piyāli wears a wild Sari, woven together of creepers and leaves. She has dressed her hair with feathers. The colour of Piyāli's body is not pitch dark; there is a bluish tinge to it. Her buttocks are heavy, flat and broad ... Her hips are slender and breasts well-formed. One does not frequently chance upon such a marvellous, graceful form.'[7] Despite unmotivated sentimental or sensual idealization, the trite obscenity of this kind of description declares itself. Whatever normative judgement a moral reformer might spell out, this only reflects the prevalent leanings of Bengali 'bābus,' for whom Piyālis are mere objects of pleasure. Piyālis, too, are not naive and at times compensate for their lot pragmatically with monetary exchange.

Doubtless these 'bābus' easily turn into targets of criticism in Santali songs. The major male-female dichotomy in the attitudes towards this pleasure-seeking affluent class is, however, interesting in the sense that the male composers disposition aims at a clear challenge or confrontation, whereas the feminine point of view reflects a specific awareness of one's own position.

---

[7] Sanyal, T. 1984: 64-65.

The riddle-songs belonging to the 'Dang-Serang' group are relevant in this connexion because they are widely sung on all occassions, madrigal or matrimonial. Their social character is pronounced, despite the uncensored private feelings or sentiments. Most of these songs with *male* motives bear the stamp of counterclaims as to their capability in empirically succeeding along with money-lenders. The song that follows substantiates this:

Money brings prestige and money brings knowledge
if you have money then you have prestige
if money leaves you then your intelligence fades away
and at the same time you are without respect.

The women, however, sing their Dang-Serangs with more lyrical introversion:

Little girl, putting your pitcher on the ground
why do you stand so silent?
- From the east and the west, from the north
and the south
the cold wind blows, I hear it.

The last two lines are, undoubtedly, the response amitted by the small girl to the 'man of action' who does not care at all for the inner world of the women. A further song, sung by a lone mother, tethered to the duty of rearing a child, amplifies the helplessness of the girl suddenly turned mother, afraid of city rowdies:

Our booth is on the crest of the hill
There a waterspring is closed
pitcher-on-head, child-at-hip
how can I really fetch water?[8]

There is a suggestive, sad note in this quatrain, which should not be confused with any kind of protest. But that is exactly what con-

[8] All these songs have been cited here by courtesy of Tapan Bandyopadhyay (1976).

nects this folk-literature with the relatively recent literature of authorship.

This stance recalls the passive wrath of Werner Herzog's Film: 'Where the Grey Ants Dream', in which aboriginal tribes in the Australian desert protest against an intruding mining concern by merely 'staring at the invaders'.[9] A sensitive love-hate relationship is involved in this way of answering properly back to those who, socially speaking, are invaders or superiors here; it prepares the ground for revolution.

If we move towards the north-eastern region of India, we come to the hilly state of Tripura[10] where the Border Security Force keeps its units alerted along the 'eastern border with Bangladesh's Chittagong hill tracts so as to prevent the possible intrusion of an extremist gang reportedly operating in the area.'[11] This 'extremist gang', we know, is constituted of Tripura Ādivāsīs who are a significant minority pledged to counter non-tribal supremacy striving for the recognition of their languages. Nripendra Chakravarti, the Chief Minister, himself belonging to the wing of C.P.I. (M.), admitted rather late, 'If I were born in a tribal family, I would have become an extremist.'[12] It is, however, in the given context, intriguing to note that the extremist minority here has not yet been able to produce a meaningful literature, oral or written, which can claim to have acquired an autonomous dimension of self-expression as in the case of Mayurbhanj Oriyas or the Santals of West Bengal.*

---

[9] Financial Times, October 19, 1984.

[10] Deb Barma, D. 1983.

[11] Amrita Bazar Patrika, October 13, 1984.

[12] Amrita Bazar Patrika, August 5, 1984.

* All the Oriya, Bengali and Santali texts are, unless otherwise specified, translated by the present author.

References

Amrita Bazar Patrika. August 5, 1984.

Id. October 13, 1984.

Archer, W.G. 1974. *The hills of flute.* London: George Allen and Unwin.

Bandyopadhyay, Tapan (ed.) 1976. *Sāoṅtalī Kavitā.* Calcutta: De Book Store.

Baske, Dhirendranath 1982. *Kudum, Sāoṅtāli Henyāli.* Calcutta: Akademi of Folklore.

De, Amalendu 1981. *Samāj o Saṃskṛti.* Calcutta: Ratna Prakashan.

Deb Barma, D. 1983. *Treatise on traditional social institutions of the Tripuri community.* Agartala.

Financial Times. October 19, 1984.

The Statesman. August 18, 1984.

Sanyal, Tapan 1984. Bangla Kathasahityer Darpane Adivasi. In *Promā* 6.3: 64-65. Calcutta.

Contributors

Günther D. Sontheimer (1934-1992) taught History of Religions and Philosophy of South Asia, traditional Hindu law (Dharmaśāstra), as well as Marathi language and literature at the South Asia Institute of the University of Heidelberg. He studied law and Indology in Tübingen and Hindu Law in Pune (1958-61). Diploma in law and Ph.D. at the SOAS in London on *The Hindu Joint Family: Its evolution as a legal institution.* (Delhi, 1975). From 1966 onwards he conducted field research on Indian folk culture, especially on the oral traditions, religion and customs of pastoral communities in Maharashtra, Andhra Pradesh and Karnataka. His publications include: *Pastoral deities in Western India,* OUP, New York, 1989; ed. with S. Settar: *Memorial stones,* Dharwad/New Delhi, 1982; ed. with H. Kulke: *Hinduism reconsidered,* New Delhi, 2nd ed., 1990. In October 1987 he received the Rabindranath Tagore Prize of Literature instituted by the Indo-German Society of Germany for his translations from Marathi.

Gilles Tarabout (1948) is currently Chargé de Recherche in Anthropology at the C.N.R.S. (Centre National de la Recherche Scientifique), Paris, and is attached to the Center for Indian and South-Asian Studies (CEIAS), and the School of Oriental Languages and Civilisations (INALCO). After fieldwork as fellow of the Indian Government (Indo-French Cultural Exchange Programme, 1980-1983), he published a thesis on Kerala religious festivals (Sacrifiér et donner à voir en pays Malabar, Paris 1986). In a number of articles he has pursued research on the traditional elite in Kerala and its relation to temples. He is presently working on trance possessions and exorcisms in Kerala.

John Richardson Freeman Jr. (1956), obtained his Master's degree in 1983 from the University of Pennsylvania, specializing in Sanskrit and Indian Philosophy. (Master's thesis: *Karma in the world-view of classical Yoga).* In 1991 he gained his Ph.D. degree in anthropology from the same university. (Title: *Sacrality, purity, and violence in the Teyyam worship of Malabar).* Besides teaching undergraduate and graduate courses in anthropology and South Asian studies at the universities of Pennsylvania and Berkeley, he has spent two years in India learning Sanskrit and Malayalam. He conducted fieldwork in Cannanore district, Kerala, on a Fulbright-Hays grant for field research for one year. He is currently academy scholar at the Harvard University Academy for International Affairs and Area Studies.

Balan Nambiar (1937), besides being a renowned modern sculptor and painter has — for the past ten to fifteen years — done extensive documentation of teyyam rituals of northern Kerala, the region where he himself was born and brought up, and whose religious and aesthetic culture deeply influences his creative work. For two years, his research was sponsored by a Nehru fellowship. He lives as a free-lance artist in Bangalore (India) and Padua (Italy).

Axel Michaels (1949), studied Indology, law and philosophy in Munich, Freiburg, Hamburg and Benares. He gained his Ph.D. in 1978 (*Beweisverfahren in der vedischen Sakralgeometrie.* Wiesbaden 1978). He was director of the Nepal Research Centre in Kathmandu (1981-83) and Spalding Visiting Fellow at Wolfson College, Oxford (1986). Presently he is professor of Comparative Religion at the University of Bern, Switzerland. Publications include *Ritual und Gesellschaft in Indien,* Frankfurt 1986. *Heritage of the Kathmandu Valley* (ed. with N. Gutschow, St. Augustin 1987); *Der indische Tanz* (ed. with F. Baldissera, Köln 1988); and *Tīrtha und Pīṭha — Der nepalische Pāśupatināth Tempel und sein rituelles Feld* (forthcoming).

Claus Peter Zoller was born in 1952 in Schwäbisch-Gmünd, Germany. In 1980 he obtained a Ph.D. in Indology with a thesis on the grammar of a hybrid (Tibetan and Indo-Aryan) dialect spoken in the Garhwal Himalayas (*Die Sprache der Rang Pās von Garhwal*, Wiesbaden). He has conducted fieldwork for the past many years in the Indian Himalayas. From 1985 to 1990 he was representative of the South Asia Institute, Heidelberg, in New Delhi. Between 1990-1992 he was assistant professor in the Institut für Indogermanistik und Indologie, University of Frankfurt. Currently he is assistant professor in the Department of Indology II (Modern Languages and Literature) at the South Asia Institute.

Elisabeth Schoembucher (1954), conducted fieldwork among the Vāḍabalija, a Telugu-speaking fishing caste on the east coast of India, between 1979 and 1981 and in 1982. Her publications, focusing on the social organization of a maritime community, include: *Die Vāḍabalijā in Andhra Pradesh und in Orissa. Aspekte der wirtschaftlichen und sozialen Organisation einer maritimen Gesellschaft.* (Wiesbaden, 1986), and: Equality and hierarchy in maritime adaptation: The importance of flexibility in the social organization of a South Indian fishing caste (*Ethnology* 27(3): 213-230). At present she is assistant professor in Anthropology at the South Asia Institute, Heidelberg University. Her current research is on spirit mediumship among the women of the Vāḍabalija.

B. A. Vivek Rai (1946), is professor and head of the department of Kannaḍa at Mangalore University, Mangalagangothri. Born and brought up in the rural Tuḷu culture of Coastal Karnataka (Dakṣiṇa Kannaḍa) he graduated in Science at Puttur, studied Kannaḍa literature at Mysore University (M.A. 1970) and joined the Kannaḍa department of the same university as a lecturer. He then concentrated on folklore studies and published several books and articles on Tuḷu culture, his major work being an extensive study of Tulu folk literature (Tuḷu Janapada Sāhitya, Bangalore 1985). During the last few years he has built up the first center for Tuḷu studies in India at the Kannaḍa department of Mangalore University.

Heidrun Brückner (1949), was trained in classical Indology, literature and linguistics (M.A. Benares 1972; Ph.D. Marburg 1978, thesis on Śaṅkara's use of similes). She spent several years in South India before joining Mainz University as assistant professor of Indology. (1982-1986). Between 1986 and 1990 she worked with G.D. Sontheimer at the South Asia Institute, Heidelberg University, on oral myths and rituals of folk deities in Tuḷunāḍu (fieldwork in 1986/87, habilitation thesis 1990 *Fürstliche Feste - Texte und Rituale der Tuḷu-Volksreligion an dẹr Westküste Südindiens,* forthcoming). Since 1990, she is professor of Indology at the department of Indology and Comparative Religion of Tübingen University. Besides oral literature and folk religion, her fields of interest include Indian Philosophy, Sanskrit drama, South Asian performance traditions, and modern Indian literature.

Peter J. Claus (1942), is professor of anthropology at California State University, Hayward. He is co-author of *The folktales of India* and *Folkloristics and Indian Folklore,* as well as many articles on the rituals and songs of Coastal Karnataka (Dakṣiṇa Kannaḍa). He is currently working on a comparative analysis of five Tuḷu *pāḍdanas.*

Aditya Malik (1959), studied Indian and Western Philosophy at the University of Delhi (B.A.) and ancient Indian history, culture and archaeology at Deccan College, University of Pune (M.A.). He has conducted fieldwork in Rajasthan between 1984-85 and 1991-92. In 1990 he obtained his Ph.D. from the University of Heidelberg with a thesis on the pilgrimage center of Puṣkara (Title: *Das Puṣkara-Māhātmya. Ein religionswissenschaftlicher Beitrag zum Wallfahrtsbegriff in Indien,* in press). In 1991 he began work with G.D. Sontheimer on a project focused on the oral epic and cult of the folk deity Devnārāyaṇ in Rajasthan. He is currently research associate in the department of Indology at the South Asia Institute, Heidelberg.

Bahadur Singh has a Ph.D. from the University of Delhi, where he was lecturer in the department of Hindi at Hindu College (1965-71). Since 1971 he has been teaching Hindi language and literature in the department of Indian studies, University of Hamburg. His publications are on Hindi and Rajasthani language and literature.

Richard Burghart (1944), studied anthropology at the University College Ibadan (Nigeria) and at the London School of Oriental and African Studies where he completed his doctorate with a study on the relation between king and ascetic in Nepal. He has conducted fieldwork between 1973-76 and 1984-85 in Janakpur, Nepal. His interests include North Indian Vaishnavism, the Hindu polity (Nepal), and the Maithili language. At present he is professor and head of the department of anthropology at the South Asia Institute, Heidelberg University.

Hugh van Skyhawk (1945), is assistant professor of Indology in the South Asia Institute, Heidelberg University. Spezialization in the devotional forms of Hinduism and popular Islam in the Deccan; medieval and modern devotional literature in Marathi. Fieldwork on *bhakti* and Hindu-Muslim religious syncretism in the Deccan. Major publications: *Bhakti und bhakta: Religionsgeschichtliche Untersuchungen zum Heilsbegriff und zur religiösen Umwelt des Śrī Sant Eknāth* (Stuttgart, 1990); *'Minorities' on themselves* (ed., Stuttgart, 1986); articles on devotional religion in the Deccan and on the image of women in Marathi literature. More recently fieldwork on the language, religion, and culture of Gilgit and Hunza (northern Pakistan).

Alokeranjan Dasgupta (1933) went to Tagore's school, Santiniketan, and the University of Calcutta. Between 1957 and 1976 he was Reader in the Department of Comparative Literature and Bengali, Jadavpur University, Calcutta. In 1971/72 he was awarded a fellowship of the Alexander von Humboldt Foundation. Over the past years he has been teaching at the South Asia Institute, University of

Heidelberg. In addition to several volumes of poems in Bengali, German and English, he has also published a number of academic works: *The Lyric in Indian Poetry,* Calcutta, 1962; *Goethe and Tagore,* Wiesbaden, 1974. Dasgupta was awarded the Rabindranath Tagore Prize for Literature from the Indo-German Society of Germany in 1987, and the Shiromani Award, Calcutta, in 1991.

GENERAL INDEX

INDEX OF SOUTH ASIAN TERMS